Educating Adolescents: Challenges and Strategies

A volume in
Adolescence and Education

Educating Adolescents Challenges and Strategies

Edited by

Tim Urdan

Santa Clara University

Frank Pajares

Emory University

INFORMATION AGE
PUBLISHING

80 Mason Street • Greenwich, Connecticut 06830 • www.infoagepub.com

Library of Congress Cataloging-in-Publication Data

Educating adolescents : challenges and strategies / editors, Frank
Pajares and Tim Urdan.
    p. cm. — (Adolescence and education)
  Includes bibliographical references and index.
  ISBN 1-59311-153-3 (pbk. : alk. paper) — ISBN 1-59311-154-1
(hardcover : alk. paper)
  1. High school teaching—United States. 2.
Teenagers—Education—United States. 3. Identity (Psychology) in
adolescence—United States. I. Pajares, Frank. II. Urdan, Timothy C.
III. Series.
  LB1737.U6E36 2004
  373.1102—dc22

                                                2004020317

LIST OF CONTRIBUTORS

Gerald R. Adams　　　　　*University of Guelph*
　　　　　　　　　　　　　　Ontario, Canada

Ron Avi Astor　　　　　　*University of Southern California*

Rami Benbenishty　　　　*Hebrew University of Jerusalem*

Gerald W. Bracey　　　　*George Mason University*

Donna Eder　　　　　　　*Indiana University*

Daniel J. Flannery　　　*Kent State University*

Deborah Garvey　　　　　*Santa Clara University*

Sandra Graham　　　　　*University of California*
　　　　　　　　　　　　　　Los Angeles

Nancy D. Kellogg　　　　*University of Texas*
　　　　　　　　　　　　　　Health and Science Center at San Antonio

Valerie E. Lee　　　　　*University of Oregon*

Janice McCabe　　　　　*Indiana University*

Heather A. Meyer　　　　*Wells College*

Susan Palijan　　　　　　*University of Guelph*
　　　　　　　　　　　　　　Ontario, Canada

Douglas D. Ready　　　　*University of Oregon*

Geoffrey L. Ream　　　　*Cornell University*

Michelle Elena Rosemond　*University of Southern California*

Karen D. Rudolph　　　　*University of Illinois*
　　　　　　　　　　　　　　Urbana-Champaign

Ritch C. Savin-Williams　*Cornell University*

Tim Urdan　　　　　　　*Santa Clara University*

Kelly L. Wester　　　　　*University of North Carolina at Greensboro*

To my brother Matt, who taught me even more than he takes credit for.
—Tim Urdan

To John Bengston, with affection and respect.
I'm trying not to formalize, Johnny.
—Frank Pajares

CONTENTS

FOREWORD

Beginning with G. Stanley Hall's description of adolescents as victims of their own raging hormones, psychologists have viewed the second decade of life as a turbulent period of "storm and stress." Although this view has been tempered by psychological research indicating that most adolescents cope well with the myriad changes they experience, the general public still tends to view adolescence as a tumultuous period of development. Indeed, many middle and high school teachers believe that their efforts to teach their students are compromised by the allegedly short attention spans, obsessions with sex, and personal insecurities of adolescents.

This volume of *Adolescence and Education* is devoted to an exploration of the challenges facing adolescents and their teachers as well as some of the strategies that have been adopted to address these challenges. Although it is true that most adolescents survive this period of development with few enduring academic or psychological problems, it is also true that a substantial proportion experience depression, bullying and violence in school, sexual harassment, and a widening gap between their personal and academic needs. Many of these problems emerge for the first time during adolescence.

This volume of the series begins with five chapters describing the various psychological and contextual problems that adolescents often experience. First, Daniel Flannery and Kelly Wester provide a broad overview of a variety of risk and protective factors at the individual, family, and school levels that are related to academic achievement during adolescence. Next, Karen Rudolph examines depression as both an antecedent and a consequence of academic difficulties. Chapter 3 provides an overview of research on sexual harassment and abuse experienced by adolescents and the effects of such abuse on academic behavior. In this chapter Nancy Kellogg describes the reasons that sexual abuse is often not reported by adolescents, and she provides various strategies for preventing sexual abuse. Sandra Graham follows with a chapter in which she examines the association between peer harassment and ethnic identity. She provides and discusses empirical evidence showing an association between ethnic majority status in a school and the consequences of being harassed by peers. Her research suggests that ethnic diversity has numerous benefits in classrooms and schools. This section concludes with a chapter by Ron Astor, Rami Benbenishty, Heather A. Meyer, and Michelle Elena Rosamond. In this chapter the authors examine adolescents' exposure to a variety of weapons on school grounds (e.g., guns, knives, clubs, and other weapons) in Israel and the United States.

The next section of the volume includes four chapters that focus on cultural and contextual factors that influence the academic experiences of adolescent students. In Chapter 6, Gerald Bracey considers international comparisons of adolescent achievement. He notes problems with the validity of such cross-national comparisons as the TIMSS-R and the Program of International Student Achievement (PISA), and he questions how the media portray the results of such tests. Next, Tim Urdan and Deborah Garvey examine the achievement and motivation profiles of first-, second-, and third-generation adolescent students using a variety of data sources. They discuss factors that vary across generational groups, including facility with the English language and connection to the native cultural beliefs and values of immigrants that can influence motivation and achievement. In Chapter 8, Valerie Lee and Douglas Ready take a critical look at the school-within-school (SWS) model for high schools. They note that although the SWS model was designed to reduce the problems many students experience in large, impersonal high schools, implementing such a model faithfully is difficult and rarely achieved. The last chapter in this section considers the more intimate context of peers and friends. Donna Eder and Janice McCabe describe the effects of various school structures and practices on adolescents' developing ethnic and social identities. They note that schools can foster the development of either positive peer cultures that help promote adaptive academic identity or negative peer cultures that undermine the commitment students feel to achieve academically.

The final section of the book includes two chapters that examine adolescent identity in greater detail. In Chapter 10, Gerald Adams and Susan Palijan describe six ways that the educational environment can influence the identity development of adolescent students. They note that although the connection between education and identity development has not been well researched and remains difficult to understand, there are specific aspects of the educational experience that can affect both identity and psychological well-being. In the final chapter of the volume, Geoffrey Ream and Ritch Savin-Williams consider the religious identity of adolescents. They argue that adolescents incorporate spirituality and religious beliefs into their self-perceptions in a wide variety of ways. They contend that various educational experiences, ranging from teachings of the church to public schools to less formal social organizations such as youth groups, influence adolescents' religious beliefs and spiritual identities.

Together, these chapters provide an overview of some of the most critical challenges that adolescents, and those who raise and educate them, must address. In addition to describing the challenges, the authors in this volume have provided suggestions for how to meet these challenges. These strategies will not be easy for educators to implement. In some cases they may require a fundamental rethinking of school structures and educational practices. By providing information regarding the scope and types of challenges that adolescents face, as well as strategies for addressing these challenges, we hope to further the ongoing discussion regarding how to best educate adolescent students.

Tim Urdan and Frank Pajares

CHAPTER 1

RISK FACTORS RELATED TO ACADEMIC ACHIEVEMENT IN ADOLESCENCE

Daniel J. Flannery
Kelly L. Wester

Obtaining an education has long been viewed as a key ingredient to adult functioning and success. The higher the level of completed years of education, the more likely people are to achieve economic success and the less likely they are to be unemployed (Price, 2002). The same holds true for adolescents. Recent research via the National Longitudinal Study of Adolescents shows that the longer a child stays in school and the more attached and involved the child and parent are in school, the less likely the child will be to engage in delinquent behavior, experiment with substance use, or fail academically (Blum, Beuhring, & Rinehart, 2000; Resnick et al., 1998). Despite awareness of the importance of staying in school and the link between academic achievement and long-term functioning, the Carnegie Council on Adolescent Development (1989) estimates that about one quarter of adolescents are at high risk of academic failure and other behavior problems. Another quarter is considered moderately at risk. The National Commission on Children (1991) estimated that as many as 40% of youth in the United States are at risk for school failure.

Educating Adolescents: Challenges and Strategies, 1–31
Copyright © 2004 by Information Age Publishing
All rights of reproduction in any form reserved.

Academic achievement is typically operationalized as an individual child's performance on a standardized test or their awarded grade in a particular subject matter (Fraser, Welch, & Walberg, 1986; Walberg & Tsai, 1981). Many factors can influence actual achievement including motivation (Wentzel, 1997, 1999), child behavior problems (Magdol, 2003), teacher expectations (Wentzel, 2002), social factors outside of the individual child's direct control, like parent support for school (Ekstrom, Goertz, Pollack, & Rock, 1986; Fan, 2001; Price, 2002), or cultural differences in the importance placed on academic achievement (Powell, 1990). We review some of these factors in more detail below.

The converse of achievement is academic failure, and many studies have examined risk of academic failure for adolescents (Beauvais, Chavez, Oetting, Deffenbacher, & Cornell, 1996; Price, 2002). Risk factors do not operate in a vacuum, but are interdependent and accumulate over time (Flannery, 1997). No single factor can account for all of an individual adolescent's academic achievement, nor will individual risk factors affect all adolescents equally. Some adolescents are significantly affected by one risk factor, depending on its intensity, the timing of its occurrence, or the duration of its influence. Still other adolescents seem to be highly resilient, able to maintain a positive developmental course despite facing a multitude of risk with little social support.

This chapter focuses on risk factors associated with academic achievement in adolescence at the individual level, the family level, and the school level. Space precludes us from a comprehensive review of all risk factors at all levels during all phases of adolescent development. Generally, we focus on research for early and middle adolescents, defined here as youth in middle and high school. Some of the risk factors we briefly review are covered in greater detail in other chapters in this volume. These include disruptive behavior, ethnicity, schools within schools, and social relationships.

INDIVIDUAL-LEVEL RISK FACTORS

Risk factors are those aspects of an adolescent's life that are associated with an increased likelihood of poor outcomes, in this case, risk of academic failure, including behaviors that can threaten their overall health and well-being (Blum, Beuhring, & Rinehart, 2000). Individual-level risk factors can be biological (i.e., the influence of particular genes, chemicals in the brain, personality factors, puberty), social (i.e., how is the individual child socialized), attitudinal (i.e., motivation to achieve), cognitive (i.e., low IQ or learning disability), and behavioral (i.e., poor school attendance, oppositional behavior, conflict with the teacher or peers, inattention). We focus in this section on the social and behavioral factors that place an individual adolescent at risk for academic failure. This includes research on delinquency and substance use, and the impact of truancy and school dropout on adolescent academic achievement.

Delinquent Behavior

In this section the term "school failure" refers to the child's failure to achieve academically at school. The association between academic failure and delinquency is clear even very early in elementary school (Hinshaw & Lahey, 1993; Tremblay et al., 1992). When school failure is present it tends to be associated with other negative outcomes such as disruptive and delinquent behavior (Barone et al., 1995; Brier, 1989, 1995; Elliott, 1996; Frick et al., 1991; Hinshaw, 1992; Maguin & Loeber, 1996). Elementary school behavior problems and academic problems often precede high school dropout and academic failure (Cairns, Cairns, & Neckerman, 1989; Hinshaw, 1992; Magdol, 2003; Tremblay et al., 1992), and early problems seem to characterize a general pattern of behavior and performance problems at school that leads to eventual academic failure (Bryant, Schulenberg, Bachman, O'Malley, & Johnston, 2000). For example, elementary students who are highly aggressive are less likely to graduate from high school or to pursue college training (Lambert, 1988), and are more likely to be disciplined or suspended from school (Ekstrom et al., 1986). Simmons and Blyth (1987) found that a low grade point average in sixth grade was associated with increased school behavior problems (e.g., suspension and truancy) in seventh grade.

In a more recent longitudinal study, 25% of youth who were categorized as delinquent failed to acquire basic skills in reading, spelling, and writing relative to nondelinquent youth. By second grade, 45% of the delinquent youth were delayed in reading and 36% were delayed in writing. By junior high school, 50% of the delinquent youth were delayed in all academic areas, compared to approximately 18% of nondelinquent youth (Meltzer, Levine, Karniski, Palfreg, & Clarke, 1984). Zagar, Arbit, Hughes, Busell, and Busch (1989) found similar results. They conducted a study on 2000 urban delinquent youth and found that 14-year-old delinquent youths who were currently in eighth grade had severe academic deficits. Zagar and colleagues found that delinquent youths' academic achievement scores in math, reading, and vocabulary ranged from mid-third grade level to early fourth grade level. These studies have found that academic achievement levels of adolescent-aged delinquents rarely exceed elementary grade school levels (Amster & Lazurus, 1984; Murphy, 1986; Zagar et al., 1989) and is consistent with the finding that fewer than 20% of adjudicated youth earn a high school diploma or General Equivalency Diploma (Murphy, 1986).

Longitudinal studies have also shown that the relationship between delinquent behavior and academic achievement is reciprocal over time—as one increases, the other decreases and vice versa (Bryant et al., 2000). Maguin and Loeber (1996) conducted a rigorous meta-analysis of studies that examined the developmental sequence of delinquency and academic failure. They found that poor academic performance predicts delinquency, independent of socioeconomic status; therefore, lower levels of offending and aggression were associated with higher academic achievement. Fergusson, Horwood, and Lynskey (1994) also found that improvements in academic performance were associated with desistance in delinquent and aggressive behavior. Students who do poorly in school are more likely to drop out, and once they drop out they are more likely to spend their available, unmonitored time associating with delinquent peers who have also dropped out of school (Elliott, 1996; Resnick et al., 1998) The longer they remain out of school, the less likely they are to return, and the more likely the cycle of delinquent behavior and academic failure is to be reinforced and perpetuated.

Moffitt, Gabrielli, Mednick, and Schulsinger (1981) found that lack of school success may limit a child's opportunities of obtaining external rewards from the school environment. If the school environment fails to provide enough support and attention, youth may turn to delinquent behavior to achieve social status. A pattern of failure tends to provide few opportunities for students to receive positive reinforcement (Farrington et al., 1990; Moffitt, 1994; Ward & Tittle, 1994). From the failing student's perspective, school then takes on aversive properties that increase the likelihood of escape, rebellion, uncooperativeness, and other negative behaviors (McEvoy & Welker, 2001). This cycle often results in school failure, dropping out of school, and involvement with delinquent peers (Elliott, 1996; Loeber, Farrington, Stouthamer-Loeber, Moffitt, & Caspi, 1998; Moffitt, 1993).

Other researchers have posed that delinquency leads to academic failure due to the fact that delinquent youths have been found to be deficient in processing information, as well as in basic reading and math skills (Beebe, 1993). Maguin and Loeber (1996) suggested that cognitive deficits and attention problems are common correlates of both academic performance and delinquency. By age 17 or 18, children who are hyperactive are more likely to achieve poorly, attend a special school, or drop out (Lambert, 1988). They are also more likely to skip classes and be absent or late (Magdol, 2003), and be disciplined or suspended (Ekstrom et al., 1986).

These aversive behaviors will affect a student's ability to learn to attend to and fulfill academic expectations and requirements (McEvoy & Welker, 2001). Aversive, disruptive behavior also affects the academic performance of others. Any time a teacher needs to take time out to discipline an individual child, time is taken away from instruction or academic engagement time and affects the general order and organization of the classroom.

Student attitudes about school are also related to their academic achievement. Students who have negative attitudes are more likely to get into trouble at school, affecting their ability to achieve academically over time. Berndt and Mekos (1995) found that students who had a negative perception or attitude about school in the fall of seventh grade tended to increase in the amount of behavior problems and misconduct they engaged in throughout the year.

School staff perceptions of a student also have been found to play a role in academic achievement and misbehavior. Students who are perceived by teachers or staff to be at risk of engaging in antisocial or delinquent behavior are more likely to be punished, excluded, and controlled than have their problems addressed appropriately by the school (Walker et al., 1996). The lack of appropriate intervention at school can further perpetuate the likelihood of academic failure because over time students viewed as troublemakers are not typically provided with many opportunities to succeed. By using aversive consequences, school officials may be increasing student apathy toward school and academics generally (McEvoy & Welker, 2001).

Substance Use

Individual adolescent substance use (alcohol and other drugs) is associated with a host of negative school behaviors and outcomes including academic failure (Lambert, 1988), truancy, dropping out (Ponsford & Lapadat, 2001; Tanner, Krahn, & Hartnagal, 1995), alienation from school, and misbehavior at school (Hawkins, Catalano, & Miller, 1992; Petraitis, Flay, & Miller, 1995). Jeynes (2002) examined the relationship between substance use and academic achievement in a national sample of 18,726 adolescent students who participated in the National Educational Longitudinal Study (NELS). He found that increased frequency of cigarette smoking and being under the influence of marijuana, cocaine, and alcohol had a significant negative impact on student academic achievement. Jeynes reported that when examining all types of substance use together, smoking, drinking, and using alcohol at school consistently produced the most significant effects.

Although adolescents can use and have access to a variety of illegal substances, most of the research that has been conducted examining academic achievement has looked at its relationship to adolescent cigarette or tobacco use. Cigarette use in and of itself may not appear to be problematic, but adolescents who report current tobacco use also tend to report engaging in other substance use and at-risk behaviors (Everett, Malarcher, Sharp, Husten, & Giovino, 2000). Tobacco use is also a gateway drug to more serious substance use, which is often comorbid with delinquent behavior (Blum, Beuhring, & Rinehart, 2000). For example, students with low grade point averages initiate and maintain cigarette use more than students with high grade point averages (Brunswick & Messeri, 1984; Schulenberg, Bachman, O'Malley, & Johnston, 1994). School failure, indicated by low grade point average, is one of the most consistent risk factors for substance use (Dryfoos, 1990; White, Pandina, & LaGrange, 1987).

What is less clear is the direction of the relationship between academic achievement, school failure, and substance use. Similar to research on delinquent behavior, substance use is inversely related to academic achievement—as academic achievement increases, youth report using less alcohol and other drugs. Many different theories regarding whether cigarette and drug use occur prior to school problems or school problems come first and lead to tobacco and other drug use have been posed (Bryant et al., 2000).

It is also unclear whether the relationship between substance use and academic achievement is direct or indirect. Studies of mediating or moderated effects show that school misbehavior (i.e., engaging in disruptive behavior at school) and poor academic achievement are associated both directly and indirectly with increased cigarette use among at-risk youth and also among youth with low-risk backgrounds (Bryant et al., 2000). Bryant and colleagues (2000) found strong support for the view that early school misbehavior and low academic achievement are key risk factors for increased cigarette use during adolescence. In two independent nationally representative samples of adolescents, it was found that school misbehavior contributed to increased cigarette use and decreased academic achievement between 8th and 10th grades, and increased cigarette use and decreased school bonding (i.e., attachment to school and belief that school is important) between grades 10 and 12 (Bryant et al., 2000). In addition, lower levels of academic achievement contributed to increased school misbehavior between 8th and 10th grades and increased cigarette use between 8th and 10th grades and between grades 10 and 12. Overall, a great deal of evidence suggests there is an indirect relationship between adolescent misbehavior, poor academic achievement, and cigarette use.

In their recent report using data from the National Longitudinal Study of Adolescent Health, Blum and colleagues (2000) showed that adolescents who were having problems with schoolwork were more likely than others to experience or be involved with a variety of risky behaviors including cigarette and alcohol use. These findings were maintained for both boys and girls, and for adolescents from different ethnic groups. Other studies have shown an association between poor academic achievement and more serious substance use. Kirk and Ward (1999) found that low-achieving students tend to also use more alcohol, marijuana, cocaine, and inhalants than do average- and high-achieving students. Magdol (2003) reported that average achievers are twice as likely to have used marijuana in the past week (12.9%) as high achievers (6.6%). In a longitudinal study of the relationship between substance use and school motivation among African American adolescents, Zimmerman and Schmeelk-Cone (2003) found a significant relationship between alcohol and marijuana use and lower educational motivation. They also found that students who used alcohol and marijuana were less likely to graduate from high school.

Truancy and Dropout

Students cannot achieve at school if they do not attend school on a regular basis. Truancy is typically defined as a prolonged absence from school with or without the consent of parents (Irfan, Igbal, Sandhu, & Singh, 1993). There are many reasons students cite for being truant or chronically absent from school. These include being afraid for one's safety, getting into trouble for bad behavior at school, hanging out with delinquent peers who also do not attend school, lack of attachment at school, poor parental monitoring, or academic failure (Berndt, 1999). Irfan and colleagues (1993) found that truants were more maladjusted in the areas of emotional, social, and educational functioning than nontruants. Overall adjustment at school was poorer for truants compared to nontruants. Students who are truant have poor achievement motivation compared to students who are not truant (Barth, 1984). Achievement motivation, defined as an internalized tendency to strive for a standard of excellence (McClelland, 1953), is a critical factor underlying high academic achievement. Students rarely achieve at a high level when they lack the motivation to excel.

Chronic school absence and truancy are well-known precursors of school failure (Reyes & Hedeker, 1993). One prospective study found school absence to be one of the best predictors of school failure and dropout (Pallas, 1986). For adolescents who experience academic failure and dropout, attendance begins to decline in sixth grade or earlier. Once a student stops attending school regularly he becomes more and more disengaged from school over time, increasing the difficulty of transitioning into high school (Roderick, 1994). The higher the number of truancies and school absences, the more likely the student will not achieve academic success and the higher the likelihood of dropping out. The academic performance of high-absence students worsened over time compared with the low- and middle-absence groups (Reyes & Hedeker, 1993). Being absent or truant from school may be one of the earliest indicators of future school problems and academic failure (Bryant et al., 2000). Barrington and Hendricks (1989) found that compared with high school graduates, dropouts had been absent twice as often by the fifth grade and three times more often by the ninth grade.

The overall dropout rate during the past decade has been reported as approximately 11% (U.S. Department of Education, n.d.). Students typically drop out of school for three reasons: (a) school-based reasons (e.g., lack of attachment to school, find school boring, being truant, not getting along with teachers, negative experiences at school); (b) wanting or needing to find a job; and (c) personal reasons (e.g., not getting along with parents, expelled from home, friends dropping out, getting pregnant, or using/abusing drugs or alcohol) (Ponsford & Lapadat, 2001; Tanner et al., 1995).

Summary of Individual-Level Risk Factors

Early school failure and misbehavior are indicators of a negative developmental trajectory that begins in early elementary school and persists through adolescence, characterized by multiple school problems and health risks (Bryant et al., 2000). Substance use, delinquency, attitudes toward school, school engagement, and truancy all tend to interact to provide an overall risk of academic failure. As the number of risk factors experienced by adolescents increases, the likelihood that they will be high academic achievers decreases. Keep in mind, however, that even though significant individual risk factors may be present, other risk and protective factors may exist within the family and at school that can either act to increase risk or provide a buffer against academic failure.

FAMILY-LEVEL RISK FACTORS

The family can be a source of risk or can be a buffer of protection when it comes to factors that influence the academic success of adolescents. We briefly review some of the family-level factors found to be significantly related to academic achievement: socioeconomic status, parental involvement, and parenting styles.

Socioeconomic Factors

The level of poverty in a family is a significant predictor of academic failure for adolescents at age 16 (Pagani, Boulerice, Vitaro, & Tremblay, 2001). An adolescent from a family of lower socioeconomic status is more likely to leave high school before finishing (Ekstrom et al., 1986) and is less likely to attend college (Lambert, 1988). Allington and Cunningham (2002) reported schools that enroll a large number of students from poor families rank among the lowest performing schools, not just in overall achievement but also in school attendance, high school completion rates, and college attendance after graduation.

Economic conditions can affect adolescent academic performance because of the financial pressures they generate, particularly with respect to how parents respond to stressors or the conflicts the stressors cause in the home (Conger, Conger, & Scaramella, 1997). One such pressure may be for the adolescent to leave school and get a job in order to support the family. Alternatively, Pagani and colleagues (2001) suggested that the relationship between socioeconomic status and academic achievement may be due more to the fact that poor families experience multiple risk factors, and thus children tend to suffer in the academic domain. Adolescents who live in poverty and experience persistent financial hardship throughout their childhood might also be more at risk of poor academic performance by virtue of their limited exposure to environmental stimuli (e.g., books, culture, scientific and verbal activities). High academic achievers are more likely to live in homes that are filled with reading material, family conversation, educational games, and writing activities that allow children to practice reading skills and master the written language (Price, 2002). According to Price (2002), "experts agree that children whose parents create a home environment that encourages learning and who get really involved in their children's education from preschool through elementary school actually earn higher grades than youngsters whose parents aren't involved" (p. 94).

Parental Involvement

The 2000 National Assessment of Educational Progress (NAEP) report showed that parental involvement, both at home and in school, is a significant contributor to a youth's academic success (cf. Price, 2002). Fan (2001) describes involved parents as those who have aspirations for their children's academic achievement, communicate with their children about education and school matters, participate in school activities, communicate with teachers about their children, and supervise their children at home.

Many different types of studies have shown that parental involvement in a child's education enhances the child's ability to learn and to succeed at school. Eccles and Harold (1993) suggested that parental involvement is important throughout a student's entire academic career, at least all the way through high school. Parental involvement has been shown to affect academic achievement (Paulson, 1994; Steinberg, Lamborn, Dornbusch, & Darling, 1992; Trusty, 1996), positive attitudes toward school (Trusty, 1996), likelihood of staying in school (Rumberger, 1995), and time spent on homework (Keith, Reimers, Fehrmann, Pottebaum, & Aubey, 1986). When parents are involved in their child's education, children perform better academically and are more engaged in school overall, reporting more effort, concentration, and attention (Bogenschneider, 1997; Gonzalez, 2002).

One particularly important aspect of parental involvement includes the educational aspirations and expectations a parent has for his or her child. When a parent sets high standards, youth tend to work harder, resulting in higher levels of school achievement (Natriello & McDill, 1986). For example, high school dropouts report that parents had low academic expectations for them (Ekstrom et al., 1986). High school dropouts also report a history of family members dropping out of school (Mahan & Johnson, 1983), suggesting that family norms and expectations play a large role in student motivation and their own expectations to achieve. Davies and Kandel (1981) suggested that high aspirations and expectations may be especially important to adolescents from low socioeconomic backgrounds because it may provide a strong influence for their children to overcome the multiple disadvantages and risk factors that they face.

Another form of parental involvement is engaging in school activities at the school and at home, such as attending parent–teacher conferences, helping with homework, and watching children participate in sports or school-related activities. When parents are not involved, their children receive lower grades, are more likely to drop out, and have poorer homework habits (Baker & Stevenson, 1986; Epstein, 1982). Gonzalez (2002) examined the relationship between parental involvement and mastery orientation to learning in a sample of high school students. Similar to other studies, when parents showed interest in their child's education by being actively involved, students were more likely to seek challenging tasks, persist through academic challenges, and experience satisfaction in their schoolwork. The critical influence of parent involvement on adolescent academic achievement and school success has been illustrated regardless of student ethnicity, parent education, and family structure (Blum et al., 2000; Bogenschneider, 1997).

Many studies have shown a direct effect of parental involvement on adolescent academic achievement and school success, but others have also found indirect effects. For example, parental involvement may affect academic achievement depending on a number of student personal characteristics such as self-concept, self-esteem, causal-attribution patterns in specific academic success and failure situations (e.g., exam results), and aptitudinal competence for academic learning (Gonzalez-Pienda et al., 2002). Parental involvement does seem to directly influence student academic self-concept, which in turn has a powerful effect on academic achievement.

As parents become involved in their child's education, either through communicating with the child and the school, going to various school functions, helping the student with homework, and holding high academic expectations and aspirations, they can provide an environment that encourages and supports academic achievement. Parental involvement, which clearly involves a whole host of different parenting behaviors, can operate as a strong protective factor that can help to buffer the influence of other risk factors. However involvement is defined, the research is clear on this point: parental involvement is significantly related to child and adolescent academic achievement and school success—the more the better (Blum et al., 2000; Resnick et al., 1998). Steinberg and colleagues (1992) suggested that parental involvement is even more beneficial to students' school success when it occurs within the context of an authoritative parenting style.

Parenting Styles

The way parents tend to interact with and discipline their children (i.e., parenting style) influences both the overall emotional health and the academic achievement of adolescents (Lamborn, Mounts, Steinberg, & Dornbusch, 1991; Shucksmith, Hendry, & Glendinning, 1995). The quality of the parent–child relationship may have an effect on academic performance even more than socioeconomic status or other demographic factors (Magdol, 2003). At the extremes, parent–child relationships can be characterized as the parent being overly strict and not allowing the child to think for him- or herself, or being too permissive and neglectful, in effect allowing the child to act without consequence and without much monitoring. Parenting at either extreme, either too permissive or too strict, appears to negatively affect adolescent academic performance (Dornbusch, Titter, Leiderman, Roberts, & Fraleigh, 1987). Family structure may indirectly affect parenting style and adolescent achievement. For example, single mothers tend to engage in a more permissive style of parenting than adults in two-parent households (Dornbusch et al., 1987). Single parents often have less ability to effectively supervise and monitor their adolescent, and have less time and energy to be involved in school and help children with their homework.

Students who described their parents as neglectful reported the poorest outcomes of all parenting styles. These include increased problem behaviors, lower grade point average, and less positive orientation to school (Lamborn et al., 1991). The frequent use of harsh and coercive discipline (as may be characteristic of authoritarian parents) can also contribute to youth aggressive and antisocial behavior, placing a child at increased risk for academic failure (Avery, Duncan, Duncan, & Hops, 1999; McEvoy & Welker, 2001).

The authoritative parenting style has the most positive impact on adolescent outcomes and academic achievement. Authoritative parenting can be characterized as a style that is demanding but responsive; parents are warm and nurturing but they also have high expectations for their child and set realistic limits with consequences for misbehavior. Baumrind (1989) found that authoritative parents tend to have children who are more academically and socially competent than parents who utilize more authoritarian, neglectful, or permissive styles. In a study of about 10,000 9th- through 12th-grade students, adolescents who characterized their parents as authoritative reported higher levels of academic achievement and competence, significantly lower levels of problem behavior, and significantly higher levels of psychosocial development than adolescents from authoritarian, indulgent, or neglectful households (Lamborn et al., 1991).

Researchers have struggled to identify which specific aspect of parenting behavior is associated most strongly with child outcomes such as positive academic achievement. Ponsford and Lapadat (2001) suggested that family support and high expectations, along with being warm and caring, tend to be important to social and academic achievement. Roberts-Gray and Steinberg (1999) agree, and stated that adolescents appear to fare better academically when they report high levels of parental involvement and autonomy, but feel that their parents have used modest levels of supervision, monitoring, and support, characteristics of an authoritative parenting style. Research on teacher–child relationships and their impact on academic motivation and achievement mirror the findings from the parent–child literature, that teachers who have high expectations of their students, who are viewed as responsive but demanding, have high-achieving students in their classrooms (Wentzel, 2002).

Although substantial evidence suggests that an authoritative style of parenting is often associated with optimum academic, social, and psychological development of children in the United States (Baumrind, 1967; Kim & Rohner, 2002), little research has examined the differences of parenting style among youth of different ethnic groups. One study that examined parenting styles among Korean American students found that an authoritative parenting style (by fathers but not mothers) was associated with higher academic achievement (Kim & Rohner, 2002; see also Steinberg, Dornbusch, & Brown, 1992).

Summary of Family-Level Risk Factors

A variety of family factors can place an adolescent at significant risk of academic failure or, conversely, provide protection from poor achievement, becoming truant, and dropping out of school. Some of these family factors are directly related to the individual parent or adolescent, and include parenting style, the level of parental involvement in their adolescent's school success and academic achievement, and the way that parents and adolescents interact with each other on a daily basis. Some family-level risk factors are more distal and not under the direct control of the parent or adolescent such as family socioeconomic status. Across studies, a consistent finding highlights the important role that parental involvement plays in adolescent academic achievement. Parents who have high standards for their child's academic achievement, who communicate with their child about the importance of education, who actively participate in school-related activities, who spend time with their child on schoolwork at home, and who communicate with their child's teachers are more likely to have a high-achieving adolescent than parents who are less involved on a daily basis in their child's academic life.

SCHOOL-LEVEL RISK FACTORS

Students spend most of their waking hours at school, so it makes sense to examine school-level organization and culture as factors that may influence adolescent academic achievement and behavior at school. Adolescents bring with them to school a myriad of experiences, histories, family backgrounds, levels of risk, expectations, variations in learning style and ability, and capacity to learn. Characteristics of the school and staff interact with these individual- and family-level factors to influence the likelihood of adolescent academic achievement. Some of the school-level factors related to academic achievement for adolescents are exposure to violence at school, school climate, school size, the availability of resources, and the quality of the student–teacher relationship.

Exposure to Violence

School violence affects the lives of children in schools—where they walk, how they dress, where they go, and who their friends are (Epp & Watkinson, 1997). Violence at schools also affects a children's ability to focus on education. Although the overall level of violence in schools has been declining in recent years (Kingery, Coggeshall, & Alford, 1998), the rate of exposure to violence at school remains a serious problem (U.S. Department of Education, 2000). The percentage of children and adolescents exposed to violence remains high. In a recent study, 56% to 87% of adolescents reported they had witnessed at least one violent incident at school, while up to 44% of students reported they had been a victim of school violence (Flannery, Wester, & Singer, in press). School violence ranges from incidents of bullying (Nansel et al., 2001; Olweus, 1993), and threats (Singer & Flannery, 2000) to weapon carrying (Centers for Disease Control, 2000), homicide (Kachur et al., 1996) and spree-shootings and fatalities (Anderson et al., 2001; Moore, Petrie, Braga, & McLaughlin, 2003).

Violence occurs at schools in urban, suburban, and rural settings, and affects children from elementary through high school (Flannery, 1997). Some studies estimate that 70% to 90% of youth will experience ongoing psychological or physical harassment at some point during their school years, characterized by exposure to bullying or being threatened with violence at school (Hazler, 1996; Hoover & Juul, 1993; Hoover & Oliver, 1996; Oliver, Young, & LaSalle, 1994; Singer & Flannery, 2000). In one study, 8% of students reported being bullied one or more times per week (Hoover & Oliver, 1996), with an average of one bullying incident occurring at school every 7½ minutes (Ross, 1996).

Bullying and threatening behavior can lead to more serious violence or consequences. In a 2-year period (1992 to 1994), 105 school-associated violent deaths were identified, with an equal number of deaths occurring in classes or other school-related activities (44%; Kachur et al., 1996). Between 1994 and 1999, 220 violent incidents at school resulted in 172 homicides, 30 suicides, 11 homicide-suicides, 5 legal intervention deaths, and 2 unintentional firearm deaths, with students accounting for 68% of these deaths (Anderson et al., 2001). In 2000, students between the ages of 12 and 18 were victims of 1.9 million total crimes of violence or theft, and about 128,000 were victims of serious violent crimes at school (e.g., rape, sexual assault, or aggravated assault; U.S. Department of Education, 2002). According to the 1999 Youth Risk Behavior Survey, 17% of youth reported that they had carried a weapon in the past 30 days, with 7% of youth reporting they had brought the weapon to school (Centers for Disease Control, 2000). Between 1993 and 2001, nearly 10% of students in grades 9 through 12 reported they had been threatened or injured by a weapon on school property within the last 12 months (U.S. Department of Education, 2002).

Exposure to violence, as a witness or a victim, is related to a number of emotional and behavioral problems that can have a considerable impact on adolescent academic achievement. These include anxiety, anger, depression, dissociation, and self-destructive and aggressive behavior (Breslau, Davis, Andreski, & Peterson, 1991; Flannery, 1999; Flannery, Singer, & Wester, 2001, 2003; Hurt, Malmud, Brodsky, & Giannetta, 2001; Overstreet & Braun, 2000; Schwab-Stone et al., 1995). Along with emotional and behavior problems, exposure to violence at school can disrupt appropriate development and socialization. For example, even the threat of being the victim of physical harm can suppress maximal educational growth and development of students (Furlong & Morrison, 2001).

Studies of victimization from violence at school have shown repeat victimization to have detrimental effects on a student's emotional and social development (Batsche & Knoff, 1994; Brockenbrough, Cornell, & Loper, 2002; Hoover, Oliver, & Thomson, 1993; Olweus, 1993). Being a victim is associated with low self-esteem, depression, social anxiety, and school avoidance (Austin & Joseph, 1996; Crick & Bigbee, 1998; Slee & Rigby, 1993).

About 8% of children report that bullying affects their lives so much so that they have attempted suicide, run away, or refused to go to school (Cullingford & Morrison, 1995), and 17% report suffering from academic problems due to bullying (Hazler, 1996). Across three national Youth Risk Behavior Surveys (Kann et al., 1995, 1996, 1998), approximately 4% to 5% of secondary school students reported staying home at least one time in the past month because of safety concerns at or on the way to school. Fourteen percent of high school students and 22% of fourth through eighth graders reported that bullying and school violence diminished their ability to learn in school (Hoover & Oliver, 1996). It is hard for children to concentrate on school when they are constantly worrying about the next time they will be harassed, what they can do to get revenge on their tormentor, or if they will become the next victim.

Flannery and colleagues (in press) found that adolescents exposed to high levels of violence at school, regardless of the amount of violent behavior they engaged in, were significantly more likely to experience higher levels of anxiety than students who reported low levels of violence exposure at school. Students who are anxious and feel unsafe in their surrounding environment are less likely to be able to pay attention in the classroom, are less likely to report that they enjoy going to school, and are overall less likely to be engaged in and attached to school. All of these factors have been associated with increased risk of poor academic achievement.

Adolescents who are exposed to violence at school also report being significantly more likely to engage in violent behavior (Singer, Anglin, Song, & Lunghofer, 1995), bring a weapon to school (Roberts, 1988), and to miss a significant number of days of school (Cairns et al., 1989; Cullingford & Morrison, 1995; Hinshaw, 1992; Lambert, 1988). As we have previously discussed, students who are aggressive, delinquent, and violent are at increased risk for truancy, dropping out of school, and academic failure.

School Climate

Effective schools can exert a positive influence on student behavior and achievement despite conditions in the home, socioeconomic status, delinquent behavior, or other risk factors. Originally, it was argued that the school could not make a difference or overcome deficits, such as poverty (Jencks et al., 1972), or help a child overcome multiple risk factors. However, more recent research has shown that some high-achieving schools are located in some extremely economically depressed urban neighborhoods (McEvoy & Welker, 2000). Level of academic achievement can also vary school to school, regardless of community or neighborhood characteristics. School climate is one factor that has recently been implicated in student academic achievement and school success. Brookover and Erickson (1975) conducted a study in middle schools and found that school climate factors accounted for 63% of variation in the mean school achievement for both low- and high-achieving schools, even after controlling for socioeconomic status and race.

The climate of a school helps to shape the interactions between students, teachers, administrators, parents, and the community. School climate consists of the attitudes, beliefs, values, and norms that underlie the instructional practices, level of academic achievement, and the operation of the school (Brookover, Erickson, & McEvoy, 1997). Some researchers have suggested that the lack of an orderly classroom environment (Linney & Seidman, 1989; National Commission on Children, 1991) and a lack of a sense of safety (Good & Weinstein, 1986) are major ingredients to a negative school climate. Students who do not feel safe and who believe they are in a highly disorganized place where adults have little interest in their well-being are more likely to suffer academically than students who rate their school more positively with respect to climate.

Perceptions of danger in the school setting are likely to have a negative influence on a student's ability to pay attention and their readiness to learn (Furstenberg & Hughes, 1995). Devine (1995) reported that community norms and behaviors of violence have invaded schools. If students fear for their safety they are less able to focus on education and learning, and instead begin to focus on their protection and well-being. Along with violence coming from other students and individuals within the school, violence can also come from the school. This violence is called systematic violence.

Systematic violence is defined as "any institutional practice or procedure that adversely impacts on individuals/groups by burdening them psychologically, mentally, culturally, spiritually, economically, or physically" (Epp & Watkinson, 1997). Applied to education, systematic violence refers to practices and procedures that prevent students from learning, resulting in 'harm" to the students (Epp & Watkinson, 1997). Examples of systematic violence include exclusionary practices that eliminate the ability for specific students to engage or participate in various school activities, clubs, or organizations. Epp and Watkinson (1997) also suggested that an overly competitive learning environment is considered to be systematic violence, and in turn creates a negative school climate, one in which students are competing against each other for grades, attention, and rewards.

The toleration of abuse is another form of systematic violence from a school. If teachers and school personnel do not intervene when bullying, threats, or violence occur, students begin to think that these behaviors are condoned at the school. This can increase behavior problems, delinquency, and exposure to violence, significant risk factors for academic failure. Unmonitored areas on school grounds are places where students can be exposed to violence or victimized by violence. Often these are physical locations that teachers and administrators claim are not part of their responsibilities (e.g., restrooms), so supervision of these areas is lax (Astor, Meyer, & Behre, 1999). Transition times (e.g., class changes) and areas where more disorganized behavior occurs (e.g., lunchrooms, playgrounds) also contribute to higher rates of disruptive and inappropriate behavior.

A school's disciplinary policies can also contribute to a culture of systematic violence, especially if those policies are rooted in principles of exclusion and punishment (Epp & Watkinson, 1997). When students are consistently punished, suspended, or expelled based on who they are (e.g., those perceived to be at risk for violent behavior or delinquency), they may start to have negative attitudes or aversive feelings toward school, ultimately becoming distanced from school, activities, and education. Schools have an obligation to create a safe environment for everyone, and school security should be a core task, developed to the point where professional standards and evaluation criteria can be applied to determine effectiveness and outcomes (Furlong & Morrison, 2001).

Other aspects of a school that influence school climate include the learning curriculum and standards, expectations of teachers in regards to mastery and achievement, and student attitudes and commitment to education. McEvoy and Welker (2000) discussed five required elements schools need to achieve a positive climate. The first requirement is a safe environment where students and teachers can focus on academic and social skills development instead of worrying about safety and security. The second is a sequenced curriculum that is understood and supported by teachers and students that also demands a high level of mastery from all students. Thus, they suggest that students do not receive credit for work that fails to demonstrate competence or does not meet standards of performance.

A third requirement suggested by McEvoy and Welker (2000) is a commitment from the school administration and personnel to conduct ongoing assessments that reflect the goals and mission of the school. Such assessments would identify any weaknesses or limitations in the curriculum or educational plan that need to be redesigned, or any policies that are no longer serving the purpose of creating a positive school climate. Schools can conduct formal assessments of environment and safety via models like Crime Prevention Through Environmental Design (CPTED), available through organizations like the National Crime Prevention Council (NCPC). The fourth requirement for a positive school climate is the elimination of school practices that are based on the assumption that many students cannot and will not be academically successful. Such policies include ability grouping or tracking, where some students are placed into low-achieving "groups" or "tracks" with low expectations for academic success. This strategy lowers child academic performance and behavior (Oakes, 1985, 1990) and can dramatically affect a student's academic self-concept, or contribute to a sense of futility (McEvoy & Welker, 2000).

The fifth necessary element to achieving a positive school climate is the affirmation and celebration of achievement for the purpose of enhancing commitment to academic progress for students and teachers, and to the mission of the school. Brown (1999) suggests a simple way schools can do this is by sponsoring and conducting awards programs so that students are recognized for their achievements. Overall, positive school climates exist when students have the opportunity to succeed and be rewarded for effort. This enhances student motivation, achievement, and has other positive school outcomes (Bryant et al., 2000; Masten, 1994).

School Size and Resources

Another school-level factor that affects school climate and thus student academic achievement is the size of the school. Smaller schools may be better for at-risk students because they tend to have better teacher-to-student ratios, and school personnel often have a better idea of who their students are, making it easier to interact with them on a personal level to establish a sense of attachment and engagement (Boyer, 1983). This can help students gain a positive attitude toward school and add to the social support network should a student's academic performance begin to suffer. In a larger school, a student who is perceived to be at risk for academic failure or is viewed by teachers or peers as a discipline problem may not get as much personalized attention academically and may tend to get lost in the number of students within the school. It makes it easier for struggling students to become truant or to drop out without necessarily being noticed or without specific academic intervention.

Although larger schools have the disadvantage of being more impersonal, they also often have the advantage of more available resources than a smaller school (Magdol, 2003). Lee, Smerdon, Alfeld-Liro, and Brown (2000) reported that larger schools were better able to serve students at the extremes of ability (i.e., low and high learning ability) within the curriculum structure as it currently existed. Larger schools also tend to be able to develop specialized programs to address individual student needs that arise.

This does not tend to be the case in small schools. Smaller schools are often forced to limit their course offerings due to financial and staffing limitations. They must focus the limited resources they have on their core programs. This can create a problem for students that are at either end of the academic achievement distribution (e.g., low- or high-achieving students) who may be excluded from basic programs or absorbed into programs that may not meet their needs (Lee et al., 2000; Monk, 1987; Monk & Haller, 1993). If a school has limited ability to expand the courses offered to students, youth who have high aspirations and are at the high end of the academic achievement scale may suffer because there are fewer choices that may prepare them for college or that are challenging. Students who are struggling to achieve or are at risk for academic failure can also suffer if they are placed into classes where they do not have the ability to succeed. This can lead to persistent experiences of failure, resulting in school aversion and a higher likelihood of dropping out.

Although staff in smaller schools do not usually view this inclusion method as desirable, they recognize that they are fiscally limited by what they can do or in what they can offer to students (Lee et al., 2000).

Teacher–Student Relationships

Teachers are a primary source of social support for students at school (Bowen & Bowen, 1999). As adults, teachers can play an important role in helping students make sense out of confusing, and potentially dangerous, situations at school. Bowen and Bowen (1999) suggested that teachers serve as both a role model and refuge for students who face situations that they may define as beyond their control or comprehension. A supportive teacher can shift the balance from risk to resilience for an at-risk student in need of a support system, mentor, or role model.

Teachers are in a position not only to educate students, but to reach out to help them make positive connections to their school, and to assist in creating a safe environment, or at least the perception of one. In schools where a culture of violence has invaded the classrooms and hallways, how a teacher responds to behavior problems is important. If teachers approach potentially violent situations with a "hands-off" attitude, or avoid intervening when they witness an act of aggression or violence, it could be interpreted by students that violence is not taken seriously in that school. In these types of settings, incidents of violent behavior, absenteeism, and truancy could increase, while academic achievement declines. On the other hand, if teachers intervene appropriately in problem situations, students may tend to perceive the school climate as safer, which can serve as a protective factor that enhances student academic achievement. Teachers are in a position to reach out to students and encourage an interest in academics, engage them in the school experience, and provide them a mechanism to help them cope with violence. Unfortunately, in our own work we have found that few adolescents talk to teachers or counselors as a way to cope with violence in their lives (Flannery et al., 2003). Finally, teachers can play a key role in directing efforts to increase school safety and helping students develop concrete strategies for addressing school crime and violence (Bowen & Bowen, 1999).

In a qualitative study that attempted to gain information of what was important to students, Ponsford and Lapadat (2001) found that most adolescent students recognize the importance of the teacher–student relationship. Students reported that they preferred teachers who did not attempt to judge or intimidate them, but related to them on a personal level. Students said it was important for a teacher to take the time to get to know them on a personal level, to solicit their opinions and perceptions, and to not base current decisions on past performance or family history (e.g., an older brother or sister's academic ability and behavior in school). Students reported striving for academic achievement when teachers cared about good teaching, communicated democratically, treated students equally without showing favoritism, recognized students as unique individuals, and geared instruction to the variety of individual learning styles in the classroom (Ponsford & Lapadat, 2001; Wentzel, 1997).

Student academic achievement is clearly linked to how flexible teachers are in the classroom. Students are more academically successful when their teachers use a variety of activities and instructional methods to accommodate individual student learning styles and are willing to introduce new material when students are ready (Ponsford & Lapadat, 2001). Instruction that is flexible suits a variety of learning styles and may prevent students from becoming discouraged and dropping out (Gadwa & Griggs, 1985). The curriculum needs to take into account the various demographic backgrounds of students, instead of assuming that students are at the same level and have the same experiences, values, and abilities.

Just as parental educational expectations and aspirations are important, so are teachers' expectations. Brookover and colleagues (1997) argued that teacher expectations for student performance and teacher judgments of student capabilities influence student achievement levels through their effect on students' perceptions of themselves. This is important because student perceptions tend to influence their opinions about their own academic abilities, what they are able to achieve, and their sense of academic futility (i.e., students' beliefs about whether the school system is stacked against them regardless of ability). McEvoy and Welker (2000) reported that academic futility and student perceptions together affect students' decisions regarding their academic behavior (e.g., study, doing homework, and dropping out). Teachers can have a significant impact on students based on their relationships and willingness to care, as well as their expectations for behavior and academic success.

Summary of School-Level Risk Factors

Even though students bring with them to school a constellation of individual and family risk, schools and teachers can still have a tremendous protective impact on students' academic achievement. Individual schools may be limited with respect to their curriculum and resources, but they do have control over the school climate that is created for students and staff. Students who feel safer in school and perceive the school climate to be positive are much more likely to be academically successful than students who are anxious, inattentive, and feel disengaged from school. Teachers play an important role in a student's academic achievement and attitude toward school. By developing more personal, caring relationships that show respect and concern, teachers can influence students' academic achievement in a positive way.

CONCLUSION

Many factors underlie an adolescent's educational performance and academic achievement. To improve students' academic achievement we must address risk factors at multiple levels and not just confine ourselves to approaches that focus solely on the individual adolescent. The solutions do not lie in reducing risk in a single arena. A comprehensive, multidimensional approach needs to be taken, especially given our understanding that risk operates at the individual, family, and school levels. Schools and teachers certainly play a significant role in helping or hindering adolescent academic achievement, but parents also matter a great deal. Parents' involvement in their children's school lives is a crucial determinant of whether an adolescent is likely to become a high achiever or, conversely, is at risk for school failure, truancy, or dropping out.

The solutions are not easy. The effects of risk are not always direct or easily measurable. Sometimes risk factors interact in complicated ways, over a long period of time, to affect an individual child's chances of academic success or failure. What seems clear is the need to start early in a child's academic life. If we want to help ensure adolescent academic achievement, then we must make sure that we provide elementary school students, parents, and teachers the tools, resources, and opportunities to succeed early on. If they do not do well as children, if they do not stay in school, if they lose interest in school, then children will have little chance of doing well as adolescents.

REFERENCES

Allington, R. L., & Cunningham, P. M. (2002). *Schools that work: Where all children read and write* (2nd ed.). Boston: Allyn & Bacon.

Amster, J. B., & Lazarus, P. J. (1984). Identifying learning problems in youthful offenders: Rationale and model. *Journal of Offender Counseling Services and Rehabilitation, 8*(4), 65–77.

Anderson, M., Kaufman, J., Simon, T. R., Barrios, L., Paulozzi, L., Ryan, G., et al. (2001). School-associated violent deaths in the United States, 1994–1999. *Journal of the American Medical Association, 286,* 2695–2702.

Astor, R., Meyer, H., & Behre, W. (1999). Unowned places and times: Maps and interviews about violence in high schools. *American Educational Research Journal, 36,* 3–42.

Austin, S., & Joseph, S. (1996). Assessment of bully/victim problems in 8 to 11 year-olds. *British Journal of Educational Psychology, 66,* 447–456.

Avery, D. V., Duncan, T. E., Duncan, S. C., & Hops, H. (1999). Adolescent problem behavior: The influence of parents and peers. *Behavior Research and Therapy, 37,* 217–230.

Baker, D. A., & Stevenson, D. L. (1986). Mothers' strategies for children's school achievement: Managing the transition to high school. *Sociology of Education, 59,* 155–166.

Barone, C., Weissberg, R. P., Kasprow, W. J., Voyce, C. K., Arthur, M. W., & Shriver, T. P. (1995). Involvement in multiple problem behaviors of young urban adolescents. *Journal of Primary Prevention, 15,* 261–283.

Barrington, B. L., & Hendricks, B. (1989). Differentiating characteristics of high school graduate, dropouts and non-graduates. *Journal of Educational Research, 82,* 309–319.

Barth, R. P. (1984). Reducing nonattendance in elementary schools. *Social Work in Education, 6,* 151–166.

Batsche, G. M., & Knoff, H. M. (1994). Bullies and their victims: Understanding a pervasive problem in the schools. *School Psychology Review, 23,* 165–174.

Baumrind, D. (1967). Childcare practices anteceding three patterns of preschool behavior. *Genetic Psychology Monograph, 75,* 43–88.

Baumrind, D. (1989). Rearing competent children. In W. Damon (Ed.), *Child development today and tomorrow* (pp. 349–378). San Francisco: Jossey-Bass.

Beauvais, F., Chavez, E. L., Oetting, E. R., Deffenbacher, J. L., & Cornell, G. R. (1996). Drug use, violence, and victimization among White American, Mexican American, and American Indian dropouts, students with academic problems, and students in good academic standing. *Journal of Counseling Psychology, 43,* 292–299.

Beebe, M. C. (1993). Categorical offenses of juvenile delinquents and the relationship to achievement. *Journal of Correctional Education, 44,* 193–198.

Berndt, T. J. (1999). Friends' influence on students' adjustment to school. *Educational Psychologist, 34,* 15–26.

Berndt, T. J., & Mekos, D. (1995). Adolescents' perceptions of the stressful and desirable aspects of the transitions to junior high school. *Journal of Research on Adolescence, 5,* 123–142.

Blum, R. W., Beuhring, T., & Rinehart, P. M. (2000). *Protecting teens: Beyond race, income and family structure.* Minneapolis: Center for Adolescent Health, University of Minnesota.

Blum, R. W., Beuhring, T., Shew, M. L., Bearing, L. H., Sieving, R. E., & Resnick, M. D. (2000). The effects of race/ethnicity, income and family structure on adolescent risk behaviors. *American Journal of Public Health, 90*(12), 1879–1884.

Bogenschneider, K. (1997). Parental involvement in adolescent schooling: A proximal process with transcontextual validity. *Journal of Marriage and the Family, 59*(3), 718–733.

Bowen, N. K., & Bowen, G. L. (1999). Effects of crime and violence in neighborhoods and schools on the school behavior and performance of adolescents. *Journal of Adolescent Research, 14,* 319–342.

Boyer, E. L. (1983). *High school: A report on secondary education in America* (The Carnegie Foundation for the Advancement of Teaching). New York: Harper & Row.

Breslau, N., Davis, G. C., Andreski, P., & Peterson, E. (1991). Traumatic events and posttraumatic stress disorder in an urban population of young adults. *Archives of General Psychiatry, 48,* 216–222.

Brier, N. (1989). The relationship between learning disability and delinquency: A review and reappraisal. *Journal of Learning Disabilities, 22,* 546–553.

Brier, N. (1995). Predicting antisocial behavior in youngsters displaying poor academic achievement: A review of risk factors. *Developmental and Behavioral Pediatrics, 16*(4), 271–276.

Brockenbrough, K. K., Cornell, D. G., & Loper, A. B. (2002). Aggressive attitudes among victims of violence at school. *Education and Treatment of Children, 25*(3), 273–287.

Brookover, W., & Erickson, E. L. (1975). *Sociology of education.* Homewood, IL: Dorsey Press.

Brookover, W. B., Erickson, F. J., & McEvoy, A. W. (1997). *Creating effective schools: An in-service program for enhancing school learning climate and achievement.* Holmes Beach, FL: Learning Publications.

Brown, D. (1999). *Proven strategies for improving learning and academic achievement.* Greensboro, NC: CAPS Publications.

Brunswick, A. F., & Messeri, P. A. (1984). Origins of cigarette smoking in academic achievement, stress and social expectations: Does gender make a difference. *Journal of Early Adolescence, 4,* 353–370.

Bryant, A. L., Schulenberg, J., Bachman, J. G., O'Malley, P. M., & Johnston, L. D. (2000). Understanding the links among school misbehavior, academic achievement, and cigarette use: A national panel study of adolescents. *Prevention Science, 1*(2), 71–87.

Cairns, R. B., Cairns, B. D., & Neckerman, H. J. (1989). Early school dropout: Configurations and determinants. *Child Development, 60,* 1437–1452.

Carnegie Council on Adolescent Development. (1989). *Turning points: Pre-paring American youth for the 21st century.* New York: Carnegie Corporation of New York.

Centers for Disease Control. (2000). Youth Risk Behavior Surveillance—United States, 1999. *MMWR, 29,* SS-5.

Conger, K. J., & Conger, R. D., & Scaramella, L. V. (1997). Parents, siblings, psychological control and adolescent adjustment. *Journal of Adolescent Research, 12,* 113–138.

Crick, N. R., & Bigbee, M. A. (1998). Relational and overt forms of peer victimization: A multi-informant approach. *Journal of Consulting and Clinical Psychology, 66,* 337–347.

Cullingford, C., & Morrison, J. (1995). Bullying as a formative influence: The relationship between the experience of school and criminality. *British Educational Research Journal, 21,* 547–561.

Davies, M., & Kandel, D. B. (1981). Parental and peer influences on adolescents' educational plans: Some further evidence. *American Journal of Sociology, 87*, 363–387.

Devine, J. (1995). Can metal detectors replace the panopticon? *Cultural Anthropology, 10*(2), 171–195.

Dornbusch, S. M., Titter, P. L., Leiderman, P. H., Roberts, D. F., & Fraleigh, J. J. (1987). The relation of parenting style to adolescent school performance. *Child Development, 58*, 1244–1257.

Dryfoos, J. G. (1990). *Adolescents at risk: Prevalence and prevention.* London: Oxford University Press.

Eccles, J. S., & Harold, R. D. (1993). Parent school involvement during the early adolescent years. *Teachers College Record, 94*, 568–587.

Ekstrom, R. B., Goertz, M. E., Pollack, J. M., & Rock, D. A. (1986). Who drops out of high school and why? Findings from a national study. *Teachers College Record, 87*, 356–373.

Elliott, D. S. (1996). Delinquency, school attendance and dropout. In D. F. Greenberg (Ed.), *Criminal careers: Vol. 2. The international library of criminology, criminal justice and penology* (pp. 377–384). Aldershot, UK: Dartmouth.

Epp, J. R., & Watkinson, A. M. (Eds.). (1997). *Systemic violence in education: Promise broken.* Albany: State University of New York Press.

Epstein, J. L. (1982). *Student reactions to teachers' practices of parent involvement.* Paper presented at the annual meeting of the American Educational Research Association, New York.

Everett, S. A, Malarcher, A. M., Sharp, D. J., Husten, C. G., & Giovino, G. A. (2000). Relationship between cigarette, smokeless tobacco, and cigar use, and other health risk behaviors among U.S. high school students. *Journal of School Health, 70*(6), 234–240.

Fan, X. (2001). Parental involvement and students' academic achievement: A growth modeling analysis. *Journal of Experimental Education, 70*(1), 27–61.

Farrington, D. P., Loeber, R., Elliott, D. S., Hawkins, J. D., Kandel, D. B., Klein, M. W., et al. (1990). Advancing knowledge about the onset of delinquency and crime. In B. B. Lahey & A. E. Kazdin (Eds.), *Advances in clinical child psychology: Vol. 13* (pp. 283–342). New York: Plenum Press.

Fergusson, D. M., Horwood, L. J., & Lynskey, M. T. (1994). A longitudinal study of early childhood education and subsequent academic achievement. *Australian Psychologist, 29*, 110–115.

Flannery, D. J. (1997). *School Violence: Risk, Preventive Intervention and Policy.* Monograph for The Institute of Urban and Minority Education, Columbia University and the ERIC Clearinghouse for Education, Urban Diversity Series No. 109.

Flannery, D. J. (1999). *Exposure to violence and victimization at school* (Choices Briefs, number 4). New York: Institute for Urban and Minority Education, Columbia University.

Flannery, D. J., Singer, M. I., & Wester, K. L. (2001). Violence exposure, psychological trauma, and suicide risk in a community sample of dangerously violent adolescents. *Journal of the American Academy of Child and Adolescent Psychiatry, 40*, 435–442.

Flannery, D., Singer, M., & Wester, K. (2003). Violence, coping and mental health in a community sample of adolescents. *Violence and Victims, 18*, 1–16.

Flannery, D. J., Wester, K. L., & Singer, M. I. (in press). Impact of violence exposure at school on child mental health and violent behavior. *Journal of Community Psychology.*

Fraser, B. J., Welch, W. W., & Walberg, H. J. (1986). Using secondary analysis of National Assessment data to identify predictors of junior high school students' outcomes. *Alberta Journal of Educational Research, 32,* 37–50.

Frick, P. J., Kamphaus, R. W., Lahey, B. B., Loeber, R., Christ, M. A., Hart, E. L., et al. (1991). Academic underachievement and disruptive behavior disorders. *Journal of Consulting and Clinical Psychology, 59,* 289–294.

Furlong, M., & Morrison, G. (2001). The school in school violence. In H. M. Walker & M. H. Epstein (Eds.), *Making schools safer & violence free: Critical issues, solutions, & recommended practices* (pp. 5–16). Austin, TX: Pro-Ed.

Furstenberg, F. F., & Hughes, M. E. (1995). Social capital and successful development among at-risk youth. *Journal of Marriage and the Family, 57,* 580–592.

Gadwa, K., & Griggs, S. A. (1985). The school dropout: Implications for counselors. *The School Counselor, 33,* 9–17.

Gonzalez, A. (2002). Parental involvement: Its contribution to high school students' motivation. *Clearing House, 75*(3), 132–134.

Gonzalez-Pienda, J. A., Nunez, J. C., Gonzalez-Pumariega, S., Alvarez, L., Roces, C., & Garcia, M. (2002). A structural equation model of parental involvement, motivational and aptitudinal characteristics, and academic achievement. *Journal of Experimental Education, 70*(3), 257–287.

Good, T. L., & Weinstein, R. S. (1986). Schools make a difference: Evidence, criticisms, and new directions. *American Psychologist, 41,* 1090–1097.

Hawkins, J. D., Catalano, R. F., & Miller, J. Y. (1992). Risk and protective factors for alcohol and other drug problems in adolescence and early adulthood: Implications for substance abuse prevention. *Psychological Bulletin, 112,* 64–105.

Hazler, R. J. (1996). *Breaking the cycle of violence: Interventions for bulling and victimization.* Washington, DC: Accelerated Development.

Hinshaw, S., & Lahey, B. B. (1993). Issues of taxonomy and comorbidity in the development of conduct disorder. *Developmental Psychopathology, 5,* 31–49.

Hinshaw, S. P. (1992). Externalizing behavior problems and academic underachievement in childhood and adolescence: Causal relationships and underlying mechanisms. *Psychological Bulletin, 111,* 127–155.

Hoover, J. H., & Juul, K. (1993). Bullying in Europe and the United States. *Journal of Emotional and Behavioral Problems, 2,* 25–29.

Hoover, J. H., & Oliver, R. (1996). *The bullying prevention handbook: A guide for principals, teachers and counselors.* Bloomington, IN: National Educational Services.

Hoover, J. J., Oliver, R. L., & Thomson, K. A. (1993). Perceived victimization by school bullies: New research and future direction. *Journal of Humanistic Education and Development, 32,* 76–84.

Hurt, H., Malmud, E., Brodsky, N. L., & Giannetta, J. (2001). Exposure to violence: Psychological and academic correlates in child witnesses. *Archives of Pediatric Adolescence Medicine, 155,* 1351–1356.

Irfan, M., Igbal, N., Sandhu, B. X., & Singh, P. (1993). School adjustment and achievement motivation among truants and non-truants studying in private school. *Journal of Clinical Psychology 20*, 17–20.

Jencks, C., Smith, M. Acland, H. Bane, M., Cohen, D., Gintis, H., et al. (1972). *Inequality: A reassessment of the effect of family and schooling in America.* New York: Basic Books.

Jeynes, W. H. (2002). The relationship between the consumption of various drugs by adolescents and their academic achievement. *American Journal of Drug and Alcohol Abuse, 28*(1), 15–35.

Kachur, S. P., Stennies, G. M., Powell, K. E., Modzeleski, W., Stephens, R., Murphy, R., et al. (1996). School-associated violent deaths in the United States, 1992–1994. *Journal of the American Medical Association, 275*, 1729–1733.

Kann, L, Kinchen, S. A., Williams, B. I., Ross, J. G., Lowry, R., Hill, C. V., et al. (1998). Youth risk behavior surveillance. United States, 1997. *Journal of School Health, 68*, 355–369.

Kann, L., Warren, C. W., Harris, W. A., Collins, J. L., Douglas, K. A., Collins, M. E., et al. (1995). Youth risk behavior surveillance, 1993. *Journal of School Health, 65*, 163–171.

Kann, L., Warren, C. W., Harris, W. A., Collins, J. L., Douglas, K. A., Williams, B. I., et al. (1996). Youth risk behavior surveillance. United States, 1995. *Journal of School Health, 66*, 365–377.

Keith, T. Z., Reimers, T. M., Fehrmann, P. G., Pottebaum, S. M., & Aubey, L. W. (1986). Parental involvement , homework, and TV times: Direct and indirect effects on high school achievement. *Journal of Educational Psychology, 78*, 373–380.

Kim, K., & Rohner, R. P. (2002). Parental warmth, control, and involvement in schooling predicting academic achievement among Korean American adolescents. *Journal of Cross-Cultural Psychology, 33*(2), 127–140.

Kingery, P. M., Coggeshall, M. B., & Alford, A. A. (1998). Violence at school: Recent evidence from four national surveys. *Psychology in the Schools, 35*, 247–258.

Kirk, P. J., & Ward, M. E. (1999). *Academic achievments and risk behaviors among middle scholl students: 1997 North Carolina risk behavior survey.* Retrieved on August 14, 2003, from http://www.dpi.state.nc.us. Public Schools of North Carolina, State Board of Education.

Lambert, N. M. (1988). Adolescent outcomes for hyperactive children: Perspectives on general and specific patterns of childhood risk for adolescent educational, social and mental health problems. *American Psychologist, 43*, 786–799.

Lamborn, S. D., Mounts, N. S., Steinberg, L., & Dornbusch, S. M. (1991). Patterns of competence and adjustment among adolescents from authoritative, authoritarian, indulgent and neglectful families. *Child Development, 62*, 1049–1065.

Lee, V. E., Smerdon, B. A., Alfeld-Liro, C., & Brown, S. L. (2000). Inside large and small high schools: Curriculum and social relations. *Educational Evaluation & Policy Analysis, 22*(2), 147–171.

Linney, J. A., & Seidman, E. (1989). The future of schooling. *American Psychologist, 44*, 336–340.

Loeber, R., Farrington, D. P., Stouthamer-Loeber, M., Moffitt, T. E., & Caspi, A. (1998). The development of male offending: Key findings from the first decade of the Pittsburgh Youth Study. *Studies on Crime and Crime Prevention, 7*, 141–171.

Magdol, L. (2003). *Risk factors for adolescent academic achievement* (Wisconsin Youth Futures Technical Report #3). University of Wisconsin-Madison Cooperative Extension. Retrieved April 4, 2003: from http://www.uwex.edu

Maguin, E., & Loeber, R. (1996). Academic performance and delinquency. In M. Tonry (Ed.), *Crime and justice: A review of research, Vol. 20* (pp. 94–126). Chicago: University of Chicago Press.

Mahan, G., & Johnson, C. (1983). Portrait of a dropout: Dealing with academic, social, and emotional problems. *NASSP Bulletin, 6*, 80–83.

Masten, A. S. (1994). Resilience in individual development: Successful adaptation despite risk and adversity. In M. C. Wang & E. W. Gordon (Eds.), *Educational resilience in inner-city America* (pp. 3–25). Hillsdale, NJ: Erlbaum.

McClelland, D. C. (1953). *The achieving society.* New York: Appleton Century Crofts.

McEvoy, A., & Welker, R. (2000). Antisocial behavior, academic failure, and school climate: A critical review. *Journal of Emotional and Behavioral Disorders, 8*, 130–140.

Meltzer, L. J., Levine, M. D., Karniski, W., Palfreg, J. S., & Clarke, S. (1984). An analysis of the learning style of adolescent delinquents. *Journal of Learning Disabilities, 17*, 600–618.

Moffitt, T. E. (1993). Adolescence-limited and life-course-persistent antisocial behavior: A developmental taxonomy. *Psychological Review, 100*, 674–701.

Moffitt, T. E. (1994). Natural histories of delinquency. In E. G. M. Weitekamp & H. J. Kerner (Eds.), *Cross-national longitudinal research on human development and criminal behavior* (pp. 3–61). Boston: Kluwer Academic.

Moffitt, T. E., Gabrielli, W. F., Mednick, S. A., & Schulsinger, F. (1981). Socioeconomic status, IQ, and delinquency. *Journal of Abnormal Psychology, 90*, 152–156.

Monk, D. (1987). Secondary school size and curriculum comprehensiveness. *Economics of Education Review, 6*, 137–150.

Monk, D., & Haller, E. J. (1993). Predictors of high school academic course offerings: The role of school size. *American Educational Research Journal, 30*, 3–21.

Moore, M., Petrie, C. V., Braga, A. A., & McLaughlin, B. L. (2003). *Deadly Lessons: Understanding lethal school violence.* Washington, DC: National Academies Press.

Murphy, D. M. (1986). Educational disadvantagement: Associated factors, current interventions and implications. *Journal of Negro Education, 55*, 495–507.

Nansel, T. R., Overpeck, M., Pilla, R. S., Ruan, W. J., Simons-Morton, B., & Scheidt, P. (2001). Bullying behaviors among US youth: Prevalence and association with psychosocial adjustment. *Journal of the American Medical Association, 25*, 2094–2100.

National Commission on Children. (1991). *Beyond rhetoric: A new American agenda for children and families.* Washington, DC: Author.

Natriello, G., & McDill, E. L. (1986). Performance standards, student effort on homework, and academic achievement. *Sociology of Education, 59,* 18–31.

Oakes, J. (1985). *Keeping track: How schools structure inequality.* New Haven, CT: Yale University Press.

Oakes, J. (1990). *Multiplying inequalities: The effects of race, social class, and tracking on opportunities to learn mathematics and science.* Santa Monica, CA: Rand.

Oliver, R. L., Young, T. A., & LaSalle, S. M. (1994). Early lessons in bullying and victimization: The help and hindrance of children's literature. *School Counselor, 42,* 137–146.

Olweus, D. (1993). *Bullying at school: What we know and what we can do.* Cambridge, MA: Blackwell.

Overstreet, S., & Braun, S. (2000). Exposure to community violence and post-traumatic stress symptoms: Mediating factors. *American Journal of Orthopsychiatry, 70,* 263–271.

Pagani, L., Boulerice, B., Vitaro, F., & Tremblay, R. E. (2001). Effects of poverty on academic failure and delinquency in boys: A change and process model approach. *Journal of Child Psychology and Psychiatry, 40*(8), 1209–1219.

Pallas, A. M. (1986). *School dropouts in the United States.* Washington, DC: National Center for Educational Statistics.

Paulson, S. E. (1994). Relations of parenting style and parental involvement with ninth-grade students' achievement. *Journal of Early Adolescents, 14,* 250–267.

Petraitis, J., Flay, B. R., & Miller, T. Q. (1995). Reviewing theories of adolescent substance use: Organizing pieces in the puzzle. *Psychological Bulletin, 117,* 67–86.

Ponsford, K. R., & Lapadat, J. C. (2001). Academically capable students who are failing in high school: Perceptions about achievement. *Canadian Journal of Counseling 35*(2), 137–156.

Powell, L. (1990). Factors associated with the under representation of African Americans in mathematics and science. *Journal of Negro Education, 59,* 292–298.

Price, H. B. (2002). *Achievement matters: getting your child the best education possible.* New York: Kensington.

Resnick, M. D., Bearman, P. S., Blum, R. W., Bauman, K. E., Harris, K. M., Jones, J., et al. (1998). Protecting adolescents from harm: Findings from the National Longitudinal Study on Adolescent Health. *Journal of the American Medical Association, 278,* 823–832.

Reyes, O., & Hedeker, D. (1993). Identifying high-risk students during school transition. *Prevention in Human Services, 10,* 137–150.

Roberts, M. (1988). School yard menace. *Psychology Today, 22,* 52–56.

Roberts-Gray, M., & Steinberg, L. (1999). Unpacking authoritative parenting: Reassessing a multidimensional construct. *Journal of Marriage and Family, 61,* 574–587.

Roderick, M. (1994). Grade retention and school dropout—Investigating the association. *American Educational Research Journal, 31,* 729–759.

Ross, D. M. (1996). *Childhood bullying and teasing: What school personnel, other professionals, and parents can do.* Alexandria, VA: American Counseling Association.

Rumberger, R. W. (1995). Dropping out of middle school: A multilevel analysis of students and schools. *American Educational Research Journal, 32*, 583–625.

Schulenberg, J., Bachman, J. G., O'Malley, P. M., & Johnston, L. D. (1994). High school educational success and subsequent substance use: A panel analysis following adolescents in young adulthood. *Journal of Health and Social Behavior, 35*, 45–62.

Schwab-Stone, M. E., Ayers, T. S., Kasprow, W., Voyce, C., Barone, C. Shriver, T., et al. (1995). No safe haven: A study of violence exposure in an urban community. *Journal of the American Academy of Child and Adolescent Psychiatry, 34*, 1343–1352.

Shucksmith, J., Hendry, L. B., & Glendinning, A. (1995). Models of parenting: Implications for adolescent well-being within different types of family contexts. *Journal of Adolescence, 18*, 253–270.

Simmons, R. G., & Blyth, D. A. (1987). *Moving into adolescence: The impact of pubertal change and school context.* New York: Aldine de Gruyter.

Singer, M. I., Anglin, T. M., Song, L., & Lunghofer, L. (1995). Adolescents' exposure to violence and associated symptoms of psychological trauma. *Journal of the American Medical Association, 273*, 477–482.

Singer, M. I., & Flannery, D. J. (2000). The relationship between children's threats of violence and violent behavior. *Archives of Pediatric Adolescent Medicine, 154*, 785–790.

Slee, P. T., & Rigby, K. (1993). Australian school children's self appraisal of interpersonal relations: The bullying experience. *Child Psychiatry and Human Development, 23*, 273–282.

Steinberg, L., Dornbusch, S., & Brown, B. (1992). Ethnic differences in adolescent achievement: An ecological perspective. *American Psychologist, 47*, 723–729.

Steinberg, L., Lamborn, S. D., Dornbusch, S. M., & Darling, N. (1992). Impact of parenting practices on adolescent achievement: Authoritative parenting, school involvement, and encouragement to succeed. *Child Development, 58*, 1266–1281.

Tanner, J., Krahn, H., & Hartnagal, T. F. (1995). *Fractured transitions from school to work: Revisiting the dropout problem.* Toronto: Oxford University Press.

Trusty, J. (1996). Counseling for dropout prevention: Applications from multicultural counseling. *Journal of Multicultural Counseling and Development, 24*, 105–117.

Tremblay, R., Masse, B., Perron, D., LeBlanc, M., Schwartzman, A., & Ledingham, J. (1992). Early disruptive behavior, poor school achievement, delinquent behavior, and delinquent personality: Longitudinal analyses. *Journal of Consulting and Clinical Psychology, 60*, 64–72.

U.S. Department of Education. (2000). *Indicators of school crime and safety.* Washington, DC: U.S. Department of Justice, Office of Justice Programs.

U.S. Department of Education. (2002). *Indicators of school crime and safety: 2002.* Washington, DC: U.S. Department of Justice, Office of Justice Programs.

U.S. Department of Education. (n.d.). *School Dropout Prevention Program.* Retrieved September 14, 2003, from http://www.ed.gov/programs/dropout/index.html

Walberg, H. J., & Tsai, S. (1981). Productive learning in social studies among early adolescents. *Journal of Early Adolescence, 1*, 245–256.

Walker, H. M., Horner, R. H., Sugai, G., Bullis, M., Sprague, J. R., Bricker, D., et al. (1996). Integrated approaches to preventing antisocial behavior patterns among school-age children and youth. *Journal of Emotional and Behavioral Disorders, 4,* 194–209.

Ward, D. A., & Tittle, C. R. (1994). IQ and delinquency: A test of two competing explanations. *Journal of Quantitative Criminology, 10,* 189–212.

Wentzel, K. R. (1997). Student motivation in middle school: The role of perceived pedagogical caring. *Journal of Educational Psychology, 89,* 411–419.

Wentzel, K. R. (1999). Social-motivational processes and interpersonal relationships: Implications for understanding students' academic success. *Journal of Educational Psychology, 91,* 76–97.

Wentzel, K. (2002). Are effective teachers like good parents? Teaching styles and student adjustment in early adolescence. *Child Development, 73,* 287–301.

White, H. R., Pandina, R .J., & LaGrange, R. L. (1987). Longitudinal predictors of serious substance use and delinquency. *Criminology, 25,* 715–740.

Zagar, R., Arbit, J., Hughes, J. R., Busell, R. E., & Busch, K. (1989). Developmental and disruptive behavior disorders among delinquents. *Journal of the American Academy of Child and Adolescent Psychiatry, 28,* 437–440.

Zimmerman, M.A., & Schmeelk-Cone, K.H. (2003). A longitudinal analysis of adolescent substance use and school motivation among African American youth. *Journal of research on Adolescence, 13*(2), 185–210.

CHAPTER 2

A SELF-REGULATION APPROACH TO UNDERSTANDING ADOLESCENT DEPRESSION IN THE SCHOOL CONTEXT

Karen D. Rudolph

Dispelling historical beliefs that adolescent depression reflects normative and transient experiences of "storm and stress," research suggest that the transition to adolescence represents a sensitive period for the onset of a variety of psychological difficulties, including depression, that may set the stage for long-term developmental trajectories (Nolen-Hoeksema & Girgus, 1994; Petersen & Hamburg, 1986; Rudolph, Hammen, & Daley, in press). Despite this shift in conceptions of adolescent depression, it is often overlooked within educational settings due to the more salient disruption created by adolescent behavior problems such as attention deficits, violence, and substance use. Yet, theory and research suggest that adolescents suffering from depression may experience severe disruption and impairment across many areas of their lives (for a review, see Rudolph et al., in press). Because school is one critical context for youth

Educating Adolescents: Challenges and Strategies, 33–64
Copyright © 2004 by Information Age Publishing
All rights of reproduction in any form reserved.

socialization and development (Kellam, Rebok, Mayer, Ialongo, & Kalodner, 1994; Roeser & Eccles, 2000; Roeser, Midgley, & Urdan, 1996), understanding the interface between depression and school adjustment is a high priority for theory, intervention, and policy regarding both the mental health and education of adolescents.

This chapter provides an overview of adolescent depression in the school context. First, a brief description of adolescent depression is provided. Second, a theoretical model is presented that hypothesizes transactions between educational experiences and depression, wherein depression is viewed as both an antecedent and a consequence of school-related difficulties. Integral to this model is the role of self-regulatory processes in linking school-related and emotional adjustment. Third, findings are summarized from an empirical investigation of depression during the adolescent transition. These findings lend support to the proposed transactional model and suggest several directions for school-based interventions and educational reform.

DESCRIPTION OF ADOLESCENT DEPRESSION

Depression may be conceptualized in several ways, including as a symptom (i.e., a depressed mood), a syndrome (i.e., a set of symptoms that tend to co-occur), or a clinical disorder (i.e., a specific set of symptoms that meet criteria for a diagnosis) (Compas, Ey, & Grant, 1993). Some debate exists about whether these three conditions merely reflect differing severity of depression, or whether they represent qualitatively different experiences. Regardless of these distinctions, however, each of these conditions is important to consider in the school context.

As a clinical disorder, adolescent depression is characterized by a combination of emotional, cognitive, and physiological symptoms, which include depressed or irritable mood, anhedonia (loss of pleasure), weight or appetite changes, sleep changes, psychomotor agitation (i.e., restlessness) or retardation (i.e., slowing down), fatigue, feelings of worthlessness or guilt, concentration problems or indecisiveness, and thoughts of death or suicide (*Diagnostic and Statistic Manual-IV-TR*; American Psychiatric Association, 2000). Depression often co-occurs with other mental health problems such as anxiety, conduct problems, and attention-deficit hyperactivity disorder.

A large body of research indicates that rates of depression increase sharply during adolescence. Approximately 15% of adolescents experience an episode of major depression by age 18 (Kessler & Walters, 1998). However, an additional 10–20% of adolescents experience significant depressive symptoms that do not meet criteria for a clinical diagnosis

(Cooper & Goodyer, 1993; Kessler & Walters, 1998). Up to 40% of adolescents may experience a depressed mood at any particular point in time (Compas et al., 1993). Both clinical disorders and subclinical levels of symptoms are associated with significant short- and long-term distress and impaired functioning (Kovacs, 1997; Kovacs & Goldston, 1991; Rao et al., 1995). Moreover, research findings suggest that rates of adolescent depression have increased in recent years compared to previous decades (Kessler, Avenevoli, & Merikangas, 2001), and depression is likely to be chronic or recurrent throughout the adolescent years (e.g., Lewinsohn, Clarke, Seeley, & Rohde, 1994; for a review, see Rudolph et al., in press). The escalation in depression from childhood to adolescence, the increasing rates of adolescent depression in recent years, and the likelihood for recurring or long-term experiences of depression collectively highlight the vital importance of understanding how depression during this life stage influences, and is influenced by, school-related experiences and outcomes.

ECOLOGICAL CONTEXT OF ADOLESCENT DEPRESSION

Although the symptoms and associated characteristics of depression involve a focus on individual adaptation, a contextualized approach to understanding adolescent depression is essential (Hammen, Rudolph, Weisz, Rao, & Burge, 1999; Rudolph et al., in press). The school environment represents one salient development context for adolescents (Eccles et al., 1993). As such, schools are critical contexts in which to understand mental health difficulties such as depression (Roeser & Eccles, 2000; Roeser, Eccles, & Sameroff, 1998). In particular, dynamic and reciprocal transactions are likely to emerge between trajectories of psychological and school adjustment over time. This interface between mental health and school adjustment may involve many facets of school-related experiences, including (a) beliefs about education and achievement (e.g., achievement motivation, self-efficacy beliefs, academic investment and values), (b) academic engagement (e.g., effort, persistence), (c) behavioral engagement (e.g., school conduct, truancy, school dropout), (d) classroom performance and achievement, and (e) subjective and objective aspects of the school environment (e.g., feelings of affiliation/belongingness versus alienation, perceptions of the classroom and school environment, teacher–student relations). Adolescent mental health is likely to both influence, and be influenced by, these school-related experiences, resulting in a mutually reinforcing cycle across development. The intertwining of these trajectories highlights the importance, for both theory and practice, of integrating educational and mental health perspectives on adolescent development (Roeser & Eccles, 2000; Roeser et al., 1996). Jointly considering psychological and school adjustment difficulties will contribute to more comprehensive theories regarding the emergence and maintenance of mental health problems, such as depression, within the school context. Moreover, understanding the developmental course of co-occurring mental health and school adjustment difficulties will contribute to the creation of educational environments that optimize adolescent development.

TRANSACTIONAL MODEL OF
SCHOOL ADJUSTMENT AND DEPRESSION

Research generally supports a link between depression and a range of school-related difficulties (for reviews, see Hammen & Rudolph, 1996; Kovacs & Goldston, 1991), including a negative academic self-concept (Asarnow, Carlson, & Guthrie, 1987), concentration problems (Ialongo, Edelsohn, Werthamer-Larsson, Crockett, & Kellam, 1996), compromised academic achievement (Ialongo et al., 1996; Puig-Antich et al., 1993), problematic school conduct (Puig-Antich et al., 1993), and less positive relations with teachers (Puig-Antich et al., 1993). Despite this evidence, integrative theoretical formulations that elucidate the processes underlying this link are scarce (for an exception, see Roeser & Eccles, 2000).

In the following section, an integrative model is proposed that considers transactions between depression and school-related difficulties during adolescence. According to this model, depression may both *undermine* adolescents' educational attitudes and endeavors and *emerge from* stressful school-related perceptions and experiences. In particular, depression is believed to compromise school adjustment through its adverse effect on both personal characteristics of youth and characteristics of their school contexts, which then place youth at risk for further depression. This risk for depression is likely heightened within school contexts that fail to support adolescents' needs (Roeser et al., 1998) and during periods of change or challenge in school contexts such as school transitions (Rudolph, Lambert, Clark, & Kurlakowsky, 2001).

The proposed integrative model emphasizes self-regulatory processes as links between depression and school adjustment (see Figure 2.1). Self-regulation involves cognitive, behavioral, and evaluative processes that guide goal-directed action and emotions. Theories of self-regulation in the achievement domain (e.g., Bandura, 1986; Deci & Ryan, 1985; Eccles, Adler, & Meece, 1984; Pajares & Schunk, 2001; Scheier & Carver, 1982) emphasize how appraisal processes, such as one's expectations regarding outcomes (e.g., perceptions of competence, self-efficacy beliefs) and one's personal investment in outcomes (e.g., goals, standards, values), contribute to behavior and emotion. Theory and research suggest that adaptive self-regulatory beliefs yield positive behavioral and emotional consequences such as constructive learning strategies, mastery-oriented behavior, high levels of achievement, and positive emotions, whereas maladaptive self-regulatory beliefs yield negative consequences such as poor learning strategies, helpless behavior, compromised performance, and negative emotions (Bandura, Pastorelli, Barbaranelli, & Caprara, 1999; Harter & Connell, 1984; for reviews, see Dweck & Leggett, 1988; Pajares & Schunk, 2001; Skinner, Zimmer-Gembach, & Connell, 1998). According to the model proposed in this chapter (see Figure 2.1), maladaptive self-regulatory processes in the school context both emerge from, and create a risk for, depression. Specifically, depression may be linked to a departure from traditional norms of school-related values, attitudes, behaviors, perceptions, and experiences conducive to successful adaptation in the educational context.

Self-regulatory processes are likely to play a particularly important role in explaining the link between school adjustment and mental health during adolescence. During this time, changes in school structure and teacher–student relations, particularly those associated with the transition from grade schools to secondary schools, frequently result in more controlling and less supportive classroom and school environments that may compromise students' sense of autonomy, competence, and belonging (Eccles & Midgley, 1989; Eccles, Midgley, & Adler, 1984; Roeser et al., 1996). At the same time, responsibility for academic progress often is shifted toward students, as they are expected to meet academic demands with less external monitoring and support (Harter, Whitesell, & Kowalski, 1992). Reflecting the difficulty of these changes, many studies document normative declines in adolescents' perceived academic competence, academic motivation, achievement, and classroom engagement, and increases in school-related concerns and negative affect during this time (Blyth, Simmons, & Carlton-Ford, 1983; Harter et al., 1992; Seidman, Allen, Aber, Mitchell, & Feinman, 1994; Skinner et al., 1998; for reviews, see Eccles & Midgley, 1989; Eccles, Midgley, & Adler, 1984).

Successfully negotiating these challenges and continuing along (or returning to) positive psychological and school adjustment trajectories requires that adolescents demonstrate a great deal of self-motivation and engage in more independent self-regulatory efforts than in earlier school years. Circumstances that interfere with adolescents' ability to assume personal responsibility for academic success are therefore likely to foster declining school adjustment. Experiences of depression during this life stage represent one such challenge to the development of adaptive self-regulatory resources. In turn, failure to develop these resources is likely to further heighten vulnerability to depression during this high-risk period.

Depression as an Antecedent of School-Related Difficulties

Researchers have suggested that an episode of depression may leave a developmental "scar" (Lewinsohn, Steinmetz, Larson, & Franklin, 1981) by interfering with critical developmental milestones and resulting in permanent changes in functioning. Even mild or transient symptoms of depression may interrupt the normative acquisition of skills and competencies. Within the school context, the experience of depression during adolescence may disrupt each stage of the self-regulatory process (see Figure 2.1).

Self-Regulatory Cognitions

Contemporary theories of achievement motivation incorporate a wide range of achievement-oriented self-regulatory cognitions. One integrative framework (Eccles, Wigfield, & Shiefele, 1998) organizes these cognitions in terms of three broad motivational questions. The first set of cognitions relates to the question "Can I do this task?" These cognitions include appraisals of one's own competence and efficacy in academic settings, perceptions of control over outcomes, expectancies for success and failure, and attributions for success and failure. The second set of cognitions relates to the question "Do I want to do this task and why?" These cognitions include academic investment and values (e.g., subjective interest in academic tasks, personal importance of academic success, beliefs that education is important for life success), as well as specific goals that guide academic pursuits (e.g., intrinsic versus extrinsic motivation, learning versus performance goals). The third set of cognitions relates to the question "What do I have to do to succeed on this task?" These cognitions include beliefs that guide selection and application of learning strategies aimed at accomplishing academic tasks, monitoring of one's behavior, evaluation of one's performance, and reactions to one's performance. According to this framework (Eccles et al., 1998), theories of self-regulation emphasize the third set of cognitions. However, these theories also incorporate many of the cognitions from the first two sets, such as self-efficacy beliefs, attributions, and goal-setting. Thus, in this chapter, the construct of self-regulatory cognitions refers to all three sets of beliefs.

Depression may undermine the development of adaptive achievement-oriented self-regulatory cognitions. Depressed youth typically experience low self-worth, diminished perceptions of their competence, and low perceived control over their environments (for reviews, see Garber & Hils-

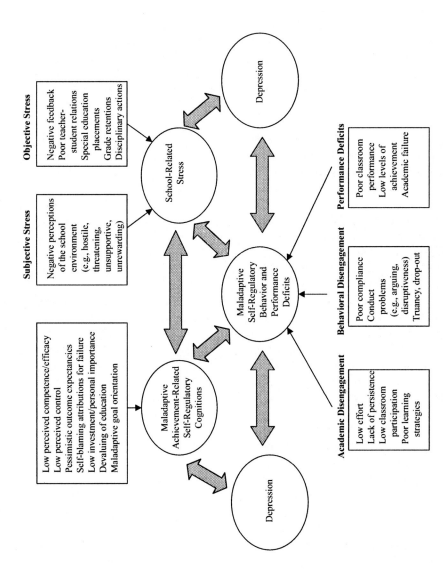

Figure 2.1.   Self-regulation model of depression in the school context.

man, 1992; Rudolph et al., in press). Thus, depressed adolescents may feel ineffective in their schoolwork, regardless of their actual level of performance, and may feel overwhelmed by the demands of school. Indeed, longitudinal research demonstrates that depression and associated emotional distress predict lower levels of academic self-concept (Cole, Peeke, Dolezai, Murray, & Canzoniero, 1999; Roeser et al., 1998), uncertainty about how to meet standards for academic performance (Pomerantz & Rudolph, 2003), and an underestimation of academic competence relative to actual performance over time (Cole, Martin, Peeke, Seroczynski, & Fier, 1998; Cole, Martin, Peeke, Seroczynski, & Hoffman, 1998; Pomerantz & Rudolph, 2003). This negative self-evaluation may undermine adolescents' investment in academics, leading them to devalue the importance of education and academic success in an effort to protect themselves from perceived failure. Moreover, a sense of hopelessness about the future may dampen excitement about, or investment in, future educational attainments.

Depression also may activate maladaptive styles of processing information, leading to self-regulatory difficulties. For example, theory and research suggest that a depressed mood can cause a narrowing of attention and memory toward negative experiences and perceived flaws (Lyubormisky, Caldwell, & Nolen-Hoeksema, 1998; Pyszczynski & Greenberg, 1987). Thus, depressed adolescents may attend to and recall academic failures more than academic successes, and they may ruminate about their perceived or actual academic weaknesses. Furthermore, depressed adolescents are prone to negative interpretations of events (for reviews, see Garber & Hilsman, 1992; Rudolph et al., in press), reflected in a tendency to attribute failure to internal, global, and stable factors, and success to external, specific, and unstable factors. When depressed adolescents experience academic problems (e.g., failing a test), they may therefore blame these problems on their lack of ability (e.g., "I am a poor student"). Consistent with this pathway, emotional distress predicts subsequent pessimistic attributional style (Nolen-Hoeksema, Girgus, & Seligman, 1986, 1992), including negative attributions about academic performance (Pomerantz & Rudolph, 2003).

Depression also may influence adolescents' goal orientation. Theories of achievement goal orientation (Dweck & Leggett, 1988; Elliott & Harackiewicz, 1996; Harter & Connell, 1984; Pintrich, 2000) distinguish between goals that focus on internal motivation, such as learning, developing knowledge and competence, or being challenged (e.g., intrinsic motivation; task–goal, mastery, or learning orientation) versus external motivation, such as demonstrating one's ability, receiving favorable evaluations of competence, or outperforming others (e.g., extrinsic motivation, performance goal orientation). Goals and accompanying achievement-related behaviors also have been distinguished as approach-oriented versus avoidance-oriented (Elliot & Thrash, 2001; Middleton & Midgley, 1997; Urdan, Ryan, Anderman, & Gheen, 2002). Approach-oriented goals involve a motivation to move *toward* academic endeavors for the purpose of developing or demonstrating knowledge, and they are associated with high levels of effort and persistence. Avoidance-oriented goals involve a motivation to move *away from* academic endeavors for the purpose of avoiding negative judgments of one's ability, and they are associated with withdrawal of effort and avoidance of challenge. Heightened negative self-evaluation and excessive focus on perceived academic incompetence may lead depressed adolescents to adopt a narrow set of goals. For example, self-determination theory suggests that feeling competent and self-determined leads people to be intrinsically motivated (Deci & Ryan, 1985). The negative self-evaluation characteristic of depressed adolescents may undermine their sense of self-determination and create a tendency toward extrinsic motivation. Moreover, negative mood states and an excessive focus on poor performance may lead depressed youth to divert their psychological resources away from mastery-oriented goals, and toward performance-oriented goals (Roeser & Eccles, 2000), particularly goals that emphasize avoiding future failure (Linnenbrink & Pintrich, 2002). Indeed, findings suggest that negative mood states may lead to lower mastery orientation (for a review, see Linnenbrink & Pintrich, 2002).

Self-Regulatory Behavior and Performance

Depression also may contribute to maladaptive self-regulatory behavior and performance deficits. In particular, depression may lead to problematic achievement-related behaviors that undermine learning and performance, as well as to general disengagement from academic pursuits. Depressive symptoms may have *direct* negative consequences for academic and behavioral engagement. For example, symptoms of depression such as sadness and anhedonia may cause disinterest in classroom activities and a lack of effort or productivity. Fatigue and concentration difficulties may impair adolescents' ability to absorb new academic material and to successfully complete academic tasks, leading to decrements in learning and performance (Kovacs & Goldston, 1991). These symptoms also may cause adolescents to avoid demanding tasks and to show less persistence when they are faced with academic challenges. Sleep and appetite disturbances may threaten adolescents' physical well-being, thereby impairing their academic performance. Depressed adolescents whose mood is characterized by irritability may demonstrate problematic classroom conduct, such as frequent arguing with teachers and peers or refusal to complete assignments. In extreme cases, depressed adolescents' disengagement from school may become severe, as reflected in frequent truancy or school dropout.

Depression also may have an *indirect* effect on academic engagement and performance through its influence on self-regulatory cognitions. Depressed youth who develop pessimistic beliefs about their academic self-efficacy, self-blaming attributions for academic failure, a low investment in academic success, and a goal orientation characterized by avoidance of failure are less likely to engage in mastery-oriented behavior. This profile of *learned helplessness*—that is, negative achievement-related attributions and reduced perceptions of control over academic outcomes, coupled with a lack of effort and persistence when faced with challenge—has been linked to a range of motivational, behavioral, and emotional deficits likely to undermine school adjustment, such as decreased initiation of tasks, poor-quality problem-solving strategies, low expectations for future success, a preference for easy over challenging tasks, and negative task-related emotions, such as anxiety, frustration, and boredom (Dweck & Leggett, 1988; Pintrich, 2000; Urdan, 1997).

Research supports these proposed negative effects of depression on academic engagement and performance (see Kovacs & Goldston, 1991). For example, depression and associated negative emotions predict the subsequent display of helpless behavior in challenging academic situations (Nolen-Hoeksema et al., 1992) and poor academic achievement (Chen & Li, 2000; Ialongo, Edelsohn, Werthamer-Larsson, Crockett, & Kellam, 1993; Roeser et al., 1998) during middle childhood and adolescence. Early-onset psychiatric disorders, including depression, also predict lower levels of educational attainment (Kessler, Foster, Saunders, & Stang, 1995).

Subjective and Objective Characteristics of the School Environment

Finally, depression may contribute to *evaluative* aspects of self-regulation, as reflected in perceptions of the school environment, as well as to objective characteristics of the environment. Due to perceptual biases and low perceived coping efficacy, depressed adolescents may overestimate the stressfulness of normative academic challenges or school-related hassles. Moreover, the social withdrawal that is characteristic of many depressed youth may lead to social isolation and a lack of peer support (Kovacs & Goldston, 1991), creating a sense of alienation from school. Beyond adolescents' perceptions of the school environment, academic disengagement and performance deficits actually may cause adolescents to *create* more stressful circumstances. For example, depressed adolescents who demonstrate low effort or frequent academic failures may elicit negative feedback from their teachers and parents or, at more extreme levels, may experience repercussions such as placement in remedial classes or grade retentions. Behavioral disengagement or problematic conduct may result in disciplinary actions at the classroom level (e.g., reprimands by teachers) or school level (e.g., detentions, suspensions), thereby creating a stressful environment and reinforcing depressed adolescents' views of school as hostile, punitive, and unrewarding.

Little longitudinal research has examined directly the influence of depression on adolescents' perceptions of the school environment or actual experience of school-related stress. Research has shown that depressive symptoms as early as first grade predict placement in remedial classes and grade retention during early adolescence (Ialongo, Edelsohn, & Kellam, 2001). Moreover, teachers report feeling overwhelmed by the emotional and behavioral difficulties of their adolescent students (Roeser & Midgley, 1997), suggesting that teachers may respond in less effective ways to depressed youth. Concurrent data suggest that depressed youth with co-occurring behavioral problems experience particularly high levels of school-related stress (Rudolph et al., 2000).

Transactions among Self-Regulatory Processes

As reflected in the bidirectional arrows in Figure 2.1, the proposed self-regulatory processes likely are reciprocal (see also Bandura, 1986; Pajares, 1996). For example, school-related stress, such as a sense of alienation from school or negative relations with teachers, may undermine adolescents' investment in traditional academic goals, diminish their sense of academic competence and control over academic success, and lead them to disengage from the school environment. Indeed, research suggests that adolescents' perceptions of the school psychological environment as unsupportive of their competence and autonomy predict lower levels of perceived academic competence, less value placed on academics, and poorer academic performance over time (Roeser et al., 1998). Similarly, adolescents who experience multiple academic failures may engage in self-defensive processes that cause them to devalue the importance of education and academic success.

Depression as a Consequence of School-Related Difficulties

According to the proposed transactional model, depression not only may adversely *affect* adolescents' school adjustment, but also may *emerge from* maladaptive school-related self-regulatory processes. Accommodating to the school environment is a central developmental task of adolescence; failure to adequately negotiate this task may therefore compromise

emotional well-being and place adolescents at risk for mental health difficulties such as depression (Eccles, Lord, Roeser, Barber, & Jozefowicz,
1997; Roeser et al., 1998; Rudolph, Lambert et al., 2001).

Self-Regulatory Cognitions, Behavior, and Performance

Several theories of the etiology of adolescent depression highlight the
role of maladaptive self-regulatory cognitions, such as low self-efficacy, a
decreased sense of control, and negative attributional style, in the onset
or exacerbation of depression (for reviews, see Garber & Hilsman, 1992;
Rudolph et al., in press). In a complementary fashion, several theories of
achievement motivation (Dweck & Leggett, 1988; Linnenbrink & Pintrich, 2002; Urdan et al., 2002) highlight possible negative emotional
consequences of particular motivational orientations, most prominently
reflected in profiles indicative of learned helplessness (e.g., theories of
intelligence as fixed, avoidance of challenge and failure, ability-oriented
attributions for failure, lack of persistence). Adolescents who feel ineffective at school, lack a personal investment in academic success, adopt
avoidance goals, and attribute academic failure to enduring characteristics of themselves may develop motivational deficits and accompanying
feelings of self-doubt, low self-worth, hopelessness, and sadness characteristic of depression. Youth with these beliefs may be particularly at risk for
depression during adolescence due to the novelty and challenges associated with the school transitions that occur during this period (Rudolph,
Lambert, et al., 2001). Moreover, adolescents who adopt traditional cultural values related to the importance of school and educational attainment are likely to feel more connected to society and to experience a
sense of emotional well-being. In contrast, those who reject mainstream
values may experience a poor match between their needs and the school
environment, and may therefore experience alienation, hopelessness, and
emotional distress (Eccles & Midgley, 1989; Roeser et al., 1998). Risk for
depression may be exacerbated by the academic disengagement and performance deficits resulting from these beliefs. That is, helpless behavior,
lack of participation in classroom and school activities, and poor academic performance stemming from a lack of investment in academics
likely confirm adolescents' negative beliefs about their worth and reinforce their sense of hopelessness, leading to depression.

Consistent with the proposed impact of maladaptive achievement-
related self-regulatory cognitions and behavior on depression, longitudinal research reveals that low perceived academic competence, a pessimistic attributional style, uncertainty about meeting academic performance
standards, low levels of academic motivation (e.g., a lack of intrinsic motivation, a decreased emphasis on the importance of education for life success), and helpless responses to academic challenge predict heightened

depression and associated emotional distress over time (Hankin, Abramson, & Siler, 2001; Nolen-Hoeksema et al., 1986, 1992; Pomerantz & Rudolph, 2003; Roeser et al., 1998). Negative achievement-related self-regulatory cognitions are particularly likely to predict subsequent depression when youth experience academic failure (Hilsman & Garber, 1995).

Subjective and Objective Characteristics of the School Environment

Adolescents' subjective and objective experiences of heightened school-related stress also may create a risk for depression. Perceptions of the school environment as supportive and nurturing of adolescents' needs (e.g., the need for competence and autonomy) are likely to promote adolescents' emotional well-being, whereas perceptions of the school environment as threatening, hostile, or otherwise unsupportive are likely to undermine adolescents' emotional well-being (Eccles et al., 1993; Roeser et al., 1998). Moreover, actual stress in the day-to-day school environment may exacerbate feelings of depression. This stress may result from the structure of the classroom and school environment (e.g., high teacher expectations, demanding workload) or may be a consequence of adolescents' own behavior (e.g., conflict with teachers due to disruptive behavior, detentions due to incomplete assignments).

A few studies support the adverse influence of negative perceptions of the school environment and school-related stress on emotional well-being. Concurrent data suggest that adolescents with positive perceptions of teacher–student relationships experience more positive school-related affect due to their stronger feelings of belonging at school (Roeser et al., 1996). Moreover, adolescents who perceive the school environment as less supportive of their needs for autonomy and personal regard demonstrate higher levels of depression and anger over time (Roeser et al., 1998). More generally, the experience of daily school hassles predicts heightened depression over time (Robinson, Garber, & Hilsman, 1995).

Summary of the Integrative Model

According to the proposed model (see Figure 2.1), depression may lead adolescents to adopt a profile of self-regulatory cognitions and behavior that undermine their effective engagement in educational endeavors, foster perceptions of school as a stressful and unwelcoming environment, and elicit negative feedback from teachers and parents. This disengagement and stress reinforces students' negative views and further interferes with their successful adjustment to school, perpetuating the depressive experiences. This cycle is likely to be exacerbated during particularly stressful or challenging times, such as the transition to secondary school that occurs during early adolescence.

EMPIRICAL INVESTIGATION OF DEPRESSION IN THE SCHOOL CONTEXT

Several lines of research establish preliminary support for the proposed reciprocal-influence model of adolescent depression and school impairment, yet comprehensive investigations that integrate educational and mental health perspectives on adolescent school functioning are limited. Theory and research drawing from educational perspectives primarily focus on cognitive and behavioral aspects of self-regulation, with less attention paid to emotional antecedents and consequences of achievement-related self-regulatory processes. Although some researchers have begun to call for the integration of emotion into theories of motivation and achievement, work in this area primarily focuses on specific task- or school-related affect (e.g., anxiety, boredom) or transient emotions, rather than on global emotional well-being (e.g., Linnenbrick & Pintrich, 2002; Meyer & Turner, 2002; for an exception, see Roeser & Eccles, 2000). Complementing this approach, theory and research drawing from mental health perspectives primarily consider global school adjustment problems (e.g., academic failure, school dropout) linked to psychological difficulties such as depression, with less attention paid to understanding specific aspects of the self-regulatory process.

Moreover, although educational research has elucidated the significant role of schools as ecological contexts for the development of achievement-related beliefs and behaviors, less emphasis has been placed on schools as contexts for emotional development. As one example, a great deal of research illustrates how school transitions present challenges for students' self-regulatory beliefs, school engagement, and perceptions of the school environment. However, minimal research examines how school transitions serve as salient developmental contexts for the emergence of individual differences in emotional difficulties such as depression. Thus, little is known about why some adolescents navigate these transitions with relative ease, whereas others experience significant stress and emotional distress during this time.

Prior research on depression within the school context is also characterized by methodological limitations. With a few notable exceptions, much of this research is based on concurrent designs that provide no information about the direction of influence between depression and school-related impairment. Research that does use longitudinal designs tends to focus on a single direction of influence, rather than on testing reciprocal-influence models (for an exception, see Roeser et al., 1998).

This section describes results from the University of Illinois Transition to Adolescence Project (UI-TAP), a longitudinal investigation of youth adjustment during the transition to adolescence (Caldwell, Rudolph, Troop-Gordon, & Kim, in press; Gazelle & Rudolph, 2004; Rudolph & Clark, 2001; Rudolph & Conley, in press; Rudolph, Kurlakowsky, & Conley, 2001; Rudolph, Lambert, et al., 2001). UI-TAP used a person x environment perspective to understand how attributes of youth and their environments jointly contribute to adolescent development. A particular focus was placed on investigating the precursors and consequences of depression over the course of the early adolescent transition. A central component of the study involved a focus on adolescent depression within the school context. This study addressed several conceptual and methodological limitations of prior theory and research by (a) examining the role of depression as both an antecedent and a consequence of a wide range of school-related adjustment indices, including academic investment and perceived control, goal orientation, classroom engagement, academic performance, and school-related stress, (b) using a longitudinal design to investigate the reciprocal influences between depression and school adjustment, (c) exploring the role of the middle school transition in the emergence of individual differences in depression, and (d) considering how the family context influences the development of achievement-related self-regulatory processes linked to depression.

Two cohorts of early adolescents participated in the UI-TAP study. The first cohort consisted of 624 adolescents (318 girls, 306 boys; mean age = 11.5; SD = .68; 67% white, 33% ethnic minority, primarily African American) who completed two assessment waves during the spring of fifth or sixth grade and the fall or spring of the following school year (79% of the original sample completed the second wave). The second cohort consisted of 586 adolescents (296 girls, 290 boys; mean age = 11.7; SD = .68; 62% white, 38% ethnic minority, primarily African American) who completed three assessment waves during the spring of fifth or sixth grade and the fall and spring of the following school year (91% and 81% of the original sample completed the second and third waves, respectively). Adolescents were recruited from elementary and middle schools in small urban and rural areas of the Midwest. The sample was heterogeneous in socioeconomic status, with approximately 43% of the adolescents receiving federally subsidized school lunches. The 1,210 adolescents comprising the two cohorts included 96% of eligible fifth and sixth graders in the targeted schools, reflecting a highly representative sample of adolescents in the geographic region.

Adolescents and their teachers completed a series of questionnaires assessing many different domains of adolescent experiences and adjustment. Relevant to the present focus, questionnaires examined achievement-related cognitions and behavior, academic performance, academic and general school-related stress, family context, and depressive symptoms.

Prevalence of Depressive Symptoms

Based on one of the most widely used measures of youth depression (Children's Depression Inventory; Kovacs, 1980/81), 13% of adolescents endorsed severe symptoms of depression occurring in the prior 2 weeks (CDI scores of 19 or greater). Although endorsement of symptoms on this measure may reflect the presence of psychological distress other than depression, adolescents who report severe symptoms are likely to qualify for clinical diagnoses of depression. An additional 12% of adolescents endorsed moderate symptoms of depression (CDI scores from 13 to 18). Notably, 30% of the adolescents reported moderate to severe suicidal ideation ("I think about killing myself but I would not do it" or "I want to kill myself").

Depression as an Antecedent of School-Related Difficulties

One goal of UI-TAP was to investigate the influence of depression on adolescents' subsequent school adjustment. Consistent with the proposed model, we hypothesized that depression would undermine adolescents' school adjustment by compromising achievement-related self-regulatory cognitions, fostering disengagement and performance deficits, creating negative perceptions of the school environment, and causing school-related stress. Findings from this study support the contention that depression interferes with each stage of the self-regulatory process (Rudolph & Pomerantz, 2004).

Self-Regulatory Cognitions
With regard to achievement-oriented self-regulatory cognitions, we anticipated that depressed adolescents would show reduced perceptions of control over academic success and lower levels of academic investment over time. We also anticipated that depression would contribute to subsequent self-blaming attributions about academic failure and decreased self-perceived coping efficacy. To assess these beliefs, adolescents completed measures tapping perceptions of academic control (e.g., "I can get good

grades at my schoolwork if I try"; Weisz, Southam-Gerow, & McCarty, 2000), global investment in academic success (e.g., "It is important for me to do well in school and get good grades"), self-blaming attributions for academic failure (e.g., "How much do you think having problems with your schoolwork is caused by things that you do?"), and perceived coping efficacy (e.g., "When you have problems with your schoolwork, can you make things better if you try?"). In addition, two specific aspects of academic investment were assessed: investment in learning (e.g., "How important is it to you to learn interesting things in school?") and investment in performance (e.g., "How important is it to you that other kids think you are smart?").

Regression analyses were conducted to examine whether depression predicted maladaptive self-regulatory beliefs 6 months and 1 year later, after adjusting for earlier self-regulatory beliefs. The second cohort of adolescents was used for these analyses due to the availability of the measures of interest. As anticipated, depressed adolescents reported significantly lower perceptions of control over academic success, decreased overall academic investment and lower investment in both academic mastery and performance, more self-blaming attributions for academic failure, and decreased coping efficacy. The majority of these associations held over 6-month and 1-year periods.

Self-Regulatory Behavior and Performance

We also anticipated that depression would foster deficits in goal-directed behavior (e.g., effort, persistence) and performance (e.g., grades, classroom performance). Teachers completed the Academic Helplessness Scale (Fincham, Hokoda, & Sanders, 1989; Nolen-Hoeksema et al., 1992) to provide reports of students' mastery-oriented versus helpless behavior in the context of academic challenge (e.g., "Gives up when you correct him/her or find a mistake in his/her work," "When s/he encounters an obstacle in schoolwork s/he gets discouraged and stops trying"). Teachers also rated several aspects of students' classroom engagement, including their display of effort, the appropriateness of their classroom behavior, the amount that they were learning, and their positive affect (how happy they were) in the classroom. As expected, heightened depression contributed significantly to lower levels of engagement on each dimension both 6 months and 1 year later, after adjusting for prior levels of engagement.

Three indexes of academic performance were used. First, teachers provided a global rating of academic achievement (1 = *Bottom of the class; doing very poorly* to 7 = *Top of the class; doing very well*). Second, teachers provided separate ratings (1 = *Far below grade* to 5 = *Far above grade*) of students' performance in specific academic subject areas (e.g., science, math, English). The average of these specific subject area ratings was calculated. Third, students' grades were collected from school records. In addition, we assessed adolescents' subjective perceptions about their academic performance (i.e., "How upset or stressed have you been about the way things are going with your schoolwork?").

Depressive symptoms at the first wave predicted lower levels of teacher-rated academic performance and poorer grades at subsequent waves, after adjusting for initial performance and grades, but these associations were weaker than those found for academic and behavioral engagement. Although these objective indexes did not reveal very large declines in performance, depressed adolescents reported significantly higher levels of stress about their schoolwork at subsequent waves.

Perceptions of the School Environment

Finally, we expected that depression would contribute to negative evaluations of the school environment and school-related stress. Due to perceptual biases, depressed adolescents may view school more negatively and may ruminate about everyday stressful experiences. Moreover, depressed adolescents' lack of engagement and compromised academic performance may cause them to generate more school-related stress such as negative feedback from teachers and parents. Because the effects of classroom and school contexts may be mediated through youths' *perceptions* of the environment (Roeser et al., 1998), we focused on adolescents' perceptions of their school experiences.

Adolescents completed four measures of stress in the school environment. First, they reported on their experience of specific stressful school-related events. Because of our interest in understanding whether depressed adolescents actually *generate* higher levels of stress, we focused in particular on events to which adolescents were likely to contribute (i.e., failing a test, failing a class, getting into trouble with the principal/receiving a detention or suspension). Adolescents first reported on whether or not they had experienced each event. For each experienced event, they then rated the degree of stress associated with the event. Scores were calculated by summing adolescents' ratings of stress across the events. Second, adolescents completed the academic subscale of the Child Chronic Strain Questionnaire (Rudolph et al., 2001), which assesses their experience of ongoing school-related stress, such as receiving negative feedback from teachers and parents (e.g., "Does your teacher tell you that you need to work harder on your schoolwork?"). Third, adolescents completed the academic subscale of the Role Disruption Questionnaire (Rudolph et al., 2001), which assesses their experience of disruptions in their academic lives since the previous school year (e.g., "Classwork is much harder"). Fourth, adolescents completed an abbreviated version (Rudolph et al., 2001) of the School Hassles Questionnaire (Robinson et al., 1995), which assesses their perceptions of daily school-related hassles. The hassles involve many different aspects of the classroom and school environment, such as relations with authority figures (e.g., "The principals and teachers don't respect you, or they treat you like you're stupid or can't be trusted"), academic expectations (e.g., "The teachers expect too much from you," "You have had too much homework"), school structure (e.g., "You have had problems finding your way around school," "School is large and crowded"), and scheduling issues (e.g., "The periods between classes are too short to get to your next class on time," "You don't have enough time to eat lunch").

As anticipated, depression significantly predicted subsequent perceptions of academic and school-related stress after adjusting for earlier stress. Specifically, depressive symptoms contributed to higher levels of stressful events and academic role disruption 6 months and 1 year later. Depression at the initial wave also predicted higher levels of chronic strain and stressful perceptions of the everyday school environment 6 months later.

Summary

Results from UI-TAP support the proposed detrimental influence of adolescent depression on a range of school-related self-regulatory processes. Adolescents who experienced depressive symptoms in the spring of one school year displayed a pattern of achievement-related self-regulatory cognitions associated with learned helplessness the following school year, even after adjusting for initial levels of these beliefs. Specifically, these adolescents believed that they had less control over their ability to succeed at school, they were less invested in academic success and learning, and they blamed themselves for their academic failures while believing that they had little ability to overcome these failures. Consistent with these maladaptive beliefs, depressed adolescents demonstrated lower levels of classroom engagement over 6-month and 1-year periods, as reflected in decreased effort, persistence, and learning; less appropriate classroom behavior; and less positive affect in the classroom. Although depressed adolescents did not experience large declines in their academic performance, they perceived the school environment as more stressful and less supportive the following school year. Overall, these findings suggest that depression may significantly impair adolescents' motivation and engagement at school. It is possible that over time the cumulative impact of these disturbances would translate into more substantial academic failure or complete avoidance of school, reflected in truancy or school dropout.

Depression as a Consequence of School-Related Difficulties

A second goal of UI-TAP was to examine the influence of disturbances in achievement-related self-regulatory processes on the emergence or exacerbation of depression. Specifically, according to the proposed model, adolescents who lack an investment in academics, have a diminished sense of control over academic success, disengage from the school setting, and experience high levels of school-related stress are more vulnerable to experiencing depression, particularly when faced with challenging academic contexts such as school transitions.

Self-Regulatory Processes and the Middle School Transition

A particular emphasis of UI-TAP was to investigate why some adolescents experience significant difficulties, including the emergence of depressive symptoms, during the transition to middle school, whereas others cope quite well with the transition (Rudolph, Lambert, et al., 2001). We predicted that adolescents with maladaptive self-regulatory cognitions prior to the transition would be more vulnerable to school-related stress and depressive symptoms over the course of the transition than those with more adaptive pretransition cognitions. Specifically, adolescents who believe that they have little control over their academic success and who place little investment in academic success may feel overwhelmed by the new challenges presented in middle school, whereas those with more adaptive beliefs may feel better able to cope with these challenges. This hypothesis was tested in two subgroups from our first cohort of students: one group of adolescents who experienced a transition to middle school between the fifth and sixth grades, and one group of adolescents who remained in the same school between the fifth and sixth grades. Self-regulatory cognitions included adolescents' perceptions of control and their global investment in academic success. Academic engagement included the teacher reports of effort, helpless behavior, and academic performance described earlier. School-related stress included adolescents' reports of chronic strain and a subgroup of the school hassles presumed to be associated with the school transition.

Consistent with our predictions, maladaptive self-regulatory cognitions predicted subsequent higher levels of perceived school-related stress and depressive symptoms in adolescents who experienced a transition to middle school, but not in adolescents who remained in a stable school environment. We also were interested in elucidating the process through which maladaptive self-regulatory cognitions influenced the experience of depressive symptoms over the middle school transition. Consistent with our model, we hypothesized that adolescents with low pretransition perceptions of academic control and low academic investment would be more likely to disengage from the academic environment in middle school. These adolescents may give up more easily when faced with academic challenges, may invest less effort in their schoolwork, and, consequently, may show poorer academic performance. This disengagement likely generates negative perceptions of the school environment and greater school-related stress, leading to depressive symptoms. As expected, analyses revealed that maladaptive self-regulatory cognitions prior to the middle school transition predicted academic disengagement following the transition. Academic disengagement was, in turn, associated with heightened reports of school-related stress, which predicted higher levels of depressive symptoms, after adjusting for pretransition symptoms. Moreover, academic disengagement and school-related stress accounted for the association between maladaptive self-regulatory cognitions and depressive symptoms.

These findings support the proposal that maladaptive achievement-related self-regulatory cognitions, behavior, and experiences represent vulnerability factors for adolescent depression. Moreover, adolescents with self-regulatory deficits may be particularly vulnerable to depression when they face normative developmental challenges associated with the middle school transition.

Achievement Goal Orientation and Depression

Although a global investment in academics may foster greater affiliation with the school environment, and consequent academic and psychological well-being, certain types of motivation may provide adolescents with particular advantages. Research generally links achievement goals that focus on internal motivation (e.g., intrinsic motivation, mastery orientation) with positive task- and school-related affect (e.g., enjoyment, interest), and achievement goals that focus on avoidance of failure with negative task- and school-related affect (e.g., anxiety, boredom) (Ames & Archer, 1988; Dweck & Leggett, 1988; Roeser & Eccles, 2000; Ryan, Hicks, & Midgley, 1997; for a review, see Linnenbrink & Pintrich, 2002). Research has provided a more mixed picture of the emotional consequences of performance-approach goals (e.g., proving that one is smart) (Elliot & Thrash, 2001). Very little is known about the more global and long-term emotional consequences of different achievement goal orientations.

An additional aim of UI-TAP was therefore to examine how different aspects of academic investment contribute to future depressive symptoms (Conley & Rudolph, 2004). Consistent with recent theory and research that consider *profiles* of achievement goals, a cluster-analytic technique was used to identify subgroups of adolescents with distinct patterns of academic investment, based on the measure described earlier that assessed adolescents' investment in learning and performance. The second cohort of adolescents was used due to the availability of this measure. This cluster analysis yielded four groups: (1) high investment, composed of adolescents who were highly invested in both learning and performance-approach; (2) learning preference, composed of adolescents who were more strongly invested in learning than performance-approach; (3) performance-approach preference, composed of adolescents who were more strongly invested in performance-approach than learning; and (4) low investment, composed of adolescents who were not highly invested in either learning or performance-approach.

Comparisons of these groups revealed that adolescents who were highly invested in both learning and performance-approach experienced significantly lower levels of concurrent depressive symptoms than the learning preference, performance-approach preference, and low investment groups. Adolescents with a learning preference experienced fewer concurrent symptoms than low-invested adolescents. Furthermore, adolescents in the high investment and learning preference groups experienced lower levels of depressive symptoms 6 months later, adjusting for earlier symptoms, than those in the low investment group. These findings suggest that adolescents who are invested in both learning and performance-approach are less vulnerable to depressive symptoms. However, investment in learning and academic challenge may provide an especially strong boost to adolescents' emotional well-being.

Origins of Self-Regulatory Cognitions and Behavior

Given that adaptive achievement-related self-regulatory cognitions and behavior protect adolescents from depressive symptoms, it is critical to determine how these processes develop. UI-TAP examined two possible origins of these self-regulatory processes. Specifically, we examined how social-contextual and developmental factors contribute to perceptions of academic control and mastery-oriented versus helpless behavior (Rudolph et al., 2001).

According to the proposed reciprocal-influence model, achievement-related cognitions and behavior not only *influence* adolescents' perceptions of the school environment and experience of stress, but also *are influenced by* environmental experiences. Indeed, research suggests that objective and subjective aspects of classroom and school contexts affect academic motivation, self-efficacy, values, and goal orientation (Harter et al., 1992; Roeser et al., 1996, 1998; Skinner et al., 1998; Urdan, Midgley, & Anderman, 1998). Adolescents exposed to school-related stress, failure, and negative feedback are likely to become overwhelmed and to feel that they lack control over their success, resulting in low persistence when faced with future academic challenges. Consistent with these predictions, findings from UI-TAP revealed that adolescents who reported significant academic and school-related stress demonstrated diminished perceptions of academic control and higher levels of academic helplessness concurrently and 6 months later.

Beyond the proximal influence of school, experiences in other contexts may shape achievement-related self-regulatory processes. We were particularly interested in how the family influences adolescents' self-regulatory cognitions and behavior. Because family experiences form the basis for the development of competence and mastery, we expected that significant disruptions in family relationships would undermine adolescents' sense of self-efficacy and sense of the world as predictable and controllable. Three aspects of family disruption were examined: separation or loss in parent–child relationships (e.g., parent separation or divorce, parent death, parent abandonment), exposure to interparental conflict, and maladaptive parent socialization styles (i.e., low autonomy granting, high rejection, inconsistent discipline). As expected, adolescents exposed to these forms of family disruption demonstrated diminished perceptions of academic control and more academic helplessness.

These findings support the proposal that developmentally salient family socialization experiences, as well as proximal aspects of school-related experiences, contribute to the emergence of achievement-related self-regulatory processes characteristic of depressed adolescents. Thus, conceptualizations of depression within the school context would benefit from a consideration of how family experiences influence school adjustment.

Summary of UI-TAP Findings

Findings from UI-TAP provide considerable support for the proposed transactional model of adolescent depression and school adjustment. Depression during early adolescence predicts future self-regulatory difficulties, including maladaptive achievement-related beliefs, disengagement from academic endeavors, and negative evaluations of the school environment. These difficulties, in turn, place adolescents at risk for further depression, particularly when faced with challenges associated with school transitions. Although depressed adolescents' achievement did not appear to be severely compromised within the 1-year follow-up period, these adolescents did feel more stressed about their schoolwork over time. It is possible that following these youth across longer periods of time would reveal declines in achievement that would be expected given their profiles of achievement orientation. This study also suggests that the family environment plays a role in the development of maladaptive achievement-related self-regulatory processes linked to depression.

This research suggests that integrating mental health and educational perspectives on youth development is a fruitful approach to understanding adolescent depression. In particular, this study elucidates how trajectories of depression and school adjustment difficulties fuel each other in a mutually reinforcing cycle during the adolescent years. Moreover, this research extends prior work demonstrating links between depression and global aspects of school adjustment by demonstrating how depression serves as a critical antecedent and consequence of specific academic self-regulatory processes. Finally, this study demonstrates the importance of considering the role of developmentally salient contexts (e.g., family disruption) and experiences (e.g., school transitions) in models of depression within the school context.

FUTURE DIRECTIONS

Current research on the intersection between adolescent mental health and school adjustment focuses primarily on achievement-related processes. However, fully understanding adolescents' adjustment at school requires a consideration of the broader social context of their lives. For example, adolescents' peer environment at school may play a large role in their academic and emotional adjustment. Peer relationships become increasingly important during adolescence, as youth begin to rely on friends to provide emotional support, intimacy, and security (Berndt, 1996; Fenzel & Blyth, 1986; Furman & Buhrmester, 1992). At the same time, adolescence is associated with higher levels of loneliness and alienation (Cotterell, 1982) and with heightened exposure to interpersonal stress (Rudolph & Hammen, 1999). Changes in the peer system may be particularly salient over the course of the middle school transition (Eccles & Midgley, 1989; Simmons, Burgeson, Carlton-Ford, & Blyth, 1987) when peer relationships are disrupted due to physical separation from friends, shifts in the criteria for popularity, decreases in social support, and the reformulation of social networks (Seidman et al., 1994). Similar to the mismatch noted between academic environments and adolescents' developmental needs for competence and autonomy (Eccles et al., 1993), a mismatch may arise during adolescence between the social context of school (increased alienation from familiar peer groups, instability of friendships) and normative developmental needs and expectations (increased dependence on peer group support, greater emphasis on closeness and intimacy). This mismatch may similarly place adolescents at risk for feelings of alienation from school and accompanying depressive symptoms.

Beyond the peer group, other aspects of adolescents' lives may interact with school experiences to place youth at risk for depression. For example, if adolescents are dealing with multiple stressors outside of school (e.g., family stress, financial difficulties, health problems), psychological and tangible coping resources may be diverted away from dealing with school-related challenges. Outside stressors also may deplete the amount of time, energy, and focused attention available for normative school-related tasks (e.g., completing homework, engaging in after-school activities). These disruptions may foster higher levels of academic stress, a decreased sense of belonging at school, and a sense of helplessness that place youth at risk for depression. Thus, it is critical to consider how adolescents' broader social contexts influence adaptation at school.

IMPLICATIONS FOR INTERVENTION AND POLICY

Overall, research indicates that depression and school adjustment problems co-occur during adolescence. The transactional nature of these co-occurring problems suggests that depression and school maladjustment may become intertwined in a self-perpetuating cycle that escalates through the school years. However, not all depressed adolescents experience school difficulties, and not all adolescents with school difficulties are depressed. Indeed, research reveals four groups of adolescents: those at low risk for both types of difficulties, those at high risk for both types of difficulties, those who devalue academics but show high levels of emotional well-being, and those who show poor emotional adjustment but continue to value school and maintain high levels of perceived academic competence (Roeser et al., 1998). A critical goal of school-based programs and educational reform should be to disentangle trajectories of mental health and school-related difficulties to avoid the downward spiral that may result when either type of difficulty emerges. Both individual-level and school-level efforts may contribute to achieving this goal.

At the individual level, because declines in school motivation and engagement may create stress in adolescents' lives that puts them at risk for depression, identifying and intervening with adolescents who are beginning to disengage from school or who show declines in academic performance may facilitate efforts to prevent the onset or progression of depressive symptoms. Relatedly, attempts to identify adolescents at risk in the school context should focus not only on those who demonstrate significant academic difficulties or disruptive behaviors, which are the typical focus of concern for school personnel and parents, but also those who display early signs of depression, such as sadness and withdrawal. This group may actually be an appropriate target for interventions aimed at preventing declines in academic motivation and engagement, particularly during stressful school transitions. Because some research suggests that the combination of depression and behavior problems presents particular challenges for school adjustment (Rudolph et al., 2000), adolescents with both of these types of problems may be an especially important group to target.

Beyond adolescent-focused prevention and intervention efforts, the interface between mental health and school difficulties suggests the importance of school-level efforts to improve adolescent mental health. As one of the most salient contexts of development during this life stage, schools play a critical role in providing supportive environments that optimize adolescents' emotional well-being. Specifically, the development of resources for effective self-regulation has a powerful influence not only on adolescents' academic achievement and proximal adjustment at school, but also on more global and long-term emotional well-being. Schools therefore have a responsibility to provide environments that encourage the growth of these skills (Pajares & Schunk, 2001). Educational theory and research suggest many strategies for designing classroom and school environments that support adolescents' needs, including the use of classroom structures and teaching practices that promote adaptive achievement-related beliefs and classroom engagement (Eccles & Midgley, 1989; Pajares & Schunk, 2001; Roeser & Eccles, 2000). Given the observed links between school adjustment and mental health, efforts to promote these types of classroom environments not only may have the intended consequences of enhancing learning and school adjustment, but also may enhance adolescents' emotional well-being. Because teachers' efficacy beliefs influence their instructional practices and relationships with students, which then contribute to students' achievement and psychological well-being (Pajares & Schunk, 2001), increasing teachers' knowledge about depression and its effects on school adjustment would be an important component of such educational reform.

Finally, an integrative perspective on education and mental health has implications for policy aimed at maximizing positive youth development. In particular, better integration of mental health services into school settings may provide a prime opportunity both for reaching underserved youth, and for creating and implementing services that consider youth in context.

ACKNOWLEDGEMENTS

Preparation of this chapter and the research described in this chapter were supported by a University of Illinois Beckman Award, William T. Grant Foundation Faculty Scholars Award, and National Institute of Mental Health Grant Nos. MH59711 and MH56327 awarded to Karen D. Rudolph. Assistance with data collection and project management for the Transition to Adolescence Study was provided by Melissa Caldwell, Alyssa Clark, Colleen Conley, Alison Dupre, Megan Flynn, Tamara Gathright, Kathryn Kurlakowsky, Sharon Lambert, and Lori Osborne. We thank Eva Pomerantz for her helpful comments on an earlier draft of this manuscript.

REFERENCES

American Psychiatric Association (2000). *Diagnostic and statistical manual of mental disorders* (4th ed.-TR). Washington, DC: Author.

Ames, C., & Archer, J. (1988). Achievement goals in the classroom: Students' learning strategies and motivation processes. *Journal of Educational Psychology, 80*, 260–267.

Asarnow, J. R., Carlson, G. A., & Guthrie, D. (1987). Coping strategies, self-perceptions, hopelessness, and perceived family environments in depressed and suicidal children. *Journal of Consulting and Clinical Psychology, 55*, 361–366.

Bandura, A. (1986). *Social foundations of thought and action: A social cognitive theory*. Englewood Cliffs, NJ: Prentice Hall.

Bandura, A., Pastorelli, C., Barbaranelli, C., & Caprara, G. V. (1999). Self-efficacy pathways to childhood depression. *Journal of Personality and Social Psychology, 76*, 258–269.

Berndt, T. J. (1996). Transition in friendship and friends' influence. In J. A. Graber & J. Brooks-Gunn (Eds.), *Transitions through adolescence: Interpersonal domains and context* (pp. 57–84). Mahwah, NJ: Erlbaum.

Blyth, D. A., Simmons, R. G., & Carlton-Ford, S. (1983). The adjustments of early adolescents to school transitions. *Journal of Early Adolescence, 3*, 105–120.

Caldwell, M. S., Rudolph, K. D., Troop-Gordon, W., & Kim, D. (in press). A transactional model of relational self-views, social disengagement, and peer stress during early adolescence. *Child Development*.

Chen, X., & Li, B. (2000). Depressed mood in Chinese children: Developmental significance for social and school adjustment. *International Journal of Behavioral Development, 24*, 472–479.

Cole, D. A., Martin, J. M., Peeke, L. A., Seroczynski, A. D., & Fier, J. (1999). Children's over- and underestimation of academic competence: A longitudinal study of gender differences, depression, and anxiety. *Child Development, 70*, 459–473.

Cole, D. A., Martin, J. M., Peeke, L. G., Seroczynski, A. D., & Hoffman, K. (1998). Are cognitive errors of underestimation predictive or reflective of depressive symptoms in children: A longitudinal study. *Journal of Abnormal Psychology, 107*, 481-496.

Cole, D. A., Peeke, L., Dolezai, S., Murray, N., & Canzoniero, A. (1999). A longitudinal study of negative affect and self-perceived competence in young adolescents. *Journal of Personality and Social Psychology, 77*, 851–862.

Compas, B. E., Ey, S., & Grant, K. E. (1993). Taxonomy, assessment, and diagnosis of depression during adolescence. *Psychological Bulletin, 114*, 323–344.

Conley, C. S., & Rudolph, K. D. (2004). *Academic goal investment: Contextual, cognitive, and emotional processes in early adolescence.* Manuscript in preparation.

Cooper, P. J., & Goodyer, I. (1993). A community study of depression in adolescent girls I: Estimates of symptom and syndrome prevalence. *British Journal of Psychiatry, 163*, 369–374.

Cotterell, J. (1982). Student experiences following entry into secondary school. *Educational Research, 24*, 296–302.

Deci, E. L., & Ryan, R. M. (1985). *Intrinsic motivation and self-determination in human behavior.* New York: Plenum Press.

Dweck, C. S., & Leggett, E. L. (1988). A social-cognitive approach to motivation and personality. *Psychological Review, 95*, 256–273.

Eccles, J. S., Adler, T. F., & Meece, J. L. (1984). Sex differences in achievement: A test of alternate theories. *Journal of Personality and Social Psychology, 46*, 26–43.

Eccles, J. S., Lord, S. E., Roeser, R. W., Barber, B. L., & Jozefowicz, D. M. (1997). The association of school transitions in early adolescence with developmental trajectories through high school. In J. Schulenberg, J. L. Maggs, & K. Hurrelmann (Eds.), *Health risks and developmental transitions during adolescence* (pp. 283–320). New York: Cambridge University Press.

Eccles, J. S., & Midgley, C. (1989). Stage-environment fit: Developmentally appropriate classrooms for young adolescents. In R. E. Ames & C. Ames (Eds.), *Research on motivation in education* (Vol. 3, pp. 139–181). New York: Academic Press.

Eccles, J. S., Midgley, C., & Adler, T. F. (1984). Grade-related changes in the school environment: Effects on achievement motivation. In J. H. Nicholls (Ed.), *The development of achievement motivation* (Vol. 3, pp. 283–331). Greenwich, CT: JAI Press.

Eccles, J. S., Midgley, C. M., Wigfield, A. L., Buchanan, C., Reuman, D., Flanagan, C., et al. (1993). Development during adolescence: The impact of stage-environment fit on young adolescents' experiences in schools and in families. *American Psychologist, 48*, 90–101.

Eccles, J. S., Wigfield, A., & Schiefele, U. (1998). Motivation to succeed. In N. Eisenberg (Ed.) & W. Damon (Series Ed.), *Handbook of child psychology: Vol. 4. Personality and social development* (pp. 1017-1095). New York: Wiley.

Elliott, A. J., & Harackiewicz, J. M. (1996). Approach and avoidance achievement goals and intrinsic motivation: A mediational analysis. *Journal of Personality and Social Psychology, 70*, 461–475.

Elliot, A. J., & Thrash, T. M. (2001). Achievement goals and the hierarchical model of achievement motivation. *Educational Psychology Review, 13*, 139–156.

Fenzel, L. M., & Blyth, D. A. (1986). Individual adjustment to school transitions: An exploration of the role of supportive peer relations. *Journal of Early Adolescence, 6*, 315–329.

Finch, F. D., Hokoda, A., & Sanders, R., Jr. (1989). Learned helplessness, text anxiety, and academic achievments: A longitudinal analysis. *Child Development, 60*, 138-145.

Furman, W., & Buhrmester, D. (1992). Age and sex differences in perceptions of networks of personal relationships. *Child Development, 63*, 103–115.

Garber, J., & Hilsman, R. (1992). Cognitions, stress, and depression in children and adolescents. *Child and Adolescent Psychiatric Clinics of North America, 1*, 129–167.

Gazelle, H., & Rudolph, K. D. (2004). Moving toward and away from the world: Social approach and avoidance trajectories in anxious solitary youth. *Child Development, 75*, 829-849.

Hammen, C., & Rudolph, K. D. (1996). Childhood depression. In E. J. Marsh & R. A. Barkley (Eds.), *Child psychopathology* (pp. 153-195). New York: Guildford.

Hammen, C., & Rudolph, K. D. (2003). Childhood mood disorders. In E. J. Mash & R. A. Barkley (Eds.), *Child psychopathology* (Vol. 2, pp. 233–278). New York: Guilford Press.

Hammen, C., Rudolph, K. D., Weisz, J. R., Rao, U., & Burge, D. (1999). The context of depression in clinic-referred youth: Neglected areas in treatment. *Journal of the American Academy of Child and Adolescent Psychiatry, 38*, 64–71.

Hankin, B. L., Abramson, L. Y., & Siler, M. (2001). A prospective test of the hopelessness theory of depression in adolescence. *Cognitive Therapy and Research, 25*, 607–632.

Harter, S., & Connell, J. P. (1984). A model of the relationships among children's academic achievement and their self-perceptions of competence, control, and motivational orientation. In J. H. Nicholls (Ed.), *The development of achievement motivation* (pp. 214-250). Greenwich, CT: JAI Press.

Harter, S., Whitesell, N., & Kowalski, P. (1992). Individual differences in the effects of educational transitions on young adolescents' perceptions of competence and motivational orientation. *American Educational Research Journal, 29*, 777–807.

Hilsman, R., & Garber, J. (1995). A test of the cognitive diathesis-stress model of depression in children: Academic stressors, attributional style, perceived competence, and control. *Journal of Personality and Social Psychology, 69*, 370–380.

Ialongo, N. S., Edelsohn, G., & Kellam, S. G. (2001). A further look at the prognostic power of young children's reports of depressed mood and feelings. *Child Development, 72*, 736–747.

Ialongo, N., Edelsohn, G., Werthamer-Larsson, L., Crockett, L., & Kellam, S. G. (1993). Are self-reported depressive symptoms in first-grade children developmentally transient phenomena? A further look. *Development and Psychopathology, 5*, 433–457.

Ialongo, N., Edelsohn, G., Werthamer-Larsson, L., Crockett, L., & Kellam, S. G. (1996). Social and cognitive impairment in first-grade children with anxious and depressive symptoms. *Journal of Clinical Child Psychology, 25*, 15–24.

Kellam, S. G., Rebok, G. W., Mayer, L. S., Ialongo, N., & Kalodner, C. R. (1994). Depressive symptoms over first grade and their response to a developmental epidemiologically based preventive trial aimed at improving achievement. *Development and Psychopathology, 6*, 463–481.

Kessler, R. C., Avenevoli, S., & Merikangas, K. R. (2001). Mood disorders in children and adolescents: An epidemiologic perspective. *Biological Psychiatry, 49*, 1002–1014.

Kessler, R. C., Foster, C. L., Saunders, W. B., & Stang, P. E. (1995). Social consequences of psychiatric disorders, I: Educational attainment. *American Journal of Psychiatry, 152*, 1026–1032.

Kessler, R. C., & Walters, E. E. (1998). Epidemiology of DSM-III-R major depression and minor depression among adolescents and young adults in the National Comorbidity Survey. *Depression and Anxiety, 7*, 3–14.

Kovacs, M. (1980/81). Rating scales to assess depression in school-aged children. *Acta Paedopsychiatry, 46*, 305–315.

Kovacs, M. (1997). Depressive disorders in childhood: An impressionistic landscape. *Journal of Child Psychology and Psychiatry, 38*, 287–298.

Kovacs, M., & Goldston, D. (1991). Cognitive and social cognitive development of depressed children and adolescents. *Journal of the American Academy of Child and Adolescent Psychiatry, 30*, 388–392.

Lewinsohn, P. M., Clarke, G. N., Seeley, J. R., & Rohde, P. (1994). Major depression in community adolescents: Age at onset, episode duration, and time to recurrence. *Journal of the American Academy of Child and Adolescent Psychiatry, 33*, 809–818.

Lewinsohn, P. M., Steinmetz, J. L., Larson, D. W., & Franklin, J. (1981). Depression-related cognitions: Antecedent or consequence? *Journal of Abnormal Psychology, 90*, 213–219.

Linnenbrink, E. A., & Pintrich, P. R. (2002). Achievement goal theory and affect: An asymmetrical bi-directional model. *Educational Psychologist, 37*, 69–78.

Lyubomirsky, S., Caldwell, N. D., & Nolen-Hoeksema, S. (1998). Effects of ruminative and distracting responses to depressed mood on retrieval of autobiographical memories. *Journal of Personality and Social Psychology, 75*, 166–177.

Meyer, D. K., & Turner, J. C. (2002). Discovering emotion in classroom motivation research. *Educational Psychologist, 37*, 107–114.

Middleton, M., & Midgley, C. (1997). Avoiding the demonstration of lack of ability: An underexplored aspect of goal theory. *Journal of Educational Psychology, 85*, 710–718.

Nolen-Hoeksema, S., & Girgus, J. S. (1994). The emergence of gender differences in depression during adolescence. *Psychological Bulletin, 115*, 424–443.

Nolen-Hoeksema, S., Girgus, J. S., & Seligman, M. E. P. (1986). Learned helplessness in children: A longitudinal study of depression, achievement, and explanatory style. *Journal of Personality and Social Psychology, 51*, 435–442.

Nolen-Hoeksema, S., Girgus, J. S., & Seligman, M. E. P. (1992). Predictors and consequences of childhood depressive symptoms: A 5-year longitudinal study. *Journal of Abnormal Psychology, 101*, 405–422.

Pajares, F. (1996). Self-efficacy beliefs in academic settings. *Review of Educational Research, 66*, 543–578.

Pajares, F., & Schunk, D. H. (2001). Self-beliefs and school success: Self-efficacy, self-concept, and school achievement. In R. J. Riding & S. G. Rayner (Eds.), *Self perception* (pp. 239-265). Westport, CT: Ablex.

Petersen, A. C., & Hamburg, B. A. (1986). Adolescence: A developmental approach to problems and psychopathology. *Behavior Therapy, 17,* 480–499.

Pintrich, P. R. (2000). Multiple goals, multiple pathways: The role of goal orientation in learning and achievement. *Journal of Educational Psychology, 92,* 544–555.

Pomerantz, E. M., & Rudolph, K. D. (2003). What ensues from emotional distress? Implications for competence estimation. *Child Development, 74,* 329–345.

Pyszczynski, T., & Greenberg, J. (1987). Self-regulatory perseveration and the depressive self-focusing style: A self-awareness theory of reactive depression. *Psychological Bulletin, 102,* 1–17.

Puig-Antich, J., Kaufman, J., Ryan, N. D., Williamson, D. E., Dahl, R. E., Lukens, E., et al. (1993). The psychosocial functioning and family environment of depressed adolescents. *Journal of the American Academy of Child and Adolescent Psychiatry, 32,* 244–253.

Rao, U., Ryan, N. D., Birmaher, B., Dahl, R. E., Williamson, D. E., Kaufman, J., et al. (1995). Unipolar depression in adolescents: Clinical outcome in adulthood. *Journal of the American Academy of Child and Adolescent Psychiatry, 34,* 566–578.

Robinson, N. S., Garber, J., & Hilsman, R. (1995). Cognitions and stress: Direct and moderating effects on depressive versus externalizing symptoms during the junior high school transition. *Journal of Abnormal Psychology, 104,* 453–463.

Roeser, R. W., & Eccles, J. S. (1998). Adolescents' perceptions of middle school: Relation to longitudinal changes in academic and psychological adjustment. *Journal of Research on Adolescence, 8,* 123–158.

Roeser, R. W., & Eccles, J. S. (2000). Schooling and mental health. In A. J. Sameroff, M. Lewis, & S. M. Miller (Eds.), *Handbook of developmental psychopathology* (pp. 135–156). New York: Plenum Press.

Roeser, R. W., Eccles, J. E., & Sameroff, A. J. (1998). Academic and emotional functioning in early adolescence: Longitudinal relations, patterns, and prediction by experience in middle school. *Development and Psychopathology, 10,* 321–352.

Roeser, R. W., & Midgley, C. M. (1997). Teachers' views of aspects of student mental health. *Elementary School Journal, 98,* 115–133.

Roeser, R. W., Midgley, C. M., & Urdan, T. C. (1996). Perceptions of the school psychological environment and early adolescents' psychological and behavioral functioning in school: The mediating role of goals and belonging. *Journal of Educational Psychology, 88,* 408–422.

Rudolph, K. D., & Clark, A. G. (2001). Conceptions of relationships in children with depressive and aggressive symptoms: Social-cognitive distortion or reality? *Journal of Abnormal Child Psychology, 29,* 41–56.

Rudolph, K. D., & Conley, C. S. (in press). Socioemotional costs and benefits of social-evaluative concerns: Do girls care too much? *Journal of Personality.*

Rudolph, K. D., & Hammen, C. (1999). Age and gender as determinants of stress exposure, generation, and reactions in youngsters: A transactional perspective. *Child Development, 70,* 660–677.

Rudolph, K. D., Hammen, C., Burge, D., Lindberg, N., Herzberg, D., & Daley, S. E. (2000). Toward an interpersonal life-stress model of depression: The developmental context of stress generation. *Development and Psychopathology, 12,* 215–234.

Rudolph, K. D., Hammen, C., & Daley, S. E. (in press). Adolescent mood disorders. In E. J. Mash & D. A. Wolfe (Eds.), *Behavioral and emotional disorders in adolescents.* New York: Guilford Press.

Rudolph, K. D., Kurlakowsky, K. D., & Conley, C. S. (2001). Developmental and social-contextual origins of depressive control-related beliefs and behavior. *Cognitive Therapy and Research, 25,* 447–475.

Rudolph, K. D., Lambert, S. M., Clark, A. G., & Kurlakowsky, K. D. (2001). Negotiating the transition to middle school: The role of self-regulatory processes. *Child Development, 72,* 929–946.

Rudolph, K. D., & Pomerantz, E. M. (2004). *The consequences of depression during early adolescence.* Manuscript in preparation.

Ryan, A. M., Hicks, L., & Midgley, C. (1997). Social goals, academic goals, and avoiding seeking help in the classroom. *Journal of Early Adolescence, 17,* 152–171.

Scheier, M. F., & Carver, C. S. (1982). Cognition, affect, and self-regulation. In M. S. Clark & S. T. Fiske (Eds.), *Affect and cognition: The seventeenth annual Carnegie Symposium on cognition* (pp. 157–183). Hillsdale, NJ: Erlbaum.

Seidman, E., Allen, L., Aber, J. L., Mitchell, C., & Feinman, J. (1994). The impact of school transitions in early adolescence on the self-system and perceived social context of poor urban youth. *Child Development, 65,* 507–522.

Simmons, R. G., Burgeson, R., Carlton-Ford, S., & Blyth, D. A. (1987). The impact of cumulative change in early adolescence. *Child Development, 58,* 1220–1234.

Skinner, E. A., Zimmer-Gembeck, M. J., & Connell, J. P. (1998). Individual differences and the development of perceived control. *Monographs of the Society for Research in Child Development, 63*(2-3, Serial No. 254).

Urdan, T. C. (1997). Achievement goal theory: Past results, future directions. In M. L. Mahr & P. R. Pintrich (Eds.), *Advances in motivation and achievement* (Vol. 10, pp. 99–141). Greenwich, CT: JAI Press.

Urdan, T., Midgley, C., & Anderman, E. M. (1998). The role of classroom goal structure in students' use of self-handicapping strategies. *American Educational Research Journal, 35,* 101–122.

Urdan, T., Ryan, A. M., Anderman, E. M., & Gheen, M. H. (2002). Goals, goal structures, and avoidance behaviors. In C. Midgley (Ed.), *Goals, goal structures, and patterns of adaptive learning* (pp. 55–83). Mahwah, NJ: Erlbaum.

Weisz, J. R., Southam-Gerow, M. A., & McCarty, C. A. (2000). Control-related beliefs and depressive symptoms in clinic-referred children and adolescents: Developmental differences and model specificity. *Journal of Abnormal Psychology, 110,* 97–109.

CHAPTER 3

ABUSIVE, WANTED, AND ILLEGAL SEXUAL EXPERIENCES IN ADOLESCENCE

Nancy D. Kellogg

According to recent estimates, approximately half of school-age teenagers in the United States have had sexual intercourse (Centers for Disease Control and Prevention, 2002). Some adolescent sexual experiences are coercive or unwanted and some occur as a result of acquiescence rather than active consent. Adolescents may have sexual partners that are verbally or physically abusive. Some adolescents may experience sexual abuse or suffer the effects of childhood sexual abuse during adolescence. While legal definitions provide some guidance as to which sexual experiences are illegal or abusive, the adolescent's perception of the experience may have a greater impact on the legal outcome, as well as the emotional and behavioral sequelae. For example, some sexual abuse victims (as defined by criminal law) do not consider their abusive experiences to be forced or unwanted (Kellogg, Burge, & Taylor, 2000), and may deny any physical or emotional symptoms; these cases are difficult to criminally prosecute because the victim does not appear "victimized." Conversely, a

Educating Adolescents: Challenges and Strategies, 65–84
Copyright © 2004 by Information Age Publishing
All rights of reproduction in any form reserved.

proportion of adolescents engaged in "consensual" sexual experiences report initial, even sustained, resistance prior to acquiescence, and may suffer debilitating emotional or physical consequences of their experiences. Cultural and family factors further influence adolescents' participation in, and interpretation of, their varied sexual experiences. An understanding of the adolescent's perception of a sexual experience is critical to the detection and effective intervention of unsafe, unwanted, or abusive sexual encounters.

A 1995 survey study of 1,909 American adolescents (Ryan, Manlove, & Franzetta, 2003) provides valuable insight regarding first experiences of sexual intercourse during adolescence. Eighty-five percent viewed their relationship with their first sexual partner as romantic, although teen boys were less likely than girls to view their relationship as such. Most teens in romantic relationships initiated sexual intercourse within the first 3 months of the relationship, and the average duration of a sexual relationship was 6 months. Teen girls were more likely than boys to have an older first sexual partner, and 19% had a partner that was 4 or more years older; these latter experiences would be considered illegal in many states, and would therefore be reportable to authorities. Girls that became involved in a sexual relationship at a younger age were more likely than older girls to have much older partners, and less likely to use contraception at least some of the time. These findings are similar to the adolescent sexual experiences of those with a history of child sexual abuse.

Overall, only 59% of adolescents discussed the use of contraception with their sexual partner, and more than 20% never used contraception. Teens that delayed sexual intercourse until later adolescent years were more likely to use contraceptives consistently. Among those that used contraception, 72% used condoms and 26% used birth control pills. Nine percent of adolescents reported that their first sexual relationship was characterized by physical violence (pushing, shoving, throwing objects that could hurt) and 24% reported verbal abuse (name-calling, insults, swearing, disrespectful treatment, threats of violence) by their sexual partner. Hispanic females were more likely than Anglos or African Americans to experience physical violence, and less likely to use contraceptives. This study offers the following suggestions for programs that address adolescent sexuality: (a) encourage young adolescents to delay sexual intercourse and seek romantic relationships that do not involve sex; (b) discourage long-term relationships with one partner since this increases the risk of early sexual involvement; (c) emphasize early communication between partners regarding contraceptive use and consistent use for every sexual encounter; and (d) establish culturally sensitive programs to address the specific problems seen among Hispanic females.

Other studies have addressed the way that sexual abuse affects relationships among peers during adolescence. Sexual abuse victims that experience significant levels of shame and self-blame feel less capable of forming satisfying relationships with their peers and potential romantic partners. They have fewer close friendships and are less likely to feel accepted by peers, but are more likely to feel they are attractive as dating partners (Feiring, Rosenthal, & Taska, 2000). This finding is similar to that seen in adult survivors of child sexual abuse and may represent a tendency for victims to form multiple and superficial sexual relationships that deteriorate when interpersonal intimacy develops (Briere & Runtz, 1993).

Sexual abuse is a common, but underreported, problem of childhood, with prevalence estimates of 25% among females under the age of 18 in the United States (Hopper, 1997; Lechner, Vogel, Garcia-Shelton, Leichter, & Steibel, 1993; Lewin, 1997). Sexual abuse is not considered a random event. Research studies have documented the following risk factors: presence of a stepfather or other father figure; living without the mother at some interval; lack of maternal education (mother did not complete high school); lack of emotional closeness to the mother; sexually repressive mother; lack of physical affection from the father; family income less than $10,000 per year; fewer than three friends in childhood (Finkelhor, 1979).

Approximately 80% of sexual abuse victims are female, and 85% of sexual offenders are well known to the victim. In one study of adolescent victims and young adults abused during childhood or adolescence (Kellogg & Hoffman, 1995), 36% of sex offenders were family members, 24% were adult acquaintances, 15% were peers, 15% were strangers, and 6% were peer family members. When the sexual offender is a family member or adult, unequivocal obedience is expected and physical escape from abuse is generally not possible. As with abusive adolescent partners, most adult sex offenders use deception to gain control and secure the silence and cooperation of their victims. Four percent of this study population described their sexual assault as "gang-related." The vast majority (98%) of the perpetrators in this study were male. Male victims of unwanted sexual experiences were as likely to be abused by a male as by a female. Sexual abuse is likely to be chronic and severe: about half are abused for more than one year and 51% percent report that the abuse involved some type of penetrating trauma. When victims are asked to characterize their feelings about unwanted sexual experiences, most report feelings of being threatened, forced, and scared (70%) and blame the abuser (60%). Almost half experience uncertainty ("I wasn't sure what to do, so I went along with it") and nearly a third blamed themselves or "didn't know it was wrong at the time." Feelings of self-blame and being "drunk or high" were more commonly reported by victims of peer perpetrators than victims of adult perpetrators.

Similar to the characteristics of an adolescent's first experience of intercourse, cultural factors also influence a victim's experience of sexual abuse. Hispanic females are more likely to have self-blame and ambivalence about abusive sexual experiences in childhood when compared with Anglo females (Kellogg & Hoffman, 1995). Also in this study, it was found that child sexual abuse was significantly less common in Hispanic than in Anglo females, but the self-denigrating tendencies of the Hispanic group may have nullified their perception that a sexual experience was abusive or unwanted. Other studies, utilizing different definitions for sexual abuse, have found that sexual abuse is more common among Hispanics (Kercher & McShane, 1984). Sanders-Philips, Moisan, Wadlington, Morgan, and English (1995) found that sexually abused Hispanic girls were more likely to be depressed than sexually abused African American girls. In addition, the degree of family support may differ among ethnic groups; sexually abused Hispanic girls were more likely than African American girls to report high levels of family conflict and lower levels of maternal support following their sexual abuse disclosure (Sanders-Philips et al., 1995). All of these factors may attenuate or exacerbate the adolescent victim's emotional trauma.

School may be a haven for sexual abuse victims. If an adolescent is a victim of intrafamilial abuse, school may represent a tangible escape from victimization. Abused adolescents may also disclose their abuse to school personnel, although one study (Kellogg & Huston, 1995) found that school programs influenced disclosure of sexual abuse in only 28% of victims. Educators may also provide information that enables adolescents to effectively evaluate and interpret their sexual experiences, enhancing the likelihood that an abusive experience will be identified and reported by the victim. Important reasons for disclosure can be presented by educators and may provide needed incentive for the adolescent to reveal the abuse. For example, many abused adolescents do not realize that sexual offenders often victimize more than one child, and may be prompted to disclose if they feel they can prevent others from being hurt.

Schools also harbor an "underground railroad" of students that are aware of victims who have never disclosed or reported their abuse to an adult. Child sexual abuse victims are most likely to confide in a friend prior to confiding in an adult (Kellogg & Huston, 1995). This study also indicated that sexual abuse victims disclose to an average of three or four peers prior to disclosing to an adult. Educators have an opportunity to impart information to this network of supportive peers in order to encourage disclosure and reporting of sexual abuse to appropriate and safe adults.

Schools may also be the source of secondary victimization once abuse has been revealed, particularly if the abuser is another student. Vicious rumors are often started by the accused assailant in order to deflect blame or further traumatize and intimidate the victim. Such harassment can have debilitating effects on the victim's school performance. For severe cases, home schooling or transfer to another school is sometimes the only effective option for the victim to complete school. School personnel can be critical to curtailing secondary victimization and academic compromise.

DEFINITIONS

The legal definition for sexual abuse varies somewhat, depending on the age of the victim. For example, in Texas, sexual abuse of a child under the age of 17 is "touching of the anus, breasts or any part of the genitals .... with intent to arouse or gratify the sexual desire of any person"; "penetration of the anus or female sex organ of a child by any means"; "penetration of the mouth of a child by the sex organ of another person"; and "causing the sexual organ of the child to contact or penetrate the mouth, anus, or sexual organ of another person" (Texas Penal Code Sections 22.021 and 43.01). However, if the child is between 14 and 17 years of age and the assailant/partner is between 14 and 17 years of age, the assailant may claim as a defense that they were within 3 years in age of the other individual. In effect, the law suggests that while an individual under the age of 17 cannot consent to any sexual activity, sexual contact between two minors ages 14–17 is defensible under certain circumstances as long as both parties are consenting. In reality, few of the latter situations are reported or prosecuted. While the strict interpretation of Texas law requires that an individual report any sexual contact involving an individual younger than 17 years of age, the purpose and effect of such reporting are obscure.

The disclosure and eventual reporting of abuse first depends on the adolescents' perception that the sexual contact was coercive, inappropriate, or unwanted. "Unwanted sexual experience" is a term first described by Erickson and Rapkin (1991) as "any kind of sexual touching or action that made you feel uncomfortable, bad, uneasy, or regretful" . . . that involves "some other teenager or an adult, someone you knew well or didn't know well at all." Based on this definition, 10% of legally defined sexual abuse victims, most of whom were abused by adult perpetrators and who were Hispanic, did not consider their abusive experiences "unwanted" (Kellogg & Hoffman, 1995).

Wanted sexual experiences may be legal or illegal. The "age of consent" and hence the parameters of what defines an illegal sexual experience vary from state to state. Many wanted illegal sexual experiences are clearly abusive; one 15-year-old female that presented her story to a sexual abuse clinic described unwanted sexual experiences with two peers but also indicated that her first wanted sexual experience was with her grandfather when she was 6 years old (Kellogg & Hoffman, 1995).

Another smaller subset of adolescents is simply unable or unwilling to interpret their sexual experiences as either wanted or unwanted. When these adolescents describe the characteristics of their sexual experiences, most indicate that they had no plan or desire to engage in sexual contact but either they resisted then "gave up," or they did not resist (Kellogg & Hoffman, 1995). When adolescents indicate they said "no" to the sexual contact either with their words or with their body, it should be considered an unwanted or abusive sexual experience. Many adolescents reason that if they did not physically struggle to the point of receiving bodily injury, then the experience must have been consensual by default.

DETECTION AND BARRIERS TO DISCLOSURE

Once an adolescent has defined his or her sexual experience as abusive and knows that it is reportable, the next obstacle to disclosure of abuse occurs during careful consideration of the potential consequences of reporting. For example, does the benefit of reporting sexual abuse by a father outweigh the risks of not being believed and disruption of the family unit? Almost half of sexual abuse victims delay disclosure because they think that no one will believe them (Kellogg & Menard, 2003). Other barriers to disclosure include fear of being taken away from one's family, self-blame, fear of causing emotional distress and possibly violence among family members, fear of abuse "stigma," embarrassment, shame, fear of losing one's abusive partner, and fear of peer ridicule and rejection.

Many of these fears are derived from threats that the sexual offender has made. Typically sexual abuse victims are coerced into secrecy with threats tailored to most effectively arouse that victim's specific fears. For example, female adolescents who are sexually assaulted by a male peer are typically told that the assailant will tell others that the victim is a "slut," or that the victim initiated the sexual activity. He exacts a promise of silence in exchange for not making her a social outcast among her peers. In cases of intrafamilial sexual abuse, the sexual offender places the burden of paradoxical responsibility on the child by suggesting that her disclosure would result in destruction of the family unit and dissipation of her mother's love. If disclosure does occur and the family is disrupted or the mother chooses not to believe the child, the child victim is likely to recant her statement of abuse, preferring the risk of further victimization to the loss of her mother's love.

Given these cumbersome obstacles to disclosure, it is not surprising that many victims either do not disclose their abuse or delay considerably before disclosing. In one study, the average and median times to disclosure were 2.3 years and 5–6 months, respectively (Kellogg & Huston, 1995). Disclosure was more likely among victims that felt the abuse was coercive or was the fault of the perpetrator (Kellogg & Hoffman, 1995). In addition, victims of rape or attempted rape are more likely to disclose abuse than victims of other types of sexual contact (Kellogg & Hoffman, 1995). Self-blame, ambivalent feelings about the abuse or abuser, and "allowing" an USE to occur in order to sustain a relationship or anger a peer or family member are all associated with a lower frequency of disclosure.

Child and adolescent sexual abuse victims choose to disclose their abuse for a variety of reasons. The most common reason for disclosure was the inability to keep it in any longer. Among 144 sexually abused females, 76% indicated that one reason they disclosed their abuse was because "I couldn't hold it in any longer"; this reason was statistically more common among Hispanic victims when compared with Anglo victims (Kellogg & Huston, 1995). In this study, the majority of respondents selected several reasons for their disclosure. Only 56% disclosed because they wanted their abuser punished and half disclosed because they were afraid someone else would be abused by the perpetrator (Kellogg & Huston, 1995). External influences, such as school programs or being convinced by a friend to tell, were relatively uncommon reasons cited for disclosure. When compared with Anglo females, Hispanic female victims were more likely to disclose because of a school program and fear of being hurt if they didn't tell (Kellogg & Huston, 1995).

Approximately 90% of female children and adolescents that disclose vaginal–penile penetration have normal examinations; penetration can occur without causing visible injury, and injuries that do occur tend to heal quickly and completely within a matter of days. In a study of 36 pregnant adolescent females undergoing a sexual assault examination, 82% had normal "intact" hymens (Kellogg, Menard, & Santos, 2003). Forensic evidence is time-sensitive and recoverable in only 25% of victims that present themselves to authorities within 72 hours of vaginal–penile penetration. Fewer than 10% of victims contract a sexually transmitted disease from their sexual assault or abuse. In addition, physical symptoms may be nonspecific, or may not correlate with examination findings. For example, many victims of sexual abuse or assault complain of genital pain or vaginal discharge, but most have normal examinations that do not explain the symptoms. Genital pain may be related to "body memory"; the recall of abuse may produce flashback experiences of pain. Although such symptoms are certainly important during clinical assessment and treatment, sexual abuse is rarely uncovered based on the physical symptoms of the victim. Ninety percent of abusive or coercive sexual experiences are first discovered when the victim discloses to someone; the remainder of cases are discovered when the abuse is witnessed, or when a victim presents with physical or behavioral symptoms (Kellogg & Menard, 2003). The most effective and reliable way to detect sexual abuse, abusive sexual relationships, and other unwanted sexual experiences is to provide a supportive and receptive environment that enhances the likelihood that disclosure will occur.

INVESTIGATIVE INTERVENTIONS

The investigation and prosecution of sexual abuse/assault relies upon the victim's history, not the presence of injuries or other material evidence. Two agencies conduct investigations: child protective services, whose goal is to ensure the safety of the child, and law enforcement, whose goal is to establish whether a crime has been committed. Because there is a considerable overlap of information gathered by each agency, many states have mandated joint investigations to make the process more efficient and to reduce the trauma to the victim caused by recounting their history numerous times. Child protective services only investigate cases of child abuse involving family members. Child protective services generally complete their investigation within 30 days, and determine each case as "abuse," "no abuse," or "unable to determine." In many states, including Texas, the burden of proof has been raised from 50 to 80%, causing the proportion of cases ruled "abuse" to become smaller; the child protective services validation rate for child and adolescent sexual abuse is less than 25% in San Antonio (Texas Department of Family and Protective Services, 2003). Child protective services also ensure that the nonabusive parent is able to protect the child victim; 19% of nonabusive custodial parents do not report or believe their child's abuse (Kellogg & Menard, 2003). Child protective services may also provide long-term follow-up and other services for the victim and family.

Law enforcement determines whether there is reasonable evidence of a crime. Most law enforcement agencies have specialized units to handle child and adolescent sexual abuse and are cognizant of the fact that physical evidence is typically lacking. Rural jurisdictions may be less aware of such knowledge, and may rely upon the presence of material evidence to prosecute a case. Law enforcement is responsible for gathering the facts and forwarding the case to the district attorney's office, where the case is reviewed for consideration by the grand jury. Many of the investigations conducted by law enforcement are delayed by lack of cooperation (by the victim or the assailant) or by lack of information (insufficient contact information). In San Antonio, Texas, it takes up to 6 months for law enforcement to prepare a case and forward it to the district attorney's office. Cases are either cleared to the district attorney's office, dismissed for insufficient evidence, or pending further investigation. If a victim views the abuse as wanted, or feels it is not a rape because she did not physically resist, then she is less likely to cooperate to the extent necessary to generate an adequate police case; many of these cases are therefore dismissed. In San Antonio, approximately 500 of the 1,400 cases per year processed by the police are forwarded to the district attorney's office and presented to the grand jury.

The district attorney's office is typically comprised of a unit that handles child protective services cases and a unit that handles criminal cases of child abuse, each operating with different goals and timeframes. In rural areas, the same attorneys may handle both types of proceedings.

Child protective services hearings determine whether the nonabusive parent is adequately protecting the child and whether it is safe to return to the child home. If the nonabusive parent fails to demonstrate adequate parental care and protection, the child may be retained in the state's custody on either a temporary or permanent basis. The vast majority of victims are returned home eventually. Child custody hearings generally occur within 10 days, 3 months, 6 months, and 1 year of the time that the state first takes custody. In large cities, criminal proceedings take place 2–4 years from the time of the initial report. However, fewer than 10% of the cases accepted by the district attorney's office reach trial; the remainder of cases result in guilty pleas, are "no-billed" by the grand jury, or are dismissed (for a variety of reasons). The likelihood of a trial resulting from a sexual abuse report is therefore very small in most regions.

The role of the health professional in the evaluation of adolescent victims of abusive sexual experiences varies from region to region. Large metropolitan areas usually have specialized programs within hospitals, clinics, or children's advocacy centers that provide expert assessments and treatment of victims. The health professional has a dual role: to recover forensic information and to address the physical and emotional consequences of the abuse. In general, an adolescent who is the victim of a recent assault (within 72 hours) or who is actively bleeding or in pain should be referred for an emergency medical evaluation. Most victims, however, do not present within an acute time frame and can be referred for a medical evaluation within a few days. A children's advocacy center or rape crisis center can provide guidance regarding the urgency of medical attention and the resources most qualified to provide the best care.

School personnel may be important witnesses for sexual abuse cases. The first person over the age of 18 that the victim discloses abuse to is called an "outcry witness." An outcry witness may testify about what the victim told them. For this reason, it is advisable for school personnel to document their questions and the victim's statements soon after the encounter. School personnel may also provide vital support and understanding to the victim during the prolonged investigative period through confidential advisory or counseling sessions, allowing the adolescent to vent any confusion or frustrations within the investigative processes. It is not advisable, however, to query the victim regarding details of the abuse as this may inhibit the investigation. Table 3.1 provides guidelines for talking with potential or actual victims of abuse.

SHORT- AND LONG-TERM CONSEQUENCES

Short-term effects of abusive sexual experiences can be pervasive, and include depression, anxiety, dissociative symptoms, aggressiveness, defects in social interactions, posttraumatic stress disorder, poor academic performance, suicide ideation, and inappropriate sexual behavior (Deblinger, McLeer, Atkins, Ralphe, & Foa, 1989; Inderbitzen-Pisaurk, Shawchuck, & Hoier, 1992; Kiser, Heston, Millsap, & Pruitt, 1991; Lanktree, Briere, & Zaidi, 1991; Tong, Oates, & McDowell, 1987). Intimate partner abuse among adolescents is associated with sequelae similar to those seen in sexually abused adolescents. In a study by Roberts, Klein, and Fisher (2003), an intimate partner relationship was considered abusive if characterized by any of the following: (1) insults, name-calling, or disrespectful treatment in front of other people; (2) swearing at partner; (3) threat of violence; (4) partner is pushed or shoved; or (5) throwing an object that could hurt at a partner. As defined, intimate partner abuse was associated with increased levels of depression in both males and females, and increased involvement in illegal drug use, antisocial behavior, and suicidal behavior among female adolescents (Roberts, Klein, & Fisher, 2003). This study concluded,

> Educators should be involved in teaching healthy conflict-resolution techniques and foster an environment intolerant of violence and abuse. In the clinical setting, recognition of involvement in an abusive relationship should prompt intervention with supportive education, assistance and assessment of personal safety, referral to community agencies, and more intense screening for involvement in other risk behaviors. (Roberts et al., 2003, p. 880)

Table 3.1.   What to Say and What to Do
When You Suspect Sexual Abuse

BEFORE YOU ASK

1. Earn, don't assume, the teen's trust.

2. Be honest, informative, and respectful to the teen.

3. Give the teen permission to talk to you about anything that worries them or that makes them feel uncomfortable, confused, or threatened: "I talk with a lot of teens about problems they may have. Sometimes they tell me about things that have happened to them or their body that they didn't like. I want you to know that it's okay to talk to me if something like this happened to you."

ASKING THE QUESTION: LISTEN AND LOOK, DON'T LEAD

1. Talk in a quiet, private place.

2. Sit facing the teen at their eye level, and not with a desk between you.

3. Keep the information confidential (inform only those who need to know).

4. Explain the rationale for your concern prior to asking the question: "I'm worried about you because you've seemed afraid to go home over the last 2 weeks. Has anything happened to make you feel differently about going home?" or "You have been asking a lot of good questions about private parts. Has anything happened that would make you more worried about this?"

WHEN A TEEN DISCLOSES ABUSE

1. Be open, receptive, and supportive; NOT judgmental, analytical, shocked, or surprised.

2. Make no assumptions about what the teen is saying; ask for clarification: "You said your brother does nasty stuff. What is nasty stuff? Does nasty stuff involve another person, or not?"

3. Verify information by repeating the teen's words back to him or her; do not paraphrase or interpret what he or she has said.

4. Some teens may prefer to write rather than verbalize what happened.

5. Ask for only minimum information required to report and make any immediate safety plans; that is, WHO the abuser is, WHEN it happened (or most recent event), and WHAT the abuse involved (sexual contact).

6. Acknowledge their feelings and their fears, however different they may be from your own feelings (they may still love the abuser!).

7. DON'T make promises you can't keep (DO NOT say things like: "We'll get this stopped right away so it will never happen to you again").

8. Tell the teen your plan (unless the abuser is present): who you are going to call and what you are going to do.

9. Thank the teen for talking with you. Have a follow-up confidential meeting within a day or two.

WHAT TO DO

1. Report immediately to your child protective services or law enforcement agency in accordance with your state laws.

2. Do NOT wait to report until further investigation.

3. Do NOT delegate responsibility for reporting.

(Continued on next page)

Table 3.1.   Continued

WHAT TO DO (continued)

4. Write down what you asked and what the teen said as soon as possible, using exact quotes when possible.

5. When appropriate, ask the child if he or she feels safe going home. A parent who is an abuser, or who is nonbelieving of the teen, may be unable to protect the teen; some victims may even be punished for "telling." Do not inform the parent of the report or the abuse if it may endanger the teen. If the teen does not feel safe or you are concerned for the teen's safety, call child protective services immediately.

6. If you think the teen may need immediate medical attention or evaluation (if abuse has occurred within 3 days or teen has symptoms of pain and/or bleeding), call your regional children's hospital, children's advocacy center, or the designated medical facility for sexual abuse/assault victims.

Source: Adapted from the *Child Abuse Pocketguide: What to Say and What to Do When You Suspect Child Abuse,* Texas Pediatric Society, Committee on Child Abuse

Abusive sexual experiences frequently influence the adolescent's ability to function socially and academically within their school environment. Among 580 children and adolescents that were surveyed in a child sexual abuse assessment facility (Alamo Children's Advocacy Center, CARE program data, San Antonio, Texas, 2003), approximately half (49%) reported that their grades changed because of the abuse; grades either declined during the time the abuse was occurring, or grades improved immediately subsequent to disclosure. Thirty-eight percent of this group reported that they got in trouble at school more often during the time they were being sexually abused. This same group of children and adolescents reported other difficulties that may manifest in a school setting. Almost half had difficulty sleeping, and half suffered intrusive thoughts of abuse that interfered with concentration on schoolwork. Almost a third had thought of hurting themselves, and 9% had engaged in self-injurious behavior. While 36% had considered running away from home, 12% reported they had run away from home, usually during the same time interval as the abuse. Thirty-eight percent did not confide in either of their parents when they were worried about something, and 32% blamed themselves for the abuse. Male victims were more likely than females to run away and to have problems with behavior at school, and were less likely to confide in a parent. Female victims were more likely than males to have suicidal thoughts, self-injurious behaviors, self-blame regarding the abuse, and intrusive thoughts regarding the abuse.

The deleterious effects of child sexual abuse can persist into adolescent and adult years. Long-term outcomes include sexual dysfunction (Courtois, 1988; Kinzl, Traweger, & Biebl, 1995), sexual revictimization (Kellogg & Hoffman, 1997), substance abuse (Berenson, San Miguel, &

Wilkinson, 1992b; Hussey & Singer, 1993), and mental health disorders (Koopmans, 1994; Lanktree et al., 1991; VanHasselt, Ammerman, Glancy, & Bukstein, 1992). Revictimization rates at the hands of another sex offender occur in 40% of victims (Kellogg & Hoffman, 1997). Victims of child sexual abuse are 2.4 times more likely than children who have not been sexually abused to be victimized by a peer during adolescent years (Kellogg & Hoffman, 1997).

TEENAGE PREGNANCY:
A MODEL OF MULTIDIMENSIONAL VARIABLES

Several studies (Berenson, San Miguel, & Wilkinson, 1992a; Boyer & Fine, 1992; Butler & Burton, 1990; DeFrancis, 1969) have established an association between sexual abuse and teenage pregnancy; one study found that 68% of teenage mothers have been sexually abused (Boyer & Fine, 1989). Sexual abuse and pregnancy tend to be associated with similar social, environmental, and family factors (Stevens-Simon & Reichert, 1992), including family dysfunction and violence, child physical abuse, and substance abuse. Family life appears to influence an adolescent's risk for unwanted or abusive sexual experiences, as well as health risk behaviors, such as unprotected intercourse and substance abuse. Butler and Burton (1990) found similarities among the families of sexually abused children and the families of pregnant adolescents: a patriarchal family structure, devaluation of the mother, and a daughter who assumes a maternal role. They also found that sexually abused girls were more likely to become pregnant intentionally than sexually active girls who were not abused.

One study (Kellogg, Hoffman, & Taylor, 1999) proposed a model to explain the timing and relationships between adolescent sexual experiences, family violence and dysfunction, and health-risk behaviors among pregnant or parenting adolescents. This model provides a basis for understanding the multi-factorial context within which adolescent sexual experiences occur.

In this study, 166 pregnant or parenting adolescent females enrolled in a school-age parenting program completed an anonymous survey. The purpose of this study was not to determine risk factors for teenage pregnancy, but rather to determine which factors *lowered* the age an adolescent first became pregnant.

The study focused on the presence or absence of family violence and substance abuse, and the ages at which an adolescent was first sexually active, first sexually or physically abused, and first had, or participated in, health risky behaviors (ran away, used illegal drugs, first got drunk, pregnancy, eating/weight difficulties). Overall, 45% of pregnant adolescents had an unwanted sexual experience, 47% did not, and 8% did not know how to characterize their sexual experiences. The responses of the latter group were indistinguishable from those who had unwanted sexual experiences. Unwanted sexual experiences were more common for adolescents who had family members who used illegal drugs or who had an "alcohol problem." Females with an unwanted sexual experience were also more likely to be hit in the face (59% vs. 38%) or hit with a fist (32% vs. 16%) by a family member than females without an unwanted sexual experience. Runaway behavior, illegal drug use, and alcohol use were significantly more common among the pregnant adolescents with histories of unwanted sexual experiences. Similar behaviors have been reported among girls who have experienced date violence or rape; these adolescents were 4–5 times more likely to be substance abusers, 3–4 times more likely to engage in unhealthy weight control behaviors, 2–8 times more likely to engage in risky sexual behaviors, and 7–9 times more likely to have suicide ideation (Silverman, Raj, Mucci, & Hathaway, 2001).

Based on the ages that an adolescent first engaged in, or was subject to, abusive experiences, sexual experiences, and health-risk behaviors, a timeline of events can be constructed from the results of this study (Kellogg et al., 1999). Family factors, such as spousal violence and substance abuse, are present during early childhood and extend through adolescence. Family dysfunction does predispose caretakers to use excessive corporal punishment, reduces the likelihood of a close intimate bond between parent and child, and may increase child vulnerability to sexual abuse. In the study by Kellogg and colleagues (1999), the average age of one's first unwanted sexual experience was 11.6 years. On the timeline, this milestone occurs about the same time one is first hit with a belt or object (9.3 years), hit in the face (12.7 years), and first hit with a fist (13.4 years) by a family member. Physical maltreatment by a family member, coupled with a sexually abusive experience, may compound feelings of isolation, helplessness, and guilt. This was further supported by the finding that when adolescents did disclose their sexual abuse to adults, only half of the adults reported the abuse to authorities or otherwise stopped the abuse. These youngsters struggle with the effects of an unwanted or abusive sexual experience and realize that home is not a safe haven. As a consequence, a variety of health-risk and delinquent behaviors begin within a year of the time they are first hit with a fist. Vomiting or laxative use to control weight begins around age 14, and adolescents first try illegal drugs at age 14.2. They first get drunk at age 14.4, then run away beginning at age 14.5. These behaviors occur during a time when adolescents face the developmental challenge of separating from their parents and establishing their identity. A dysfunctional and nonprotective family environment may either decrease the ability of adolescents to resist or avoid deleterious or self-destructive behaviors or may drive them to seek such behaviors to ameliorate suffering or more ostensibly demonstrate rebellion. Adolescents' first wanted sexual experience begins at age 14.8, and those with a history of unwanted sexual experiences were more likely to have this experience with an individual who is at least 4 years older. The older partner may also be the supplier of drugs and alcohol to the teen, and may demand sex in exchange for his wares. The mean age of first pregnancy in this study was 15.9 years.

Four factors lowered the age of first pregnancy. As expected, the younger an adolescent was when she began to have wanted sexual experiences, the younger she was when she became pregnant. Approximately two-thirds either did not use contraception or used contraception less than half of the time they engaged in sexual activity. Sexual abuse indirectly affected this relationship; the younger one was when she was first sexually abused, the younger she was when she had her first wanted sexual experience. The presence of a family member with an "alcohol problem" lowered the age of first pregnancy by 5 months. The third factor was also related to family environment; the younger an adolescent was when she was first hit with a belt, the younger she was when she became pregnant. Finally, the younger an adolescent was when she first got drunk, the younger she was when she became pregnant for the first time. Other factors had indirect effects on the age of first pregnancy: the younger one was when she was first hit with a fist, the younger she was when she first got drunk; the presence of a family member that used illegal drugs lowered the age of one's first unwanted sexual experience by 9.5 months and lowered the age that one first got drunk by 2.9 months. These relationships are summarized in the following equation derived from the model:

Age first pregnancy = 4.00 + .54 (age first wanted sexual experience) + .22 (age first got drunk) + .11 (age first hit with a belt) − .42 (× 1 if family member with an alcohol problem; × 0 if not)

The formula would be utilized as follows: if an adolescent had her first wanted sexual experience at age 14.1 years, first got drunk at age 13.5, was first hit with a belt at age 7.8 and there were no family members with alcohol problems, then the predicted age of first pregnancy would be:

4.00 + .54 (14.1) + .22 (13.5) + .11 (7.8) − .42 (0) = 15.4 years

(If any of the first three factors are not present, the equation cannot be used to predict pregnancy age.)

This model demonstrates the close and complex relationships between adolescent sexual experiences and experiences within the home as well as among peers. The model suggests that the risk factors for abusive sexual experiences, which in turn affect wanted sexual experiences, begin in childhood. Effective intervention must address family life, early sexual experiences, and health-risk behaviors, focusing on physical and sexual abuse, substance abuse, and reduction of violence within the home.

PREVENTION

The goals of primary prevention of child and adolescent sexual abuse are to: (a) reduce the likelihood that a potential sexual offender will act on his desires by making confidential, nonincriminating treatment available; (b) reduce the appeal of potential victims with programs that promote self-esteem and emphasize the importance of disclosure; and (c) decrease sexual desire for children by eliminating child pornography and other material that portray children in sexual ways. Schools typically provide programs that address primary prevention by promoting self-esteem and healthy decision making in order to avoid unwanted sexual encounters. Sexual harassment, date rapes, partner violence, and bullying have become notable problems among adolescents, occurring even within schools. Several schools have employed harsh punishments and "bullyproof" programs to address the problems of sexual harassment and bullying.

The goal of secondary prevention is to stop ongoing abuse by promoting victim disclosure and reporting of abuse. Secondary prevention provides guidance to adults on how to talk to children when abuse is suspected and provides rationale to adolescents regarding the importance of disclosure. Most primary prevention programs for sexual abuse also incorporate secondary prevention goals by encouraging the victim to share the secret. As discussed previously, schools may also target peer confidants of the victim in order to secure their assistance in promoting the victim's disclosure to an adult.

Tertiary prevention entails comprehensive and effective treatment of victims in order to reduce the likelihood that an adolescent victim will become an abusive partner or revictimized. Effective tertiary prevention also promotes the recovery of the victim so they will seek healthy relationships and avoid health-risk behaviors. Counselors or therapists that specialize and have expertise in sexual victimization are best suited to address the varied needs of the adolescent. Rape crisis centers and children's advocacy centers can provide or refer adolescents for such services.

INTERVENTION STRATEGIES FOR SCHOOLS

Schools have both opportunities and obligations regarding adolescent sexual experiences. Schools may assist in the *prevention, detection, reporting,* and *treatment* of unwanted, coercive, illegal, or abusive sexual experiences that may occur during adolescence.

Prevention

1.   Promote the development of decision-making and conflict-resolution skills that help the adolescent avoid unsafe relationships (that may or may not include sex), illegal drugs, delinquent activities, and other self-injurious behaviors.
2.   Increase awareness of sexual, physical, and verbal abuse within the context of adult–child and peer relationships. Provide resources and counselors within the school that can offer confidential advice and guidance regarding relationships. Consider implementation of available programs (may be available through rape crisis agencies) that address bullying, date rape, and abusive relationships.
3.   Adopt a "no tolerance" policy for violence and abuse.

Detection

1.   Give adolescents opportunity and explicit permission to talk about any uncomfortable, coercive, or confusing sexual experiences. Use Table 3.1 as a guideline for how to broach such topics appropriately.
2.   Provide education regarding the importance of disclosing abuse—not only to prevent abusive experiences from escalating, but also to prevent other people from being victimized. Provide guidance to peer confidants of victims so they may encourage their friends to disclose abuse and seek help.
3.   Be aware of cultural factors that may affect the adolescent's abusive experience and their willingness to disclose. For example, Hispanic females are more likely to experience self-blame and more family conflict as a result of their abuse.

Reporting

1.   When an illegal sexual experience is identified, whether or not the adolescent feels it is abusive, report promptly to authorities in

accordance with state laws. Know the age parameters of what defines an illegal (reportable) sexual experience among adolescents within your state.

2. When reporting abuse to authorities, ensure that the victim feels safe going home. He or she may fear parental repercussions, disbelief, or nonsupport. Report any perceived lack of parental support to child protective services.

Treatment

1. Ensure that any information gathered from the adolescent is kept confidential and shared only with the necessary adults and agencies. Take firm, decisive measures to reduce secondary victimization created by vicious rumors among adolescent peer groups.
2. Publicize community resources that can provide assistance, medical treatment, and mental health services to victims of unwanted, illegal, or abusive experiences.

REFERENCES

Berenson, A. B., San Miguel, J. D., & Wilkinson, G. S. (1992a). Prevalence of physical and sexual assault in pregnant adolescents. *Journal of Adolescent Health, 13*, 466–469.

Berenson, A. B., San Miguel, J. D., & Wilkinson, G. S. (1992b). Violence and its relationship to substance use in adolescent pregnancy. *Journal of Adolescent Health, 13*, 470–474.

Boyer, D., & Fine, D. (1989). *Teen parent victimization: A preliminary report to the Department of Health and Social Services.* Seattle, WA: Washington Alliance Concerned with School-Aged Parents.

Boyer, D., & Fine, D. (1992). Sexual abuse as a factor in adolescent pregnancy and child maltreatment. *Family Planning Perspectives, 24*(1), 4–19.

Briere, J., & Runtz, M. (1993). Childhood sexual abuse: Long-term sequelae and implications for psychological assessment. *Journal of Interpersonal Violence, 8*, 367–379.

Butler, J. R., & Burton, L. M. (1990). Rethinking teenage childbearing: Is sexual abuse a missing link? *Family Relations, 39*, 73–80.

Centers of Disease Control and Prevention. (2002). Trends in sexual risk behaviors among high school students—United States, 1991–2001. *MMWR, 51*(38), 856–859.

Courtois, C. A. (1988). *Healing the incest wound.* New York: W.W. Norton.

Deblinger, E., McLeer, S. V., Atkins, M. S., Ralphe, D., & Foa, E. (1989). Posttraumatic stress in sexually abused, physically abused, and nonabused children. *Child Abuse & Neglect, 13*, 403–408.

DeFrancis, V. (1969). *Protecting the child victim of sex crimes committed by adults*. Denver, CO: American Humane Association.

Erickson P., & Rapkin, A. J. (1991). Unwanted sexual experiences among middle and high school youth. *Journal of Adolescent Health, 12*, 319–325.

Feiring, C., Rosenthal, S., & Taska, L. (2000). Stigmatization and the development of friendship and romantic relationships in adolescent victims of sexual abuse. *Child Maltreatment, 5*(4), 311–322.

Finkelhor, D. (1979). *Sexually victimized children*. New York: Free Press.

Hopper, J. (1997). *Prevalence, lasting effects, and resources*. Retrieved from http://www.jimhopper.com/male-ab#studies

Hussey, D. L., & Singer, M. (1993). Psychological distress, problem behaviors, and family functioning of sexually abused adolescent inpatients. *Journal of American Academy of Child and Adolescent Psychiatry, 32*, 954–961.

Inderbitzen-Pisaruk, H., Shawchuck, C. R., & Hoier, T. S. (1992). Behavioral characteristics of child victims of sexual abuse: A comparison study. *Journal of Clinical Child Psychology, 21*, 14–19.

Kellogg, N. D., Burge S., & Taylor E. R. (2000). Wanted and unwanted sexual experiences and family dysfunction during adolescence. *Journal of Family Violence, 15*(1), 55–68.

Kellogg, N. D., & Hoffman, T. J. (1995). Unwanted and illegal sexual experiences in childhood and adolescence. *Child Abuse & Neglect, 19*(12): 1457–1468.

Kellogg, N. D., & Hoffman, T. J. (1997). Child sexual revictimization by multiple perpetrators. *Child Abuse & Neglect, 21*, 953–964.

Kellogg N. D., Hoffman T. J., & Taylor E. R. (1999). Early sexual experiences among pregnant and parenting adolescents. *Adolescence, 34*, 292–303.

Kellogg, N. D., & Huston R. L. (1995). Unwanted sexual experiences in adolescents: Patterns of disclosure. *Clinical Pediatrics, 34*(6), 306–312.

Kellogg, N. D., & Menard S. M. (2003). Violence among family members of children and adolescents evaluated for sexual abuse. *Child Abuse & Neglect, 27*, 1367-1376.

Kellogg, N. D., Menard, S. M., & Santos, A. (2004). *Genital findings in pregnant adolescents: "Normal" does not mean "nothing happened." Pediatrics, 113*(1), e67-e69.

Kercher, G. A., & McShane, M. (1984). The prevalence of child sexual abuse victimization in an adult sample of Texas residents. *Child Abuse & Neglect, 8*, 495–501.

Kinzl, J. F., Traweger, C., & Biebl, W. (1995). Sexual dysfunctions: Relationship to childhood sexual abuse and early family experiences in a nonclinical sample. *Child Abuse & Neglect, 19*, 785–792.

Kiser, L. J., Heston, J., Millsap, P. A., & Pruitt, D. B. (1991). Physical and sexual abuse in childhood: Relationship to post-traumatic stress disorder. *Journal of the American Academy of Child and Adolescent Psychiatry, 30*, 776–783.

Koopmans, M. (1994). Self-reports of sexual, mental health status, and perceived confusion of family roles: A retrospective study of college students. *Psychological Reports, 75*, 339–347.

Lanktree, C., Briere, J., & Zaidi, L. (1991). Incidence and impact of sexual abuse in a child outpatient sample: The role of direct inquiry. *Child Abuse & Neglect, 15*, 447–453.

Lechner, M. E., Vogel, M. E., Garcia-Shelton, L. M., Leichter, J. L., & Steibel, K. R. (1993). Self-reported medical problems of adult female survivors of sexual abuse. *Journal of Family Practice, 36*, 633–638.

Lewin, T. (1997, October 1). Young victims often turn to alcohol, drugs, risky sex and suicidal thoughts. *New York Times*, p. 12.

Roberts, T.A., Klein, J. D., & Fisher, S. (2003). Longitudinal effect of intimate partner abuse on high-risk behavior among adolescents. *Archives of Pediatric and Adolescent Medicine, 157*, 875–881.

Ryan, S., Manlove, J., & Franzetta, K. (2003). The first time: Characteristics of teens' first sexual relationships. *Child Trends Research Brief*. Retrieved from www.childtrends.org/PDF/FirstTimeRB.pdf

Sanders-Philips, K., Moisan, P. A., Wadlington, S., Morgan, S., & English, K. (1995). Ethnic differences in psychological functioning among black and Latino sexually abused girls. *Child Abuse & Neglect, 19*, 691–706.

Silverman, J. G., Raj, A., Mucci, L. A., & Hathaway, J. (2001). Dating violence against adolescent girls and associated substance use, unhealthy weight control, sexual risk behavior, pregnancy, and suicidality. *Journal of the American Medical Association, 286*, 572–579.

Stevens-Simon, C., & Reichert, S. (1992). Sexual abuse, adolescent pregnancy and child abuse: A developmental approach to an intergenerational cycle. *Archives in Pediatric Adolescent Medicine, 148*, 23–27.

Tong, L., Oates, K., & Mcdowell, M. (1987). Personality development following sexual abuse. *Child Abuse & Neglect, 11*, 371–383.

VanHasselt, V. B., Ammerman, R. T., Glancy, L. J., & Bukstein, O. G. (1992). Maltreatment in psychiatrically hospitalized dually diagnosed adolescent substance abusers. *Journal of the American Academy of Child and Adolescent Psychiatry, 31*, 868–874.

CHAPTER 4

ETHNICITY AND PEER HARASSMENT DURING EARLY ADOLESCENCE

Exploring the Psychological Benefits of Ethnic Diversity from an Attributional Perspective

Sandra Graham

If we were to ask adolescents what they worry about at school, a generation ago they probably would have said passing examinations and being promoted to the next grade. Today, adolescents' school concerns often revolve around safety as much as achievement, including the specter of peer harassment. Survey data indicate that anywhere from 40% to 80% of school-aged youth report that they personally have experienced victimization from others, ranging from relatively minor instances of verbal abuse and intimidation to more serious forms of victimization, including assault, property damage, and theft (e.g., Boney-McCoy & Finkelhor, 1995; Nansel, Haynie, & Simons-Morton, 2003). Not surprisingly, over 60% of 8- to 15-year-olds rate bullying as a major concern in

Educating Adolescents: Challenges and Strategies, 85–108
Copyright © 2004 by Information Age Publishing

their lives (Kaiser Family Foundation and Children Now, 2001). In the aftermath of recent school shootings, bullying has now been recognized as a major public health concern, as the perpetrators of such abuse are becoming more violent and the targets of their abuse are feeling more vulnerable.

In this chapter, I describe a program of research that my colleagues and I have undertaken to understand the social and emotional adjustment difficulties of early adolescents who are victims of others' harassment. We have a particular focus on ethnic group membership and the role that it might play in understanding the psychological consequences of peer victimization. A good deal of peer relations research, including the study of victimization, is conducted in urban school contexts where multiple ethnic groups are represented, but very little of that research has systematically examined ethnicity-related variables. That is disappointing because so much of peer relations—for example, the formation and maintenance of friendships, the dynamics of peer acceptance and rejection, and the factors that exacerbate aggression and harassment—all are likely to be influenced by such context factors as the ethnic composition of schools and neighborhoods, as well as the social and ethnic identities that are most significant to youth.

One of my goals in writing this chapter is to propose a framework for infusing ethnicity and ethnic context in the study of peer harassment. That framework draws on my intellectual roots in attribution theory, where I have examined the perceived causes of success and failure in both the academic and social domains, and how those attributions influence how a person subsequently thinks, feels, and behaves (e.g., Graham, 1997). Here I apply attributional analyses to examine how victims from multiple ethnic groups construe the reasons for their plight and how particular causal perceptions influence adjustment. I hope to make a case for the importance of causal beliefs as a theoretical scaffold and ethnicity as a central context variable, both of which can aid our understanding of the dynamics of peer harassment.

The research that I describe was conducted with early adolescents who have transitioned to middle school. That means that I have a particular interest in understanding the phenomenon of peer harassment as an adolescent experience. The transition to middle school is accompanied by major shifts in the importance of the peer group, as well as heightened concern about finding one's niche, fitting in, and peer approval in general. Ethnicity also takes on added significance in larger and typically more diverse middle schools as adolescents attempt to define their identity in relation to affiliation with similar others (e.g., Hamm, 2000; Shrum, Cheek, & Hunter, 1988). In light of these developmental concerns, early adolescents who are victims of peer harassment might be particularly vulnerable to adjustment difficulties.

PEER HARASSMENT: A BRIEF OVERVIEW

I define peer harassment as the types of bullying, taunting, name-calling, and intimidation that takes place in and around school, especially when adult supervision is minimal. Such harassment may be either direct, entailing face-to-face confrontation; or indirect, typically involving a third party and some form of social ostracism. It has been suggested that the more direct forms of physical harassment decline from childhood to adolescence (e.g., Nagin & Tremblay, 1999), whereas the more indirect forms increase (e.g., Crick et al., 2001). But that developmental pattern is not so clear since most of the research documenting age-related change in the forms of harassment has not been conducted with multi-ethnic child and adolescent samples. Note also that my definition of peer harassment does not include the more lethal sorts of peer-directed hostilities such as those seen in the widely publicized school shootings. Although many of those shootings may have been precipitated by a history of peer abuse (Leary, Kowalski, Smith, & Phillips, 2003; Verlinden, Herson, & Thomas, 2000), they remain rare events. My definition and focus here is on more typical and widespread types of peer harassment that affect the lives of many youth and that may have far-reaching and uncertain consequences.

During the past decade, a growing empirical literature has documented the negative psychological, social, and academic consequences of being a victim of peer harassment (see Juvonen & Graham, 2001). Victims tend to have low self-esteem and to feel more lonely, anxious, unhappy, depressed, and insecure than their nonvictimized peers. Victims also are very disliked by their peers, particularly during the middle school years. In general, early adolescents appear to be unsympathetic toward victims and to endorse the belief that they are responsible for their plight and bring their problems on themselves (Graham & Juvonen, 2002; Hoover, Oliver, & Hazler, 1992; Rigby & Slee, 1991). The psychological and social adjustment difficulties of peers often stand in stark contrast to that of their perpetrators (i.e., bullies), who more often have positive self-views during adolescence and enjoy high social standing among peers (Juvonen, Graham, & Schuster, 2003). Although studies linking victim status to academic achievement are fewer, there is evidence that victimization is associated with negative attitudes toward school and/or poor performance as early as kindergarten and extending into the adolescent years (Graham, Bellmore, & Juvonen, 2003; Juvonen, Nishina, & Graham, 2000; Kochenderfer & Ladd, 1996). It is not difficult to imagine the chronic victim who becomes so anxious about going to school that she or he tries to avoid it at all costs (e.g., Batsche & Knoff, 1994).

VIEWING PEER HARASSMENT THROUGH AN ATTRIBUTIONAL LENS

Acknowledging the known relationships between peer victimization and adjustment problems, as an attribution theorist, I was especially interested in *why*. That is, what processes or mediating mechanisms might explain why some victimized youth might feel lonely, anxious, and have negative self-views?

One such mechanism might relate to how victims construe the reason for their plight. For example, a history of peer abuse and the perception of being singled out for such harassment might lead a victim to ask "Why *me?*" In the absence of disconfirming evidence, some victims might come to blame themselves for their peer relationship problems. Such an adolescent might conclude, for example, that, "I'm the kind of kid who deserves to be picked on." Self-blame and accompanying negative affect can then lead to many negative outcomes, including low self-esteem, loneliness, anxiety, and depression.

Relevant to this focus, Janoff-Bulman (1979) has made a distinction between behavioral and characterological self-blame for coping with rape (another obvious form of victimization). Janoff-Bulman described the two types of self-blame as follows:

> Behavioral self-blame is control related, involves attributions to a modifiable source (one's behavior), and is associated with a belief in the future avoidability of a negative outcome. Characterological self-blame is esteem related, involves attributions to a relatively nonmodifiable source (one's character), and is associated with a belief in personal deservingness for past negative outcomes. (p. 1978)

In attributional language, behavioral self-blame is *internal* ("It's me"), *unstable* ("Things can change"), and *controllable* ("I can do something about it"). That self-ascription resembles lack of effort as a cause of failure in the achievement domain (Weiner, 1986). In contrast, characterological self-blame is also *internal* ("It's me"), but *stable* ("Things will always be that way"), and *uncontrollable* ("There's nothing I can do to change it"). That attribution is more akin to low aptitude as a cause of achievement failure. The maladaptive consequences of low aptitude compared to lack of effort in the achievement domain are well documented (see Weiner, 1986). Indeed, a whole program of empirical research, labeled attribution-retraining, has documented the motivational benefits of teaching students to attribute their academic failures to lack of effort rather than lack of aptitude (see Fosterling, 1985).

In a similar vein, a number of researchers have documented that individuals who make characterological self-attributions for negative social outcomes cope more poorly, feel worse about themselves, and are more depressed than individuals who make behavioral self-attributions (see reviews in Anderson, Miller, Riger, Dill, & Sedikides, 1994; Frazier, 1990; Janoff-Bulman, 1992). Research with early adolescents also revealed that characterological self-blame for academic and social failure resulted in heightened depression (Cole, Peeke, & Ingold, 1996). Such findings are also compatible with research on learned helplessness, where it has been shown that children and adults with pessimistic explanatory styles (i.e., failure attributions to internal, stable, and global factors) are more psychologically impaired than their peers with optimistic explanatory styles (i.e., internal, unstable, and specific) (Peterson, 2000). Thus two motivational sequences hypothesized by attribution theorists that might be relevant to peer victimization are:

Victimization → Behavioral → Perceived causes → More adaptive responses
 -self-blame controllable by (e.g., higher self-esteem, self and unstableless anxiety)

Victimization → Characterological → Perceived causes → Maladaptive responses
 -self-blame uncontrollable by (e.g., low self-esteem, anxiety) self and stable

Attributions about Peer Harassment: A First Study

In our first study on peer harassment in middle school, my colleagues and I adopted the distinction between characterological and behavioral self-blame to examine the attributions that young adolescents endorse to explain harassment from their peers (Graham & Juvonen, 1998). We recruited a sample of about 400 sixth graders from 18 homeroom classes in a multiethnic middle school located in a working-class community in Los Angeles, and that qualified for compensatory education federal funding. Thus our participants were predominantly of low socioeconomic status (SES). Mirroring the ethnic breakdown of the school, our sample was approximately 30% African American and 30% Latino, with the remaining 40% comprised equally of four ethnic groups: whites, Persian/Middle Easterners, Asian/Pacific Islanders, and biracial youth. Ethnic identification was based on self-report.

All data were gathered via questionnaires that participants filled out during their homeroom period. The first part of the questionnaire consisted of self-report and peer nomination measures of victimization. For example, we asked participants to rate the extent to which they felt like "someone who gets picked on a lot" and we asked peers to nominate classmates who fit various behavioral descriptions that portrayed victimization (e.g., "Name three classmates who get put down or made fun of by others"). Those self-report and reputational measures were later used to classify respondents into victim subgroups. In the second part of the questionnaire that assessed psychological adjustment, respondents completed well-validated and widely used measures of self-esteem, loneliness, and social anxiety.

In the third part of the questionnaire we developed a new measure to assess attributions for harassment. Participants were asked to imagine that they had experienced two types of victimization at school (being humiliated in the locker room, being physically threatened in the restroom). For example, they read a hypothetical vignette such as the following:

> Imagine that when you are in the restroom in your school, you see a couple of kids smoking. When they see you, one of them blocks the door so you can't get out, while the other presses you against the wall.

After reading the scenario and being instructed to imagine that such an incident actually happened to them, participants were asked to rate how much they agreed with 32 statements that captured their causal thoughts, feelings, and behavioral reactions to the victimizing incident. The thoughts included attributions designed to tap characterological self-blame (e.g., "This sort of thing is more likely to happen to me than to other kids"; "Why do I always get into these situations?") and behavioral self-blame (e.g., "I should have been more careful this time"), as well as external attributions pertaining to others. Factor analyses confirmed the existence of these causal constructs (see Graham & Juvonen, 1998).

Based on self-reported subjective experiences with victimization and having a reputation as a victim based on peer report, we identified the subgroup in our sample who could appropriately be classified as chronic victims ($n = 40$, about 10% of the sample). We compared their ratings on the two self-blame measures and the three adjustment indices to the subgroup who did not perceive themselves as victims and did not have that reputation among their peers ($n = 165$, about 40% of the sample). The results of those analyses are shown in Table 4.1. The two self-blame measures are reported as standard scores, with a mean of zero and a standard deviation of one. Loneliness and social anxiety are 5-point rating scales, whereas self-esteem is measured on a 4-point scale. Higher numbers on

Table 4.1.   Psychological Adjustment as a Function of Victim Status

	Victim Group	
Variable	Victims	Nonvictims
Characterological self-blame	$.30^a$	$-.12^b$
Behavioral self-blame	$.03^a$	$-.11^a$
Loneliness	2.2^a	1.8^b
Social anxiety	2.6^a	2.0^b
Self-esteem	2.9^a	3.2^b

Note: Row means for victims and nonvictims with different superscripts are significantly different at $p < .05$. Characterological self-blame and behavioral self-blame scores are standardized. Scores range from 1 to 5 for loneliness and social anxiety, and from 1 to 4 for self-esteem.
Source: Data from Graham and Juvonen (1998).

these scales indicate more loneliness, more social anxiety, and higher self-esteem.

Table 4.1 shows that victims compared to nonvictims endorsed significantly more characterological self-blaming attributions for imagined peer harassment. There were no differences between the groups on the theoretically less maladaptive behavioral self-blame attributions, suggesting that all of the young adolescents in this study to some degree blamed their own (controllable) behavior when explaining peer harassment. Consistent with much of the research literature, victims were also lonelier, more socially anxious, and lower in self-esteem than their nonvictimized classmates.

From an attributional perspective, we hypothesized that the relationship between peer victimization and psychological maladjustment might be mediated by attributions that implicate one's character. The results of a path analysis supported that mediational hypothesis. That is, much of the relation between self-reports of being a victim and maladjustment were explained by characterological self-blaming attributions. A similar analysis with behavioral self-blame as the mediator failed to show any mediated effects. Thus, the data were consistent with our attributional analysis of the maladaptive consequences of attributions for victimization that are internal, stable, and uncontrollable. It is as if the victim is saying to himself or herself: "It's something about me, things will always be that way, and there is nothing I can do to change it." Those causal thoughts are then predicted to result in greater psychological distress. In some cases, the attributional sequence that I hypothesize may reveal cyclical or even bidirectional effects. Over time, for example, youth who feel increasingly lonely and socially anxious can become more vulnerable to self-blaming attributions. And in the real world, of course, many antecedent conditions, such as whether victimization is chronic or short-lived or perpetrated by many versus a few peers, will influence the likelihood that a vulnerable child will conclude that "it must be *me*." To my knowledge, however, this is the first study to systematically document that particular kinds of causal attributions for peer harassment might be related to particular adjustment consequences.

Bringing Ethnicity to the Analysis

Thus far I have not said anything about ethnicity, despite the fact that our sample was multiethnic. I can say at the outset that there were no ethnic differences in the attributions that individuals endorsed for imagined peer harassment or in the relations between attributions and adjustment. That should not be surprising. There is no theoretical or empirical rationale for hypothesizing that attributions should vary as a function of victim ethnicity per se. Comparative racial research on attributions, albeit largely confined to African Americans and whites, does not find systematic differences between racial groups in the content of their causal beliefs (see review in Graham, 1994). Despite some popular beliefs to the contrary—probably a legacy of an older locus of control literature—African American youth are not more likely than their white counterparts to attribute failure to internal and/or uncontrollable causes. Furthermore, studies of attributional process that examine attribution–adjustment linkages similar to those that we investigate also document more racial similarity than difference (e.g., Graham & Long, 1986). Although comparative attribution research involving other ethnic groups is sparse, there is no reason to expect systematic differences in either attributional content or process simply as a function of respondent (victim) ethnicity.

I do believe that ethnic variation and ethnicity of victim are important variables for understanding causal beliefs about victimization and their psychological consequences. But rather than focus on ethnicity per se, I want to make a case for examining ethnicity within a particular school or classroom context, where that context varies by ethnic composition. To illustrate, let me turn to what we know about the contextual antecedents of peer victimization.

According to Olweus (1994), victimization is most likely to occur in settings where there is an imbalance of power between perpetrator and victim. Such asymmetric power relationships can take many forms, as when the strong bully the weak, older kids harass younger targets, or the intellectually superior deride their less competent peers. Building on Olweus's ideas about power relationships, it also is possible that the ethnic makeup of a setting can signal an imbalance of power and can therefore function as an antecedent of victimization. That is, in a racially diverse school setting, one might hypothesize that students whose ethnic group is the statistical minority (i.e., less powerful in the numerical sense) would be more vulnerable to victimization. On the other hand, statistical majority groups (i.e., more powerful in the numerical sense) would be expected to have more perpetrators than targets of peer harassment. Racial dissonance in the numerical sense is likely to exacerbate perceptions of "us" versus "them" (e.g., Tajfel & Turner, 1986) and ingroup–outgroup disparities (Hewstone, 1989), which are known antecedents of interpersonal conflict.

We tested the relations between victim status and majority/minority ethnic group composition in our multi-ethnic middle school sample described above (Graham & Juvonen, 2002). Recall the ethnic composition of that sample. At 30% each, African Americans and Latinos were the two majority groups. At about 10% each, whites, Persians, Asians, and biracial youth were the four minority groups. Within each of those ethnic groups, we examined how many youth had reputations as victims versus aggressors based on peer nominations.

Those data, displayed in Figure 4.1, were consistent with our expectations. The two groups who were the numerical majorities (African Americans and Latinos) had more members perceived as aggressive and fewer members perceived as victims than what would be expected if there was no relationship between ethnicity and victim status. That pattern was particularly true for African American majority group members, among

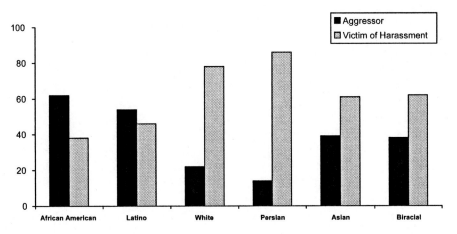

Source: Graham and Juvonen (2002).

Figure 4.1.   Percentage of nominations for being a victim of harassment or an aggressor in each ethnic group.

whom 64% of their nominations were for behaviors describing an aggressor compared to 38% for behaviors describing a victim. In contrast, for the groups who were the numerical minorities (whites, Persians, Asians, biracial), we found a pattern of overnominating peers from these groups as victims relative to what would be expected by chance and undernominating peers from these same groups as aggressive. For example, four times more white and Persian students were nominated as victims of harassment than as aggressors. Similar findings with other ethnic groups who were numerical minorities in their school have been reported in both American (Hanish & Guerra, 2000) and European research (Verkuyten & Thijs, 2002). All of these studies therefore suggest that individuals' ethnic representation within context may be more important than their specific ethnic group in predicting their vulnerability to peer harassment.

Now what about the youth in these ethnic groups who do indeed have reputations as victims? In terms of the kind of adjustment variables that we have been examining, does it make a difference whether you are a victim in the majority or minority ethnic group? On the one hand, one could argue that ethnic minority victims would be the most vulnerable to loneliness, anxiety, low self-esteem, and self-blaming tendencies. That would be consistent with the way we think about an imbalance of power and the reality that minority group victims may have fewer same-ethnicity friends to either ward off potential harassers or buffer the consequences of victimization (e.g., Hodges, Boivin, Vitaro, & Bukowski, 1999).

On the other hand, consider what it must be like to be a victim *and* a member of a numerical majority group. Being a victim when your ethnic group holds the numerical balance of power and has a stronger reputation as aggressive might be especially debilitating because you deviate from what is perceived as normative for your group. Wright, Giammarino, and Parad (1986) adopted the label *social misfit* to describe individuals whose problem social behavior deviated from group norms. In a study of boys living in cottages while attending summer camp, Wright and colleagues found that aggressive boys were most rejected when their cottage was low in perceived aggressiveness based on counselor and peer ratings and withdrawn boys were most rejected when their cottage was low in behaviors associated with social withdrawal. The negative consequences of being a social misfit, that is, deviating from the local norms, have been replicated in other social contexts such as laboratory play groups (Boivin, Dodge, & Coie, 1995) and naturalistic classrooms that could be characterized in terms of high and low levels of aggression and social withdrawal (Stormshak et al., 1999).

In our next analyses, we examined the adjustment outcomes of victims and nonvictims as a function of majority/minority ethnic group status (see Figure 4.2). African Americans and Latinos had sufficient numbers to be

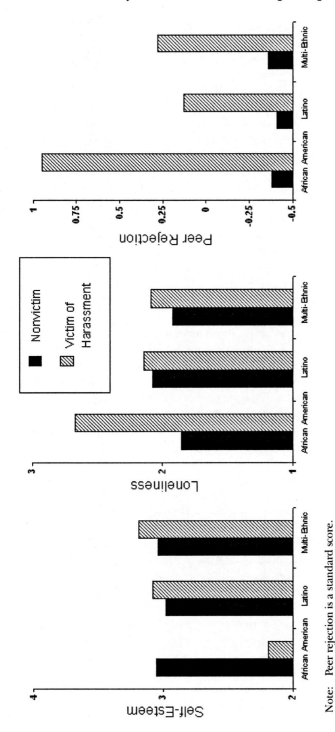

Note: Peer rejection is a standard score.
Source: Graham and Juvonen (2002).

Figure 4.2.   Mean differences in self-esteem (left panel), loneliness (middle panel), and peer rejection (right panel) as a function of ethnicity and victim subgroup.

retained as separate groups in these analyses. Because the pattern of victim nominations was similar across the four minority groups, each relatively small in number, we combined those groups into one cluster that we called multiethnic. That strategy was not ideal, but to achieve statistical power, it was a compromise we had to make when the analysis involved extreme social groups (i.e., victims and nonvictims) within ethnic groups that already were small by virtue of being in the numerical minority.

Figure 4.2 shows the results of these analyses for the psychological adjustment variables of self-esteem and loneliness. We also included a measure of peer rejection because of the well-documented association between that variable and peer victimization and because prior studies of the social misfit effect have focused on interpersonal evaluation. The pattern of findings in Figure 4.2 is similar across the three outcomes. Within each of the three ethnic groups, it was the African American victims who fared worse than nonvictims. Furthermore, across victim groups, African American targets had lower self-esteem, felt lonelier, and were more rejected than Latino victims or victims in the multiethnic group. In contrast, the adjustment outcomes of Latino victims were similar to those of multiethnic victims. The findings for African American victims are compatible with what we know about the consequences of being a social misfit, or someone whose own behavior deviates from what is perceived as normative for their group. African American students were not expected to be perceived as victims, given both their numerical majority status (their group held the numerical balance of power) and the perception of their ethnic group as aggressive (relatively few African Americans had reputations as victims and relatively more had reputations as being aggressive). Being a victim of peer harassment and a member of an ethnic majority group where aggressiveness is the perceived norm can be especially debilitating, both psychologically and socially.

How do these findings relate back to our attributional analyses of how victims construe the reasons for their plight? I propose as a working hypothesis that early adolescent victims who have characteristics that deviate from group norms will be particularly vulnerable to characterological self-blaming attributions ("It must be *me*"). African American victims of harassment best fit that description in the above analyses. Compared to Latinos (the other majority ethnic group), perceived aggressiveness was higher within the African American sample.

Because our study was carried out in only one middle school with one particular configuration of ethnic groups, we cannot know for sure whether the relations between ethnicity and the consequences of peer harassment were really due to majority/minority status, as we hypothesized, or to the specific ethnic groups that comprised those classifications. I believe that the process of vulnerability to characterological self-blame for non-normative behavior should generalize across different ethnic groups who hold the numerical balance of power in different contexts. In the next study I turn to such tests of generality.

Ethnicity and Peer Harassment in Context: Multilevel Effects

The data for our next analysis come from the first wave (fall of Grade 6) of an ongoing longitudinal study of peer harassment across middle school (see Graham et al., 2003; Juvonen, Graham, & Schuster, 2003). The demographics of the sample for this study improves upon many of the shortcomings of the sample that was studied in Graham and Juvonen (1998, 2002). Rather than 400 multiethnic sixth graders selected from 18 classrooms in one Los Angeles middle school, we recruited about 2,000 sixth graders selected from 99 classrooms in 11 middle schools located throughout the city. The schools (and classrooms) were carefully selected to vary in ethnic composition. That selection strategy yielded the ethnically diverse sample that is shown in Table 4.2. Because Latinos comprise about 70% of students enrolled in the Los Angeles Unified School District, they make up our largest group at 45%. About two-thirds are of Mexican heritage, with the remaining one-third coming mainly from Central America. Asian youth are primarily Korean (70%), with the remaining 30% comprised of Vietnamese and Pacific Islanders. About three-fourths of the Latino and Asian participants were U.S.-born children of immigrants. African American and white youth tended to be ethnically homogeneous and again there was a small subgroup that identified themselves as biracial. The sample is also well balanced by gender ($n = 909$ boys and 1,094 girls). To avoid confounding ethnicity with social class in our analyses, all of the schools were located in predominantly low-SES neighborhoods and all qualified for Title I funding.

Note also in Table 4.2 that the 11 schools can be divided into three types that vary in ethnic diversity. Latino majority and African American majority schools were those where Latinos and African Americans, respectively, were at least 60% of the population and no other ethnic group exceeded 30% of the population. Schools were classified as diverse when no ethnic group held the numerical majority within the school and there were at least three different ethnic groups represented.

Given our interest in diverse ethnic groups that hold the numerical balance of power, the reader might wonder why we did not include schools where, for example, white and Asian students were the numerical majority. The answer to that question highlights the challenges of studying ethnic diversity in Los Angeles public schools. Among those chal-

Table 4.2.   Ethnic Breakdown of the Longitudinal Sample, as a Function of School Type

Ethnicity	Latino Majority (n = 3)	African American Majority (n = 3)	Diverse Schools (n = 5)	Total
Mexican American/Latino	491	137	282	910 (45%)
African American/Black	106	293	112	511 (26%)
Asian/Pacific Islands	75	9	128	212 (11%)
White	50	2	136	188 (9%)
Biracial	57	29	96	182 (9%)
Total	779	470	754	N = 2,003

lenges are the residential segregation of many ethnic groups, the lure of suburbia for the middle class, and the loss of confidence in public schools for many Los Angeles residents who can afford private alternatives. Because schools in the Los Angeles Unified School District (LAUSD) and neighboring low-SES districts are over 70% Latino, it has become increasingly difficult to find middle schools where Latinos are not the majority group. For example, only four middle schools in LAUSD have a clear African American majority and three of those schools are a part of this sample. Schools that are majority Asian tend to be located in more affluent communities, reflecting the economic prosperity of groups with East Asian roots (e.g., Japan, Korea, and Taiwan). In low-SES communities that do attract Asians, such as where we recruited, the students share their school turf with Latinos.

Those challenges notwithstanding, we set out to test the moderating influence of majority/minority ethnic status on the relations between peer victimization and psychological adjustment with a much larger sixth-grade sample drawn from many different middle schools that varied in ethnic composition. As in the prior study, we had reputational (peer nomination) measures of peer victimization as well as self-report measures of loneliness, social anxiety, and self-blaming attributions for imagined peer harassment.

We also created two new measures of ethnic diversity, one at the individual level and one at the classroom level, that were central to our analytic approach. Recall that the 2,000 participants in this sample were recruited from 99 classrooms, 77 of which had sufficient numbers to be used in this analysis. For each participant, we created an individual-level variable that we labeled *percent same ethnicity*. That variable described the proportion of peers in an individual's classroom who shared his or her ethnicity. The larger the proportion, the more likely an individual student is to be a member of the ethnic majority group. Thus the variable allowed us to examine the effects of being in a classroom with mostly same-ethnicity classmates (numerical majority status) in contrast to being a numerical minority.

The second measure of diversity that we created was at the classroom level. Classroom ethnic composition can influence the range of individual *percent same ethnicity* scores. For example, the range of same ethnicity scores will be greater if there are many ethnic groups represented in the classroom in differing proportions than if there are few groups and one group is clearly the majority. We therefore wanted a measure of classroom-level diversity that took into account both the number of ethnic groups and the relative proportion of each within that classroom. Controlling for classroom-level diversity permitted us to approach the kind of generality we wanted—that is, to examine the role of majority/minority status on victimization–adjustment relations, independent of one's specific ethnic group and independent of the variability associated with being in one type of classroom with a particular ethnic mix versus residing in another classroom with a different ethnic configuration.

To assess ethnic diversity at the classroom level, we adapted a measure first used in the ethology literature, known as Simpson's index of diversity (Simpson, 1949):

$$Diversity\ index\ =\ 1 - \sum_{1}^{g} p_i^2$$

where p is the proportion of students in a particular ethnic group and i and g is the number of groups. The index calculates the probability that any two students selected at random in a classroom will be from different ethnic groups. Possible values range from 0 to 1, where higher values (probabilities) indicate greater diversity.

Figure 4.3 illustrates the meaning of the classroom diversity index in relation to the individual diversity variable (percent same ethnicity) for three hypothetical examples. The first pie graph depicts a classroom of Latino and African American students with low diversity ($d = .18$). Ninety percent of the students are Latino and 10% are African American. The middle pie graph shows a classroom with the same two ethnic groups, but in this case they are equally represented. That classroom is the more diverse by our definition ($d = .50$). Finally, the third pie graph captures the most diverse classroom ($d = .72$). It is comprised of four ethnic groups, 40% of whom are Latino, with the remaining three groups equally represented at 20% each. Thus one of the advantages of this diversity index is that it takes into account both the number of ethnic groups within a given context and the representation of each group. The 77 classrooms used in our analysis achieved a good range of ethnic diversity. The average diversity score was .47 (*sd* = .22), with values ranging from 0 (three classrooms that were entirely ethnically homogeneous) to .77 (see Bellmore, Witkow, Graham, & Juvonen, in press).

Given the nested structure of our data (individual students of different ethnicities nested in classrooms that vary in diversity), we used hierarchical linear modeling (HLM) as our main analytic tool (Raudenbush, Bryk, & Congdon, 2000). One benefit of HLM is that it controls for dependencies in the data that result from students sharing the same classroom context. Thus we used HLM to examine whether the relationship between victim reputation and psychological adjustment was influenced by ethnic majority/minority status (i.e., percent same ethnicity) when controlling for the variability associated with classroom diversity. Another benefit of HLM is that it allowed us to test whether the relationships between victim reputation and adjustment was moderated by the higher-order classroom variable. That is, we examined whether youth with reputations as victims reported more (or less) adjustment difficulty depending on the ethnic diversity of their classroom.

Some readers may question our rationale for studying ethnic diversity at the classroom rather than the school level. Because classrooms in our study largely mirrored school ethnic diversity, that focus especially suited our needs because of the greater statistical power that it provided for multilevel modeling (i.e., 77 classrooms rather than 11 middle schools). Moreover, classrooms and the middle schools were organized such that sixth graders spent much of the day with the same classmates. A disadvantage of this approach is that we do not capture how peers in other sixth-grade classrooms or other grades in the school contribute to an individual's reputation as a victim. I acknowledge this shortcoming,

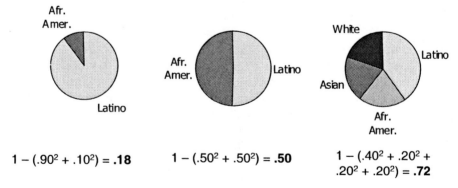

Figure 4.3.   Illustrations of the classroom diversity index.

although I still believe that it is appropriate and meaningful to study classrooms as the unit of analysis in middle school. As students move into middle adolescence and the highly departmentalized high school environment, I realize that it will be necessary to study school-level rather than classroom-level effects.

Controlling for classroom diversity in middle school, and independent of particular ethnic groups, the HLM analysis showed that victimization was related to more loneliness and social anxiety. More importantly for our purposes, that relationship was significantly moderated by ethnic majority–minority group status. Figure 4.4 shows the nature of that moderation for each adjustment outcome. Plotted here are the regression slopes predicting loneliness and social anxiety at high and low levels of victim reputation (one standard deviation above and below the mean) for students who were high and low in the proportion of classmates who shared their ethnicity. Consistent with our predictions, the regression slopes describing the relations between victim reputation and both outcomes were steeper for sixth graders who shared their classroom with a larger percentage of same-ethnicity classmates (i.e., the numerical ethnic majority). In other words, and in agreement with a social misfit analysis, loneliness and social anxiety were greatest for victims who were members of the ethnic majority group.

At the classroom level, scores on the diversity index did not moderate the victimization–adjustment relationship in a systematic way. However,

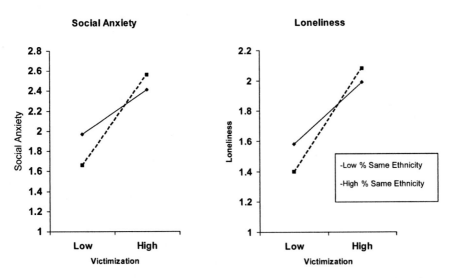

Figure 4.4.   The relationship between victimization and adjustment as a function of ethnic majority/minority status (percent same ethnicity).

there were significant intercept effects suggesting that classroom ethnic diversity influenced average levels of loneliness and anxiety, independent of victim reputation or majority/minority status. Students were less lonely and less socially anxious in classrooms that were high in ethnic diversity.

What about the moderating role of characterological self-blame? We conducted the same HLM analysis with both types of self-blame as dependent variables. Victimization predicted characterological self-blame but not behavioral self-blame, as in our previous research (Graham & Juvonen, 1998). At Wave 1 in the fall, the moderating role of percent same ethnicity only approached significance ($p < .07$). However, by the spring of the school year (Wave 2), that effect was significant and consistent with the findings for loneliness and social anxiety. As Figure 4.5 shows, victimization was a stronger predictor of characterological self-blame for students whose classmates shared their ethnicity. These short-term longitudinal analyses suggest that being a victim and a majority group member does influence self-blaming attributions, but that causal construals emerge gradually over time. In addition, like the intercept analyses for loneliness and social anxiety, more classroom diversity also predicted less characterological self-blame. There is something about membership in a more ethnically diverse classroom that promotes more positive self-views for all of the class members, independent of their victim reputation, ethnic group, or majority/minority status.

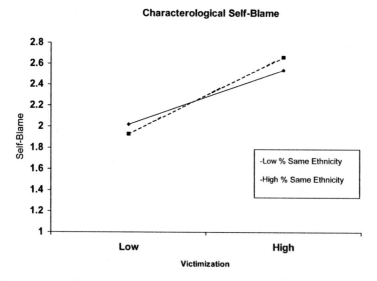

Characterological Self-Blame

Figure 4.5. The relationship between victimization and characterological self-blame as a function of ethnic majority/minority status (percent same ethnicity).

In sum, the multilevel analysis provided an opportunity to study how ethnicity within context, as opposed to ethnicity per se, influences victimization–adjustment relations. We made the distinction between ways in which all students in the same classroom are more similar to each other than to students in another classroom (diversity), but also differ from each other based on their individual characteristics (ethnicity and percent same ethnicity). Taking into account classroom-level variance allowed us to have more confidence in our finding that victims whose group is the ethnic majority in a particular context may be at risk for greater maladjustment.

SUMMARY AND CONCLUSIONS

In this chapter, I set out to make a case for examining the role of ethnicity in understanding the dynamics of peer harassment during early adolescence. The analyses presented here lead me to the following conclusions:

First, ethnicity is an important context variable for understanding the experiences of early adolescents who are harassed by their peers. But it is not so much ethnic group per se as it is ethnicity within a particular school context. I do not think that it is productive to expect any particular ethnic group to be more or less at risk for being the target of peer abuse. Rather, I suspect that the critical variable is whether any one ethnic group does or does not hold the numerical balance of power. Numerical ethnic minority group members may be more vulnerable to experiencing harassment.

Second, being a victim and a member of the ethnic majority group has its own unique vulnerability. Like social misfits (Wright et al., 1986), when victims deviate from what is perceived as normative for their group they are more likely to feel bad about themselves and to be rejected by the peer group. If one's ethnic group holds the numerical balance of power, then causal construals about the reasons for of harassment are more likely to implicate the self.

Third, ethnic diversity in context—where no one group holds the numerical balance of power—may have particular psychological benefits. Independent of victim reputation and ethnic group membership, we found that students in classrooms that were more ethnically balanced felt less lonely, less socially anxious, and over time were less likely to endorse characterological self-blaming attributions. I suggest as a working hypothesis that ethnic diversity creates enough attributional ambiguity to ward off self-blaming tendencies. Greater diversity among ethnic groups who share the balance of power discourages attributions for failure to the self ("It must be *me*") while allowing for attributions to external factors that protect self-esteem ("It could be *them*"). There is a vast empirical literature in adult social psychology on the self-protective functions of attributions to external causes among stigmatized groups (see Crocker & Major, 1989; Crocker, Major, & Steele, 1998). The time seems right to bring that literature to developmental social psychology and to studies of coping with the social stigma of chronic harassment by peers.

Although I focus on an attributional explanation, there surely are other factors that can explain the positive effects of classroom ethnic diversity in these analyses. For example, it may be that teachers in more diverse classrooms are doing something different than teachers in nondiverse classrooms (e.g., addressing equity issues or promoting more cultural awareness). Or it could be that diversity fosters strong ethnic identity, which then acts as a buffer against general feelings of vulnerability. These are only speculations, but they merit further study.

Some Caveats

I did not talk at all about gender in this chapter, despite the fact that our samples are very well balanced by gender so that we can examine whether the pattern of findings is different for adolescent boys and girls. In our analyses we have not found meaningful differences between boys and girls in the experience of peer harassment or the relations between harassment and adjustment. The absence of gender differences is consistent with other large-scale studies of peer victimization in school (Nansel, Overpeck, Pilla, Ruan, & Simons-Morton, 2001). In some ways that is comforting. The absence of effects of gender or of ethnicity per se tells us that having a reputation as a victim of harassment cuts across gender and ethnic divides. No one gender or ethnic group is inherently more vulnerable than another. But had we studied the perpetrators of harassment rather than their victims, the story would have been different. In our research and almost every study that I know of where ethnicity and gender are examined, it is males—and African American males—who are more likely to be perceived as aggressive (see Noguera, 2003). Perceiving African American males as aggressive may have as much to do with pervasive cultural stereotypes about black males as violent and aggressive (e.g., Graham & Lowery, in press) as with their actual behavior. Thus I am not sure how much the associations between having a reputation as aggressive and being an African American male adolescent vary as a function of ethnic majority/minority status, but that is an intriguing question for future research.

Also related to the study of perpetrators rather than victims, it is less clear that external attributions ("It could be *them*") are the most functional. A very robust finding in the peer aggression literature is that aggressive boys display an attributional bias—that is, they overattribute hostile intent to their peers, especially in situations of ambiguous provocation (see review in Coie & Dodge, 1998). A low threshold for assigning (rather than accepting) blame has been linked to anger and escalating aggressive behavior. Thus it is important to recognize that the underlying dynamics of aggression and victimization are not the same for perpetrators and victims, and that different analytic frameworks may be needed.

Final Thoughts

The research described in this chapter reveals positive effects of ethnic diversity on coping with peer harassment at both the individual and classroom level. I highlighted the benefits of more diversity as a way of lessening the negative consequences of being a victim of peer harassment. No doubt there are many other psychological benefits of multiethnic school environments, just as there are some contexts in which being a part of the ethnic majority group has self-enhancing functions.

For some readers, my conclusions about the psychological benefits of ethnic diversity may seem obvious and not in need of attributional analyses. Social scientists have been concerned with the consequences of ethnic diversity in schools since the early studies on school desegregation that followed *Brown v. Board of Education* in 1954. But a careful look at the developmental literature after Brown reveals very little systematic research on the social consequences of ethnic diversity. That research, which yielded inconsistent and largely disappointing findings, all but disappeared after 1980, with little evidence that increased ethnic contact in desegregated schools enhanced the self-views and social adjustment of ethnic minority youth (Schofield, 1991). Ironically, one of the lasting legacies of desegregation research was that African American children and adolescents report higher self-esteem when they attend segregated rather than integrated schools (Gray-Little & Hafdahl, 2000).

I believe that the time is right to revisit that legacy. The 50th anniversary of *Brown v. Board of Education*, the known benefits of ethnic diversity on college campuses that have shaped the affirmative action debate (Milem, 2003), and the changing ethnic landscape revealed by Census 2000 are powerful signals that developmental psychologists should be undertaking new programs of research that examine how ethnic diversity can promote healthy social development in children and adolescents. I hope that the conceptual analysis and research presented in this chapter will stimulate new ways to think about ethnicity in context, ethnic diversity, and coping with peer harassment during adolescence.

REFERENCES

Anderman, E. M., & Kimweli, D. M. S. (1997). Victimization and safety in schools serving early adolescents. *Journal of Early Adolescence, 17,* 408–438.

Anderson, C., Miller, R., Riger, A., Dill, J., & Sedikides, C. (1994). Behavioral and characterological attributional styles as predictors of depression and loneliness: Review, refinement, and test. *Journal of Personality and Social Psychology, 66,* 549–558.

Batche, G., & Knoff, H. (1994). Bullies and their victims: Understanding a pervasive problem in the schools. *School Psychology Review, 23,* 165–174.

Bellmore, A., Witkow, M., Graham, S., & Juvonen, J. (in press). Beyond the individual: The impact of ethnic context and classroom behavioral norms on victims' adjustment. *Developmental Psychology.*

Boivin, M., Dodge, K. A., & Coie, J. D. (1995). Individual-group behavioral similarity and peer status in experimental play groups of boys: The social misfit revisited. *Journal of Personality and Social Psychology, 69,* 269–279.

Boney-McCoy, S., & Finkelhur, D. (1995). Special populations: Psychological sequelae of violent victimization in a national youth sample. *Journal of Consulting and Clinical Psychology, 63,* 726-736.

Coie, J., & Dodge, K. (1998). Aggression and antisocial behavior. In N. Eisenberg (Ed.), *Handbook of child psychology. Volume 3: Social, emotional, and personality development* (pp. 779–862). New York: John Wiley.

Cole, D., Peeke, L., & Ingold, C. (1996). Characterological and behavioral self-blame in children: Assessment and developmental considerations. *Development and Psychopathology, 8,* 381–397.

Crick, N., Nelson, D., Morales, J., Cullerton-Sen, C., Casas, J., & Hickman, S. (2001). Relational vixtimization in childhoodand adolescence: I hurt you through the grapevine. In J. Juvonen & S. Graham (Eds.), *Peer harassment in school: The plight of the vulnerable and victimized* (pp. 196–214). New York: Guilford Press.

Crocker, J., & Major, B. (1989). Social stigma and self-esteem: The self-protective properties of stigma. *Psychological Review, 96,* 608–630.

Crocker, J., Major, B., & Steele, C. (1998). Social stigma. In D. Gilbert, S. Fiske, & G. Lindzey (Eds.), *The handbook of social psychology* (4th ed., Vol. 2, pp. 504–553). Boston: McGraw-Hill.

Fosterling, F. (1985). Attribution retraining: A review. *Psychological Bulletin, 98,* 495–512.

Frazier, P. (1990). Victims' attributions and postrape trauma. *Journal of Personality and Social Psychology, 59,* 298–304.

Graham, S. (1994). Motivation in African Americans. *Review of Educational Research, 64,* 55–117.

Graham, S. (1997). Using attribution theory to understand academic and social motivation in African American youth. *Educational Psychologist, 31,* 167–180.

Graham, S., Bellmore, A., & Juvonen, J. (2003). Peer victimization in middle school: When self and peer views diverge. *Journal of Applied School Psychology, 19,* 117–137.

Graham S., & Juvonen J. (1998). Self-blame and peer victimization in middle school: Anattributional analysis. *Developmental Psychology, 34,* 587–599.

Graham, S., & Juvonen, J. (2002). Ethnicity, peer harassment, and adjustment in middle school: An exploratory study. *Journal of Early Adolescence, 22,* 173–199.

Graham, S., & Long, A. (1986). Race, class, and the attributional process. *Journal of Educational Psychology, 78,* 4–13.

Graham, S., & Lowery, B. (in press). Priming unconscious racial stereotypes about adolescent offenders. *Law and Human Behavior.*

Gray-Little, B., & Hafdahl, A. (2000). Factors influencing racial comparisons of self-esteem: A quantitative review. *Psychological Bulletin, 126,* 26–54.

Hamm, J. V. (2000). Do birds of a feather flock together? The variable bases for African American, Asian American, and European American adolescents' selection of similar friends. *Developmental Psychology, 36,* 209–219.

Hanish, L. D., & Guerra, N. G. (2000). The roles of ethnicity and school context in predicting children's victimization by peers. *American Journal of Community Psychology, 28,* 201–223.

Hewstone, M. (1989). *Causal attributions: From cognitive processes to collective beliefs.* Oxford, UK: Blackwell.

Hodges, E. V. E., Boivin, M., Vitaro, F., & Bukowski, W. M. (1999). The power of friendship: Protection against an escalating cycle of peer victimization. *Developmental Psychology, 35,* 94–101.

Hoover, J., Oliver, R., & Hazler, R. (1992). Bullying: Perceptions of adolescent victims in midwestern USA. *School Psychology International, 13,* 5–16.

Janoff-Bulman, R. (1979). Characterological and behavioral self-blame: Inquiries into depression and rape. *Journal of Personality and Social Psychology, 37,* 1798–1809.

Janoff-Bulman, R. (1992). *Shattered assumptions: Toward a new psychology of trauma.* New York: Free Press.

Juvonen, J., & Graham, S. (2001). *Peer harassment in school: The plight of the vulnerable and victimized.* New York: Guilford Press.

Juvonen, J., Graham, S., & Schuster, M.. (2003). Bullying among young adolescents: The strong, the weak, and the troubled. *Pediatrics, 112,* 1231–1237

Juvonen, J., Nishina, A., & Graham, S. (2000). Peer harassment, psychological well-being, and school adjustment in early adolescence. *Journal of Educational Psychology, 92,* 349–359.

Kaiser Family Foundation, Children Now. (2001). *Talking with kids about tough issues: a national survey of parents and kids.* Retrieved from http://www.kff.org/content/2001/3105/summary.pdf

Kochenderfer, B., & Ladd, G. (1996). Per victimization: Cause or consequence of children's school adjustment difficulties? *Child Development, 67,* 1305–1317.

Leary, M., Kowalski, R., Smith, L., & Phillips, S. (2003). Teasing, rejection, and violence: Case studies of the school shootings. *Aggressive behavior, 29,* 203–214.

Ma, X. (2001). Bullying and being bullied: To what extent are bullies also victims? *American Educational Research Journal, 38,* 351–370.

Milem, J. (2003). The educational benefits of diversity: Evidence from multiple sectors. In M. Chang, D. Witt, J. Jones, & K. Hakuta (Eds.), *Compelling interest:*

Examining the evidence on racial dynamics in colleges and universities (pp. 126–169). Stanford, CA: Stanford University Press.

Nagin, D., & Tremblay, R. (1999). Trajectories of boys' physical aggression, opposition, and hyperactivity on the path to physically violent and nonviolent juvenile delinquency. *Child Development, 70,* 1181–1196.

Nansel, T., Haynie, D., & Simons-Morton. The association of bullying and victimization with middle school adjustment. *Journal of Applied School Psychology, 19,* 45–61.

Nansel, T., Overpeck, M., Pilla, R., Ruan, W., & Simons-Morton, B. (2001). Bullying behaviors among US youth: Prevalence and association with psychosocial adjustment. *Journal of the American Medical Association, 285,* 2094–2100.

Noguera, P. (2003). The trouble with black boys: The role and influence of environmental and cultural factors of the academic performance of African American males. *Urban Education, 38,* 431–459.

Olweus, D. (1994). Annotation: Bullying at school: Basic facts and effects of a school-based intervention program. *Journal of Child Psychology and Psychiatry, 35,* 1171–1190.

Peterson, C. (2000). The future of optimism. *American Psychologist, 55,* 44–55.

Raudenbush, S. W., Bryk, A. S., & Congdon, R. (2000). *HLM for Windows. Version 5* [Computer software]. Lincolnwood, IL: Scientific Software International, Inc.

Rigby, K., & Slee, P. (1991). Bullying among Australian school children: Reported behavior and attitudes toward victims. *Journal of Social Psychology, 131,* 625–627.

Schofield, J. (1991). School desegregation and intergroup relations: A review of the literature. *Review of Research in Education, 17,* 335–409.

Shrum, W., Cheek, N. H., & Hunter, S. M. (1988). Friendship in school: Gender and racial homophily. *Sociology of Education, 61,* 227–239.

Simpson, E. H. (1949). Measurement of diversity. *Nature, 163,* 688.

Stormshak, E. A., Bierman, K. L., Bruschi, C., Dodge, K. A., Coie, J. D., & The Conduct Problems Prevention Research Group. (1999). The relation between behavior problems and peer preference in different classroom contexts. *Child Development, 70,* 169–182.

Tajfel, H., & Turner, J. (1986). *The social identity theory of intergroup behavior.* In D. Worchel & W. Austin (Eds.), *Psychology of intergroup relations* (2nd ed., pp. 7–4). Chicago: Nelson-Hall.

Verkuyten, M., & Thijs, J. (2002). Racist victimization among children in The Netherlands: The effect of ethnic group and school. *Ethnic and Racial Studies, 25,* 310–331.

Verlinden, S., Hersen, M., & Thomas, J. (200). Risk factors in school shootings. *Clinical Psychology Review, 20,* 3–56.

Weiner, B. (1986). *An attributional theory of motivation and emotion.* New York: Springer-Verlag.

Wright, J. C., Giammarino, M., & Parad, H. W. (1986). Social status in small groups: Individual-group similarity and the social "misfit." *Journal of Personality and Social Psychology, 50,* 523–536.

CHAPTER 5

ADOLESCENT VICTIMIZATION AND WEAPON USE ON SCHOOL GROUNDS

An Empirical Study from Israel

Ron Avi Astor, Rami Benbenishty, Heather A. Meyer, and Michelle Elena Rosmond

The school shootings in the United States from the mid-1990s to 2000s have heightened public awareness worldwide with regard to the use of lethal weapons in schools (Furlong & Morrison, 2000; Kingery, Coggshall, & Alford, 1999; Kingery, Pruitt, Heuberger, & Brizzolara, 1995; May, 1999; Simon, Crosby, & Dahlberg, 1999). The research on youth possession and use of guns is quite extensive (see reviews in McKeganey & Norrie, 2000; Mercy & Rosenberg, 1998). However, most research studies focus solely on the possession and use of guns and only peripherally address other social aspects associated with weapons on school grounds. For example, a student may see a weapon on school grounds, may be directly threatened by another student with a weapon, or may even be injured by a weapon. Looking at all these different forms of victimization by weapons is important because they may have differential effects on the

Educating Adolescents: Challenges and Strategies, 109–129
Copyright © 2004 by Information Age Publishing

students involved. Although seeing a weapon on school grounds may constitute a serious threat, it differs significantly from being a victim of a direct threat by a weapon. Additionally, suffering a weapon-related injury represents a much more significant victimization than a threat. Furthermore, the dynamics surrounding lethal victimization by weapons appear to be present in schools in many cultures and countries throughout the world, but current literature focuses almost exclusively on gun violence in U.S. schools (Astor, Benbenishty, Zeira, & Vinokur, 2002; Benbenishty, Zeira, & Astor, 2000; Bronner, 1999; Burnett, 1998; Paetsch & Bertrand, 1999; Smith et al., 1999).

There are many theories as to the reasons why students carry weapons to school. Some studies explore the relationship between victimization on school grounds and weapon carrying and use as a form of protection (e.g., Kingery et al., 1995; May, 1999). This belief has been strengthened by the recent spree of mass school shootings in the United States (e.g., Columbine High School, Littleton, Colorado) where it was speculated that the shooters were avenging years of bullying and victimization. Other theories have focused on the relationship between weapon carrying, juvenile delinquency, gang affiliation or contact, and an array of negatively oriented peer group behaviors that include drug use and criminal activity (Kingery et al., 1999; Lizotte, Howell, Tobin, & Howard, 2000; Page & Hammermeister, 1997; Simon et al., 1999; Yexley, Borowsky, & Ireland, 2002). Theories that focus on the "spillover" effects of community and family violence suggest that youth weapon use on school grounds stems primarily from growing up in a violent family, the presence of weapons in households, and community beliefs that are accepting of weapon use.

In this chapter we examine the issue of weapons on school grounds from a number of perspectives intended to further theory, methodology, conceptual development, and interventions. First, we selectively review some major concepts regarding weapon carrying in schools, including perspectives that focus on (a) delinquency, (b) community and family violence, (c) self-protection, (d) the types of weapons students carry (e.g., are there cultural, regional, or other differences?), and (e) the relationship between prior victimization and weapons possession. Second, the chapter presents an empirical study of student victimization and weapon possession in Israeli schools. In our Israeli empirical case example, we explore the relationships between victimization on school grounds and weapon use on school grounds.

There is a need for inquiries that explore the reasons behind school weapon carrying and use in countries outside of the United States. A broader exploration could help uncover cross-cultural or culturally specific explanations for weapon carrying in schools that could inform both theory and practice. Hence, this chapter also presents an analysis of patterns of relationships between prior victimization and weapon carrying and use on school grounds using data on Jewish and Arab school-aged children in schools in Israel. To our knowledge, this is the first nationally representative sample on such issues for any country in the Middle East. Ultimately, we hope the questions we put forth in this chapter will further the research on weapon use in schools across cultures by discussing both common themes and differences.

CONCEPTUAL OVERVIEW

Delinquency

Studies have found strong associations between overall delinquent behaviors and weapon use (Kingery et al., 1999; Lizotte et al., 2000; Lowry, Powell, Kann, Collins, & Kolbe, 1998; Simon et al., 1999; Yexley et al., 2002). In the delinquency literature, weapon use and possession are not studied as separate behaviors, but are instead seen as part of an overall delinquency profile. For example, Lizotte and associates (2000) demonstrated that youth delinquency was related to gang membership, substance abuse, drug selling, and weapon possession. Studies often show that the weapon carrier is involved in a broad array of antisocial behaviors and that weapon carrying is the result of negative social environments where the negative social groups desensitize, indoctrinate, and normalize the use of weapons (Kingery et al., 1999; Lizotte et al., 2000; Simon et al., 1999; Yexley et al., 2002).

Although aspects of juvenile delinquency theory are supported by the empirical literature (e.g., Furlong & Morrison, 2000), there are some alternative explanations that focus on prior victimization. For example, it is quite possible that some of these "delinquent" students might have also suffered severe victimization that later contributed to these antisocial tendencies. Furthermore, a broader epidemiological exploration of students who carry weapons might reveal that there is a large subgroup of students who are not "delinquents" per se, but who carry weapons to school due to fear. These students may possess a need for self-protection based on prior victimization experiences in schools.

Community Influences

There has been considerable research on the relationships between school violence and the "spillover" effects of community violence, especially in high-crime urban areas (Kupersmidt, Shahinfar, & Voegler-Lee,

2002; Valois, MacDonald, Bretous, Fischer, & Drane, 2002). For example, Garbarino (1992) found that many children growing up in violent and dangerous communities also have impaired psychological development. Schools within high-risk communities can either serve as a refuge from violence or mirror the violence rates in the larger community. Some researchers find that community rates of weapon use clearly *influence*, but are not the same as, school rates of weapon use (Simon et al., 1999). On the whole, weapon use and possession in communities are consistently higher than those in schools (see Simon et al., 1999). This is especially evident after the enactment of the "zero tolerance" school policies in the late 1990s. Government data suggest that within the same samples of students who report using weapons in the community, significantly fewer bring weapons onto school grounds (see Astor, Benbenishty, & Marachi, 2004; Astor, Pitner, Benbenishty, & Meyer, 2002; Rapp-Paglicci, Roberts, & Wodarski, 2002).

Another large-scale national study examined whether students who carry weapons in the community also carry weapons on school grounds (Simon et al., 1999). Approximately one-half of adolescents who reported that they carried weapons in the community also carried weapons on school grounds. This study also found that a wide range of delinquent behaviors and prior victimization at school were key variables in weapon carrying on school grounds. Simon and colleagues (1999) reported that students who received an offer to use drugs on school grounds, had property stolen or damaged, were threatened or injured with a weapon on school grounds, or missed school because they felt it was unsafe were more likely to report carrying a weapon both off and on school grounds. The results speak to the potentially important role that school victimization plays in weapon possession on school campuses. Currently, about 9% of students report victimization involving other students using weapons at school (U.S. Department of Justice, 2002).

Family Influences: Household Beliefs about Weapons

Similar to community violence beliefs, "spillover" assumptions are made about students who are raised in families that use violence as a means of expression or solving problems. Empirical research has found that children who are raised in violent households are more likely to carry weapons, act aggressively, and perpetrate violence (Corvo & Williams, 2000; Orpinas, Murray, & Kelder, 1999). In fact, Yexley and associates (2002) found a relationship between different experiences of family physical violence and violent adolescent behaviors including attempted suicide, fighting, and gun carrying at school. Another study (Ding, Nelsen,

& Lassonde, 2002) examined adolescent aggressiveness in relation to household gun ownership, beliefs about guns, and experiences with guns. Children in families that owned guns tended to react aggressively to frustration in school and were more likely to believe that gun carrying was not dangerous or problematic. Several other studies suggest that family attitudes and access to weapons at home increase the risk of youth bringing those weapons to school (see Yexley et al., 2002).

Nevertheless, this literature on family influences seems to be overwhelmingly focused on firearms and students' access to firearms, as almost no other kinds of weapons have been carefully examined. This is surprising, considering the availability of other items in children's homes that could easily be used as weapons. For example, all children have access to sharp knives in their kitchens in addition to bats/clubs, box cutters, and pocket knives that could cause serious injury and are easy to conceal. Again, very little epidemiological or conceptual work has been conducted on family or community patterns for different types of weapon use on school campuses.

Weapons for Self-Protection

When students are asked for the reason why they bring weapons to school, self-protection is most commonly cited (Furlong & Morrison, 2000; Kingery et al., 1995). In fact, the right to bear arms for self-protection is embedded in the U.S. constitution and culture; a common assertion used by the National Rifle Association (NRA) to defend weapon use (mainly guns) by "noncriminal" citizenry. Consequently, numerous inquiries on the use of weapons for protection emerge out of the defensive gun use (DGU) literature (e.g., Schnebly, 2002; Wells, 2002). These studies are based on the theory that gun carriers see these weapons as an effective tool for preventing and interrupting crimes. However, some DGU studies have suggested that with criminal populations, gun carriers' motivations often go beyond protection alone, and guns are often needlessly utilized in some situations. For instance, Wells (2002) collected data on the DGU with male inmates and found that 27% of the claimed defensive gun use situations may have involved more than just simple defensive gun use. For example, the victim may fire on a retreating perpetrator when he or she has the opportunity to escape the situation. In addition, some studies suggest a relationship between carrying a gun and finding oneself in a potentially violent social situation (Schnebly, 2002; Wells, 2002). In other words, people who carry guns are far more likely to enter dangerous situations and in turn become victimized (e.g., Schnebly, 2002).

These types of DGU studies have mainly been conducted in the United States and have focused on incarcerated adults or youth outside the context of the school (Schnebly, 2002; Wells, 2002). It is not clear if the results from DGU studies on firearm use and possession are applicable to non-firearm weapons on school grounds. Also, we suspect that these findings may vary across cultures where perspectives on weapons and weapon use may vary.

In addition, research on DGU has not fully explored issues of prior victimization and gun use and carrying. After the U.S. and international school shootings, the media made many links between chronic victimization and using a weapon in school. The FBI and Secret Service Reports of 2002 mentioned the relationship between being bullied and bringing a weapon to school and shooting it (see also Vossekuil, Reddy, Fein, Borum, & Modzeleski, 2000). Therefore, we can suspect that this extreme population of students who are being victimized in school may be more prone to bring a weapon to school, either for self-defense or for revenge (American Psychological Association, 1993; DuRant, Krowchuk, Kreiter, Sinal, & Woods, 1999).

Type of Weapons and Victimization

As mentioned earlier in this chapter, the weapon possession literature tends to focus on gun usage (Ding et al., 1999; Kingery et al., 1995; Lizotte et al., 2002; May, 1999; Ruddell & Mays, 2003; Schnebly, 2002; Wells, 2002; Yexley et al., 2002), which is understandable as guns allow an individual to perpetuate maximal damage with minimal effort. Most U.S. surveys lump together different types of weapons, ask about "a weapon," and do not distinguish between guns, knives, and other weapons. For instance, the YRBSS (Youth Risk Behavior Surveillance System), an ongoing national survey of students in grades 9–12, includes only one item that asks: "During the past 30 days, on how many days did you carry a weapon such as a gun, knife, or club on school property?" (for other examples, see Bailey, Flewelling, & Rosenbaum, 1997; Kodjo, Auinger, & Ryan, 2003).

Although guns are lethal weapons, students are victimized by a number of other potentially lethal weapons such as bats/clubs, knives, rocks, and box-cutters (Corvo & Williams, 2000; Kingery et al., 1999; Simon et al., 1999; Stolzenberg & D'Alessio, 2000). An exploration of the patterns behind the use of a wider array of weapons on school grounds is virtually absent from the research literature. A specific kind of weapon may be selected if it is easy to conceal and the consequences for getting caught with a particular weapon are minor. For example, a school may have a "zero tolerance" for weapons policy, but a student may still be able to carry and conceal an "exacto" knife, which is commonly used in student art classes. Despite being something that is used in art class, this kind of knife is small, easily concealed, and could be a potentially lethal weapon. Researching other widely accessible weapons such as knives could expand the existing theory.

Different kinds of weapons vary in many respects (most obviously lethality), although there are also distinctions in terms of symbolic and cultural meaning. For instance, Kingery and colleagues (1995) found that there were ethnic differences in preference for weapons. Non-Hispanic blacks preferred guns, while Hispanics and non-Hispanic whites preferred knives. When students use guns regularly for hunting with their parents (i.e., in rural areas, see Devine & Lawson, 2003), the meaning of bringing a gun to school is different than when the possession of firearms in the community is rare (i.e., in suburban areas). Researchers have just begun to look at some of the patterns of gun, knife, and other weapon use and whether patterns are similar across age, gender, culture, and ethnicity. Our research will attempt to shed more light on these important issues.

School-based Victimization and Weapon Possession on School Grounds

Although it is clear that weapon carrying occurs both in school and in the community surrounding the school, we focus on how prior victimization *on school grounds* influences weapon carrying and use on school grounds. A school-based study by Kingery and colleagues (1999) assessed factors associated with youth gun possession on school grounds. The findings suggested that students who possessed weapons were mainly perpetrators, rather than victims, of violence. In addition, students who brought weapons onto campus were more likely to threaten to use a weapon, to pull out a weapon during a fight, and/or to shoot or stab someone. Nevertheless, the study also provided alternative evidence suggesting that students who were victims of extreme violence or who witnessed extreme violence were more likely to carry a weapon to school. From this school-based study it is not fully clear if students are bringing weapons to campus because they are fearful of being threatened or injured, or in order to perpetrate violence. The recent FBI (2002) and Secret Service Reports on "school shooters" also suggest a complex relationship between the prior victimization of the shooters and the perpetration of these homicidal acts.

Furlong, Bates, and Smith (2001) examined the correlation between an item asking how many times a student has brought a weapon to school and the School Risk Index. This index tallies the number of risk factors present for the student, such as missing school due to fear of violence, being threatened and injured with a weapon in school, and the use of cigarettes and drugs on school property. The authors combined three data waves that administered the YRBSS in the United States and examined the prevalence of weapon possession, its relation to grade level, ethnicity/race, and gender. The correlations between weapon possession and the various items included in the index were low (range .13 to .26), but the correlation with the combined School Risk Index was higher ($r = 0.36$), providing support for the hypothesis that bringing weapons to school is associated with being victimized in school.

Similarly, Paetsch and Bertrand (1999) reported that in their sample of Canadian youth, students who self-reported weapon possession were more likely to report higher levels of victimization, both in and out of school. Thus, of the students who reported having a weapon at school, 49% reported a moderate/high level of victimization at school, 22.1% reported a low level, and only 15.7% reported no victimization at all. The levels of victimization among the students who did not report involvement with weapons were much lower.

It is possible that students bring weapons to schools because they fear for their safety without being directly victimized. A study by May (1999) assessed the impact of fear of crime and victimization on gun possession by adolescents on school campuses. He found that there is a significant association between fear of criminal victimization and gun possession in school, even after controlling for the other explanations. In addition, students who carried weapons to school perceived their neighborhoods to be more dangerous and had increased fear of criminal victimization. However, more studies are needed that clearly delineate the contribution of school-based social dynamics on weapon use.

AN EMPIRICAL EXPLORATION OF WEAPON USE IN ISRAEL

The second section of this chapter provides an empirical examination of weapon use, surrounding concepts discussed in the first section of the chapter. We explore some of these questions using data but also provide a case example of two other cultures and school violence. This is the first such published data on Arab and Jewish children and weapon use in schools.

Israel presents an interesting arena with regard to weapons. Visitors to Israel are often astonished by the number of guns they see in the streets. There are many male and female uniformed soldiers on their way to and from their army base carrying their personal rifles. There are also many young Israeli men in their civilian clothes who live in the occupied territories (West Bank and Gaza Strip) and openly carry either a rifle or a handgun. School guards are most often armed with a handgun. This weapon is intended to protect from outside danger and never to be used against students. Thus, weapons are quite common in everyday life in Israel, are associated with safety and protection from terrorist attacks, and are not seen as a threat. Nevertheless, one needs a license to carry a handgun, and this license is given only to those who are deemed to live in, or travel through, dangerous areas. Weapon carrying among youth is totally unacceptable and is associated with criminal activities. Hence, despite the extensive presence of guns in Israel, guns in schools are seen as very rare and extremely dangerous.

Methodology

Sample

The study is part of a larger national ongoing study on school violence in Israeli schools (Benbenishty, 2002; Benbenishty et al., 2000). Our sample was designed to represent all Jewish and Arab students in grades 7–11 (ages 12–17) in the public school system supervised by the Israeli Ministry of Education. It should be noted that in Israel, Jews and Arabs attend separate schools, so it is rare that Arab students attend a Jewish school and vice versa. As a group, the Arab population is more disadvantaged than the Jewish population on every socioeconomic indicator. These circumstances may strongly affect school victimization, because neighborhood poverty and high crime rates may influence the schools and the social dynamics that influence victimization and its consequences (Lorion, 1998).

For the purposes of the study reported here, we used a probability sampling method that consisted of a two-stage stratified cluster sample. The sample was stratified on both age-related school type (middle and high schools) and ethnicity (Jewish and Arab). First, we randomly selected schools from the complete list of all schools that belong to that stratum and second, in each of these schools, we selected one class randomly from each of the grade levels. Participants were students who attended that class during the time of the survey. Stratification was nonproportional and all analyses used sampling weights computed to ensure that our sample represented the entire school population in Israel (Nirel & Saltzman, 1999). Our sampling procedure yielded a total of 10,400 students.

Procedure and Instruments

The study was conducted with the cooperation and funding of the Israeli Ministry of Education and its procedures were approved by their

Chief Scientist and are in accordance with the ethical guidelines for human subjects at the Hebrew University. All the students participated in the study on a voluntary basis and with informed consent. Participants could withdraw from the study for any reason at any time. Principals of the schools in the sample received a formal request to participate in the study from the Chief Scientist and the Director General of the Ministry of Education. The vast majority of the schools cooperated; there was an excellent response rate of 92%. A member of the survey team gave the questionnaire to students in their classes with clear instructions and support for clarifying any misunderstandings on survey items.

The questionnaire used in this study is an adapted version of the California School Climate Survey (Furlong, 1999; Rosenblatt & Furlong, 1997) that was modified to address issues of interest to the researchers and to the Israeli context. The research instrument contained more than 100 questions pertaining to six areas:

1. *Personal victimization by peers* (over a range of low level, such as pushing and shoving, to severe, such as extortion, serious beating, and gun threats). We also included a scale describing various aspects of sexual harassment in secondary schools (Zeira, Astor, & Benbenishty, 2002).

2. *Weapons in school* (carrying, seeing others, threats with weapons)

3. *Personal victimization by staff* (emotional, physical, sexual)

4. *Risky behaviors in school* (peers and staff)

5. *Feelings and assessments regarding school violence* (severity of the problem, fear of attending school, feeling safe at school)

6. *School climate* (teachers' support of their students, policies against violence, student participation).

The original items were translated from English to Hebrew and Arabic. Some items were adapted to the Jewish-Israeli and Arab-Israeli culture and jargon. To ensure translation accuracy, they were retranslated into English and then multiple translations and retranslations were made and compared. We piloted the translated questionnaires in a pretest on approximately 7,000 Jewish and Arab students. The instrument was also used in a first wave of data collection that took place in the fall of 1998.

Descriptive Results

Weapon-related Behaviors Associated with Gender, School Level, and Ethnic Group

We presented the students with a series of questions on weapon-related behaviors *during the previous month and on school grounds.* Table 5.1 shows that Israeli students are exposed to knives much more than they are to guns. Whereas 2.7% of the students said that they brought a gun to school and 3.5% said that another student threatened them with a gun, 5.7% reported bringing a knife to school and 6.3% had been threatened with a knife.

More than one fifth of the students (21.3%) reported being hurt by a rock, a chair, or another object used by another student to hurt them in school. A much smaller number (5.6%) reported being cut by a knife or another sharp object. This trend is similar to the one found in the United States. DuRant and his associates (1999) reported that whereas 3% of the U.S. students they surveyed reported carrying a gun to school, 14.1% reported carrying a knife. Almost half of the Israeli students saw another student with a knife in school. It should be noted that in the first wave of data collection in our study (conducted about 4 months earlier), we found similar findings.

Table 5.1 shows that in most weapon-related behaviors, males report three to four times more exposure to weapons than females. It is interesting to note that not only are fewer females bringing weapons to school and being threatened with a weapon, but fewer females report seeing weapons in school. It seems that these weapons are being shown and known mainly to males involved in violence. These gender effects were found in many other studies on weapons in school. For instance, in a

Table 5.1.   Weapon-Related Behaviors by Gender, Ethnic Group, and School Level

		Total	Gender		Ethnic Group		School Type	
			Male	Female	Jewish	Arab	Junior	High
Brought ...	A gun	2.7	4.1	1.3	2.2	4.5	2.7	2.6
	A knife	5.7	9.1	2.3	4.8	9.2	5.5	5.9
Threatened by...	A gun	3.5	5.6	1.3	3.0	5.4	3.2	3.8
	A knife	6.3	10.3	2.5	4.2	14.5	7.2	4.9
Hurt by ...	A knife or sharp object	5.6	9.4	1.9	5.2	7.4	6.0	4.9
	A rock, chair, other object	21.3	30.3	12.6	21.8	19.6	24.1	16.3
Saw on school grounds ...	A student with a real handgun	4.4	7.6	1.2	4.0	6.1	4.0	4.8
	A student with a knife	46.4	59.2	34.2	47.4	42.7	46.2	46.8

study by DuRant and colleagues (1999), a higher percentage of adolescent boys (20.2%) reported having carried a knife or club to school than adolescent girls (7.7%).

The only behavior reported much more by junior high students than by high school students involved being hurt by an object (not necessarily a weapon), 24.1%, compared with 16.3% among high school students. In the United States, DuRant and associates (1999) reported that there was no significant relationship between school grade and carrying a gun to school. Still, eighth-grade students were more likely to carry a knife or club to school than were sixth- and seventh-grade students.

Arab students are more likely than Jewish students to report that they were involved with guns and knives. Where 4.8% of the Jewish students said they brought a knife to school, 9.2% of the Arab students made such a report. Similarly, 2.2% of the Jewish students reported that they brought a gun to school compared with 4.5% of the Arab students. Interestingly, the percentages of Jewish and Arab students who reported seeing another student in school carrying a knife were almost identical.

The finding that Arab students have more access to guns was very surprising to us considering the political climate in Israel. Gun control and regulation is very strong for the Jewish population. Because of concerns surrounding terrorism we assumed that the access to guns would be even more difficult for the Arab students. However, there is an illegal underground that makes access to guns easier than we originally hypothesized. Much of the gun use in Arab schools is related to family clan issues. Guns are used to threaten and scare in feuds among clans. This is more common especially in the Bedouin and Druze populations (who serve in the military and have access to guns), but also with other Arab groups.

Probability of Bringing a Gun or Knife to School: Comparing Victims and Nonvictims

Following these findings in the literature that indicate a possible connection between victimization and weapons in school, we asked whether Israeli students who are frequently victimized are more prone to bringing weapons to school.

Table 5.2 presents the probability that a student victimized by a specific form of violent act would bring a weapon compared with a student who has not been victimized. This table shows that students who bring weapons to school tend to be those students who are victimized much more than others. For instance, among students who were threatened with a gun there were 30.1% who brought a gun to school, compared with only 1.7% of students who were not threatened with a gun. Similarly, among students who saw another student with a gun in school, 28.5% brought a

Table 5.2.   Probability of Bringing Knives and Guns to School among Students Victimized and Not Victimized by Violent Acts

Student Victimization	Probability of Bringing a Gun to School		Probability of Bringing a Knife to School	
	Not Victimized %	Victimized %	Not Victimized %	Victimized %
A student threatened you with a gun and you saw the gun	1.7	30.1	4.8	30.6
You saw a student in school with a gun	1.5	28.5	4.4	34.2
A student seized and shoved you on purpose	1.6	20.8	4.3	29.3
A student cut you with a knife or a sharp instrument on purpose	1.6	20.8	4.3	29.3
A student gave you a serious beating	1.7	16.0	4.3	23.7
A student threatened you with a knife, and you saw the knife	1.8	15.5	4.5	23.2
You were blackmailed under threats by another student	1.7	15.4	4.4	21.6
Gang members at school threatened, harassed, and pressured you	1.6	14.6	4.3	21.1
You were involved in a fight, got hurt, and required medical attention	1.7	12.3	3.7	23.8
Students threatened you on your way to or from school	1.6	10.6	4.1	17.6
Another student took your things away from you by force	1.7	8.1	4.4	12.7
A group of students boycotted you—did not want to play/talk with you	1.9	7.8	4.4	13.7
A student used a rock or another instrument in order to hurt you	1.4	7.3	3.7	12.9
You were involved in a fist fight	1.5	5.9	2.8	13.9
A student tried to intimidate you by the way he was looking at you	1.8	5.7	3.9	11.8
You were kicked or punched by a student that wanted to hurt you	1.8	5.4	3.8	11.4
A student threatened to harm or hit you	2.0	4.2	3.4	10.5
You saw a student in school with a knife (or an "exacto knife")	1.4	4.0	1.7	10.1
A student mocked, insulted, or humiliated you	2.7	2.7	4.7	6.4
A student cursed you	3.0	2.6	4.1	6.2

gun, whereas only 1.5% of students who did not see another student with a gun carried one.

The patterns with regards to bringing a knife to school are similar. For instance, among students who reported receiving a serious beating, 23.7% brought a knife to school, whereas only 4.3% of those who were not victimized in such a way carried a knife. Among students who saw another student in school with a knife, 10.1% reported bringing a knife to school, but among those who did not see another student with a knife only 1.7% reported bringing a knife to school.

Table 5.2 shows that physical victimization and threats of physical harm were associated with bringing a weapon to school, whereas verbal victimization in the form of curses and humiliations were not related to bringing weapons to school. It is important to note, however, that social isolation/exclusion in school was associated with bringing a weapon to school. Thus, among students who reported being socially isolated and excluded, approximately 7.8% brought a gun and 13.7% brought a knife to school. The rates among students who did not report being socially excluded were much lower; only 1.9% reported bringing a gun and 4.4% reported bringing a knife. Verbal threats that involve a weapon appear to have a similar impact as physical victimization on weapon carrying. The data from Israel appear to be consistent with media reports from different countries that experiences with physical victimization, weapon threats, and social exclusion appear to be highly related to bringing a gun or a knife to school.

This implies that verbal behaviors need to be seen in two different ways. First, verbal threats that involve a weapon really behave similarly to physical victimization. Second, even though social exclusion is different than both verbal threats involving a weapon and physical victimization, it still is related to bringing a lethal weapon to school. In addition, verbal name-calling and non-weapon-related threats are not related to bringing a gun or knife to school. This is important because name-calling by itself is not connected to bringing a weapon, suggesting that there needs to be greater distinctions between specific types of verbal and emotional forms of victimization.

Multiple Forms of Victimization and Bringing a Weapon to School

In order to get an overall picture of the relationships between victimization and weapon-related behaviors in school, we created a Physical Victimization Index where the number of different types of student physical victimization experienced in the previous month was tallied.

Figure 5.1 shows that the prevalence of bringing a weapon to school is highly associated with physical victimization. Whereas the prevalence of bringing a gun to school among students who do not report any type of physical victimization is 1.5%, it goes up to 2.7% for students reporting three types of victimization, to 10.3% among students who report five types of victimization, and to 28.4% among students who report being victims of six types of violent events. Possession of guns and knives on campus follows the same pattern, suggesting that the social factors influencing them are similar. However, we see a slightly higher possession rate for knives than guns. We suspect that access may be an explanation for this (note, however, that the differences between guns and knives are relatively minor considering how many students have access to knives). In addition, students tend to experience multiple victimization incidences prior to bringing weapons to school.

Figure 5.1 suggests that the relationship between physical victimization and bringing weapons to school is not a linear one. It seems that there is a qualitative difference between students who report up to three out of the six types of victimization we addressed, and students who experience almost all of the different victimization types. This finding calls for focusing the efforts to prevent weapons in school on the small group of students who are extreme in their levels of victimization. Targeting these students may raise issues of labeling and stigmatizing. Nevertheless, we think that spreading the efforts thin among the whole student population may not be as effective as identifying the students who are most extreme in their victimization levels and addressing their specific needs.

Fear and Bringing a Weapon to School

We examined whether reports on bringing a weapon to school were related to students' reports that they feared going to school in the last month. We found that missing school due to the fear of being victimized was highly related to bringing a weapon to school—specifically, 4.4% of the students who did not miss school in the last month due to fear reported bringing a knife to school, whereas about 20% of the students who missed school once or twice reported that they brought a gun to school. Among the small number of students who reported missing school due to fear more than twice in the last month, almost 40% report that they brought a knife to school! A similar pattern is evident with regard to bringing a gun to school—1.7% of those who did not miss school reported that they brought a gun to school, while 34.4% of the students who missed school more than twice reported bringing a gun to school.

These findings are similar to those reported by Simon and colleagues (1999) who showed that among students who missed school due to fear, the probability of bringing a weapon to school was six times higher than among those who did not report missing school due to fear. Interestingly, Wilcox and Clayton (2001) reported that despite strong relationships between weapon carrying on school grounds and previous

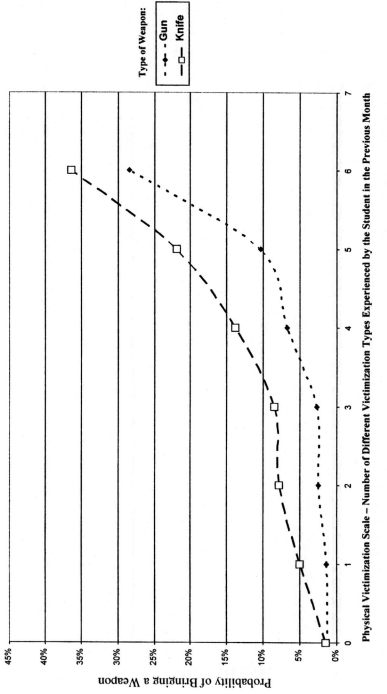

Figure 5.1.   The probabilty of bringing a weapon to school as a function of physical victimization.

victimization, little evidence was found for the predictive power of school-associated fear.

Clearly, our findings indicate that missing school due to fear is a strong predictor for bringing a weapon to school. Simon and his associates (1999) interpret this finding as a possible indication that this behavior is fulfilling the perceived need for personal safety. They argue, therefore, that if students feel unsafe in school without a weapon, the threat of punishment might be ineffective in deterring weapon carrying in school. The implication is that personal safety should be increased before we can expect students to refrain from bringing weapons to school.

The relationship between being a victim and the act of bringing or using a weapon may not be explained only from an "intent" perspective. For instance, it is not entirely clear if students who bring a weapon are only "afraid" and a weapon is their means of protection, or if there are also elements of retribution/revenge involved. For example, students who bring weapons because they are socially excluded may do so in retribution rather than self-defense. A similar point was made by Page and Hammermeister (1997) who indicate that although a common reason that youth gave for carrying weapons is that they were afraid someone would "jump" them, there are many indications that weapon carrying is related more to perpetration and criminal activity than to victimization and fear. These kinds of issues need to be explored further to better understand the motivations (fear, revenge, retribution, self-defense, and normative acceptance) that underlie weapons carrying and use on school grounds.

CONCLUSIONS AND SUMMARY

Research on weapon carrying and use in schools has been primarily focused on exploring issues of juvenile delinquency, family and community violence, and access to firearms, with limited research on the role of prior victimization. In addition, there has been an almost exclusive focus on firearm carrying and violence in the United States. In this chapter, we have attempted to move beyond a focus on guns to an exploration of different kinds of weapons and different kinds of victimization both in the United States and cross-culturally.

Our study shows that there are many ways weapons on school grounds can victimize students including seeing a weapon, being injured by a weapon, and being threatened by a weapon. Each type of victimization can produce different outcomes in the behavior of students. For example, a large proportion of students share common experiences with specific forms of weapon victimization (e.g., about one fifth of students claimed to have been injured by an object at school). Also, there are clear associations between being victimized at school and bringing weapons. More specifically, students who are chronically victimized are more likely to bring both guns and knives to school. In addition, the patterns associated with victimization and weapon use for knife and gun use are almost identical. Experiencing physical victimization, threats, and social exclusion are related to bringing a weapon to school, whereas verbal-social victimization is not related to weapon use.

Some patterns of victimization and weapon use are clearly associated with gender and culture. Gender patterns in Israel are similar to those in the United States in that males report three to four times the level of victimization and weapon use than females. In addition, Israeli students are more likely to be exposed to knives than to guns. Arab students are more likely than Jewish students to report being involved with either guns or knives.

Lastly, fear plays a significant role in victimization and weapon carrying and use. We have found that victimization is a major predictor of students bringing weapons to school. Indeed, a sizable proportion of students who do not attend school due to fear more than twice in the past month were likely to bring either a knife or a gun to school. We believe that most of these patterns exist in other countries as well. We encourage researchers to expand their study of weapon use to include the types of victimization we explored in our study.

The pool of students who bring weapons onto school grounds is much greater than those who actually use the weapons. Nevertheless, understanding the motivations for bringing weapons could further our understanding of lethal violence on school grounds and reduce the overall risk of being injured by a weapon. Our data suggest that being victimized is related to bringing a weapon to school grounds. Hence, we suggest that strategies to reduce weapons on school grounds should also incorporate students' experiences with victimization and social exclusion.

REFERENCES

American Psychological Association. (1993). *Violence and youth: Psychology's response.* Washington, DC: Author.

Astor, R. A, Benbenishty, R. A., & Marachi, R. (2003). Violence in schools. In P. A. Meares (Ed.), *Social work services in schools* (4th ed., pp. 149–182). Allyn & Bacon.

Astor, R. A., Benbenishty, R., Zeria, A., & Vinokur, A. (2002). School climate, observed risky behaviors, and victimization as predictors of high school students' fear and judgments of school violence as a problem. *Health Education & Behavior, 29*(6), 716–736.

Astor, R. A., Pitner, R. O., Benbenishty, R., & Meyer, H. A. (2002). Public concern and focus on school violence. In L. A. Rapp-Paglicci, A. R. Roberts, & J. S. Wodarski (Eds.), *Handbook of violence* (pp. 262-302). New York: Wiley.

Bailey, S. L., Flewelling, R. L., & Rosenbaum, D. P. (1997). Characteristics of students who bring weapons to school. *Journal of Adolescent Health, 20*(4), 261–270.

Benbenishty, R. (2002). *A national study of violence in Israel—Wave III: December 2002.* Jerusalem: Israeli Ministry of Education.

Benbenishty, R., Zeria, A., & Astor, R. A. (2000). *A national study of violence in Israel—Wave II: Fall 1999.* Jerusalem: Israeli Ministry of Education.

Bronner, E. (1999, August 7). Violence among Israelis sets off national wave of soul searching. *New York Times*, p. A1.

Burnett, C. (1998). School violence in an impoverished South African community. *Child Abuse & Neglect, 22*(8), 789–795.

Corvo, K., & Williams, K. (2000). Substance abuse, parenting, styles and aggression: An exploratory study of weapon carrying students. *Journal of Alcohol & Drug Education, 46*(1), 1–13.

Devine, J., & Lawson, H. A. (2003). The complexity of school violence: Commentary from the U.S. In P. K. Smith (Ed.), *Violence in schools* (pp. 332–350). London: Routledge Falmer.

Ding, C. S., Nelsen, E. A., & Lassonde, C. T. (2002). Correlates of gun involvement and aggressiveness among adolescents. *Youth & Society, 34*(2), 195–213.

DuRant, R. H., Krowchuk, D. P., Kreiter, S., Sinal, S. H., & Woods, C. R. (1999). Weapon carrying on school property among middle school students. *Archives of Pediatrics & Adolescent Medicine, 153*(1), 21–26.

Furlong, M. J. (1999). *California school climate and safety survey.* Retrieved from http://education.ucsb.edu/~schpsych/research.html

Furlong, M. J., Bates, M. P., & Smith, D. C. (2001). Predicting school weapon possession: A secondary analysis of the youth risk behavior surveillance survey. *Psychology in the Schools. Special Issue: Appraisal and Prediction of School Violence, 38*(2), 127–139.

Furlong, M. J., & Morrison, G. (2000). The *school* in school violence: Definitions and facts. *Journal of Emotional and Behavioral Disorders, 8*(2), 71–82.

Garbarino, J. (1992). *Children in danger: Coping with the consequences of community violence.* San Francisco: Jossey-Bass.

Kingery, P. M., Coggeshall, M. B., & Alford, A. A. (1999). Weapon carrying by youth. *Education and Urban Society, 31*(3), 309–333.

Kingery, P. M., Pruitt, B. E., Heuberger, G., & Brizzolara, J. A. (1995). Violence in rural schools: An emerging problem near the United States and Mexico border. *School Psychology International, 16*(4), 335–344.

Kodjo, C. M., Auinger, P., & Ryan S. A. (2003). Demographic, intrinsic, and extrinsic factors associated with weapon carrying at school. *Archives of Pediatrics and Adolescent Medicine, 157*(1), 96–103.

Kupersmidt, J. B., Shahinfar, A., & Voegler-Lee, M. E. (2002). Children's exposure to community violence. In A. M. La Greca, W. K. Silverman, E. M. Vernberg, & M. C. Roberts (Eds.), *Helping children cope with disasters and terrorism* (pp. 381–401). Washington, DC: American Psychological Association.

Lizotte, A. J., Howell, J. C., Tobin, K., & Howard, G. J. (2000). Factors influencing gun carrying among young urban males over the adolescent-youth adult life course. *Criminology, 38*(3), 811–834.

Lorion, R. (1998). Exposure to urban violence: Contamination of the school environment. In D. Elliot, B. Hamburg, & K. Williams (Eds.), *Violence in American schools: A new perspective* (pp. 293-311). New York: Cambridge University Press.

Lowry, R., Powell, K. E., Kann, L., Collins, J. L., & Kolbe, L. J. (1998). Weapon carrying, physical fighting, and fighting related injury among U.S. adolescents. *American Journal of Preventive Medicine, 14*(2), 122–129.

May, D. C. (1999). Scared kids, unattached kids, or peer pressure: Why to student carry firearms to school? *Youth & Society, 31*(1), 100–127.

McKeganey, N., & Norrie, J. (2000). Association between illegal drugs and weapon carrying in young people in Scotland: Schools' survey. *British Medical Journal, 320*(7240), 982–984.

Mercy, J. A., & Rosenberg, M. L. (1998). Preventing firearm violence in and around schools. In D. S. Elliott & B. A. Hamburg (Eds.), *Violence in American schools: A new perspective* (pp. 159–187). New York: Cambridge University Press.

Nirel, R., & Saltzman, P. (1999). *The structure of the sample and sampling weights in the "Israel National Study of School Violence."* Israel: Laboratory of Statistics, Hebrew University.

Orpinas, P., Murray, N., & Kelder, S. (1999). Parental influences on students' aggressive behaviors and weapon carrying. *Health Education & Behavior, 26*(6), 774–787.

O'Tool, M. E. (2002). *The school shooter: A threat assessment perspective.* Washington, DC: Author.

Paetsch, J. J., & Bertrand, L. D. (1999). Victimization and delinquency among Canadian youth. *Adolescence, 34*(134), 351–367.

Page, R. M., & Hammermeister, J. (1997). Weapon-carrying and youth violence. *Adolescence, 32*(127), 505–513.

Rapp-Paglicci, L. A., Roberts, A. R., & Wodarski, J. S. (Eds.). (2002). *Handbook of violence.* New York: Wiley.

Rosenblatt, J. A., & Furlong, M. J. (1997). Assessing the reliability and validity of student self-reports of campus violence. *Journal of Youth Adolescence, 26*(2), 187–202.

Ruddell, R., & Mays, G. L. (2003). Examining the arsenal of juvenile gunslingers: Trends and policy implications. *Crime & Delinquency, 49*(2), 231–252.

Schnebly, S. M. (2002). An examination of the impact of victim, offender, and situational attributes on the deterrent effect of defensive gun use: A research note. *Justice Quarterly, 19*(2), 377–398.

Simon, T. R., Crosby, A. E., & Dahlberg, L. L. (1999). Students who carry weapons to high school. *Journal of Adolescent Health, 24*(5), 340–348.

Smith, P., Morita, Y., Junger-Tas, J., Olweus, D, Catalano, R., & Slee, P. (1999). *The nature of school bullying: A cross-national perspective.* New York: Routledge.

Stolzenberg, L., & D'Alessio, S. J. (2000). Gun availability and violent crime: new evidence from the national incident-based reporting system. *Social Forces, 78*(4), 1461–1482.

U.S. Department of Justice, Bureau of Justice Statistics. (2002). *Indicators of school crime and safety.* Washington, DC: Author.

U.S. Federal Bureau of Investigation (FBI), National Threat Assessment Center. (2002). *U.S. safe schools initiative: An interim report on the prevention of targeted violence in schools.* Washington, DC: Secret Service Reports.

Valois, R. F., MacDonald, J. M., Bretous, L., Fischer, M. A., & Drane, J. W. (2002). Risk factors and behaviors associated with adolescent violence and aggression. *American Journal of Health Behavior, 26*(6), 454–464.

Vossekuil, B., Reddy, M., Fein, R., Borum, R., & Modzeleski, W. (2000). *U.S.S.S. safe school initiative: An interim report on the prevention of targeted violence in schools.* Washington, DC: U.S. Secret Service, National Threat Assessment Center.

Vossekuil, B., Fein, R. A., Reddy, M., Borum, R., & Modezelski, W. (2002). *The final report and findings of the Safe School Initiative: Implications for the prevention of school attacks in the United States.* Washington, DC: U.S. Secret Service and U.S. Department of Education.

Wells, W. (2002). The nature and circumstances of defensive gun use: A content analysis of interpersonal conflict situations involving criminal offenders. *Justice Quarterly, 19*(1), 127–157.

Wilcox, P., & Clayton, R. R. (2001). A multilevel analysis of school-based weapon possession. *Justice Quarterly, 18*(3), 509–541.

Yexley, M., Borowsky, I., & Ireland, M. (2002). Correlation between differential experiences of intrafamilial physical violence and violence adolescent behavior. *Journal of Interpersonal Violence, 17*(2), 707–720.

Zeira, A., Astor, R., & Benbenishty, R. (2002). Sexual harassment in Jewish and Arab public schools in Israel. *Child Abuse & Neglect, 26*(2), 149–166.

CHAPTER 6

LOOKING AT ADOLESCENTS THROUGH INTERNATIONAL ASSESSMENTS

Gerald W. Bracey

Although the developers of international assessments of student achievement did not emphasize them as comparative examinations of adolescence, since 1967, a variety of such studies have been carried out, often including students in their teens. They offer information on yet another facet of the adolescent experience.

The early studies, it must be said, were not particularly sound in terms of methodology and will not be considered here. The methodology has improved significantly and all international studies now draw probability samples for the various countries. Getting the schools drawn by the samplers to participate is still a problem in some places (Statistics Canada in Ottawa and Westat in the United States are the two most common organizations utilized). The International Association for the Evaluation of Educational Achievement (IEA) studies note this in the results by putting parentheses around the countries' names or by presenting their results separately. The media and politicians, though, have cared not at all about these niceties, nor, actually, have those who have written about the studies. An exception is the methodological critique I offered of the Third Inter-

Educating Adolescents: Challenges and Strategies, 131–148

national Mathematics and Science Study's Final Year of Secondary School (TIMSS). The study is now often referred to as TIMSS-95 to differentiate it from a repeat called TIMMS-R in this country and TIMSS-99 elsewhere (Bracey, 2000).

It also remains a question whether one can administer a test in 41 nations (the number of nations that participated in TIMSS-95 at the eighth-grade level) and have the languages of the tests be fair to all students.

This chapter describes the major outcomes of *How in the World Do Students Read?* (Elley, 1992), the Third International Mathematics and Science Study (TIMSS-95) (Beaton, Martin, Mullis, Gonzalez, & Kelly, 1996; Beaton, Mullis, et al., 1996; Martin et al., 1997; Mullis et al., 1997, 1998), the Third International Mathematics and Science Study—Repeat (TIMSS-99) (Martin et al., 1999; Mullis, Martin, Gonzalez, Gregory, et al., 1999; Mullis, Martin, Gonzalez, O'Connor, et al., 1999), the Program of International Student Assessment (PISA) (Organization for Economic Cooperation and Development [OECD], 2001), and the Progress in Reading Literacy Study (TIMSS International Study Center, 2003).

Other works related to international studies include *The Learning Gap* (Stevenson & Stigler, 1992), *The Teaching Gap* (Stigler & Hiebert, 1999), and the *TIMSS 1999 Video Study* (Hiebert et al., 1999). *The Learning Gap* is not treated here because the data are dated, are not representative of the nations involved, and, in some places, misinterpreted by the authors. *The Teaching Gap* and the *TIMSS 1999 Video Study* are not treated here because the focus of this volume is on adolescence and these studies both focus on how teachers teach mathematics in different countries.

The dates given in all instances are the dates of the studies with publications coming 1–2 years later. Because different results at different ages have led to conjectures and conclusions about nations' educational systems, results for elementary students will be included where such data exist.

The major source of data from international studies has been the IEA, although in the TIMSS-95 studies and in Progress in International Reading Literacy Study (PIRLS), the bulk of the work has been accomplished through Boston College with a strong assist in TIMSS-95 from Michigan State University. Recently, the Organization for Economic Cooperation and Development (1995) in Paris has developed what will be an ongoing assessment program, PISA.

Perhaps the best known of the studies is the Third International Mathematics and Science Study. This study tested fourth graders in 26 nations, eighth graders in 41 nations, and students in their final year of secondary school in 16 to 21 nations, depending on the test. Note that TIMSS-95 referred to this last group as in their "final year of secondary school." This is because final year does not always equate to the 12th grade in the United States.

TIMSS-95 gave rise to a popular statement about the decay of American education over the grades, uttered by President Bill Clinton and numerous educators and put most crassly by former Secretary of Education, William J. Bennett, in a speech to the Heritage Foundation on its 25th anniversary: "In America today, the longer you stay in school, the dumber you get relative to your peers in other industrialized nations" (Bennett, 2001).

The results that gave rise to this comment show American students above average in mathematics at the fourth grade and third in the world in science. At the eighth-grade level, American students were average in both subjects. American high school seniors apparently finished at or near the bottom in the final year component of TIMSS-95. Thus, the older American students are, the worse they do relative to other nations.

Elsewhere I have presented a detailed critique of the final year study and will only summarize those findings here. I believe that the dropoff from grade 4 to grade 8 is real. It is cause for concern, although hardly the stuff of crisis.

Two reasons can be brought forward to explain the decline. First consider the many recent cartoons that turn on students having difficulty bearing the weight of their backpacks. These cartoons cover a serious problem: a large increase in scoliosis and other spinal problems. The weight problem arises because American textbooks are two or three times as thick as those found in most nations. In most countries, the state controls the production of textbooks, but in the United States, they are produced by large, for-profit publishing houses. These publishers, attempting to reach the widest possible market, take a kitchen-sink approach to inclusion.

Teachers for their part try to cover it all. Non-test data from TIMSS-95 show American teachers spending much less time on many more topics during the course of a year than do their counterparts abroad. The coverage is often too brief and students don't master the topic. This leads to review the next year. Teachers abroad spend little time on review. Results from TIMSS-99-Video show American teachers spending much more time on review while teachers in the other six countries in that study are introducing new material.

This leads to the second reason the decline from Grade 4 to Grade 8 is likely real. Historically, American educators have viewed the middle school years as a period of review and consolidation. Even now, after a great deal of attention to acceleration mathematics, only about 15% of American 8th graders take algebra. Indeed, a number of middle school teachers and counselors feel that the middle school years should not emphasize intellectual aspects of school, but rather attend to these youngsters' burgeoning sexuality and their search for a clearly defined personality. If *Washington Post* reporter Linda Perlstein's (2003b) characterization of the middle school years is accurate, it is indeed a time of emotional meltdown and intellectual turpitude. In an interview on National Public Radio's "All Things Considered," Perlstein (2003a) said, "Parents can take comfort knowing that middle school ends." Other developed countries show no such reticence at introducing new topics and generally considering the middle school years to be part of high school rather than the consolidation of the elementary school years.

That American seniors finished at or near the bottom in the final year study is so much a part of the popular culture it will likely never be dislodged by mere data. It fits a syndrome that I have labeled "The Neurotic Need to Believe the Worst." The perception occurred because, while the TIMSS Final Year Report made it clear that different nations had very different systems, the U.S. Department of Education's press conference presented the study as apples-to-apples, America's seniors against other nations' seniors in the case of the mathematics/science literacy score and America's most advanced seniors against other nations' most advanced seniors in the cases of Advanced Mathematics and Physics, the two subjects tested in the final year study.

Still, there are a number of questions about the accuracy of this statement, and some data that can be raised to challenge the actual placement of American scores. TIMSS-95 administered a mathematics/science literacy test to what should have been a probability sample in 21 countries, then allowed the various nations to choose the students to whom it would be appropriate to give one or both of the other two tests, physics and advanced mathematics (16 countries participated in each subject).

First, there is an unanswered question: Do other nations experience a "senior slump"? Certainly one is not likely to see it among those seniors in Germany, France, and England who are preparing for their Abitur, Baccalaureat, or A-levels, respectively. In Japan, the senior year culminates in "exam hell" of life-determining tests, and the South Koreans make the Japanese look relaxed. Many Korean mothers pray all night at temple on exam eve. Many people go to work earlier exam day to lower the chances that some student might be made late by a traffic jam. Landings at airports are curtailed and, at least through 2000, all 90 American military bases in South Korea halt training (the recent rise in tensions on the Korean peninsula might have brought this courtesy to an end).

Korean students endure these tests because they wish to gain entry at one of three elite institutions of higher education that have a collective admissions rate of 1.7%. Of course, in both Japan and Korea, those who do enter the hallowed halls go into intellectual hibernation.

In any case, American students mostly have their future, at least their immediate future, planned out before their second semester and in some cases even at the start of the senior year. The senior slump in Virginia is sufficiently severe that Virginia Governor Mark Warner has proposed permitting seniors to earn up to a full semester's worth of college credits. Yet, to get the TIMSS final year tests as close to the end of the final year as possible, they were administered in this nation in May.

Beyond these cultural considerations, there was at least one cultural condition and some methodological factors that acted to the detriment of American students. For instance, only a few of the countries met TIMSS-95 own criteria for producing valid data. Countries violated participation rates, used unapproved sampling methods, or both. For the mathematics/science literacy test, only eight of 21 countries met all criteria. For advanced mathematics, 10 of 16 met all criteria and for physics 11 of 16. No doubt being able to choose what groups to test in the latter two instances facilitated the increased proportion meeting all criteria.

Those of us who have lived abroad are never likely to trust international comparisons very far because of the numerous, but impossible to quantify cultural variables that might play a role in achievement. For instance, I have friends with grandchildren in French schools. They are appalled at the teachers' use of shame as a motivational technique. A teacher might take the worst paper on a topic, post it on a bulletin board, and make fun of it. What impact does this have? Does this ladling large dollops of shame result in the vaunted French adult display of repartee? Do French children spend a lot of classroom time thinking of clever responses that they could give if they dared?

One cultural variable that TIMSS-95 did manage to quantify was the worker/student status variable. In most countries, you are a student or a worker, not both. Most American seniors are both and it shows up in their TIMSS-95 scores. Table 6.1 provides the number of hours American students worked per week at paid jobs and the TIMSS-95 results. It also presents the same figures for Sweden, a more typical nation.

Although not wholly consistent, most research on the effect of jobs on school performance in this country finds curvilinear relations: students who work up to 20 hours a week do better in school than students who have longer work weeks or students who do not work. Once social class factors are removed, the usual explanations are in terms of time management and a sense of responsibility to others. After 20 hours, though, the job starts to consume time that should be given to sleeping, eating properly, and doing schoolwork.

One aspect of TIMSS-95 that was overlooked in media stories was the linking of TIMSS-95 eighth-grade results to 1996 NAEP eighth-grade mathematics and science results. The U.S. Department of Education con-

Table 6.1.   Hours Worked at a Paid Job and TIMSS Final Year Scores

	Number of hours worked per week			
	0 to 7	*7 to 14*	*21 to 35*	*35+*
	TIMSS Final Year Scores			
United States	39 (484)	7 (506)	27 (474)	28 (448)
Sweden	84 (563)	8 (541)	5 (511)	4 (463)
France	83 (512)	10 (488)	4 (474)	3 (463)

Notes: The curvilinear pattern is seen in TIMSS-95 results for U.S. students who work more than 20 hours a week showing declining performance, those students constituting a majority (55%) of all students. France and Sweden display more typical results. Numbers outside parentheses are the percent of students in each country who work the number of hours given in the various columns. Numbers in parentheses are scores on the TIMSS mathematics/science literacy test.
Source: Mullis et al. (1998, p. 120).

tracted with Educational Testing Service to put the results of both tests onto a single scale (National Center for Education Statistics, 1998). This permits the comparison of the 41 nations that took part in TIMSS-95 to the 40 states and District of Columbia that participated in the 1996 state-level NAEP mathematics and science assessments.

The main use of this data, other than for bragging or wailing rights among individual states, is to display the enormous variation in performance across states. Only 6 of the 41 countries scored higher than one group of states in mathematics, and only one scored higher in science. These states are Iowa, Nebraska, North Dakota, Montana, Wisconsin, Minnesota, and Maine. Alaska, Connecticut, Massachusetts, and Vermont were outscored by eight countries in mathematics and one in science. For the lowest states, though, only three countries—Colombia, Kuwait, and South Africa—scored lower, and for the District of Columbia, only South Africa. To provide an idea of how variable scores are, the 95th percentiles of the three lowest scoring countries are not as high as the 5th percentile of the highest scoring, Singapore.

As far as national results go, TIMSS-99 looked very much like TIMSS-95. This was something of a disappointment to mathematics reformers. Some had claimed that the NCTM Standards, first adopted in 1989, had not registered their full impact in upper grades when the first TIMSS-95 tests were administered. However, American eighth graders in 1999 scored only slightly better than eighth graders in 1995 and were below average among nations who participated in both assessments.

TIMSS-99 differed from TIMSS-95 in that some U.S. school districts and consortia of districts participated as well as some states. This again served to illustrate the variability of countries and the variability within this country. In mathematics, of the 65 nations, states, districts, and consortia, Naperville, Illinois, finished 6th, the First in the World Consortium (also in Illinois) 7th, and Montgomery County, Maryland, 10th. On the other hand, Chicago, Rochester, and Miami Dade finished 53rd, 57th, and 60th, respectively.

In science, Naperville outscored all other 64 entities, while the First in the World Consortium was 4th, the Michigan Invitational Group 5th, and Academy District 20th, Colorado (Colorado Springs) 6th. Rochester was 53rd, Chicago 55th, and Miami-Dade 61st.

State finishes are less representative of the range of states because none of the highest or lowest scoring states in TIMSS-95 participated. Michigan was the highest-finishing state, 24th of 65 in mathematics and 11th in science.

It is not clear why American students so consistently perform better on the international stage in science than in mathematics. If asked to guess I would conjecture that other nations—outside of Asia, at least—do not emphasize science as early as the United States does and that in no other nation does science permeate the popular culture the way it does here.

PISA:
PROGRAM FOR INTERNATIONAL STUDENT ASSESSMENT

Little attention was paid to PISA in this country, but Europe went all agog, especially Germany. American students finished average in reading, mathematics, and science, but the Germans finished low. This should have not come as any surprise in Deutschland because its scores in *How in the World Do Students Read?* and TIMSS-95 had not been especially good either.

PISA officials declared that they were not trying to determine how well students had mastered their school subjects, but how well they could apply them to new settings and real-life problems and how well they could reflect on what they read. Descriptions of the science materials sound quite a bit like the Science Reading tests in the early ACT battery.

PISA assessed 15-year-olds. Most of the problems are too complicated to be described here but here is one example. The student is presented with a map of Antarctica, which contains a legend for distance. The student's problem is to estimate the area of the continent. The student can enclose the continent in a rectangle and use the formula for finding the area of a rectangle or, more accurately given the shape of the land mass, draw a circle around the continent and use the formula for calculating the area of a circle. Thus, the student has to know something learned in school—area formulas—but also to recognize their applicability to the problem at hand.

Among the 32 countries, American 15-year-olds were 15th, 19th, and 14th in reading, mathematics, and science, respectively. German students finished 21st, 20th, and 20th, respectively. German scores were not all that much lower than American scores, 10 points in reading, 3 in mathematics, and 12 in science, each on a 600-point scale.

German media, though, looked at ranks, not scores. "Dummkopf!" exclaimed *The Economist*, "PISA Debacle" declared Munich's *Süddeutsche Zeitung*. The cover of *Der Spiegel* asked "Are German Students Stupid?" *Frankfurter Allgemeine Zeitung* demanded the country "Fix Our Schools." "Now you have it. Germany, the land of poets and philosophers, is struck down," mused Andreas Schleicher, PISA's director at OECD. All in all, German media devoted over 700 pages to reporting the disaster, hurling accusations and trying to figure out what went wrong. Americans, who by this time had had almost 20 years to get over "A Nation At Risk," no doubt experienced at least some shivers of *schadenfreude*.

In looking for an answer, Germans turned to their short school day, to weak early childhood education, but, most of all, to tracking. Germany is one of the few remaining developed countries to track students early on, beginning at age 10. Critics contended that tracking at such an early age invariably meant tracking by social class, and, in many urban areas, tracking by immigration status. Thus, children who had limited mastery of German were stuck in classes that did not meet their needs. One German teacher was cited as saying it was hard to teach children in German when they chattered in Turkish and Arabic.

As with all international comparisons, PISA scores were strongly correlated with wealth, but the relationship was strongest in Germany. Tracking was also held to be responsible for Germany scoring highest on the "Inequality Index," the ratio of the top 10% readers' average score to the bottom 10%. For Germany that ratio was 1.8. Once again indicating the variability of scores in this country, the United States had the third worst Inequality Index at 1.6 (Finland, Japan, and Canada had the smallest ratios).

Most embarrassing, it seemed, was the fact that Germany scored lower than the United States. This had been true in *How In the World Do Students Read?*, but German and American eighth graders had finished in a virtual tie in TIMSS-95, with German scoring slightly higher in mathematics, 509 versus 500, the U.S. edging it out in science, 534 versus 531 (Germany did not participate at other grade levels). After the reading study appeared, I was sent an engineering research journal wherein one article reported that in that study, "German standards were exceeded even in the United States." Even. It appears that the worst way to lose face in international comparisons is to finish lower than America. German officials managed to hand off blame in that instance to the families for not encouraging reading.

Der Spiegel observed that German educators had repeatedly characterized Japanese schools as suffering from *gakkyu hokain* (collapsing discipline), *ijime* (bullying), and *junken jigoku* (exam hell). If these qualities so dominate the Japanese education system, asked the magazine slyly, why did they do so well on PISA? Japanese students finished 7th in reading, 1st in mathematics, and 2nd in science.

Rather than explain why the Japanese did so well, the Germans, and most other Europeans, turned to Finland for answers and guidance. Finland outscored all other nations in reading, finished fourth in mathematics, and third in science. The mathematics and science finishes placed them first if only European nations were considered.

"For six weeks German delegations have been going weekly to Finland to visit Finnish schools and teachers," reported the Geneva daily, *Le Temps*. At the time of the article the data had been published only 6 weeks, so the northbound caravans must have started almost immediately. *Le Temps* also sent one of its reporters, Francois Modoux, up north to see what he could see.

Modoux found the Finns spending a lot of money on schools, with schools in poor areas receiving more funds than affluent schools. All schools aimed for small classes (under 20). Despite finding some Swedes and Lapps in Finnish schools, Modoux reported Finland to be an ethnically and linguistically homogeneous nation that, without using the phrase, has a true commitment to "no child left behind." It is also a prosperous nation, ranking first in global competitiveness in the World Economic Forum's rankings of 85 nations (the U.S., which had been first, fell to second due to the Bush tax cuts, the mounting international trade deficit, and the corruption scandals among corporations and Wall Street).

There is no tracking in the first 9 years. Thus unlike German students who have differentiated curricula, which appear to lead to different outcomes, Finnish students all receive the same curriculum. Students who are having difficulties get extra attention, including those referred to by the head of one school as the "impossible cases." Finns give many tests to their students, but schools that score low get more funding. Modoux was impressed with the Internet connectedness of the country and the strong emphasis on multilingualism. And one education official told Modoux— jokingly it would seem—it was all simply a strategy for survival; given Finland's frigid climate they have to make do for themselves because it is hard to recruit immigrants.

When it comes to immigrants, the U.S. fares well in educating them, at least according to PISA scores. The difference between the scores of stu-

**Table 6.2.   PISA Reading Scores by
Immigrant Status of Parents and Children**

	Third generation	Second generation	First generation	Difference between third and first generation
United States	511	478	466	45
Germany	507	478	419	88
France	512	471	434	78
Austria	515	453	422	93
Belgium	522	411	431	91
Denmark	504	409	433	71
Switzerland	514	460	402	112
Sweden	523	485	450	73

Anglophone nations in general appear to integrate immigrants more readily than nations speaking Latinate or Germanic languages:

	Third generation	Second generation	First generation	Difference between third and first generation
Australia	532	528	513	19
U.K.	511	510	456	55
New Zealand	538	507	507	31
Canada	538	539	511	27

Note: Third generation represents native students born to native parents; second generation includes native students born to immigrant parents; first-generation students were immigrant students born to immigrant parents.
Source: Organization for Economic Cooperation and Development (2001, p. 293).

dents who were born here and who had at least one native-born parent and students born abroad with two foreign-born parents were smaller in the United States than in other nations. These results are displayed in Table 6.2.

Of course, the table does not reflect only the outcomes of nations' attempts to educate immigrants. Immigration policies can affect the table. Canada, for example, has long had a dual policy. On the one hand, it is relatively open, especially to relatives of immigrants already in the country. On the other hand, it has actively recruited well-educated immigrants. In the First International Adult Literacy Survey, both the United States and Canada had a higher percentage of immigrants than of native-borns scoring at the lowest level, but Canada also had a higher percentage of immigrants than native-borns scoring at the highest level (OECD, 1995).

An analysis of PISA by the U.S. Department of Education reveals yet another source of variability. The Department reported PISA scores by ethnic group. It is possible to imagine a situation where the entire U.S.

**Table 6.3.   U.S. Ranks on PISA (Out of 32 Nations) if
U.S. Sample Consisted of Only One Ethnic Group**

Ethnicity	Reading	Mathematics	Science
White students	2nd	7th	4th
Black students	29th	30th	30th
Hispanic Students	29th	30th	30th

Note: Asian and Native American groups too small for separate reporting.
Source: National Center for Education Statistics (www.nces.ed.gov/surveys/pisa)

sample consisted of only one ethnic group. If one then ranks the scores
for this group, the results would appear as in Table 6.3.

PIRLS: PROGRESS IN LITERACY STUDY

PIRLS was completed in 2002 and released in April 2003 to an almost
silent nation. In contrast to TIMSS and PISA, which had all received coverage from virtually all dailies, PIRLS attracted bylined stories from only
three major newspapers: the *Boston Globe,* the *Boston Herald,* and the
Washington Times. The appearance of PIRLS in the Boston papers
occurred, no doubt, because PIRLS was released through Boston College.
The *Washington Times* was founded to provide a conservative alternative to
the "liberal" *Washington Post* and in that role has been a constant critic of
the achievement of U.S. public schools. While the *Times* story provided
the basic facts of the case, commentary from persons such as Reid Lyon
served to place a negative spin on the results (Archibald, 2003). Lyon
lamented the results generally and claimed that they (somehow) reflected
that fact that "30 percent to 40 percent of U.S. 4th-graders are not proficient readers."

The Associated Press put out a short wire story that was picked up by
only 14, mostly small-market papers (that I could find, anyway). Some
papers abbreviated AP's story. The *Washington Post* was one of the few
large-market media that carried the AP story—1/12 of the back page of
the A section. The other 11/12ths were ads for a department store. The
*New York Times, Los Angeles Times, Atlanta Constitution, Houston Chronicle,
Chicago Sun, Chicago Tribune*, and most other majors carried not one
word.

The *Boston Globe*'s story ran under the headline, "U.S. Fares Well in
World Reading Test," but the text took away even as it gave. It first felt it
necessary to remind people that American kids can't do math, then said,
"They are faring better, but still not outstanding, at reading."

The cynic in me says this is another instance of "if it bleeds it leads" journalism. The results from PIRLS were good news. Among the 35 nations taking part, the United States finished 9th overall and only three nations, Sweden, England, and The Netherlands, had significantly higher scores (Finland did not participate). American students scored 542, and the three top countries landed at 561, 554, and 553, respectively. The average among the 35 countries was 500. Still not outstanding?

Most of the papers that carried the AP story also ran its headline "Reading Study Shows Mixed Results for United States." What made the results "mixed," though, were the scores of various ethnicities. White students scored 565 (higher than top-ranked Sweden), but Hispanics reached only 517 and blacks 502, still above the 500 international average. Asian students scored 551, just behind England and the Netherlands.

In recent years, international studies have taken to reporting "benchmark" scores, usually upper and lower percentiles and American students fared well there. Nineteen percent of them scored above the international 90th percentile, 41% scored above the 75th percentile, 68% above the 50th percentile, and 89% above the 25th percentile.

The most dramatic results, though, were those produced by the U.S. Department of Education showing the relationship between the PIRLS scores and poverty (Table 6.4). As usual, poverty was defined in terms of eligibility for free or reduced-price meals.

Schools with fewer than 25% of the students eligible for free meals scored above the highest country, Sweden. If students in schools with 25–50% poverty constituted a nation, it would rank fourth. Only students in schools where more than 75% of the students live in poverty do the scores fall below the international average of 500.

I wish to make a small digression here to emphasis the role of poverty in the development of children in the United States. Such a note is appropriate because in the last international study of poverty in developed

Table 6.4.   Scores on the PIRLS by Percent of Students in School Eligible for Free Meals

Percentage of students in school eligible for free lunch	Average score on the PIRLS for the school
<10%	589
10 to 24.9%	567
25 to 49.9%	551
50 to 74.9%	519
>75%	485

Source: National Center for Education Statistics (2001).

nations, the U.S. had by far the highest proportion of children in that condition, 22%. The next highest nation was Australia at 14% and no other country topped 10%. The percent has now fallen to just below 20%.

It is common to hear in politically conservative quarters the allegation that "poverty is no excuse." This is true. Poverty is not an excuse. It is a condition, like gravity, and, like gravity, it affects everything.

Two studies have appeared downplaying the role of poverty. One, *No Excuses*, from The Heritage Foundation, is, frankly, not worth treating. Persons wishing to see an analysis can find one that I wrote with Bruce Biddle of the University of Missouri at *www.asu.edu/educ/epsl/EPRU/ peer_reviews/cerai-00-19.htm* (Biddle & Bracey, 2000). The other, *Dispelling the Myth*, was conducted by the Education Trust and is at their site, *www.edtrust.org*. The "myth" in question is that poor children cannot learn, a myth I do not recall ever hearing anyone voice.

The Education Trust claimed to have found thousands of schools it designated "high-flying schools." Such schools had high poverty rates, high minority enrollment, or both, yet scored in the top third of the state on whatever a particular state used as its state test.

Closer examination, though, revealed that the criteria for "high-flying" were rather low themselves. To be designated a high-flyer, a school had only to have one grade score in the top third on only one subject in only one year. It was also pointed out that in many cases, it was the middle-class students in the school that brought the school its high-flying label. Poor students scored low (Krashen, 2002). Krashen also observed that some of the schools designated as high-poverty by the Education Trust were not high-poverty in the data they had reported to the state.

To get a better fix on the Education Trust study, I used the interactive database at the organization's website. Investigators can vary several variables and ascertain how many high-flying schools exist under these varying conditions.

I analyzed the results for California: Calfornia uses a nationally normed standardized test, the SAT9, and has done so for a few years, meaning scores would not be depressed from the novelty of a new test. I increased the achievement to the top quarter of the state, but used the Education Trust's criteria of only one subject in one grade in one year. I varied the poverty level rate only, not ethnicity. The results are as shown in Table 6.5.

At the time of the Education Trust study, there were 8,761 public schools in the Golden State. Table 6.4 shows that when the poverty rate rises above 50%, there is very little chance that the school will be designated high-flying, even with the lenient criteria for inclusion. Rather than "dispelling the myth," the Education Trust study actually provides powerful evidence for the impact of poverty on achievement.

Table 6.5.   Impact of Poverty Rates on School Achievement

Poverty rate greater than:	Number of high-flying schools
1%	1,232
5%	1,011
10%	775
25%	324
50%	74
75%	9
90%	3

Source: Education Trust, "Dispelling the Myth" Online Database.

These results should not come as a surprise. On reading tests, even those from back in the 1960s, American students have always done much better than on tests of mathematics and science. In *How in the World Do Students Read?*, IEA's predecessor to PIRLS, American 10-year-olds finished second in the world behind Finland, and American 14-year-olds finished in a tie for 8th place. The 14-year-olds' scores were sufficiently bunched that only Finland had a significantly higher score.

On *How in the World*, America's best readers—the 90th, 95th, and 99th percentile—outscored even the Finns, although the differences were likely too small to be significant (these data have not yet been forthcoming from PIRLS).

LIMITATIONS OF THE STUDIES

As noted at the beginning, the earlier international comparisons suffered various design problems and even the later ones, although attempting to obtain national probability samples, were not wholly successful in so doing.

There has been disappointingly little critical commentary on TIMSS or PISA (it is a bit early for such from PIRLS). In addition to my critique in *Educational Researcher,* an earlier article observed that for the TIMSS studies, no curriculum matches were conducted (Bracey, 1998). One would expect the sequencing of topics to differ among countries and one might even expect different countries to have different conceptual approaches that would affect what topics are taught and how. That, after all, is what the "math wars" have been about in this nation. Indeed, the curriculum study of mathematics for TIMSS was called *Many Visions, Many Aims* (Schmidt, McKnight, Valverde, Houang, & Wiley, 1996).

In other countries, curriculum experts reviewed items to see which ones represented those nations' curricula. Some items were flagged in all countries and when scores are calculated only for the items the countries judged appropriate, there is some variation in score.

The United States did no item–curriculum matching. Again, the let's-see-how-they-do mentality prevailed. In addition to possible curricu-lum–item mismatch, some items on the TIMSS science tests suffered tech-nical problems (Wang, 1998). Some, for instance, did not have only one right answer. For others, the true answer depended on information about the conditions of scientific observations and this information was not pro-vided. And some items, especially free-response items, did not take the students' cognitive development into account. For instance, the correct answer for one question was "The sun is farther away from earth than the moon." Students who said "The sun is higher up than the moon" received a zero, although many third and fourth graders use these words inter-changeably.

Such problems might be more serious in connection with PISA. Prais (2003), of the National Institute of Economic and Social Research in England, was intrigued by the PISA research. His interest was initially piqued by the fact that in both TIMSS-95 and TIMSS-99, the United Kingdom had scored some 40 points lower than Switzerland, France, Bel-gium, the Czech Republic, and Hungary. In PISA the United Kingdom had finished some 20 points *ahead*. This 60-point difference represents two-thirds of a standard deviation and thus is not an insignificant change.

Prais found several problems. First, he questioned the validity of attempting to ask "real-life" questions. He presented an example wherein students had to solve a speed and distance problem for a car on a race-track. The question assumed the students knew quite a bit about racetrack shapes. Prais commented, "Perhaps these are perfectly reasonable assumptions and reasonable questions in relation to Australian or Ger-man boys, but for girls in rural Greece or Portugal?" He also questioned the validity of the PISA enterprise in general of trying to find real-life questions:

> The questions asked in PISA were deliberately different from those in ear-lier surveys, and were ostensibly *not* intended to test mastery of the school curriculum; they can, perhaps, be said to be nearer to tests of common sense (or of IQ). No one has ever doubted the common sense of the British people nor of British youngsters: The issue has been whether or not they are as well served as they might be by their schooling system. (Prais, 2003, p. 144)

Prais also noted that by testing an age, some nations had to test various grades. While the United Kingdom has a strict calendar year approach to grouping, some other nations do not. When the scores for Belgium were published, it was noted that Belgian 15-year-olds in Grade 10 scored 564 while those in Grade 9 scored only 455, and those in Grade 8, 364. The eighth graders would have little impact, but almost one quarter of those tested in Belgium were in Grade 9.

The choice of the 15-year-olds is also problematic because of school-leaving in some nations. Some 47% of the 15-year-olds in Brazil and 48% of those in Mexico were no longer in school. In England, 15-year-olds are in their final year of obligatory schooling and preparing for a series of tests.

A national probability sample is essential to ensure the validity of the results and PISA wished to have at least 85% of the schools picked for the sample participate. They attained this in most countries, but the response rate for the United Kingdom was only 61%. Says Prais, "The missing schools on the whole were probably low-attaining schools; and there must be grave suspicions of upward bias in the average score of responding schools as a result of such a low response rate." As with NAEP in this country, PISA used an additional sample of "replacement schools" but these are likely higher performing; low-achieving schools do not readily participate.

Once the schools are chosen, students are as well. In England, only 81% of those chosen took the tests, and in some large cities on the continent, the rate dropped to 70%. "The *true* proportion of pupils participating, including all schools contributing to each country's published average score (even those with 25–50% pupil participation), has so far not been revealed. The shenanigans of the Official Mind at work here raise wider worries" (p. 151).

Finally, Prais attaches an "annex" to his article, "On the Computational Mysteries of PISA's Country Rankings." He expresses considerable astonishment over his findings when he looked at the results of 31 released items in terms of the proportion of students getting specific items correct. Although OECD had reported Britain ahead of Switzerland, Swiss students bested British students on 21 out of 31. He expresses dismay that the paper on how Rasch transformations were applied to get from raw scores to scaled scores "is not easy reading even for professional mathematicians, and makes no concessions to those who are fully adept research-psychometricians" (p. 161).

I present this exposition because of my own doubts about the accuracy of all of these internationals, my own dismay over the uncritical acceptance of the studies by so many professional researchers and policymakers alike, and the absence of critical examinations of the studies.

It seems to me that these comparisons mostly serve those who conduct them. Whole careers have been made from TIMSS. The field is a growth industry. American taxpayers coughed up over $50 million for TIMSS-95. Has it gotten a good return on that investment?

REFERENCES

Archibald, G. I. (2003, April 9). U.S. fourth-graders rank 9th overall in reading survey. *The Washington Times*, p. A1.

Beaton, A. E., Martin, M. O., Mullis, I. V. S., Gonzalez, E. J., & Kelly, D. L. (1996). *Science achievement in the middle school years*. Boston: Boston College, TIMSS International Study Center.

Beaton, A. E., Mullis, I. V. S., Martin, M. O., Gonzalez, E. J., Kelly, D. L., & Smith, T. A. (1996). *Mathematics achievement in the middle school years*. Boston: Boston College, TIMSS International Study Center.

Bennett, W. J. (2001). *The state and future of American education*. Invited address delivered to the Heritage Foundation on the 25th anniversary of its founding.

Bracey, G. W. (1998). Tinkering with TIMSS. *Phi Delta Kappan, 80*(1), 32–36.

Bracey, G. W. (2000). The TIMSS final year study and report: A critique. *Educational Researcher, 29*(4), 4–10.

Biddle, B., & Bracey, G. W. (2000). No excuses, lots of reasons [Review of the report *No excuses: Lessons from 21 high-performing, high-poverty schools*] (CERAI [00-19]). Milwaukee, WI: Center for Education Research, Analysis, and Innovation.

Elley, W. B. (1992). *How in the world do students read?* The Hague, Netherlands: International Association for the Evaluation of Educational Achievement.

Hiebert, J., Gallimore, G., Garnier, H., Bogard Giwin, K., Hollingsworth, H., Jacobs, J., et al. (1999). *TIMSS 1999 video study of eighth-grade mathematics teaching*. Washington, DC: National Center for Educational Statistics.

Krashen, S. (2002). Don't trust the education trust. *Substance, 27*(6), 3.

Martin, M. O., Mullis, I. V. S., Beaton, A. E., Gonzalez, E. J., Kelly, D. L., & Smith, T. A. (1997). *Science achievement in the elementary school years*. Boston: Boston College, TIMSS International Study Center.

Martin, M. O., Mullis, I. V. S., Gonzalez, E. J., Gregory, K. D., Smith, T. A., Chrostowski, S. J., et al. (1999). *TIMSS 1999 international science report*. Boston: Boston College, TIMSS International Study Center.

Martin, M. O., Mullis, I. V. S., Gonzalez, E. J., O'Connor, K. M., Chrostowski, S. J., Gregory, K. D., et al. (1999). *TIMSS 1999 eighth grade science benchmarking report*. Boston: Boston College, TIMSS International Study Center.

Mullis, I. V. S., Martin, M. O., Beaton, A. E., Gonzalez, E. J., Kelly, D. L., & Smith, T. A. (1997). *Mathematics achievement in the primary school years*. Boston: Boston College, TIMSS International Study Center.

Mullis, I. V. S., Martin, M. O., Beaton, A. E., Gonzalez, E. J., Kelly, D. L. & Smith, T. A. (1998). *Mathematics and science achievement in the final year of secondary school*. Boston: Boston College, TIMSS International Study Center.

Mullis, I. V. S., Martin, M. O., Gonzalez, E. J., Gregory, K. D., Garden, R. A., O'Connor, K. M., et al. (1999). *TIMSS 1999 international mathematics report.* Boston: Boston College, TIMSS International Study Center.

Mullis, I. V. S., Martin, M. O., Gonzalez, E. J., O'Connor, K. M., Chrostowski, S. J., Gregory, K. D., et al. (1999). *TIMSS 1999 eighth grade mathematics benchmarking report.* Boston: Boston College, TIMSS International Study Center.

National Center for Education Statistics. (1998). *Linking the national assessment of educational progress (NAEP) and the third international mathematics and science study (TIMSS): Eighth grade results, July, 1998.* (NCES Report 98-500). Washington, DC: Author.

Organization for Economic Cooperation and Development. (1995). *Literacy, economy, and society: Results of the first adult literacy survey.* Paris: Author.

Organization for Economic Cooperation and Development. (2001). *Program for international student assessment.* Paris: Author. Retrieved from http://www.oecd.org/index.htm. U.S.-oriented analysis retrieved from http://www.nces.ed.gov/survey/pisa

Perlstein, L. (2003a, September 9). *All things considered.* National Public Radio.

Perlstein, L. (2003b). *Not much, just chillin: The hidden lives of middle schoolers.* New York: Farrar Strauss & Giroux.

Prais, S. J. (2003). Cautions on OECD's recent educational survey (PISA). *Oxford Review of Education, 29,* 2.

Schmidt, W. H., McKnight, C. C., Valverde, G. A., Houang, R. T., & Wiley, D. E. (Eds.). (1996). *Many visions, many aims: A cross-national investigation of curricular intentions in school mathematics.* Dordrecht, The Netherlands: Kluwer.

Stevenson, H. W., & Stigler, J. W. (1992). *The learning gap: Why our schools are failing and what we can learn from Japanese and Chinese educators.* New York: Summit Books.

Stigler, J. W., & Hiebert, J. (1999). *The teaching gap: Best ideas from the world's teachers for improving education in the classroom.* New York: Free Press.

TIMSS International Study Center. (2003). *Progress on reading literacy study.* Boston College: Author. Retrieved from http://timss.bc.edu/pirls2001. U.S.-oriented analysis retrieved from http://www.nces.ed.gov/surveys/pirls

Wang, J. (1998). A content examination of the TIMSS items. *Phi Delta Kappan, 80*(1), 36–38.

CHAPTER 7

ENROLLMENT, ACHIEVEMENT, AND MOTIVATIONAL PROFILES OF IMMIGRANT AND NATIVE ADOLESCENTS

Tim Urdan and Deborah Garvey

In the United States, and particularly in California, there are increasing numbers of immigrant adolescents in school. In some schools, immigrants (i.e., first generation) and children of immigrant parents (i.e., second generation) students are the majority of the student body. It is important, therefore, to understand the characteristics of immigrant students for a variety of reasons. First, if there are differences between immigrant and native students in achievement, motivation, or approaches to schooling, educators and researchers concerned with creating optimally motivating learning environments must understand the characteristics of immigrant students. School reform efforts, school curricula, and teacher training may all need to consider the particular needs or preferences of immigrant students in order to be effective with the maximum number of students. Second, immigrant students may provide clues in educators' efforts to understand and address some vexing problems among native students, including persistent apathy and low achievement. Third, under-

Educating Adolescents: Challenges and Strategies, 149–177

standing immigrant–native differences in motivation and educational progress gives policymakers the empirical content for informing ethical education policy, including how to fairly distribute scarce resources to enhance equality of educational opportunity.

The purpose of this chapter is to examine the characteristics of immigrant students from a variety of perspectives. First, using a combination of nationally representative data and California-specific data, we describe the immigrant adolescent student population in terms of its demographics, graduation and school enrollment rates, and achievement levels. Next, examining a smaller sample of students from three California high schools, we examine differences and similarities in the motivational orientations of immigrant and native students as well as the possible mechanisms for those differences. The chapter begins with a definition of terms, including immigrant, native, and generational status. These definitions are followed by a description of the demographic characteristics of immigrant and native students, first from California and then from a national sample. Next, we summarize the results of a series of studies examining the motivational orientations of high school students and differences between generational groups in their motivational orientations. The chapter concludes with consideration of the importance of these results for educators and school reform efforts.

"Generational status" generally refers to an individual's temporal proximity to an immigrant to the United States. A person is first generation or foreign born if she was born outside of the United States and its territories to non-U.S. citizen parents. A native-born person, by contrast, was born in the United States or a U.S. territory or was born abroad to at least one U.S.-citizen parent. Natives are further classified according to their removal from the first generation. Second-generation children were born in the United States or a U.S. territory to a non-U.S. citizen mother. Third-generation individuals are native-born children of native-born mothers and include third and higher-order generations. Missing information on father's birthplace in some of the survey data used in this chapter requires that we identify second and third generation according to the mother's place of birth only.

IMPORTANCE OF THE EDUCATIONAL SUCCESS OF IMMIGRANT YOUTH

From a pragmatic perspective of fostering productivity growth and enhancing economic efficiency, society has a major stake in understanding the educational attainment of immigrant youth and developing policies to ensure immigrants' persistence in the American education system.

The convergence of two demographic and economic forces, namely, the recent rapid growth of the immigrant population and the tight link between educational attainment and earnings, render increasingly important the educational success of immigrant youth. We briefly examine each of these forces in turn.

Growth in the immigrant population has been dramatic at both the national and state levels over the past decade. Recent U.S. Census Bureau figures show that the foreign-born population in the United States grew by 64% since 1990 to over 32 million residents in 2002, comprising nearly 12% of the U.S. population (Schmidley, 2003). The immigrant population in California increased a robust 37% from 6.5 million to 8.9 million persons between the 1990 and 2000 censuses, and accounted for over 26% of the state population. Indeed, during the 1990s California experienced the largest influx of immigrants of any state in the nation, receiving almost twice as many immigrants as second-place Texas. Since 1980, California has ranked first among states in the size of its foreign-born population and the foreign-born population share. California's dominance as an immigrant-receiving state is expected to persist well into the future (Gibson & Lennon, 1999; Migration Policy Institute, 2003; Schmidley, 2001).

Increased immigration is reflected in the rapid growth of first- and second-generation youth: nationally one out of every five children under age 18 had at least one immigrant parent in 2000, triple the 1970 proportion (Ruiz-de-Velasco, Fix, & Clewell, 2000). The growth in the number of first- and second-generation youth is much higher in California. Census data indicate that, at a minimum, over 45% of California's school age population (ages 5 to 18) had at least one foreign-born parent in 2000, an increase of over 20% just since the 1990 census (Table 7.1). Thus, if current migration and immigrant settlement patterns continue, first- and second-generation immigrant youth will constitute the majority of the state's labor force within 20 years.

Recent changes in the economic value of schooling highlight the importance of identifying factors that influence the educational attainment of immigrant youth. Labor economists have documented a strong positive relationship between an individual's educational attainment and her lifetime earnings potential. Indeed, recent work suggests that the "return" to education may actually be *proportionally* higher for individuals with relatively low schooling (Card, 2001).

There has been little research on the educational attainment patterns of immigrant youth and potential differences among generational groups in the factors that influence educational outcomes. Quantitative studies of the educational achievement of immigrant children typically focus solely on first-generation immigrants and generally find that the foreign born

Table 7.1.   Race/Ethnicity and Generational Status of California Youth Ages 5–18, 1990 and 2000

Characteristic	Total	First Generation	Second Generation	Third+ Generation	Second/Third+ Generation
Generational status, 2000	100%	11.9%	34.1%	49.2%	4.8%
Generational status, 1990	100%	14.9%	23.0%	56.8%	5.4%
Race/Ethnicity, 2000					
Non-Hispanic					
White alone	35.8%	8.0%	10.6%	60.7%	28.0%
Black alone	7.0%	1.5%	1.2%	11.4%	17.2%
Asian alone	10.0%	22.8%	18.4%	1.5%	5.6%
Chinese/Taiwanese	2.2%	4.5%	4.5%	0.3%	0.6%
Filipino	2.4%	5.4%	4.6%	0.2%	1.2%
Vietnamese	1.3%	3.7%	2.5%	0.0%	0.8%
All other Asian	4.1%	9.2%	6.9%	1.0%	3.0%
Native American alone	0.5%	0.0%	0.1%	0.9%	1.5%
Other, including > 1 race	4.1%	2.9%	3.8%	4.6%	4.4%
Hispanic (any race)	42.5%	64.7%	65.9%	20.9%	43.3%
Mexican	34.2%	52.5%	53.3%	16.5%	35.8%
Other Hispanic	8.3%	12.3%	12.5%	4.5%	7.5%
Number of observations (2000)	7,179,864	853,108	2,445,448	3,535,160	346,148
Number of observations (1990)	5,733,814	852,965	1,317,323	3,255,490	308,036

Note: "Second/Third+ Generation" includes youth for whom generational status cannot be determined (see text).

Source: Authors' calculations are from the 1990 5% State and 2000 1% Census Integrated Public Use Microdata Samples (IPUMS) for California.

fare as well as their native peers in school, although certain subpopulations, notably Mexicans and Central Americans, have lagged (Hirschman, 2001). Other research examining the relationship between generational status and educational outcomes has been limited to examining high school dropout behavior (Giorguli Saucedo, White, & Glick, 2002) or the educational achievement of a particular racial or ethnic group (Driscoll, 1999).

This study seeks to address the limitations of previous research by documenting broad measures of immigrant educational attainment derived from census data, with a focus on California's immigrant youth population. Longitudinal survey data are then analyzed to provide preliminary insights into the factors that influence several measures of immigrants' attained schooling levels.

CALIFORNIA'S UNIQUE IMMIGRANT YOUTH POPULATION

A Demographic Profile of California's Immigrant and Native Youth Population

The primary data sources for our descriptive analysis are the 1990 5% State and 2000 1% Census Integrated Public Use Microdata Samples (IPUMS) for California (Ruggles, Sobek, King, Liebler, & Fitch, 2003). These data sets, constructed from the 1990 and 2000 Censuses of Population and Housing conducted by the U.S. Bureau of the Census, provide detailed demographic information on approximately 1.46 million and 339,000 randomly sampled individuals in 1990 and 2000, respectively. Individuals are assigned weights so that they are statistically representative of California's resident population on April 1 of each census year. Hence, person-weighted data are used throughout the analysis to replicate the overall state population.

California's youth population ages 5 to 18 increased from 5.80 million to 7.26 million persons (25%) between the 1990 and 2000 censuses. Slightly over 1% of youth resided in "group quarters," primarily college dormitories, and to a lesser extent, correctional facilities and other institutions. Youth living in group quarters are excluded from the analysis because their generational status cannot be determined. Not only is the youth population in group quarters numerically small, but there is also no evidence that our sample is biased by their exclusion. Foreign-born youth are as likely to reside in group quarters as native youth, and the fraction of foreign-born youth that resides in group quarters reflects their population share.

The analysis sample therefore includes the 5.73 million and 7.18 million California youth who resided in households in 1990 and 2000, respectively. Determining generational status from census data is simple only for the first generation: a youth is first generation if he reports that he was born outside of the United States and its territories to non-U.S. citizen parents. Because respondents are not asked about their parents' place of birth, distinguishing second- from third-generation youth is not straightforward. In addition, the third generation includes third and all higher-order generations since the latter cannot be separately identified. Questions on birthplace of parents were dropped after the 1970 census.

Our methodology takes advantage of IPUMS-constructed variables to identify whether a youth's biological parent(s) resides in the child's household and then uses parents' reported birthplace to determine a native-born child's generational status. Second-generation youth are identified as native-born children with at least one foreign-born biological parent present in the household. A youth is defined as third generation if she is herself native born, and one of the following conditions holds: both biological parents are native born or one biological parent is native born and the other biological parent does not live in the household. The residual category "second/third+ generation" consists of native-born youth whose generational status cannot be determined because neither biological parent lives in the household with the child.

Table 7.1 shows generational status in 1990 and 2000 and the race/ethnicity distribution of California's youth population at the 2000 census. As of 2000, about 10% of California children were foreign born, at least a third were native born to at least one foreign-born parent, and slightly under half were unambiguously third generation. The remaining 5% were native born of indeterminate generational status. Indeed, California is fast approaching the demographic threshold of a minority third-generation youth population, if it has not already passed it.

Interestingly, although the first and third generation grew slightly from 1990 to 2000, both groups' shares of the school-age population declined due to the explosive growth of the second generation, which grew over 85% during the decade. The second generation constitutes at least a third of the state's youth population. The size and population share of the second generation is expected to continue to grow rapidly because of the relative youth and higher fertility of first-generation women compared to native-born women (Tafoya, 2002).

The racial and ethnic composition of first- and second-generation youth reflects the top countries of birth of California's immigrant population: Mexico, the Philippines, China/Taiwan, and Vietnam (U.S. Bureau of the Census, 2002). Nearly two thirds of first- and second-generation youth were of Hispanic, overwhelmingly Mexican, origin, and roughly another 20% identified themselves as Asian. Whites comprised less than 11% of first- and second-generation youth, but constituted over 60% of the third generation.

The demographic characteristics of California's public elementary and secondary schools reflect those of the state's overall youth population. We used IPUMS data to determine the generational status of the state's public school population (top panel of Table 7.2). Not surprisingly, the generational status of public school pupils reflects the generational composition of the school-age population in Table 7.1. Three features are particularly noteworthy. First, California is experiencing a rapid decline in the share of its student population that is third generation. The third generation grew so modestly between the two censuses that at most no more than 53% of public school students were third generation in 2000, as compared to 62% in 1990. The rapid growth of the second generation in the population resulted in a doubling in the number of second-generation students from 1.1 million in 1990 to 2.2 million in 2000. Indeed, over a third of public school pupils were second generation in 2000. Most strikingly, at a minimum, over 47% of students attending California's public schools were the children of immigrants in 2000.

More recent data from the California Department of Education (2004) show that public school enrollment grew from 5.2 million in 1993 to over 6.1 million students in 2002, an increase of over 18%. Increasing school enrollment reflects both the rapid growth in the youth population and, to a lesser extent, secular growth in school participation rates (discussed below). The ethnic composition of public schools mirrors the rapid growth of second-generation youth: the typical public school student was less likely to be white (35% vs. 43%), and more likely to be Hispanic (44% to 36%) in 2002 than 1993. Asian and black enrollments increased proportionally so that their share of the student population remained steady over the period, at approximately 11% and 9%, respectively.

The number of public school students designated as English language learners, however, grew more than twice as fast as overall enrollment, increasing from 1.2 to 1.6 million children between 1993 and 2002. As a result, English learners comprised over a quarter of California public school pupils in 2002. Increasing enrollment of Hispanic children, who are more likely to be English learners than other ethnic groups, accounted for over 90% of the growth in the English learner population (California Department of Education, 2002). Clearly California will face an ongoing challenge of educating English language learners and encouraging their persistence in school (Tafoya, 2002).

Table 7.2.   School Enrollment and Educational Achievement of California Youth, 1990 and 2000

Characteristic	Total	First Generation	Second Generation	Third+ Generation	Second/ Third+ Generation
Public school population ages 5 to 18					
Generational status, 2000	100%	11.8%	35.3%	48.2%	4.7%
Generational status, 1990	100	14.8	23.2	56.9	5.1
Enrollment, 2000	6,143,530	722,420	2,167,366	2,962,013	291,731
Enrollment, 1990	4,665,466	688,966	1,083,000	2,656,691	236,809
School enrollment status					
Youth ages 12 to 18					
Percent in school, 2000	93.8%	85.3%	96.7%	96.2%	83.1%
Percent in school, 1990	90.5	82.9	94.7	93.5	77.1
Youth ages 16 to 18					
Percent in school, 2000	87.1	74.8	92.6	91.7	72.9
White	91.6	93.1	95.6	93.3	68.0
Asian	94.1	92.5	96.7	91.8	84.1
Hispanic	80.4	65.8	90.6	87.7	72.6
Mexican	79.5	63.8	90.3	87.6	70.5
Percent in school, 1990	83.1	73.5	91.1	88.7	65.3
Completed schooling to date, youth ages 16 to 18, 2000					
Less than ninth grade	4.8%	13.0%	2.8%	2.5%	3.4%
Ninth grade	12.6	11.6	10.7	14.7	8.1
Tenth or eleventh grade	56.6	48.7	56.8	61.8	45.2
Twelfth grade, no diploma	9.6	10.9	13.0	7.1	10.5
High school graduate/GED	10.7	10.6	11.2	8.9	20.5
Some college	5.7	5.2	5.5	5.0	12.3
Mean age	16.99	17.08	16.97	16.91	17.29
Standard deviation	0.82	0.82	0.80	0.80	0.79

Note: "Second/Third+ Generation" includes youth for whom generational status cannot be determined (see text). "Asian" and "White" are defined as non-Hispanic racial groups. "Hispanics," therefore, may be of any race. "School enrollment" refers to attending either a public or a private school. Ethnicity differences in educational attainment are not shown in Table 7.2 due to space constraints, but are available upon request.
Source: Authors' calculations are from the 1990 5% State and 2000 1% Census Integrated Public Use Microdata Samples (IPUMS) for California.

Educational Achievement of California's Immigrant and Native Youth

It is important to note that there are two drawbacks to using census data to measure educational attainment. The most important limitation is that the census only asks general questions about educational achievement, namely current enrollment, highest grade completed, and whether the individual attained a degree or diploma. The census contains no information about educational aspirations or schooling trajectories. Of lesser importance is the exclusion from our analysis of youth residing in group quarters. The fact that such individuals are disproportionately likely to be low achievers (i.e., youth living in group settings or in prison) or high achievers (i.e., youth living in college dormitories) is offset by the fact that they are no more likely to be foreign born.

Despite its limitations, the census provides useful insights into the educational achievement of immigrant and native youth. We first examine school enrollment patterns of adolescent youth as a critical baseline indicator of educational achievement and then look at approximate measures of high school completion and postsecondary schooling by generational status. IPUMS data show that almost 94% of adolescents ages 12 to 18 were enrolled in either public or private schools in 2000, a three-percentage point gain since 1990 (middle panel of Table 7.2). School participation rose within all generational status groups between 1990 and 2000, although growth was most striking for natives of indeterminate generation, 83% of whom attended school in 2000 versus 77% in 1990.

Relative gaps persist in school enrollment probabilities across generations, particularly for the immigrant generation. We restrict our attention to youth ages 16 to 18, who are no longer subject to compulsory schooling laws and for whom enrollment is a choice. Native youth of indeterminate generation and first-generation youth were significantly less likely to attend school than other generations in both census years. In 1990, only two thirds of indeterminate native youth and about 74% of first-generation youth were in school compared to roughly 90% of second- and third-generation youth, a 17- to 25-percentage point enrollment disadvantage. Indeterminate native youth narrowed their enrollment gap relative to other natives by six percentage points in 2000, as the groups' enrollment rates increased to 73% and 92%, respectively. Although first-generation enrollment increased slightly in absolute terms to nearly 75% in 2000, the gap relative to second- and third-generation youth did not narrow over the decade.

Average within-generation enrollment propensities, however, mask sharp differences across ethnic groups. We focus on Hispanic-Asian differences in school participation. The first-generation enrollment disadvantage is caused by extremely low school participation among Hispanic youth, particularly those of Mexican origin. Less than two thirds of Mexican first-generation youth ages 16 to 18 attended school in 2000, compared to over 90% of whites and Asians. Hispanic and Mexican enrollment in other generations, while still significantly lower, narrows dramatically relative to whites and Asians. Looking at *cross*-generation achievement, Hispanic, Mexican, and Asian second-generation youth are more likely to be enrolled than either their first- or third-generation counterparts.

Generational differences in youth school enrollment are reflected in high school completion status and postsecondary school enrollment. The bottom panel of Table 7.2 presents data on the highest level of schooling completed to date by generational status for youth ages 16 to 18 in 2000. We chose 16 as the cutoff age since it is a critical decision point for youth who choose to remain in school beyond the compulsory school age. School completion measures have some meaning for individuals who are approaching the end of formal schooling. However, it is highly likely that completed schooling underestimates lifetime educational attainment, with the severity of the bias directly related to the probability that a student is currently enrolled in school. Note that high school graduates and GED recipients are still considered to be "in school" if they are enrolled in post-secondary or vocational schooling.

There are distinct differences in attainment across generations. Most troubling is the experience of first-generation teens, who are four to five times more likely than other generation groups to have completed less than the ninth grade. Despite being slightly older, the first generation is also less likely to have completed 10th and 11th grade than second- and third-generation teens but is no more likely to have completed high school than the second generation. This pattern is driven by low attainment of Hispanics, especially Mexican youth, who are nine times more likely than whites and Asians (19 vs. 2%) to have less than a ninth-grade education, but only 60% as likely as whites to have a high school degree (10 vs. 17%). With less than two thirds of first-generation Hispanic youth attending school at the time of the census, this low level of achievement may persist into adulthood.

By contrast, over 56% of second-generation teens and nearly 62% of third-generation teens completed 10th or 11th grade by April 2000, despite being slightly younger on average than first-generation teens. Ethnicity differences in attainment and the Hispanic disadvantage are much smaller in the second and third generations. For example, while Hispanic second-generation youth are still more likely to have fewer than 9 years of schooling than whites and Asians, the absolute differences are small (3 vs. 1 and 2%, respectively). In addition, there is no Hispanic second-generation deficit in higher schooling levels. Similar ethnicity differences characterize third-generation educational attainment.

The educational attainment of native teens of indeterminate generation resembles that of other native generations overall. Such youth, who are the oldest on average, are also most likely to have completed high school and to have attained some postsecondary schooling. Since older youth are less likely to live in their parents' household than are younger youth, older native-born youth are more likely to be of indeterminate generational status than younger natives. Over 20% have completed high school or obtained a GED, while 12% (fully twice as many as any other generational status group) have completed some postsecondary schooling. Ethnicity differences are more pronounced than in the second and third generations but less dramatic than in the first generation. Hispanic youth (6%) are more likely than whites (2%) to have less than a ninth-grade education, but are less likely than Asians to possess a high school degree (17 vs. 34%). Hispanic youth are also less likely to have some postsecondary schooling than whites or Asians (9 vs. 18 and 12%, respectively). For the roughly one quarter of the group who are not currently enrolled in school, these measures of school completion may represent ultimate educational attainment.

A NATIONAL EDUCATIONAL PORTRAIT OF IMMIGRANT AND NATIVE YOUTH

We use data from the public-use version of the National Education Longitudinal Study of 1988 (hereafter referred to as NELS:88) to provide a national portrait of the educational characteristics of immigrant and native youth. NELS:88, a longitudinal survey conducted by the U.S. Department of Education's National Center for Education Statistics, is a two-stage stratified, nationally representative sample of approximately 1,050 schools and 24,500 students who were eighth graders in the spring of 1988.

NELS:88 is particularly well suited to an analysis of educational attainment by generational status. Hispanic and Asian students were oversampled, yielding large numbers of first- and second-generation youth. This dataset includes rich information on students' and school dropouts' educational experiences, aspirations, and nonschool activities. The youth's participating parent provided rich information on family background (including the youth's and parents' place of birth) and socioeconomic characteristics. Youth were reinterviewed every 2 years through the spring of 1994 and again in 2000 (National Center for Education Statistics,

1994). Data through the 1994 follow-up are used in this study, when most respondents were 20 or 21 years old.

Sample selection criteria in the base year (1988) initially excluded approximately 500 students from the survey whose limited command of English prevented them from completing the student questionnaire and tests. NCES reduced potential bias introduced by this exclusion criterion by including a representative sample of roughly 200 formerly excluded individuals in subsequent survey rounds. Unfortunately, questions about place of birth and parental place of birth were not asked in follow-up surveys. Although generational status cannot be determined for these individuals, we assign them an "unknown generation" status and still observe their educational outcomes. Since first-generation immigrants are more likely to be limited English proficient than other generation status groups, the first-generation NELS:88 sample may not be nationally representative. Lopez (1999) shows the probability of English language difficulties decreases in each generation. Thus youth of unknown generation are most likely to be first generation and least likely to be third generation. At most, however, 150 first-generation immigrants are included in the "unknown generation" as a result of the initial language exclusion. "Unknown generation" status is assigned to an additional 2,000 respondents with missing birthplace information either due to item nonresponse or inclusion in the NELS:88 after the base year survey. Indeed, nearly half of youth of unknown generation status identify themselves as non-Hispanic white and only 20% are Hispanic (see Table 7.3). Mother's birthplace is used rather than father's birthplace because mothers were more likely to respond to the parent questionnaires and there is much more missing information on father's birthplace.

We focus on two sets of high school achievement measures in this analysis. We first consider generational differences in participation in an academic high school program and participation in at least one advanced placement (AP) course. Both of these are indicators of college preparedness (Vernez, Abrahamse, & Quigley, 1996). We then examine how high school completion status differs across generational groups. An individual can exit high school in one of three ways: by achieving a high school diploma, completing a General Equivalency Diploma, or dropping out without obtaining a high school degree. Research has shown that labor market rewards are lower for holders of GED diplomas relative to regular high school diplomas (Cameron & Heckman, 1993).

Generational differences in mean educational attainment measures are presented in the second and third panels of Table 7.3. There were no significant differences across generational groups for participation in academic high school programs. Both first- and second-generation youth (55 and 48%) are significantly more likely than the third generation (41%) to

Table 7.3. Educational Achievement of Youth by Generational Status and Race/Ethnicity, 1994

	Total	First Generation	Second Generation	Third+ Generation	Unknown Generation
Race/Ethnicity					
White	71.4%	13.8%	33.5%	78.3%	49.6%
Asian	3.5	40.3	15.9	0.9	5.8
Hispanic	10.3	37.3	42.1	6.1	20.3
Proportion participating in:					
Academic program	63.1%	68.4%	65.6%	63.4%	55.3%
Asian		74.6	80.5	65.4	73.3
Hispanic		65.3	59.6	55.3	44.1
Advanced placement course	41.4	54.7	47.9	41.0	34.4
Asian		62.9	66.0	30.5	48.9
Hispanic		43.7	40.6	40.6	36.0
High school completion status					
Received a high school diploma	82.0%	82.2%	84.3%	82.6%	73.2%
Asian		89.3	93.4	92.1	91.7
Hispanic		76.4	79.0	74.3	64.2
Completed GED equivalency	6.0	6.5	3.7	6.0	7.9
Asian		2.0	0.7	0.9	1.0
Hispanic		6.8	4.8	7.9	8.1
No high school diploma	12.0	11.3	12.0	11.4	18.9
Asian		8.7	5.9	6.9	7.3
Hispanic		16.8	16.2	17.8	27.7
Unweighted observations	14,915	753	1,002	10,919	2,241
Weighted observations	2,967,565	101,832	179,527	2,475,653	210,552

Notes: "Asian" and "White" are defined as non-Hispanic racial groups. "Hispanics," therefore, may be of any race. Educational attainment measures are student self-reports (see text). The number of observations varies across educational outcomes due to missing data.

Source: Authors' calculations are from the public-use version of the National Education Longitudinal Study of 1988 (NELS:88), 1994 follow-up.

participate in at least one advanced placement course in high school. With the exception of a lower GED equivalency rate in the second generation than the third generation, there are no significant differences between first-, second- and third-generation youth in high school diploma receipt, GED equivalency completion, or dropout status. Youth of unknown generation are extremely disadvantaged in measures of college preparedness and to a lesser extent, high school completion, compared to all other generational status groups, particularly the first-generation group.

Generational averages mask a great deal of diversity in educational outcomes by ethnicity. As shown in the top panel of Table 7.3, Hispanics and Asians are overrepresented in the first and second generations (and to a lesser extent in the unknown generation), while whites predominate in the third generation.

To keep the discussion tractable, we examine differences in educational achievement among Hispanic and Asian youth. With the exception of second- and unknown-generation whites, whose outcomes lag behind those of their Asian counterparts, educational attainment of white youths approximates that of Asians. Looking first at *cross*-generation differences *within* ethnic group, distinct racial patterns emerge. As with overall generational averages, unknown-generation Hispanic youth have the lowest attainment among Hispanic generations, and the second generation has a significantly lower probability of GED completion than the third generation. Unlike the overall generational mean, first- and second-generation Hispanics are no more likely to take advanced placement courses than the third generation.

Asian educational attainment patterns, by contrast, differ markedly from generational averages in two ways. First, Asian youth of unknown generation generally achieve at rates similar to other Asian generations. Second, the Asian second generation exhibits a distinct advantage in academic program participation and advanced placement course taking compared to the third generation.

As was the case with the California data, the most striking *within*-generation difference in educational outcomes nationally is that Asian educational attainment exceeds that of Hispanics and generally the generational average as well. Second-generation Asians are significantly more likely to participate in an academic program than Hispanics, while first- and second-generation Asians are more likely to take at least one advanced placement course than their Hispanic counterparts. First-, second-, and third-generation Asian youth are significantly more likely to earn a high school diploma and less likely to complete a GED equivalency or drop out of school. Hispanic youth of unknown generation are particularly disadvantaged relative to their Asian counterparts, who have much higher academic program participation and high school completion rates. As discussed above, to some extent these youth are actually limited English proficient members of the first and second generations. Although not shown in Table 7.3, Hispanic unknown-generation youth have similar outcomes as do African Americans on all measures and as do whites on advanced placement participation.

Recall that California's Hispanic and Asian second-generation youth are more likely to be enrolled in school than their first- and third-generation counterparts, although there are no significant cross-generational differences in completed schooling. This result is confirmed in the NELS:88 sample.

Although first-generation students in the California sample were less likely to complete high school than second- and third-generation students, there was no such disadvantage for first-generation students in the national sample. This difference is likely due to the higher proportion of Hispanic students and the inclusion of students with limited English proficiency (LEP) in the first-generation group of the California sample. Two thirds of California's first generation is Hispanic (vs. 37% of the NELS:88 sample), of which a striking 80% hails from Mexico. Other research suggests that Mexican youth frequently migrate to the United States to work, not to attend school (Hirschman, 2001).

Does Generational Status Affect Educational Attainment?

To examine whether generational status predicts educational achievement independently of relevant family factors (i.e., family socioeconomic status, parents' education, family composition and stability, family involvement), student factors (i.e., prior achievement, race, gender, educational aspirations) and school factors known to affect academic offerings like advanced placement classes (i.e., school size, location, type), we conducted a series of logistic regressions.

Preliminary analyses suggest that family socioeconomic status, parental educational attainment, and parental involvement in a child's schooling are overwhelmingly the most important forces driving the youth educational attainment measures described in Table 7.3. As other research has found, family income and parental educational attainment are the most determinative factors of attainment, effectively swamping estimated differences in the impact of generational status. Even independent of these family background characteristics, parental aspirations have a strong additional positive impact on the probability of taking an academic high school program, and to a lesser extent, on receiving a regular high school diploma.

Interestingly, when one controls for other factors that influence educational attainment, a significant independent effect of generational status emerges for the first generation. These youth are significantly more likely to take at least one advanced placement course and receive a high school diploma than otherwise similar youth of other generational status. The first generation is also marginally more likely to participate in an academic high school program. In short, first-generation youth have better educational outcomes than would be predicted based on their observable sociodemographic and economic characteristics.

EXAMINING MOTIVATIONAL PROFILES ACROSS GENERATIONAL GROUPS

In addition to presenting the educational enrollment and attainment profiles of American and California youth across generational groups, we also want to describe motivational and achievement differences across these groups. Survey data were collected from students in three high schools over a 2-year period (Urdan & Giancarlo, 2001). The purpose of the project was to gain information regarding the motivational orientations of high school students using an achievement goal theory framework of motivation (Maehr & Midgley, 1991).

Prior Research on Generational Status and Motivation

The existing research on motivational differences between generational and cultural groups has tended to focus on two factors. First, research on differences between individuals with a collectivist self-definition and individuals with an individualistic self-definition suggests that individualists tend to value competition more than collectivists (Triandis, Bontempo, Villareal, Asai, & Lucca, 1988). Cross-cultural research has revealed that individualistic cultures tend to emphasize competition, independence, individual achievement, autonomy, and gratification of personal desires (Triandis, Leung, Villareal, & Clack, 1985). In contrast, collectivist cultures stress the importance of conformity to the ingroup, obedience, responsibility to family, sensitivity toward others, obligations, group cohesion, and subordination of personal or individual desires for the benefit of the group.

A second, related focus of research examining motivational differences between cultural/generational groups has been the influence of family. For example, Fuligni and his colleagues (Fuligni & Tseng, 1999; Fuligni, Tseng, & Lam, 1999) have reported that children of immigrants reported a stronger sense of obligation to care for family members in the future than did children of native parents. Suarez-Orozco (1991) found that children of immigrants from Latin America also felt a strong sense of family obligation and were highly motivated in school. Similarly, Gibson (1995) found that the adolescent children of Sikh immigrants tended to be highly motivated and to achieve well despite a number of potential barriers, including having a native language other than English and having an appearance (due to the clothing style of the Sikhs) that was outside of the mainstream. Gibson noted that among Sikh students there was a shared value of bringing honor to the family through academic success and avoiding bringing shame upon the family through academic failure.

Taken together, these two features of research on generational and cultural variations in motivation suggest that immigrants and children of immigrants, particularly from collectivist societies (e.g., Latin American, Asia), should be more motivated than native students and be motivated to achieve academically for different reasons. Explanations for why the children of immigrants may be more motivated include that their parents clearly express to them that a major reason for immigrating was to provide better financial opportunities for their children, opportunities that can be realized through academic achievement. Similarly, immigrants from collectivist cultures may encourage their children to succeed in school for familial purposes (e.g., bringing honor to the family, situating oneself to take care of the family later in life) rather than for individualistic reasons, such as personal pride. The mechanisms underlying generational differences in motivation, therefore, may include both a sense of family orientation (from the individualism–collectivism distinction) as well as the direct influence of the immigration experience.

The limited amount of research conducted to date exploring motivational differences between generational groups has produced modest results. Fuligni (1997) reported that first- and second-generation students placed greater value on learning the material in mathematics and English than did third-generation students and tended to achieve at least equally well. The children of immigrants also aspired to higher levels of education than did the children of native-born parents. Fuligni and Tseng (1999) also found that high school students' feelings of family obligation were positively, although modestly, associated with valuing of mathematics and English, particularly with the utility value of these subjects. They reported a curvilinear association between sense of family obligation and academic achievement such that those students highest and lowest in family obligation achieved at lower levels than did those with medium levels of family obligation.

Elliot and his colleagues, citing research on differences between collectivist and individualistic societies, argued that, whereas individualists are motivated by the desire to feel pride, collectivists are motivated more by a desire to avoid shame (Elliot, Chirkov, Kim, & Sheldon, 2001). There was evidence from this study that performance-avoid goals were pursued more often by members of collectivist cultures and were associated with perceived well-being differently among members of collectivist and individualistic countries. Specifically, performance-avoid goals were negatively related to well-being in the individualistic country (United States) but unrelated to well-being in the collectivist countries (South Korea and Russia). The results revealing cultural variations in the pursuit and effects of performance goals were statistically significant but quite weak ($r < .20$).

Goal Theory: Definitions and Theoretical Underpinnings of Cultural Differences

Achievement goal theory posits that students perceive different purposes for striving to achieve academically (see Elliot, 1997, for a review). Students may be primarily concerned with learning and understanding the material in their classes, and this desire to develop competence is referred to as a *mastery* goal. Alternatively, students may desire to demonstrate superior competence relative to other students (a *performance-approach* goal) or avoid appearing less able than others (a *performance-avoid* goal). Which goal a particular student endorses is believed to depend, in part, on the goal-related messages that are salient in the classroom. In some classrooms, learning and understanding are strongly emphasized, thereby creating a *mastery goal structure* in the classroom and encouraging students in the classroom to adopt mastery goals. In contrast, students may perceive a strong emphasis on competition and ability differences among students in the classroom, thereby observing a *performance goal structure* in the classroom.

Maehr and Nicholls (1980) argued that goals might operate differently for members of collectivist (e.g., Asian) cultures than for members of individualistic (e.g., North American) cultures. Whereas mastery goals represent a relatively selfless absorption with the task (Maehr & Kaplan, 2000), performance goals involve a self-conscious, ego-involved concern with how one appears relative to others. Therefore, individuals who differ in the way they define themselves along the individualism–collectivism dimension may also differ in their pursuit of performance goals, moreso than in their pursuit of mastery goals.

There are two primary manners in which the pursuit and effects of performance goals may differ for individuals. First, some students concerned with appearing able relative to others may focus on the approach dimension (i.e., wanting to appear smarter or more able than others), whereas others may be more inclined to adopt performance-avoid goals. It is possible that students with individualistic self-definitions may be more inclined to adopt performance-approach goals in the pursuit of feeling pride, whereas students with collectivist self-definitions might adopt performance-avoid goals due to the greater emphasis on shame and avoiding bringing shame to the family found in collectivist societies (Markus & Kitayama, 1991). Similarly, individuals in classrooms that emphasize competition and ability differences among students (i.e., classrooms with strong performance goal structures) may differ in their responses to such messages. Whereas individualistic students may be inclined to adopt performance-approach goals in such contexts, collectivists should be more likely to adopt perfomance-avoidance goals.

In addition to differences in the mean levels of performance goal adoption, students may differ in their responses to performance goals and classroom performance goal structures. As mentioned earlier, we suspect that some students (i.e., collectivists) may be more inclined to respond to classroom performance goal structures by adopting performance-avoid goals, whereas others (i.e., individualists) may be more likely to adopt performance-approach goals. These differences in the effects of classroom performance goal structures may exist even if there are no differences among students in their perception of the strength of the classroom performance goal structure. Similarly, although individualists and collectivists may both pursue performance-avoid goals, the associations between these goals and outcomes may differ for the two groups. For example, individualists may suffer more negative consequences from pursuing performance-avoid goals because for these students performance-avoid goals are more strongly associated with personal ego protection, whereas for collectivists avoidance motives may be the normative motivational stance and be more strongly tied to pleasing family members than to threats to one's ego (Elliot et al., 2001; Markus & Kitayama, 1991).

Differences between generational groups in the pursuit and consequences of performance goals may depend primarily on the individualism–collectivism distinction. In California, most immigrants are from Asia, South-East Asia (i.e., Vietnam), and Latin America. These cultures have been described as being more collectivist than the culture of the United States, which is the quintessential individualistic society. First- and second-generation students should be more strongly tied to their collectivist roots than are third-generation students because immigrant parents often try to emphasize and maintain the cultural beliefs and customs of their native lands. Third-generation students, who were born to native U.S. parents, have little direct link to collectivist ideologies and may therefore exhibit a more classic individualistic pattern. The individualism–collectivism distinction, therefore, may be one mechanism that explains generational differences in the pursuit and effects of performance goals.

Previous research on cultural and generational differences in motivation suggests that there may be mean differences between groups on a variety of motivational variables. In addition, there appear to be some cultural differences in the associations between motivational constructs and outcomes, such as achievement and well-being. The magnitude of these results tends to be small, however. In the next section we describe a series of studies that we have conducted to examine whether there are differences between generational groups in the pursuit and effects of achievement goals. We begin with a description of a research project designed to examine generational differences in the pursuit and effects of performance goals and classroom goal structures. We present the results from a number of studies from the project that indicate differences between generational groups and between those students high and low in a measure of family orientation, which we used as something of a proxy for the individualism–collectivism distinction.

THE MOTIVATION AND CRITICAL THINKING PROJECT

The Motivation and Critical Thinking Project was conducted in the San Francisco Bay Area (Urdan & Giancarlo, 2001). There were several objectives of the project, but one of the most important was to examine whether first-, second-, and third-generation students differed in their motivational profiles. The project was guided by an achievement goal theory framework. Survey data were collected from students over a 2-year period.

The Sample

In the first year of the study surveys were administered twice (once in the fall, once in the spring) to 891 students of three high schools in their English classrooms. All of the students were either native English speakers or had been deemed proficient in English by the school district. Therefore, there were few students in the sample who were recent immigrants (i.e., within the 2 or 3 years before the study began) from non-English-speaking countries. The difficulties that non-English-speaking students have in progressing through the educational system, as we described earlier, do not apply to the students in this sample. All of the students were in either the 9th or 11th grades in the first year of the study. The sample was diverse both ethnically (244 Latino students, 174 Filipino, 149 Vietnamese, 114 Caucasian, 79 Chinese) and generationally (23% were first-generation, 46% second-generation, and 31% third-generation).

In the second year of the study, 725 students of the original sample remained in the study and 275 students were added to create a total sample of 1,000 students in Grades 10 and 12. The ethnic and generational distributions were essentially the same during the second year of the study as during the first year.

The Measures

The variables of interest in this study included personal achievement goals (mastery, performance-approach, and performance-avoid), perceived classroom goal structures (mastery and performance), family orientation, self-handicapping, and achievement. The personal goals measures were adapted from Midgley and colleagues (2000) to refer specifically to the domain of English. The classroom goal structure measures were developed for this study. They include 15 items (8 mastery, 7 performance) designed to tap into students' perceptions of the shared values among students within classrooms regarding the desire to learn and understand (mastery) and the desire to compete with and outperform (or avoid being outperformed by) other students. Self-handicapping was also adapted from the PALS survey (Midgley et al., 2000) to apply to English.

Family orientation was a four-item measure designed for this study. The purpose of this variable is to assess the degree to which students want to achieve academically for the sake of family concerns, including pleasing parents, making parents proud, and putting oneself in a position to provide for the family when the student gets older. Because previous research has demonstrated that a strong sense of connection to family, as well as a desire to please family members, is a defining feature of collectivist cultures, we hoped this variable would serve as a proxy measure of individualism–collectivism. Existing measures of individualism and collectivism (e.g., Hui & Yee, 1994) were too long and inappropriate for use with high school students.

All of the survey items referred specifically to the domain of English. In addition, all were assessed using a 5-point scale (1 = "Not at all true" to 5 = "Very true"). Items within each scale were averaged to create a range from 1 to 5 on each variable. All scales had acceptable internal reliability with this sample (i.e., Cronbach's alphas greater than .70).

Teacher-assigned grades at the end of each semester of the study were collected from student records and serve as the achievement measure in this study. Grades were assessed on a 14-point scale (0 = "F" to 13 = A+).

Summary of Results

We have conducted a number of studies examining differences between first-, second-, and third-generation students and the effects of family orientation. Our examinations of mean-level differences between the generational groups have revealed that first-generation students tended to score higher on all of our motivational and achievement variables than did third-generation students (Urdan & Giancarlo, 2001). The results of the comparisons among generational groups conducted in the second semester of the first year of the study are reported in Table 7.4. There are three noteworthy trends in these results. First, the first-generation students scored significantly higher than the third-generation students on both the "good" and the "bad" forms of motivation (i.e., mastery goals and performance-avoid goals, respectively) and had higher average levels

Table 7.4.   Comparisons of Generational Groups on Motivation and Achievement

	First Generation $N = 191$	*Second Generation* $N = 384$	*Third+ Generation* $N = 262$	*F*
Year-end English grade	8.74 [a] (3.29)	7.76 [b] (3.89)	6.73 [c] (3.66)	17.58*** $\eta^2 = .04$
Mastery goals	3.93 [a] (.77)	3.71 [b] (.76)	3.53 [c] (.77)	14.92*** $\eta^2 = .04$
Performance-approach goals ^	3.04 [a] (1.09)	2.93 [ab] (.99)	2.75 [b] (1.08)	4.70** $\eta^2 = .01$
Performance-avoid goals ^	2.36 (.92)	2.23 (.97)	2.14 (.95)	2.70* $\eta^2 = .01$
Classroom mastery goal structure	3.68 [a] (.79)	3.40 [b] (.77)	3.34 [b] (.80)	11.42*** $\eta^2 = .03$
Classroom performance goal structure ^	2.97 [a] (.77)	2.77 [b] (.84)	2.71 [b] (.90)	5.67** $\eta^2 = .01$
Family obligation‡	4.14 [a] (.74)	3.99 [a] (.78)	3.64 [b] (.91)	24.12*** $\eta^2 = .06$

Notes: * indicates $p < .05$, ** $p = .01$, and *** $p < .001$.
Numbers in parentheses are standard deviations.
^ indicates generational differences became nonsignificant when controlling for family orientation.
‡ indicates generational differences remained significant when controlling for English grade.
Groups with different superscripts indicate significant differences at the $p < .05$ level using Tukey contrasts.
English grade was scored on a 14-point scale ($0 = F$ and $13 = A+$).

of achievement. As with the census and NELS:88 data, first-generation Latino students had significantly lower achievement levels than did Asian students, particularly Vietnamese immigrants. This trend also held true for the perceived classroom goal structures. Second, the effect sizes for the differences were generally quite weak. Finally, the addition of the family orientation variable as a covariate eliminated the statistically significant differences between generational groups on the three performance goal variables (performance-approach, performance-avoid, and perceived classroom performance goal structure), but not on the two mastery goal variables (mastery goals and perceived classroom mastery goal structure).

The analysis of the mean-level differences between generational groups indicated that first-generation students had a more positive motivational and achievement profile than did second-generation students, who in turn achieved higher grades and were more mastery goal oriented than were third-generation students. In addition, the analysis revealed that differences on the performance goal variables were mediated by the family orientation variable. These results suggest that students who differ in their sense of family orientation (and, by extension, sense of self on the individualism–collectivism dimension) may pursue performance goals for different purposes and may respond to performance-goal messages in the classroom in different ways. We examined such differences in a number of studies.

Urdan (in press) found that students high in their sense of family orientation were more likely than students low in family orientation to adopt performance-avoid goals when they perceived a strong classroom performance goal structure. This result was consistent with previous research indicating that in collectivist cultures there is often a strong emphasis on shame motivation (Markus & Kitayama, 1991). When placed in classrooms where ability differences among students are made salient, students with strong connections to collectivist norms and beliefs will likely be more inclined to adopt avoidance goals (with the aim of avoiding shaming the family) than will students raised with individualistic beliefs.

In the same study, Urdan found trends for two interactions involving family orientation and performance goals. In the first interaction, the negative association between performance-avoid goals and achievement in English was weaker among students with a strong sense of family orientation than for students weak in family orientation. This interaction is consistent with the finding of more negative effects of performance-avoid goals on well-being among students from individualistic cultures (Elliot et al., 2001). The second interaction trend revealed that the positive association between achievement in English and *subsequent* adoption of performance-approach goals was stronger among students who scored higher on the family orientation scale. This interaction suggests that students with an individualistic self-definition are more likely than those with a collectivist orientation to respond to positive achievement feedback by adopting performance-approach goals. Both of these interactions, though theoretically sensible, were interpreted with caution because the interactions were not quite statistically significant and because they were not replicated in other waves of data collected from the same sample.

One of our goals has been to understand whether differences between generational groups on motivation variables vary by the nationality of students. Unfortunately, in California (and elsewhere) the distribution of immigrants from various countries is not even across generational groups. In our sample, for example, there were very few third-generation Vietnamese and Filipino students. In contrast, there were almost no first-generation Caucasian or African American students in our sample. Therefore, it was difficult to determine whether there were nationality/ethnicity by generational status interactions. Using a subsample of participants, we did find that first-generation Vietnamese and Filipino students reported slightly higher scores on performance-avoid goals than students born in the United States. In contrast, Latino students born in the United States were higher in performance-avoid goals than Latino students born outside of the United States (Figure 7.1). These results may be evidence that the existence of stereotypes about ethnic groups has an effect on students' avoidance goal orientations. It seems that the longer a certain ethnic group member is in the United States, the more aware they become of the stereotype about their cultural group. The common stereotype about Asian students in the United States is that they are high achievers academically, whereas the stereotype regarding Latino students is that they are academically weak. The greater period of time that these students reside in the United States, the more cognizant they become of these ste-

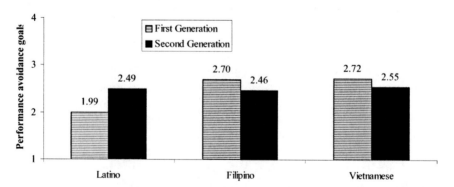

Figure 7.1.   Interaction of ethnicity and generational status of performance avoidance goals.

reotypes and the more relaxed Asians may become while the more anxious Latinos may become (Sempel, Urdan, & Giancarlo, 2001).

Taken together, these results suggest (a) that first-generation students have more adaptive motivational and achievement profiles than third-generation students, as evidenced by higher achievement in English and greater endorsement of mastery goals; (b) that generational differences in the pursuit of performance goals and perceptions of classroom performance goal structures are mediated by sense of family orientation; (c) that the associations between classroom performance goal structure, performance-avoid goals, and achievement differs according to one's level of family orientation with students high in family orientation more likely to adopt performance-avoid goals in response to perceiving a classroom performance goal structure and a less negative association between performance-avoid goals and achievement for these students; and (d) that the association between generational status and performance-avoid goal pursuit differs for students of different nationalities. More globally, these results suggest that the way students define themselves along the individualism–collectivism dimension affects the meaning and function of performance goals more so than mastery goals and that societal expectations about one's nationality can influence the adoption of performance-avoid goals.

All of these results need to be interpreted with caution. The students in this sample did not include non-English speakers. Results from the census data revealed that the ability to speak English, and to stay in school, can have dramatic effects on the achievement profiles of immigrant students. In addition, the effect sizes, particularly for analyses involving performance goals, were quite weak. Moreover, some of the effects found in one wave of data were not replicated in other waves of data. Therefore, the results indicating generational or cultural differences in motivation should be considered suggestive rather than definitive. Additional research using qualitative data in addition to survey data is needed and is currently being conducted.

IMPLICATIONS

In California, immigrants represent the fastest-growing segment of the student body. In some school districts, the children of immigrants are the majority. Therefore, it is important that we understand the achievement, enrollment, and motivational characteristics of these students. To the extent that there are differences between immigrant and native students in motivation and learning preferences, efforts to reform schools in order to enhance the motivation and achievement of students will have different effects on these two populations. These differences must be understood before either a complete understanding of student motivation or effective strategies for educating a diverse student body can be achieved.

The results of our analyses of differences between immigrant and native students in achievement, motivation, enrollment, and completion suggest that there may be important differences, and that there are several potential causes of these differences. The descriptive results from the census and NELS:88 datasets suggest there are significant differences in secondary school achievement by generational status, with California's first generation, especially Mexicans and other Hispanics, and "indeterminate" generations at greatest risk of being ill prepared to navigate the education-driven American labor market. An important implication of our findings for policymakers is that educational policies should target the vulnerable limited-English-proficient population. English language learners need to be brought "up-to-speed" linguistically so that they can handle the challenging courses necessary to prepare for postsecondary schooling and successfully complete their high school careers. It appears clear that students who lack proficiency in English are at risk for not completing school and taking advantage of the rewards associated with school completion. The multivariate analyses conducted with these data represented a "first pass" at isolating the independent effect of generation on educational achievement. Future work needs to examine how the impact of generational status differs within racial and ethnic groups. Researchers would also be well advised to analyze how various dimensions of parental engagement in schooling, family socioeconomic characteristics, and school inputs, such as the degree of teacher and administrator involvement in student learning, grading practices, and student peer influences, are mediated differently across race and ethnic groups within and across generations.

The analyses examining motivational differences between generational groups are also preliminary. Future research examining generation by ethnicity interactions is needed, as are controls for socioeconomic status and parental involvement. Future studies that include non-English-speaking students are also needed to determine whether the more adaptive motivational and achievement profiles of first-generation students in this study would remain when non-English-speaking immigrants are included. Our results suggesting differences in motivational profiles indicate that more research in this area is warranted. There is more to learn about cultural differences in motivation and achievement, and the information to be gained will be of use both to educators responsible for the education of immigrant and native students and to researchers interested in refining theoretical models.

ACKNOWLEDGMENTS

Portions of the research presented herein were supported by a grant to the first author by the W. T. Grant Foundation. Garvey gratefully acknowledges financial support from a Hackworth Grant for Faculty Research in Applied Ethics from the Markkula Center for Applied Ethics at Santa Clara University and a W.E. Upjohn Institute for Employment Research Mini-Grant. Preliminary versions of portions of this chapter were presented at the Twenty-Third Annual Association for Public Policy and Management Fall Research Conference, November 1-3, 2001, in Washington, D.C., and at the annual meeting of the Southern Demographic Association, October 10-12, 2002, in Austin, TX, under the title "The Educational Assimilation of Immigrant Youth."

REFERENCES

Bean, F. D., Chapa, J., Berg, R. R., & Sowards, K. A. (1994). Educational and sociodemographic incorporation among Hispanic immigrants to the United States. In B. Edmonston & J. S. Passel (Eds.), *Immigration and ethnicity: The integration of America's newest arrivals* (pp. 73–100). Washington, DC: Urban Institute Press.

California Department of Education, Educational Demographics Unit. (2002). *English learner (EL) students and enrollment in California public schools, 1993 through 2002.* Retrieved June 1, 2003, from http://www.cde.ca.gov/demo graphics/reports/statewide/lepstpct.htm

California Department of Education, Educational Demographics Unit. (2004). *Enrollment by ethnicity, 1981–82 through 2002–03.* Retrieved July 4, 2004, from http://www.cde.ca.gov/sd/cb/enreth.asp

Cameron, S. V., & Heckman, J. J. (1993). The nonequivalence of high school equivalents. *Journal of Labor Economics, 11*(1, Part 1), 1–47.

Card, D. (2001). Estimating the return to schooling: Progress on some persistent econometric problems. *Econometrica, 69,* 1127–1160.

Driscoll, A. K. (1999). Risk of high school dropout among immigrant and native Hispanic youth. *International Migration Review, 33,* 857–875.

Elliot, A. J. (1997). Integrating the "classic" and the "contemporary" approaches to achievement motivation: A hierarchical model of approach and avoidance achievement motivation. In M. L. Maehr & P. R. Pintrich (Eds.), *Advances in motivation and achievement* (Vol. 10, pp. 143-179). Greenwich, CT: JAI Press.

Elliot, A. J., Chirkov, V. I., Kim, Y., & Sheldon, K. M. (2001). A cross-cultural analysis of avoidance (relative to approach) personal goals. *Psychological Science, 12,* 505–645.

Fuligni, A. J. (1997). The academic achievement of adolescents from immigrant families: The roles of family background, attitudes, and behavior. *Child Development, 68,* 261–273.

Fuligni, A. J., & Tseng, V. (1999). Family obligation and the academic motivation of adolescents from immigrant and American-born families. In T. Urdan (Ed.), *Advances in motivation and achievement* (Vol. 11, pp. 159–183). Stamford, CT: JAI Press.

Fuligni, A. J., Tseng, V., & Lam, M. (1999). Attitudes toward family obligations among American adolescents with Asian, Latin American and European backgrounds. *Child Development, 70,* 1030–1044.

Gibson, C., & Lennon, E., (1999). *Historical census statistics on the foreign-born population of the United States: 1850–1990* (Population Division Working Paper No. 29). Washington, DC: U.S. Bureau of the Census.

Gibson, M. A. (1995). Additive acculturation as a strategy for school improvement. In R. G. Rumbaut & W. A. Cornelius (Eds.), *California's immigrant children: Theory, research, and implications for educational policy* (pp. 77–106). San Diego: Center for U.S.-Mexican Studies, University of California, San Diego.

Giorguli Saucedo, S. E., White, M. J., & Glick, J. E. (2002, May). *Between family, job responsibilities and school: generation status, ethnicity, and differences in the routes out of school.* Paper presented at the annual meeting of the Population Association of America, Atlanta, GA.

Hirschman, C. (2001). The educational enrollment of immigrant youth: A test of the segmented-assimilation hypothesis. *Demography, 38*(3), 317–336.

Hui, C. H., & Yee, C. (1994). The shortened individualism-collectivism scale: Its relationship to demographic and work-related variables. *Journal of Research in Personality, 28,* 409–424.

Jasinski, J. L. (2000). Beyond high school: An examination of Hispanic educational attainment. *Social Science Quarterly, 81*(1), 276–290.

Kao, G., & Tienda, M. (1995). Optimism and achievement: The educational performance of immigrant youth. *Social Science Quarterly, 76*(1), 1–19.

Lopez, M. H. (1999). *Does bilingual education affect educational attainment and labor market outcomes? Evidence from the national education longitudinal study of 1988 and high school and beyond.* Unpublished manuscript, University of Maryland.

Maehr, M. L., & Kaplan, A. (2000, April). *It might be all about the self: Self-consciousness as an organizing scheme for integrating understandings from self-determination theory and achievement goal theory.* Paper presented at the annual meeting of the American Educational Research Association, New Orleans, LA.

Maehr, M. L., & Midgley, C. (1991). Enhancing student motivation: A school-wide approach. *Educational Psychologist, 26,* 399–427.

Maehr, M. L., & Nicholls, J. G. (1980). Culture and achievement motivation: A second look. In N. Warren (Ed.), *Studies in cross-cultural psychology* (Vol. 2, pp. 221–267). New York: Academic Press.

Midgley, C., Maehr, M. L., Hruda, L. Z., Anderman, E., Anderman, L., Freeman, K. E., et al. (2000). *Manual for the Patterns of Adaptive Learning Scales (PALS).* Ann Arbor: University of Michigan.

Migration Policy Institute. (2003). *Migration information source: U.S. census data on the foreign born, fact sheet on the foreign born: California* 2002. Retrieved June 1, 2003, from http://www.migrationinformation.org/USfocus/state.cfm?ID=CA.

National Center for Education Statistics. (1994). *National education longitudinal study of 1988 second follow-up: Student component data file user's manual.* Washington, DC: U.S. Department of Education, Office of Educational Research and Improvement.

Ruggles, S., Sobek, M., Alexander, T., Fitch, C. A., Goeken, R., Hall, P. K., King, M. & Ronnander, C. (2003). Integrated Public Use Microdata Series: Version 3.0 [Machine-readable database]. Minneapolis: Minnesota Population Center [producer and distributor]. Retrieved July 2, 2003, from www.ipums.org

Ruiz-de-Velasco, J, Fix, M., & Clewell, B. C. (2000). *Overlooked and underserved: Immigrant students in U.S. secondary schools*. Washington, DC: Urban Institute.

Schmidley, D. (2001). *Profile of the foreign-born population in the United States: 2000* (Current Population Reports, Series P23-206). Washington, DC: U.S. Census Bureau.

Schmidley, D. (2003). *The foreign-born population in the United States: March 2002* (Current Population Reports, Series P20-539). Washington, DC: U.S. Census Bureau.

Sempel, J., Urdan, T., & Giancarlo, C. (2001, April). *Comparing the motivational profiles of first, second, and third generation students*. Poster presented at the annual meeting of the American Educational Research Association, Seattle, WA.

Suarez-Orozco, C., & Suarez-Orozco, M. M. (1995). *Transformations: Immigration, family life, and achievement motivation among Latino students*. Stanford, CA: Stanford University Press.

Suarez-Orozco, Marcelo (1991). Immigrant adaptation to schooling: A Hispanic case. In M. Gibson & J. Ogbu (Eds.), Minority status and schooling: A comparative study of immigrant and involuntary minorities (pp. 37-62). New York: Garland.

Tafoya, S. M. (2002). The linguistic landscape of California schools. *California Counts: Population Trends and Profiles, 3*(4).

Triandis, H. C., Bontempo, R., Villareal, M. J., Asai, M., & Lucca, N. (1988). Individualism and collectivism: Cross-cultural perspectives on self-ingroup relationships. *Journal of Personality and Social Psychology, 54*, 323–338.

Triandis, H. C., Leung, K., Villareal, M. J., & Clack, F. L. (1985). Allocentric versus idiocentric tendencies: Convergent and discriminant validation. *Journal of Research in Personality, 19*, 395–415.

Urdan, T. (in press). Predictors of academic self-handicapping and achievement: Examining achievement goals, classroom goal structures, and culture. *Journal of Educational Psychology.*

Urdan, T., & Giancarlo, C. (2001). A comparison of motivational and critical thinking orientations across ethnic groups. In D. M. McInerney & S. V. Etten (Eds.), *Research on sociocultural influences on motivation and learning* (Vol. 1, pp. 37–60). Greenwich, CT: Information Age.

U.S. Bureau of the Census. (2002). *Census 2000 summary file 3 (SF 3)—Sample data, detailed tables: PCT19. Place of birth for the foreign-born population [126]—Universe: Foreign-born population*. Retrieved July 15, 2003, from http://fact finder.census.gov/servlet/DatasetMainPageServlet?_ds_name=DEC_2000_S F3_U&_program=DEC&_lang=en.

Vernez, G., Abrahamse, A. F., & Quigley, D. (1996). *How immigrants fare in U.S education*. Santa Monica, CA: RAND.

CHAPTER 8

THE SCHOOLS-WITHIN-SCHOOLS REFORM

A Viable Solution to the Problems of Large High Schools?

Valerie E. Lee and Douglas D. Ready

For decades, researchers, pundits, and politicians have disparaged the state of the public high school (see, e.g., Angus & Mirel, 1999; Boyer, 1983; NASSP, 1996; National Commission on Excellence in Education, 1983; Powell, Farrar, & Cohen, 1985; Sizer, 1984, 1992). These indictments concentrate on three broad areas: (a) high school curricula that stratify students' social and academic experiences; (b) social environments in which students are not known well by their teachers; and (c) low levels of student engagement and achievement. These unfavorable characteristics are more frequently found in large high schools, which are educating an increasing proportion of U.S. students.

According to classic sociological theory, as organizations grow larger, their social interactions become increasingly hierarchical and formalized (Weber, 1922/1978). Sociologists of education have applied these constructs to schools, concluding that as schools grow larger, developing per-

Educating Adolescents: Challenges and Strategies, 179–206
Copyright © 2004 by Information Age Publishing
All rights of reproduction in any form reserved.

sonal relations becomes more difficult (Bidwell, 1965; Bryk & Driscoll, 1988; Bryk, Lee, & Holland, 1993). School size influences social relations largely through the opportunities students and teachers have to interact. Instead of identifying with the wider school, teachers in larger high schools tend to be "specialists" who associate with small subgroups of teachers and students, which are often defined (and limited) by subject matter and departmental structures (Newmann, 1981; Siskin, 1994). Conversely, in smaller schools students and teachers tend to play more diffuse roles. Despite their size, smaller schools generally provide a similar number of cocurricular and extracurricular offerings, resulting in increased opportunities for student and teacher participation (Barker & Gump, 1964; Schoggen & Schoggen, 1988). This increase in the diversity of settings in which teachers and students interact helps to flatten hierarchical social structures.

Academically, as high schools grow larger, they tend to offer a more diversified curriculum, which schools often see as a logical response to increased student diversity (Bryk et al., 1993; Lee, Bryk, & Smith, 1993). Unfortunately, more diversified curricula are associated with reduced learning and learning that is more strongly related to students' race and social class (Gamoran, 1987; Lee & Bryk 1989; Lee, Burkam, Smerdon, Chow-Hoy, & Geverdt, 1997; Oakes, 1985). In terms of a specific size, research suggests that students learn the most (and that learning is most equitable) in medium-sized high schools—that is, those that enroll between 600 and 900 students (Lee & Smith, 1997).

Regardless of how one defines "small" or "large," virtually no contemporary research suggests that high schools should be *larger* than they are. With the agreement that smaller high schools are generally beneficial to students' social and academic development, what policy options are available? In the current fiscal environment, it is unlikely that taxpayers would support the construction of many small high schools and the abandonment of the buildings that now house large comprehensive high schools. In many locations with large public high schools, particularly inner cities, maintaining *existing* schools is a financial challenge.

A logical (and seemingly less expensive) alternative to constructing new schools is to divide large high schools into several smaller schools that inhabit the original building. This design, often referred to as "schools-within-schools" (SWS), has recently attracted considerable interest from many of the same practitioners, researchers, foundations, and government agencies who have touted small schools. Despite the groundswell of support for this reform, the empirical base on schools-within-schools is quite sparse. Those who promote the SWS model often cite research on school size and small schools to justify their advocacy. However, it is unclear whether research on small schools and school size is directly applicable to the SWS structure.

BACKGROUND

For most adolescents, high school entry occurs at a time of substantial psychological growth and social uncertainty. Peer networks established in elementary and middle school are often interrupted as new social ties are forged. Familial relations also experience considerable transformation. Parents become less involved in the daily activities of their children's schooling and typically take a more "hands-off" approach to their students' social and academic lives (Stevenson & Barker, 1987; Useem, 1992). Conflicts and tensions with family members often arise as autonomy increases and students develop unique identities apart from the family (Buchanan, Eccles, & Becker, 1992; Steinberg, 1990). As such, school-based social relations become a crucial medium through which students receive the support that enables them to succeed (Lee & Smith, 1999).

Unfortunately, an important line of research suggests that an improper fit often exists between young adolescents' developmental needs and the school environments in which they are placed (see Eccles & Midgley, 1989; Eccles et al., 1993; Hunt, 1975). Many adolescents experience large, anonymous, and bureaucratic high schools, which may not correspond well to their social or psychological developmental needs (Bryk & Driscoll, 1988). Optimal educational environments would offer cognitive challenges and psychosocial support that matched students' developmental needs (Eccles et al., 1993). The freedom high schools often provide, however, creates opportunities for many adolescents to become "lost in the cracks."

A fundamental notion underlying the SWS structure is that by dividing themselves into smaller units, large high schools can reproduce the social relations and psychological supports typically found in small schools. A more implicit conviction is that positive social ties between students and teachers will improve student engagement and commitment, leading ultimately to increased student achievement. Although these ideas have received increased interest over the past several years, the SWS structure and the philosophies behind it claim a longer history. Forty years ago Barker and Gump (1964) suggested a "campus model" for high schools wherein

> students are grouped in semiautonomous units for most of their studies, but are usually provided a school-wide extracurricular program. The campus school provides for repeated contacts between the same teachers and stu-

dents; this continuity of associates probably leads to closer social bonds. A common sense theory is that the campus school welds together the facility advantages of the large school and the social values of the small school. (pp. 201–202)

Two decades later, Goodlad (1984) advocated a high school structure that incorporated "houses organized vertically, so that each contains students from all secondary grade levels" (p. 311). More recently, the first recommendation in *Breaking Ranks*, an influential report about secondary schools issued jointly by the Carnegie Foundation and the National Association of Secondary School Principals is that "schools must break into units of no more than 600 students so that teachers and students can get to know each other" (1996, p. 5).

Over the past several years substantial governmental and foundational support has also coalesced around the SWS reform. In 2001 the U.S. Department of Education's Smaller Learning Communities Grants program allocated $42.3 million for high schools seeking to divide themselves into smaller units (U.S. Department of Education, 2001). The program was reauthorized in 2002 under the No Child Left Behind Act, with a 2003 appropriation of $135 million.[1] The Bill and Melinda Gates Foundation has awarded over $500 million to high schools seeking to create smaller, more personalized learning environments (Gates Foundation, 2003). An early Gates Foundation initiative, the Washington State Achievers Program, offers support to high schools in that state that restructure themselves into "small, autonomous learning environments of no more than 100 students per grade level" (Gates Foundation, 2001). The Annenberg and Carnegie Foundations and the Pew Charitable Trusts have also directed substantial resources to schools implementing schools-within-schools, especially in Philadelphia and Chicago. Although the majority of this support has been directed toward urban schools enrolling substantial proportions of minority and low-income students, the SWS model is becoming increasingly popular in suburban areas (Gewertz, 2001). Rhode Island recently approved a proposal that requires *all* school districts to implement strategies that create "more personalized learning environments" in their high schools by 2005, potentially via the SWS structure (Archer, 2003).

The terminology SWS high schools use to describe their smaller units differs from school to school, with such labels as "houses," "academies," "blocks," "small learning communities," and "subschools," all referring to the smaller organizational groups within the larger school. To avoid confusion, we use the term "subunit" to describe these smaller units. Subunits are typically organized around curricular, pedagogical, or (most often) career themes. For example, a subunit might focus on the fine arts, cooperative learning, or careers in health or business (Lee, Ready, & Johnson, 2001; Oxley, 1989, 1994; Raywid, 1995). Subunits with vocational themes sometimes offer state certifications and endorsements in such vocational fields as child care, health care, or auto mechanics. Some SWS high schools organize special subunits for the school's youngest students (usually ninth graders), referred to as "freshman academies" by the Talent Development SWS reform program (McPartland, Legters, Jordan, & McDill, 1996). Beyond coursework, administrative functions including homeroom, guidance counseling, and all but the most serious discipline infractions are generally handled within the subunits (Oxley, 1989).

Although the term has come to have multiple meanings, we use "schools-within-schools" narrowly, referring to high schools where all students and most faculty are members of one of several smaller subunits. This "full-model" SWS structure is distinguished from a more common format where large high schools offer only one or two subunits, and most students remain in the regular high school program (Lee et al., 2001). These partial SWS structures often involve the creation of one or two vocationally oriented "career academies" within a larger public high school (Kemple & Rock, 1996; Kemple & Snipes, 2000; Stern, Raby, & Dayton, 1992). Other schools may have one subunit that serves disaffected and low-performing students as an alternative school. Likewise, Muncie and McQuillan (1996) investigated the implementation of several individual and self-contained Coalition of Essential Schools programs within larger high schools. None of these models are whole-school reforms, which is how our definition of SWS would be labeled. In fact, Muncie and McQuillan concluded that implementing such partial-model SWS structures within Coalition high schools was a poor idea, because they found that animosity developed between a "special" subunit and the remainder of the school.

Advocates of the SWS reform contend that one advantage of dividing large comprehensive high schools into smaller subunits is to weaken or eliminate the tracking structures that typify such schools, thereby creating a more equitable distribution of student achievement by race or class (e.g., Fine, 1994). Logic suggests that it is more difficult for individual subunits, either by design or because they enroll fewer students, to respond to students' social and academic diversity with differentiated academic programs. Thus, it would make sense for subunits to reduce the number of specialized academic programs they offer, which in turn might reduce the social and academic stratification that typically results from differentiated curricular structures. A common curriculum within a single subunit, with fewer courses that are taken by almost all students, would be a logical response to the smaller numbers of teachers and students.

However, almost all SWS high schools offer differentiation via their subunits, and permit students to select their subunit based presumably on their individual preferences and attraction to the various subunits' themes and offerings (Lee et al., 2001; McPartland et al., 1996). The goal of permitting subunit choice is to foster commitment among students and to increase their engagement with school. Allowing student choice in selecting subunits, although logical in the context of commitment-building, raises the same concerns expressed about educational choice in other contexts. Some authors interested in the SWS model have recognized the danger that such structures may actually be used to sort students into different subunits based on academic ability. For example, in commenting on the small-school movement in Philadelphia high schools, McMullan warned: "The greatest concern is that charters do not become thinly disguised tracks into which students are placed based on some arbitrary standard of performance or expectation" (1994, p. 69). Some subunits may actually be *designed* to attract certain types of students, or they may develop reputations that draw students with particular characteristics. Indeed, Oxley (1994) cautioned, "[sub]-units must not intentionally screen out particular students or inadvertently attract only certain groups of students" (p. 256). These and other authors caution that the SWS structure may produce stratification similar to that found within diversified high school curricula: the allocation of students with different social and academic backgrounds to different classes and programs.

In this chapter we use empirical evidence from our own research to examine the extent to which the SWS structure ameliorates some of the problems of large comprehensive high schools. Our discussion is organized around a series of four conclusions, which we offer in the context of five high schools employing schools-within-schools. Our findings should be of value to practitioners considering the SWS model, to policymakers interested more broadly in high school reform, and to researchers who are interested in how school structure plays out among students and faculty.

PROCEDURES

The Search for SWS High Schools

The initial phase of our work consisted of a national search for public SWS high schools. The search had three main goals. First, we sought to compile an extensive list of SWS high schools. Second, we wanted to understand the general state and prevalence of the reform in the late 1990s, and to know more about the various SWS structures in existence at that time. In short, we wanted to know about the population from which a smaller sample for intense study would be drawn. Third, we were interested in locating five SWS high schools that would represent well the larger population of SWS high schools and that were also interested in serving as sites for our research. Although we looked hard to identify a relatively affluent high school with the SWS structure, we were unable to locate even one. Schools serving high-achieving, affluent students may not see the value of the SWS reform, believing that their students are already motivated and surrounded by positive social networks.

The need to identify many high schools with the SWS structure in a short period of time suggested a telephone interview strategy. We began by contacting organizations and individuals we hoped would know of SWS high schools. These early sources included state departments of education, schools of education, the National Association of Secondary School Principals (NASSP), U.S. Department of Education regional labs, and school district administrators. We also relied heavily on the Internet, searching websites of hundreds of school districts, many of which had links to their high schools.

As we began calling schools that were suggested to us in the initial stage of our search, we soon found Patton's (1990) "snowball" or "chain" sampling strategy to be quite valuable. We ended each of our calls by asking respondents whether they knew of any SWS high schools. As we continued calling, our list of actual and potential SWS high schools "snowballed." In this national search, we made over 600 phone calls, sent dozens of e-mail requests, and spent hundreds of hours on the Internet. Of the hundreds of high schools we contacted through telephone interviews, only 55 actually had the full-model SWS structure that incorporates all students into the subunit structure. In choosing five of these schools to study, we used Patton's "maximum variation sampling" strategy, which seeks to maximize variability along as many dimensions as possible. We sought a school sample that varied by region and location, history with the SWS organization, subunit themes, and school social and academic composition. However, we also wanted to study schools in which the SWS structure was stable, so we limited our potential sample to schools that had employed the design for at least 3 years. (For more detail about the processes and conclusions drawn from this phase of the larger study, see Lee et al., 2001.)

Data Collection

The full research team of 11 members included both university faculty members and doctoral students. Two-person teams devoted two week-long visits to their assigned schools over the course of a calendar year, in the spring and fall of 1999. Each week-long visit consisted of interviews with students, teachers, guidance counselors, and school- and district-level administrators; shadowing of students; observations of interactions in hallways and other public locations; attending special events (including athletics) that occurred during our visit; mapping the physical layout of the building; collecting papers and documents pertinent to school life; and learning about the contexts in which the school operated. Our conversations with school members focused on the extent to which students' social and academic experiences depended on subunit membership, and how the SWS structure influenced the development of positive relations between students and teachers. Two team members (ourselves) visited all the schools at least once (Ready) or twice (Lee). Almost all interviews were audio taped, transcribed verbatim (unless interviewees objected), and verified. In the spring of 2001, we conducted a short round of revisits to each school. Our goal in this third round of short visits was to investigate the stability of the SWS reform by evaluating the extent to which the SWS structures in each school had changed.

SCHOOL DESCRIPTIONS AND CONTEXTS

Below we describe the five SWS schools that we studied. We assigned schools and subunits pseudonyms, and we describe them as they were in the 1998–1999 school year.

John Quincy Adams High School, the only public high school in a New England city committed to school choice, was among the first SWS high schools in the nation. It was formed in the 1970s when the city's two mostly segregated high schools were reformed into a single comprehensive high school enrolling 1,900 students. Among the five schools we studied, Adams enrolled the most racially, economically, and academically diverse student body. Many students were from affluent professional families, although other students received public assistance and lived in public housing. Every year dozens of Adams graduates attended elite colleges and universities, but an equal number left Adams (and formal education) after ninth grade. Adams enrolled substantial numbers of Caribbean, European, and Central American immigrants, as well as American-born blacks, whites, Asians, and Hispanics. Adams' SWS structure was unique, in that five of its six subunits (Alternative, College Prep, Community, Core Curriculum, and International Cooperative Learning [ICL]) were organized around pedagogical rather than career themes. One Adams subunit offered a traditional vocational curriculum (Vocational).

Ulysses S. Grant High School, an all-black high school enrolling 2,600 students, had over a decade's experience with the SWS structure. Grant was both a neighborhood and a "selective" high school, in that it enrolled students from its catchment area, but its five subunits (African American Studies, Arts, Business, Communications, and Health) also attracted students from across the city. Application rates were higher (and acceptance rates thus lower) for Business and Communications, which were selective magnet schools. Among the five SWS high schools in the study, Grant's student body had the least variability in terms of race, social class, academic achievement, and future educational plans. Although Grant's reputation had improved considerably in recent years, it was plagued by problems common to inner-city high schools. Each year it enrolled roughly 1,000 ninth graders and graduated fewer than 250, and course failure rates approached 40%. Students in this mid-Atlantic city could apply to any public high school (or subunit) in the district, which made recruiting (and subunit reputation) important. Students attending either of Grant's two feeder middle schools were guaranteed admission to any of Grant's subunits. However, students from these middle schools, which were quite small and located in one of the most blighted neighborhoods in the city, constituted only 10 to 15% of Grant's enrollment.

Benjamin Harrison High School, which enrolled 1,300 students in grades 10–12, was the only SWS high school in its mostly working-class Pacific Northwest city. Harrison had implemented four career-based subunits a decade earlier: Arts/Humanities, Health/Human Services, International Business, and Science/Technology. Among the city's four high schools, Harrison had the lowest test scores and enrolled the most socially and racially diverse student body, which led to its reputation as the "urban school." Although the district's minority enrollment increased 5% between 1994 and 1998, Harrison's minority population grew by 11.5% during the same period, adding to this public perception. This reputation belied the fact that Harrison's enrollment remained two-thirds white. Its lower test scores led district-level administrators to think Harrison needed more reform and restructuring. When this research began, the long-term viability of Harrison's SWS structure was in question.

James Monroe High School, a relatively new school, was built around the SWS structure with much commitment to the idea from district leaders who were influenced by books by Goodlad (1984) and Sizer (1984). Monroe's 1,400 mostly Hispanic students were organized into four classroom "pods" that were connected to a central area containing the library and administrative offices. In this fast-growing Southwestern school district not far from the Mexican border, some students came from professional families living in elegant homes that surrounded the school. Other students came from poor families whose homes in the surrounding desert often had dirt floors and no electricity or running water. Thus, the school evinced great social diversity but little racial diversity. Monroe's subunit structure was unusual, with two magnet school subunits and two nonthe-matic subunits in which students who did not select one of the magnet schools were randomly placed. These nonmagnet "Generics" (as they were labelled by students and staff) were "regular" high school programs without explicit themes or organizing rationales.

Zachary Taylor High School was a large "zoned" high school that enrolled 2,300 students who were not admitted to (or did not select) one of the city's several selective high schools. Taylor's enrollment—two-thirds black, one-quarter white, with small numbers of Asian and Native American students—was the most racially integrated regular high school in this mid-Atlantic city where school enrollments were overwhelmingly black. As recently as 1975, Taylor was almost all white. These changes in Taylor's racial makeup were associated with a decline in both reputation and support in the community. As part of a major restructuring effort in the early 1990s, Taylor had created six subunits, four of which were "career acade-mies": Business, Arts/Humanities, Health/Human Services, and Mechani-cal. A unique component of Taylor's SWS structure was that ninth graders did not participate in the regular career academies. Rather, they were placed into one of two "freshmen academies" without career themes, then permitted to select one of the four career academies for 10th grade.

FINDINGS

Conclusion 1: Elements of the comprehensive high school—particularly the diversified curriculum—are alive and well in SWS high schools. Many components of the comprehensive high school are incompatible with the autonomy enjoyed by small schools, both logistically and philosophically. Unlike the five SWS high schools we studied, the small autonomous high schools often praised in both academic literature and the popular press, such as Central Park East (Meier, 1995) and Urban Academy (Cook, 2000), have shed the trappings of the "shopping mall" high school (see Powell et al., 1985). This was done partly out of necessity—as they enroll fewer students and employ fewer teachers—but mostly out of a philosoph-ical agreement among staff about what students needed to know and be able to do. Specifically, these purposefully small schools offer a con-strained academic curriculum, including few AP, honors, foreign lan-guage, elective, and low-level, nonacademic courses. The result is that students are more likely to share common social and academic experi-ences.

In keeping with their comprehensive pasts, Adams, Grant, Harrison, and Taylor continued to offer courses at different levels (including AP and honors courses at Adams and Harrison), as well as the co- and extracurricular activities that define the comprehensive high school. Monroe, which was constructed with the SWS structure in mind, offered a comprehensive curriculum from the beginning. A theme that ran throughout many of our conversations with teachers and administrators in the SWS high schools we studied was the difficulty of implementing and *sustaining* the SWS structure within a preexisting comprehensive high school. These challenges stemmed from the desire to reap the benefits of small schools *and* those of a large, comprehensive high school. The result of this desire was that the schools offered expansive curricula and students often took these classes outside their subunits.

For two reasons, advanced and elective courses were rarely offered within individual subunits, and tended to enroll students from multiple subunits. First, providing courses with small enrollments in each subunit was prohibitively expensive; offering sections of Calculus, AP Physics, or French IV in every subunit—which would enroll only a few students each—was impossible. An exception occurred in Monroe, whose Math/ Science Magnet was allowed to offer subunit specific AP and honor courses with very low enrollments. This policy of unequal-sized classes fostered considerable animosity among students and teachers in the school's other subunits. Second, such elective and cocurricular courses as band, journalism, and drama were *meant* to be school-wide activities that enrolled students from every subunit. Such courses were offered in whatever subunit the teacher assigned to them was located, but they enrolled students from most or all subunits.

According to staff members at several schools, maintaining the comprehensive curriculum undermined the SWS structure. Students' curricular choices trumped attempts to keep classes "pure" (i.e., they enrolled only students from that subunit). Harrison High School described the tension between the SWS structure and the comprehensive high school quite eloquently in a recent grant proposal: "[Harrison] has two conflicting missions: (1) comprehensive high school with 13 departments all operating independently of each other, plus more than 20 cocurricular activities also operating independently; and (2) four schools-within-a-school structure attempting to integrate all subject areas into a school mission." The proposal continued, "The original design of the SWS concept was to provide strong student–faculty relationships, but due to a comprehensive high school structure, SWS have not met the original objectives." Harrison's principal, new to the school after our year-long study, told us that over the past decade, Harrison's SWS structure had slowly devolved back into a comprehensive high school:

> The staff had come to realize that the school-within-school process had failed, was failing. It deteriorated. You're running a small schools concept

that was a bastardized form of what it was supposed to be. Then you're running a comprehensive high school, *and you can't run both.*

A district-level administrator used the following metaphor to describe Harrison's desire to have both autonomous subunits *and* a comprehensive high school program: "It almost reminds me of having one foot here in a little bit of glue, and one foot over here, and you don't understand why you can't be here, but you haven't let go of this foot and brought it over." She noted that elective courses were the primary obstacle to creating subunit-specific classes, but that electives were one of the ways parents and the community judged the quality (and even legitimacy) of high schools. External perception was especially important for a high school whose reputation in the district was weak. Were Harrison to lose the traditional trappings of the comprehensive high school, she continued, its image in the community might be damaged even further:

> I know how hard it is for parents. You have the vision in your mind of a traditional high school, and all that entails.... They say they want this [the SWS structure], but they also want proms, and they want band, and they want 12 or 20 sports. That's going to be a big challenge for us.

Although Adams was the only public high school in its district, and suffered from problems of reputation only in relation to the city's several private high schools, a similar tension was evident there. Staff at Adams asserted that the parents of academically successful students often saw little need for reform. In their view, the traditional comprehensive high school with its extensive curriculum *already* worked for their children. One Adams administrator claimed that the push to maintain a wide array of course offerings generally came from these parents:

> The high-achieving population wants comprehensive. It works well for them in most cases. They were always the ones who could navigate the school no matter how big. They were the ones who could read the 80-page college-like course catalog we have, and they would be able to negotiate it. They would target the teachers that they wanted [for their children], the courses that they wanted, and quite honestly, it worked well because we satisfied their needs. We looked great.

Conclusion 2: One result of attempts to maintain the comprehensive high school was that subunit autonomy was both varied and limited. This influenced the degree to which subunits created distinctive identities and developed positive social relations. Our research has identified many social benefits resulting directly from the schools-within-schools model. Staff claimed that the SWS structure led to more positive interactions between students and teachers, and to social relations that were more often built upon notions of trust. Long-term staff also reported that improved student behavior, attendance, commitment to school, safer and more orderly school climates, and increased teacher satisfaction and feelings of self-efficacy accompanied the school's transition to the SWS organization. These are the very benefits small-school advocates have been trumpeting for decades. Indeed, several teachers at Taylor claimed that the SWS structure "saved" their school from its dubious honor as one of the worst high schools in its state.

We must be careful here not to "compare" social relations within these SWS high schools to either traditional comprehensive high schools or small autonomous schools. The SWS organizational structure *does* move schools toward social environments that differ from those commonly found in traditional high schools—a positive development. As noted, staff members consistently reported that overall school climates had improved since the adoption of the SWS reform. However, despite more positive social relations, the SWS structure does *not* appear to replicate "small schools" as some SWS advocates claim. This conclusion echoes Raywid (1995), who reserves the label "schools-within-schools" for schools whose subunits are fully autonomous and who report directly to district-level administrators and not to personnel within the building. In Raywid's lexicon, the organization of the high schools we studied could be more accurately labeled "mini-schools." Indeed, in none of the SWS high schools we studied were subunits autonomous. Rather, each subunit was tied socially, academically, and fiscally to the larger school. For example, subunits followed the same school-wide class schedule. Because of the common schedule and because in every period some students were taking courses outside their own subunit, it was almost impossible to organize subunit-specific activities during the school day. Furthermore, although most subunits had some role in choosing their teachers, principals in each building had the final decision in personnel matters. Additional evidence of this limited autonomy was financial; in no school we studied were subunits provided their own budgets. All funds were channeled through the larger high school. In several schools, subunits could draw on discretionary accounts, but these funds were generally quite small.

This limited autonomy constrained subunits' ability to foster closely-knit communities. For many students, social attachment to their subunit was quite tenuous—few of their academic or extracurricular experiences were subunit specific. Thus, the SWS structure may have created smaller learning communities for some students and not for others. The extent to which the SWS structure created personalized environments appeared to vary within a single school or subunit, depending on the courses and activities in which individual students were enrolled. For example, stu-

inherently alter schooling where it mattered most: in classroom instruction. Some argued that attempts to raise student achievement without improving the quality of academic instruction were fruitless. Offering committed, well-behaved students the same inferior instruction was unlikely to raise test scores. Although the SWS structure provides fertile ground in which innovative teaching and learning might take root, it appears that dividing students into smaller subunits *in and of itself* is unlikely to influence the nature of instruction. This is especially true in schools that permit classrooms to remain isolated spaces, and teaching to remain a solitary endeavor.

In the schools with generally low levels of student achievement, we found that support for the schools-within-schools reform often collided with outside pressure to raise test scores. For example, some Harrison staff and district-level administrators viewed the SWS structure as an *impediment* to raising student achievement, rather than a potential vehicle for reform. One district-level administrator alleged that Harrison's restructuring efforts had focused "too much on relationships" at the expense of instructional or curricular reforms, neither of which the SWS model explicitly addressed. Outside push to raise test scores created tensions in other schools as well, often because the SWS model was implemented with *social* rather than *academic* ends in mind. Several of the schools we studied expressed immediate concerns about school safety and student behavior, both of which took precedence over improving test scores. These schools asserted that improving social relations and increasing student commitment were the central motivators for implementing the SWS structure; none mentioned raising achievement. In this sense, a positive social climate was an end in and of itself.

Administrators at Adams and Taylor candidly admitted that an impetus for adopting schools-within-schools was that they could increase social control by "dividing and conquering." For example, Adams High School was created in the late 1970s when the school district merged its vocational high school with the city's comprehensive high school, mostly for desegregation reasons. Concerned about the social climate in a large school during a period of racial unrest, staff searched for ways to make the school "feel smaller and safer." Similarly, in the early 1990s, Taylor High School, which was known throughout the city as an "out-of-control" school, faced takeover by the state. Fights and vandalism were rampant, and individuals not associated with the school were often found wandering the halls. Taylor viewed restoring order as a primary goal, and the conversion to an SWS structure accomplished this goal well.

Conclusion 4: The locus of social stratification is shifted, but not ameliorated, by the SWS structure. Unfortunately, to varying degrees, subunit choice within these diversified SWS structures seemed to permit students

ments opposite Monroe. Despite Grant's limited socioeconomic variability (i.e., most students came from low-income families), students in the more selective subunits less often lived in the impoverished neighborhoods surrounding the school. This further delineated social distinctions among Grant's subunits.

In the three schools with traditional vocational subunits (Adams, Harrison, and Taylor), substantial gender differences existed between subunits because males more often selected the vocational subunits. One Harrison Science and Technology teacher lamented the fact that teachers' efforts to recruit more females had failed: "We've tried everything, but it doesn't make any difference." Students and staff at these schools told us that creating subunits that enrolled mostly males—many of whom were low-achieving—fostered climates that were less conducive to learning. When asked to describe Taylor's Mechanical subunit, which was 82% male, one Arts and Humanities student laughed and exclaimed, "It's all one big testosterone-bound place!" In explaining why so few females selected Mechanical, one subunit director asserted that the local neighborhood cultures maintained traditional "blue-collar" beliefs regarding gender roles: "You're going against a more traditional culture here. This isn't [the suburbs] where girls think they can do anything they want."

Gender differences among subunits at Adams were due largely to Vocational, which attracted a large number of males. Conversely, female students were overrepresented in Alternative, which its director attributed to the subunit's isolation on the top floor of the building, it's smaller size, and its relatively safe environment:

> For a while I thought we were becoming [an elite nearby women's college] because white girls tended to pick this [subunit] more than anybody in the last two years. They feel safe up here in this big school.

Staff in several schools justified subunit structures diversified by theme and claimed that they helped to accommodate the wide range of student academic ability; diversification was essential to "meeting students' needs." Many teachers were aware of the negative connotations association with such views, and worried that they might be perceived as supporting "tracking." Indeed, most denied that their SWS structures resembled traditional tracking, because students were permitted to *select* their subunits. As the sorting we observed by race, class, and gender was due to student *self*-selection, some staff felt it was not problematic. One Taylor teacher asserted, "I think it's not really tracking, it's just meeting their needs. I think in education we're so afraid of saying these kids are tracked that we forget about meeting everybody's needs." Another Taylor teacher decried efforts to create more heterogeneous classes and subunits, asserting that high-achieving students were often left to learn on their own:

> It's not fair to tell this kid who is smarter, "Well, you just read the book. Teach yourself. You're smart enough." No, that child is entitled to a teacher who is going to push him along at his speed. And it's not saying anybody is better than anybody else, either.

Similar to low-level courses in comprehensive high schools, vocationally oriented subunits tended to enroll many academically unmotivated students. Most of our informants viewed such subunits as the school's weakest. A teacher in Taylor's Mechanical subunit lamented, "Historically, our children are the least academic because it's hands-on manufacturing and auto mechanics. We teach the most difficult children—it's just a larger percentage of slow learners here." During our study, Adams' Vocational subunit was dismantled because it was seen as academically dysfunctional. One Adams administrator asserted, "They closed [Vocational], which was a good move from my perspective. As a [subunit] I think it was a dumping ground."

Structural Influences

Although student choice clearly influenced subunit composition, subunit procedures and processes also affected students' subunit placements. Subunits with good reputations actively recruited students. The head of Taylor's Business subunit reported sending invitation letters to all ninth graders with grade point averages of 80 or higher. They sought to have many more applicants than slots, so that their enrollees would be of higher quality. Another element of Taylor's subunit choice system further exacerbated stratification in that students received their subunit choices on a "first come, first served basis." Students who submitted their applications early generally received their first choice. A Taylor subunit head noted: "[This] really means if your attendance is good, you're going to get your choice. When it gets down to the end of the year and you haven't been attending for the last month of school, if you're promoted, then you're going to get pretty much what's left."

Grant's Business subunit received many more applications each year than it had openings, which allowed it to set high expectations for prospective students and to simultaneously maintain a large applicant pool. One Business teacher claimed that he "was able to look at the applications and not necessarily pick the best, but I was able to deny access to students who just had either terrible behavior or [whose] attendance was deplorable." Although Monroe administrators claimed that all who applied to its Math/Science Magnet were admitted, certain students were—as this one was—*encouraged* to apply:

> My counselor told me that some people [from Monroe] were going to come and give a presentation on what Math/Science Magnet was about. It sounded great to me; she said, "I think you'd be perfect for it. You'd have a lot of fun," and, "You'd like the advanced learning." She said that it was going to be way better than anything else.

At Adams the ability to appeal subgroup placements exacerbated between-subunit stratification. Because application rates were lower, students who chose Core Curriculum, ICL, or Community almost always got their first choice. However, because College Prep and Alternative received twice as many applications as openings, the school used a lottery to decide admissions. During the year of our study, students who applied to the popular subunits but were denied admission through the lottery could file a "hardship appeal" wherein they and their parents could explain why they "must" be given their first choice. For several years prior to our study, almost all appeals were successful. According to many students and staff, the appeals process was typically used by wealthier, more educated, and more politically adroit families—exactly the type of families already overrepresented in Alternative and College Prep. We heard numerous reports about parents who, after being denied their subunit choice by the lottery and appeals processes, pulled political strings to force school administrators to get their choice. A ninth grader told us (and the appeals board) that had he not received his first choice (College Prep) his mother would have enrolled him in a private school (his appeal was successful). The school did not want to lose such families.

CONCLUSIONS

Sources of Evidence

Our conclusions here are drawn from three sources. The first source comes from empirical research about the organization and structure of U.S. high schools (e.g., Bryk et al., 1993; Lee & Bryk, 1988, 1989; Lee et al., 1993; Lee & Smith, 1997, 1999). Among many conclusions we have drawn from that work, one is particularly relevant here. A constrained academic curriculum, where most students take academic courses and where few low-level courses are available, leads to increased student learning and to learning that is more equitably distributed by students' social background. Most of the high schools we studied in that research would

be typical of the comprehensive high schools we have referred to frequently in this chapter, although our research has also included many private (particularly Catholic) high schools. The type of curriculum we
describe as associated with both more learning and its more equitable distribution was unusual, but not unknown, in comprehensive public high
schools.

Our second information source is somewhat more explicit. One of us
(Lee) has conducted several studies that focus on school size, particularly
the size of high schools. This research has led to two major conclusions:
(1) that students learn more in schools that are large enough to be able to
offer a solid academic curriculum but (2) small enough that students and
faculty know one another well. That size high school, enrolling 600–900
students, seems to engender the same set of outcomes as the constrained
academic curriculum identified in the research that constitutes our first
information source (Lee & Smith, 1997).

Qualitative research on school size has helped to confirm these conclusions. Our qualitative study about school size has also convinced us that
small high schools—particularly those that are small by default—would
rather be larger than they are (Lee, Smerdon, Alfeld-Liro, & Brown,
2000). This research alerted us to a distinction not often made by those
who write about small high schools, usually with an advocacy tone. That
is, some high schools are small because they want to be small, and others
are small because they just don't have many students. These two types of
small schools should not be confused. The "small by design" high schools
have many advantages not shared by the "small by default" schools. This
has led us to be somewhat skeptical about "smallness" as an inherently
valuable characteristic of high schools. Smallness that is accompanied by
the ability to organize a school around a particular theme or ideology, to
attract students, families, and faculty to whom this theme is appealing,
and to select among applicants is a special kind of smallness, and not
really the same smallness that most small high schools experience.

Our third source of information, and clearly the one from which we
draw most explicitly in this chapter, is our 3-year qualitative study of five
U.S. high schools that were divided into schools-within-schools. We were
led to conduct this study as a direct follow-up to our other studies of
school size. "How," we asked, "could the nation create a large number of
small high schools?" The SWS reform was the main way we heard that it
was happening. We didn't know enough about the reform to design and
conduct a large-scale evaluation of the SWS reform, nor were there
enough SWS schools in the United States at the time we began our study
to conduct such research. Our field-based study of a small number of
carefully chosen SWS high schools was meant as a way to understand this

assumed that more engagement and commitment would inevitably lead to increased learning.

Choice

One of the bedrock features of SWS schools, at least among those we studied, is that students (and sometimes teachers) would choose their subunits. These schools were not in themselves schools of choice. Rather, they allowed choice within them. Virtually everyone associated with this reform advocates such choice, with the assumption that if students can choose to associate with a subunit that reflects their interests and serves their needs, increased engagement and commitment will result. However, what we saw as a result of such a full-choice model within these schools was considerable social and academic stratification.

Although technically these SWS high schools were no longer engaged in curriculum tracking, in effect we saw the same mechanism operating within the schools. That is, subunits—through their themes and their courses—were quite stratified. Motivated and high-achieving students ended up in the Math/Science Magnet at Monroe High School, whereas less motivated and lower-achieving students were in the Generic subunits. Adams' best students were in the Alternative or College Prep subunits, whereas many of the weakest students were in Vocational or Community. This type of stratification by subunit existed to some degree in each of the SWS schools we studied. Some of the schools recognized this as a natural (and not unfortunate) feature of the design. One school, Adams, recognized the stratification that had occurred over time as something they didn't want to continue. At the time of our latest visit, Adams had retained its subunit structure, but had reorganized it drastically. No longer did the subunits have themes that were associated with differentiated learning. More radically, Adams had moved to a system of random assignment of students to subunits, so that subunit social and academic characteristics were equivalent. Our point here is simple: choice almost inevitably leads to stratification. We contend that stratification is something that schools should move away from. However, we saw very little reduction in social stratification as a result of the SWS reform in the schools we studied.

What Do Schools Want To Be?

Tyack and Cuban's (1995) phrase "grammar of schooling" describes the practices and procedures that students, parents, teachers, and communities use to define what "real schools" look like. Just as native speakers of a language would react negatively to mandated changes in grammatical structures, educational reforms that deviate from cultural notions of schooling often face the greatest resistance. Thus, moving away from the "real" comprehensive high school is difficult, as "real" high schools organize their days into periods lasting between 40 and 55 minutes, have football teams, marching bands, academic departments, and offer a smorgasbord of academic and nonacademic courses. Because most SWS high schools serve communities who embrace such visions, limiting the scope of the comprehensive high school is politically untenable. Small-by-design schools can challenge the grammar of schooling in ways most SWS high schools cannot. They enroll the families and students who are attracted to their particular designs, and they can decide not to enroll students who don't fit their molds. In effect, such schools have considerable advantages that the SWS high schools we studied do not.

The major conclusion we draw from our work in the SWS high schools we studied is that schools must decide what they want to stand for, rather than letting their designs flow from what their student clienteles seem to want or need. We believe that the SWS reform would tend to be more effective and more equitable (defined in both affective and achievement terms) if the schools were able and willing to limit students' academic and social activities to their subunits. The more autonomous and "pure" subunits are, the more they would resemble small-by-design high schools that SWS advocates suggest the structure emulates. We found that each subunit's capacity to foster a solid and positive school community among its students seemed to depend on how often these students took classes within their own subunits. We saw several instances of students' affective attachments shifting from the level of the school to the subunit, which would tend to strengthen subunit community.

Our cautions about the SWS reform refer to its potential to segregate and stratify, features we feel should be avoided in all schools. Readers should not read our conclusions as an indictment of the reform, but rather as a caution to schools as they consider adopting the SWS structure, and as they plan their subunits. Many features of comprehensive high schools need to be sacrificed if schools-within-schools are to work well. In many ways, we conclude that the SWS structure offers potential solutions to the problems that plague large comprehensive high schools. A major advantage is that the SWS structure leads schools that consider and adopt it to rethink their purposes, and to consider exchanging the "shopping mall" format for a narrower program shared by all students. Equally important is the reform's potential to encourage new processes and social and academic organizations, especially in terms of curricular structures, the use of time and space, and the relationships between teaching and learning—in short, a fundamental look at what students should know, who should know what, and how adolescents' lives in school should be organized. In this sense, the dialogues in which these schools engaged as they implemented the SWS structure were themselves valuable.

ACKNOWLEDGMENT

The Spencer Foundation's generous support for the study described in this chapter is gratefully acknowledged. However, the Foundation's support does not imply its agreement with the opinions and statements expressed herein. Responsibility for errors of fact or interpretation rests solely with the authors. Authors were listed alphabetically. Both authors contributed equally to this chapter.

NOTE

1. The Smaller Learning Communities program is being evaluated by Abt Associates. Lee serves on the Technical Work Group that advises the evaluation.

REFERENCES

Angus, D. & Mirel, J. (1999). *The failed promise of the American high school, 1890–1995*. New York: Teachers College Press.

Archer, J. (2003, January 15). R.I. board backs plan to 'personalize' state's high schools. *Education Week, 22*(18), p. 10.

Barker, R., & Gump, R. (1964). *Big school, small school: High school size and student behavior*. Stanford, CA: Stanford University Press.

Bidwell, C. E. (1965). The school as formal organization. In J. G. March (Ed.), *Handbook of organizations* (pp. 972–1022). Chicago: Rand McNally.

Boyer, E. L. (1983). *High school: A report on secondary education in America*. New York: Harper & Row.

Bryk, A. S., & Driscoll, M. E. (1988). *The school as community: Theoretical foundations, contextual influences, and consequences for students and teachers*. Madison: Center on Effective Secondary Schools, University of Wisconsin.

Bryk, A. S., Lee, V. E., & Holland, P. B. (1993). *Catholic schools and the common good*. Cambridge, MA: Harvard University Press.

Buchanan, C. M., Eccles, J. S., & Becker, J. B. (1992). Are adolescents the victims of raging hormones? Evidence for the activational effects of hormones on moods and behavior in adolescence. *Psychological Bulletin, 111*, 62–107.

Cook, A. (2000). The transformation of one large urban high school: The Julia Richman Education Complex. In E. Clinchy (Ed.), *Creating new schools: How small schools are changing American education* (pp. 101-120). New York: Teachers College Press.

Eccles, J. S., & Midgley, C. (1989). Stage/environment fit: Developmentally appropriate classrooms for early adolescents. In R. E. Ames & C. Ames (Eds.), *Research on motivation in education* (Vol. 3, pp. 139–186). Greenwich, CT: JAI Press.

Eccles, J. S., Midgley, C., Wigfield, A., Buchanan, C.M., Reuman, D., Flanagan, C., et al. (1993). Development during adolescence: The impact of stage-environment fit on young adolescents' experiences in schools and in families. *American Psychologist, 48*(2), 90–101.

Fine, M. (1994). Chartering urban school reform. In M. Fine (Ed.), *Chartering urban school reform: Reflections on public high schools in the midst of change* (pp. 5-30). New York: Teachers College Press.

Gamoran, A. (1987). The stratification of high school learning opportunities. *Sociology of Education, 60*, 135–155.

Gates Foundation. (2003). *Recent small high school grants.* Retrieved from http://www.gatesfoundation.org/Education/SmallHighSchools/Grants/default.htm?showYear=2002

Gates Foundation. (2001). *School and district grants.* Retrieved from http://www.gatesfoundation.org/education/schooldistrictgrants/default.htm

Gewertz, C. (2001, May 2). The breakup: Suburbs try smaller high schools. *Education Week, 20*(33), 1, 16, 18–19.

Goodlad, J. I. (1984). *A place called school.* New York: McGraw-Hill.

Hunt, D. E. (1975). Person-environment interaction: A challenge found wanting before it was tried. *Review of Educational Research, 45*, 209–230.

Kemple, J. J., & Rock, J. L. (1996). *Career academies: Early implementation lessons from a 10-site evaluation.* New York: Manpower Demonstration Research Corporation.

Kemple, J. J., & Snipes, J. (2000). *Career academics: Impacts on students' engagement and performance in high school.* New York: Manpower Demonstration Research Corporation.

Lee, V. E., & Bryk, A. S. (1988). A multilevel model of the social distribution of high school achievement. *Sociology of Education, 61*, 78–94.

Lee, V. E., & Bryk, A. S. (1989). Curriculum tracking as mediating the social distribution of high school achievement. *Sociology of Education, 62*, 172–192.

Lee, V. E., Bryk, A. S., & Smith, J. B. (1993). The organization of effective secondary schools. In L. Darling-Hammond (Ed.), *Review of research in education* (Vol. 19, pp. 171–267). Washington, DC: American Educational Research Association.

Lee, V. E., Burkam, D. T., Chow-Hoy, T., Smerdon, B. A., & Geverdt, D. (1997). *High school curriculum structure: Effects on course-taking and achievement in mathematics for high school graduates.* Paper presented at the annual meeting of the American Sociological Association Annual Conference, Toronto.

Lee, V. E., Ready, D. D., & Johnson, D. J. (2001). The difficulty of identifying rare samples to study: The case of high schools divided into schools-within-schools. *Educational Evaluation and Policy Analysis, 23*(4), 365–379.

Lee, V. E., Smerdon, B. A., Alfeld-Liro, C., & Brown, S. L. (2000). Inside small and large high schools: Curriculum and social relations. *Educational Evaluation and Policy Analysis, 22*(2), 147–171.

Lee, V. E., & Smith, J. B. (1997). High school size: Which works best, and for whom? *Educational Evaluation and Policy Analysis, 19*(3), 205–227.

Lee, V. E., & Smith, J. (1999). Social support and achievement for young adolescents in Chicago: The role of school academic press. *American Educational Research Journal, 36*(4), 907–946.

McMullan, B. J. (1994). Charters and restructuring. In M. Fine (Ed.), *Chartering urban school reform: Reflections on public high schools in the midst of change* (pp. 63-77). New York: Teachers College Press.

McPartland, J. M., Legters, N., Jordan, W., & McDill, E. L. (1996). *The Talent Development High School: Early evidence of impact on school climate, attendance, and student promotion.* Baltimore: Center for Research on the Education of Students Placed At Risk, Johns Hopkins University.

Meier, D. (1995). *The power of their ideas: Lessons for American from a small school in Harlem.* Boston: Beacon Press.

Muncie, D. E., & McQuillan, P. J. (1996). *Reform and resistance in schools and classrooms: An ethnographic view of the Coalition of Essential Schools.* New Haven, CT: Yale University Press.

National Association of Secondary School Principals. (1996). *Breaking ranks: Changing an American institution.* Reston, VA: Author.

National Commission on Excellence in Education. (1983). *A Nation at Risk: The Imperative for Educational Reform.* Washington, DC: U.S. Government Printing Office.

Newmann, F. M. (1981). Reducing student alienation in high schools: Implications of theory. *Harvard Educational Review, 51*(4), 546–564.

Oakes, J. (1985). *Keeping track: How schools structure inequality.* New Haven, CT: Yale University Press.

Oxley, D. (1989, Spring). Smaller is better. *American Educator, 28-31*, 51–52.

Oxley, D. (1994). Organizing for responsiveness: The heterogeneous school community. In M. Wang & E. Gordon (Eds.), *Educational resilience in inner-city America: Challenges and prospects* (pp. 179-190). Hillsdale, NJ: Erlbaum.

Patton, M.Q. (1990). *Qualitative evaluation and research methods* (2nd ed.). Newbury Park, CA: Sage.

Powell, A. G., Farrar, E., & Cohen, D. K. (1985). *The shopping mall high school: Winners and losers in the educational market place.* Boston: Houghton Mifflin.

Raywid, M.A. (1995). *The subschools/small schools movement: Taking stock.* Madison: University of Wisconsin, Center on the Organization and Restructuring of Schools.

Schoggen, P., & Schoggen, M. (1988). Student voluntary participation and high school size. *Journal of Educational Research, 81*(5), 288–293.

Siskin, L. S. (1994). *Realms of knowledge: Academic departments in secondary schools.* Washington, DC: Falmer Press.

Sizer, T. R. (1992). *Horace's school: Redesigning the American high school.* Boston: Houghton Mifflin.

Sizer, T. R. (1984). *Horace's compromise: The dilemma of the American high school.* Boston: Houghton Mifflin.

Steinberg, L. (1990). Interdependence in the family; Autonomy, conflict and harmony in the parent-adolescent relationship. In S. S. Feldman & G. R. Elliot

(Eds.), *At the threshold: The developing adolescent* (pp. 255–276). Cambridge, MA: Harvard University Press.

Stern, D., Raby, M., & Dayton, C. (1992). *Career academies: Partnerships for reconstructing American high schools*. San Francisco: Jossey-Bass.

Stevenson, D. L., & Barker, D. P. (1987). The family-school relationship and the child's school performance. *Child Development, 58,* 1348–1357.

Tyack, D., & Cuban, L. (1995). *Tinkering toward utopia: A century of public school reform*. Cambridge, MA: Harvard University Press.

U.S. Department of Education. (2001). *Smaller learning communities: Overview.* Retrieved from: http://www.ed.gov/offices/OESE/SLCP/overview.html.

Useem, E. L. (1992). Middle school and math groups: Parents' involvement in children's placement. *Sociology of Education, 65,* 263–279.

Weber, M. (1978). *Economy and society.* Berkeley: University of California Press. (Original work published 1922)

CHAPTER 9

BRIDGING SOCIAL AND ACADEMIC IDENTITIES

Peer Relations, Friendship, and Educational Experiences

Donna Eder and Janice McCabe

Friends and peers play an important role in adolescents' school experiences. In fact, many youth like to attend school mainly because of the opportunity to spend time with their friends. But do these valued experiences with friends hinder or support their academic achievements? What structural factors and what processes are in place in schools to reinforce or reduce academic identities through friendship and peer relations? These questions have been raised and researched from several different perspectives over the past several decades, with increasingly complex findings.

This chapter begins with an examination of the extent to which certain social identities (athlete, club member, prep, etc.) compete with academic identities for youth today. We begin by addressing Coleman's (1961) research showing that social values compete with academic ones. We discuss how this perspective does not allow for the possibility of social roles complementing academic roles. Also, as school cultures have become

Educating Adolescents: Challenges and Strategies, 207–236
Copyright © 2004 by Information Age Publishing
All rights of reproduction in any form reserved.

increasingly diverse, more opportunities are available for today's youth to express both social and academic identities.

We then turn to an examination of the relationship between extracurricular activities and academic identities. We present research showing that a strong link exists between extracurricular involvement and academic performance, even when controlling for initial levels of achievement. In a few cases these activities do appear to detract from academic achievement, especially certain athletic activities for black and white males.

We then turn to a broader concern: that social class, race, and other background characteristics result in social identities that compete with academic ones, particularly for certain students of color and certain working-class students. We illustrate the ways in which school practices such as curriculum tracking and certain school countercultures contribute to a gap between peers' norms and school-oriented ones. At the same time, we show how some school and peer contexts help bridge this cultural gap for many students, helping them to develop a tolerance for contradictions and an ability to juggle different cultures.

Finally, we look at the experiences of college students where gender identities emerge as a new factor that can compete with academic ones for females. We also revisit the issue of social relations and identities more generally, and the degree to which college student subcultures support or detract from academic experiences. The chapter concludes with a discussion of school practices at the secondary level that promote a gap between peer norms and academic ones as well as those practices that help bridge this gap. The implications for college environments as well as suggestions for future research at each level of schooling will follow.

SOCIAL IDENTITIES AND ACADEMIC IDENTITIES

Youth hold multiple identities as family members, students, and members of peer groups as well as members of social categories like gender and race. By identity, we mean the self-characterizations and meanings individuals make based on the structural features of group memberships, roles, and categories (Stryker, 1980) and also the meanings that others attach to the self based on a person's character traits (Goffman, 1963). Social identities reflect how people are differentially located in society; each individual reflects multiple identities—those related to a youth's various roles as well as to his/her social class, race/ethnicity, gender, age, and sexual preference. These roles and group memberships can have varying degrees of salience by both the self and others. Likewise, identities related to social categories like social class and race can vary in their degree of salience (Stryker, 1980).

Identities are shaped by both structure and agency and may differ according to the social context. For this chapter we are concerned primarily with social identities related to school context. These consist not only of roles and group memberships such as student, athlete, band member, cheerleader, and peer group member, but also social class, race, and gender for many students. Often, school-based peer groups are formed around social class, racial, and gender identities, and some students find the norms related to one or more of these social categories to be relevant to embracing or rejecting the roles of student and academic leader.

One of the first studies to identify an adolescent culture was Coleman's (1961) study of adolescent values. In this study he portrayed adolescents' value of social success as being in competition with their value of academic success. At that point in time, adolescents placed more importance on being remembered as a star athlete or leader of social activities than on being remembered as a brilliant student. Later studies of European schools suggested that the presence of extracurricular activities in American schools might be responsible for some of this value conflict. For example, in their comparison of Danish and American youth, Kandel and Lesser (1972) found that leading crowds were less prominent in Danish high schools that did not offer extracurricular activities. Also, Danish youth were more likely to want to be remembered as being brilliant students than were the American youth in their study. Schools that offer opportunities to develop certain identities such as athlete and cheerleader might be promoting a status system that places more value on social than academic success.

Although Coleman (1961) portrayed these values as being in conflict, more recent research provides a much more complex view of the relationship between social and academic identities. Through the review of this research we see that for many students, involvement in extracurricular roles enhances their academic performance rather than detracts from it. Involvement in these activities may lead to more contact with academically oriented peers and greater commitment to the school culture. Even though current status systems in American schools often continue to place more emphasis on social roles than on academic ones, many bright students use their involvement in these social activities to gain peer acceptance and admiration, while simultaneously excelling in their academic roles (Brown, Morey, & Kinney, 1995).

When Coleman conducted his research in the 1950s, adolescent culture was quite homogenous. In the decades that followed, studies began to show several leading crowds within the same school (Cusick, 1973; Larkin, 1979). Today, adolescent school cultures are even more diverse, allowing students to have a greater choice of identities, including that of "brain." These multiple and more fragmented subcultural groups do not lend themselves to dichotomous identities such as social versus academic or pro-school versus anti-school and thus allow academic leaders to coexist as one of many subcultures (Kipnis, 2001).

Although early research examined extracurricular roles as the main type of social identity in schools, studies that followed began to explore the impact of social class, race, and gender as they interact to influence students' academic identities. Again, some of the early studies portrayed uniform effects of these social identities such as Willis's (1981) study of male working-class youths' resistance to school culture and Fordham's (1996) study of black youths' anti-school culture. However, much of the research published in the past decade has stressed the importance of school and community contexts as well as variation across peer groups within the same school. As we show later in this chapter, the relationship between social and academic identities is becoming increasingly complex.

EXTRACURRICULAR ACTIVITIES AND ACADEMIC IDENTITIES

For many students, extracurricular activities are central for forming friendships (Amit-Talai, 1995), and there is considerable support for the link between academic and social experiences in studies of the relationship between extracurricular involvement and academic success. Although earlier research attributed the high correlation between extracurriculars and achievement to the effect of these activities on achievement, more recent studies have identified a strong selection bias in which bright students are more likely to participate in extracurricular activities (Quiroz, Flores-Gonzalez, & Frank, 1996). This selection bias, however, is also evidence for the existence of a strong link between extracurricular involvement and academic achievement.

Additional research has carefully controlled for students' earlier academic performance in order to see which, if any, extracurricular activities contribute to an increase in academic performance. The theoretical frameworks behind these studies point to the importance of associating with peers who support academics as well as developing positive attitudes about leadership and competition (especially among girls) through involvement in various clubs, interest groups, and athletic teams. In addition, extracurricular involvements are believed to lead to more contact with teachers, which can benefit both students' actual achievement as well as their course grades.

Eccles and Barber (1999) found that all of the extracurricular activities they studied increased students' GPA, controlling for previous achievement. These included academic clubs, performing arts, team sports, and other school activities (student council, pep club, cheerleading). They found the highest rates of participation for boys to be in team sports (67%) while girls preferred both sports (46%) and performing arts (43%). A small but significant group of both boys and girls participated in academic clubs (11% and 17%, respectively).

Broh (2002) also found that many extracurricular activities boost students' grades and test performances. He differentiated between interscholastic sports and intramural sports, finding the former to benefit grades in mathematics and English as well as mathematics test scores and the latter to decrease grades as well as reading test scores. He also differentiated between music and drama within the performing arts, finding music to have a slightly more positive influence. Participation in music benefited both mathematics and English grades as well as mathematics test scores, while drama benefited English grades and reading test scores. Other extracurricular activities, such as student council and yearbook/newspaper activities, benefited students' grades but not their test performance. The only activity besides intramural sports to negatively influence students' grades was vocational clubs.

In her study of high school sophomores, Dagaz (2004) focused on changes in reading and science achievement as a result of extracurricular involvement. She found that student government, drama, and academic clubs increased reading and science test scores (controlling for eighth-grade scores) with academic clubs having the strongest effect. Some activities, such as student government, had more influence on females from lower socioeconomic classes than those from higher social classes, while drama was more beneficial for females in higher social classes. For males, student government was more influential for those from higher social classes than from lower social classes, suggesting important gender as well as social class differences. The impact of sports on changes in achievement was much smaller and varied depending on gender, social class, and type of sport with more negative effects for lower-class students than for those in higher social classes.

In his ethnographic study of high school debate teams, Fine (2001) suggested that debate encourages the development of many educational and life skills such as critical thinking, research, analysis, organization, citizenship, and self-confidence. However, the effect that participation in debate, particularly competitive high school debate, has on grades is potentially contradictory. While the debaters he studied are in the top 10% of their high school class, it is unclear whether this relationship is causal or merely correlational. Despite the many benefits of debate, the intense time commitment preparing for and attending tournaments can lower grades for some students, particularly in their least favorite classes. Friends and peers also play an important role in adolescents' experiences of debate. Many students join debate with friends and once in debate form other close ties, the relationship with their debate partner being the most significant. Within the status system of the school, debate may be a high-status or a low-status activity depending on the social arrangements of the school. Debate is central to the status system at some schools, particularly those with a long history of debate and successful debate teams. In contrast, students at other schools see debate as a stigmatized activity and debaters as "geeks" and social outsiders.

Studies that focus just on athletic teams have led to a complicated portrayal of the influence of sports on achievement. Comparing the influence of sports on white and black students, Eitle and Eitle (2002) found that although football has a positive influence on grades for whites, it has a negative influence for blacks. Furthermore, certain sports like football and basketball are negatively associated with mathematics and reading achievement for both blacks and whites.

Hanson and Krause (1998) found that sports involvement has a different effect on achievement, depending on students' gender and race. When they examined the relationship between sophomores' sports involvement and academic achievement in the 1980s (not controlling for earlier achievement), they found sports to negatively relate to mathematics and science achievement for males, whereas having a positive correlation with girls' enrollment in mathematics and science classes. In the senior year, when they were able to control for earlier achievement, they found no effect of sports on males' achievement or enrollment in mathematics and science classes, whereas varsity sports continued to have a positive effect on girls' enrollment. However, sports participation was more important for white females and those from higher social classes, whereas it had a negative influence on black females. In a more recent study of women involved in sports in the 1990s, even the effect of varsity sports on females is mixed, enhancing science achievement while decreasing mathematics achievement (Hanson & Krauss, 1999).

Taken together these findings suggest that for the most part there is a positive relationship between extracurricular involvement and academic performance. In some cases the involvement actually enhances performance in grades or on test scores. Researchers have documented that one intervening link in this process is an exposure to a higher level of peer support for academics in many extracurricular activities (Lamborn, Brown, Mounts, & Steinberg, 1992). In addition, females in particular may benefit by gaining greater comfort with a competitive atmosphere (Hanson & Krauss, 1998). At the same time, certain sports and clubs might expose students to an anti-school culture, as some research has found the level of peer support for academics to be lower in varsity sports (Lamborn et al., 1992). In addition, more demanding varsity sports can distract students from academics, making them too tired or nervous to concentrate (Hanson & Krauss, 1999; Lamborn et al., 1992). Yet, these processes are clearly influenced by students' gender and race as well as by the particular extracurricular activity.

TRACKING, FRIENDSHIP, AND SCHOOL COUNTERCULTURES

A broader concern regarding peers and achievement is related to the role of social class and race. To understand this role we first examine another school arrangement that strongly influences students' friendships—curriculum tracking. Although extracurriculars is one educational site where adolescents spend time with peers who often reinforce academic identities, other peer groups within schools may denigrate academic achievement. Tracking operates in many schools to create academically homogenous peer and friendship groups that can reinforce anti-academic attitudes. Most research findings suggest that tracking leads to academic achievement among upper-track students by surrounding them with highly motivated peers and effective teachers (Gamoran & Mare, 1989), whereas it discourages lower-track students and increases disengagment (Oakes, 1985).

Tracking influences peer relations because students tend to form friendships with others in the same track (Crosnoe, 2002; Eckert, 1989; Hallinan & Williams, 1989; Hargreaves, 1967; Hauser, Sewell, & Alwin, 1976; Karweit, 1983). High-achieving students may benefit from being surrounded by other high-achieving students who may also value academics. In addition, low-track students may suffer because their peers devalue academics or they may see themselves as anti-academic because of the label applied to students in low-track classrooms.

Tracking tends to divide and marginalize students as it separates them into tracks by linguistic ability, race, and socioeconomic status, as well as by academic ability (Brantlinger, 1993; Davidson, 1996; Oakes, 1985). The impact on identity may differ according to whether there is a rigid tracking system or one with more mobility between tracks (Gamoran, 1992). Tracking structures the opportunities for peer association and the nature of peer relations within the school; however, its influence is determined by the scope of tracking, and opportunities for—and perceived value of—peer interaction across curricular tracks (Karweit & Hansell, 1983).

Moreover, many students feel uncomfortable in classrooms dominated by racially/ethnically diverse students, an effect often attributed to academic tracking (Davidson, 1996). Self-selection of students into tracks also plays a role in creating and maintaining these divisions. Because they feel like "outsiders" in the higher tracks, minority students often avoid them, thereby limiting their future educational and occupational opportunities. Students may choose to remain in "easy" courses because they do not want to face the discomfort of entering an environment where their peers see them as different (Davidson, 1996). However, some findings suggest that minority students may be less likely to avoid the higher tracks if they have a peer group of students with similar experiences and identities in the higher track, such as the group of high-achieving lower-class Mexican American girls in Bettie's (2003) study.

Tracking, of course, is a complex process. In this review, we highlight where it may be problematic. Furthermore, the solutions to the problems with tracking are not obvious. If tracking were eliminated, this may cause other problems for students; therefore, a better solution may be a modified (de)tracking program, such as the Advancement Via Individual Determination (AVID) program studied by Mehan, Hubbard, and Villanueva (1994), which we discuss later.

Students identify academic divisions, such as those caused by tracking, as contributing to the formation of peer groups and subcultures, through separating students into these groups and defining them as academically and socially different as well as hierarchically arranged (Davidson, 1996). Students construct social identities within peer subcultures and may find them to be an alternate source of self-esteem to school success or a way to support social and school identities (Bettie, 2002; Gotto, 1997; MacLeod, 1987; Mehan et al., 1994; Proweller, 1998). Tracking affects peer relations through structuring the opportunities for and settings of peer interaction, although this is mediated by other factors such as student subcultures and extracurricular activities.

Tracking often leads to the formation of school countercultures (sometimes referred to as subcultures of resistance or oppositional subcultures). Kipnis (2001) has stressed the need to clarify the difference between school countercultures and other peer subcultures that may have aspects of resisting adult authority but are less critical of schooling overall. Unlike other subcultures, countercultures include a rejection of academic norms and values, are critical of the reproduction of societal inequalities, and express identity in critical modes.

The most commonly referenced counterculture is that found by Willis (1981) among working-class white males in Britain. The "lads" created identities in opposition to other, more school-identified peers, whom they labeled "ear'oles." They tried to undermine school authority and rebelled openly through their delinquency, truancy, and direct opposition to teachers. In addition, they were critical of schooling as it reproduces social class differences and saw no other option for themselves than continuing the factory jobs that their parents held. MacLeod (1987) found a similar counterculture among the white lower-class males that he studied in which their peer group ("the hallway hangers") valued toughness and rebellion over academic achievement and school involvement.

Countercultures have also been tied to issues of racial inequality. In Fordham's (1996) study, the black anti-school culture influenced a wide range of students, not just one clique. Like the "lads," students in this school were critical of schooling. They saw schooling as an institution that perpetuates racial inequality and equated school achievement with whiteness. Their rebellion took the form of using Black English, being silent, and ridiculing peers who did not conform to the anti-school norms. Valenzuela (1999) found a similarly strong counterculture in her study of Mexican Americans who valued education, but felt that the school they attended "subtracted" from their cultural experience and values rather than enhancing them. These peer norms led to many students in the school resisting academic roles in both direct and subtle ways, equating achievement with being "geeky." For other youth, racial and class identities are so intertwined that oppositional behaviors included those that opposed middle-class as well as white norms, such as loud talking, impolite behavior, and distinct modes of dress (Cousins, 1999).

Finally, studies of working-class girls have found peer groups that have particular ways of expressing opposition to school involving an exaggerated femininity and focus on romance. Some working-class females perceive the school's message as threatening to their future roles and use romance to escape from the dominant school culture (Christian-Smith, 1990; Gilbert & Taylor, 1991). In so doing, they assert their physical maturity, sexuality, and exaggerated femininity (McRobbie, 1978). Bettie (2003) also found that Mexican American working-class girls adopt a more sexual stance than the prep girls in their school, but notes that these girls are more interested in portraying an adult status as an alternative to prep-defined status and do not focus on romance or on males as a source of security. In summary, research findings suggest that tracking works through the peer group to structure peer relations, school countercultures, subcultures, and friendships.

RACIAL IDENTITY, ACADEMIC PERFORMANCE, AND SCHOOL AND PEER CONTEXTS

Although school countercultures have been linked to issues of class and race, many researchers have also stressed that not all students of color participate in such countercultures. Identities are not only racial in nature, but they occur in various school and community contexts (Hemmings, 1998; Lee, 1996; Phelan & Davidson, 1993; Phelan, Davidson, & Cao, 1998). Thus, students of color may turn to many strategies, not just oppositional ones, depending on their schools' structure and practices, programs in their community, their families, and their peers.

Hemmings's (1998) in-depth study of three black students highlights the critical roles that the type of school and practices within schools play along with family and peer factors in shaping students' academic identities. The schools these students attended varied in the extent to which European American traditions, attitudes, and dialect were the norm and in the ethos regarding achievement. Two of the students attended a predominantly middle-class magnet school for college-bound students with little focus on black culture. They both attempted to embrace middle-class and academic norms, but with differing experiences. For Trevor, a student from a working-class background who joined the highest academic track, embracing academic norms led to tension at home as well as isolation from peers because this track was predominantly white. For Serena, a student from a middle-class family who joined a middle-level track, there was little tension with family values and she had many more black peers to socialize with in the middle track. Finally, Eliza's experience in a working-class school with a strong counterculture made it difficult for her to fully embrace academic norms and realize her academic potential.

Akom's (2003) study of black females in a low-income, primarily black urban school found that a community religious-based program was instrumental in helping black students develop a strong academic focus. The seven females interviewed, who were all members of the Nation of Islam, drew upon the beliefs and practices of Islam to maintain strong racial pride and a belief that education was central to developing themselves and their race. These students formed informal study groups based on those formally organized at their community temple, which allowed them to merge academic and racial identities. Likewise, Horvat and Lewis (2003) found that a community-based program that developed Young Black Scholars clubs in local schools helped to promote academic achievement in black peer groups. Horvat and Lewis also focused on the agency of these black youth and their ability to navigate the school peer culture, attributing peer criticism of "acting white" to immaturity, while at the same time cultivating relationships with other academically successful peers.

Another in-depth study examined the experiences of students from many different ethnic backgrounds, finding again that school structure and practices play important roles, as do family and peers (Phelan et al., 1998). For example, one Mexican American female saw her peer culture as being vastly different from the European American culture of her high school. When she tried to participate in the school culture these strong differences created so much anxiety and stress that she turned to her peer culture to avoid further stress. Another Mexican American felt her family and peers embraced different values than the middle-class school values of individual achievement, independence, and competition. She negotiated school life by playing one role in class and a different role with her peers who value solidarity and interdependence. Although she did very well when instruction was based on peer interaction, she had few opportunities to excel academically because there was little focus on interdependent work in the lower track that she was in.

In a study of a predominantly nonwhite high school, Valenzuela (1999) found that recent immigrants were more likely to express a pro-school attitude, as they were grateful to have opportunities not available to them in Mexico. Also, their connection with Mexican culture was strong as most were fluent in Spanish. On the other hand, Mexican Americans born in the United States felt the school subtracted from their culture by placing little emphasis on Mexican tradition and values. They felt separated from both mainstream and Mexican culture and were generally less academically oriented. Students in the one peer group of United States–born Hispanics that was academically oriented had all been members of the Spanish Club and thus had a shared opportunity to focus on Spanish language and Mexican culture. They were able to build an academic identity and see it as compatible with their Mexican, Spanish-speaking selves.

When Mexican Americans attend school with white students from a wide range of social class backgrounds, other dynamics emerge. While most of the middle-class girls in Bettie's (2003) study were part of the prep culture, one group of middle-class Mexican American girls "performed" a working-class style through their clothes and behavior, identifying the prep style as "acting white." However, unlike most of the Mexican American working-class peers in their "hardcore" subculture, they were in college tracks and performed well academically. Their involvement in a Chicano student movement organization allowed them to express their racial identity and align with other Mexican Americans while also doing well academically. For these girls "acting white" was limited to social behavior and did not include academic behavior. At the same time, there were a few working-class Mexican Americans who joined the prep style and performed well academically. Their involvement in leadership roles in various minority achievement programs and Mexican cultural and political school organizations helped them to be aware of racial issues while still having high academic aspirations. Bettie (2003) points to the importance of such programs and organizations in schools for both of these groups of students. She sees them as helping facilitate new strategies for students who cope not by abandoning their racial or academic identities, but by developing a tolerance for contradictions and an ability to juggle cultures.

While Asian American students are often thought to have a strong academic peer culture, a study by Lee (1996), which examined the variety of Asian American school experiences, shows that this is not always the case. She identified four groups among the 365 Asian students attending an academically oriented high school (the school itself was 18% Asian American, 35% black, and 45% white). One of the groups, the Asian New Wave, consisted primarily of working-class and poor students from China, Vietnam, and Cambodia. They generally were more concerned with peer acceptance than with achievement, believing that achievement often interfered with getting to know non-Asians. Because of the highly competitive atmosphere at this school, only the top track was considered smart and many students in the Asian New Wave refused to participate in an academic experience that made them feel like "dummies," opting to be "cool" instead. The most politically active of the four groups, the Asian Americans identified, combined a highly critical identity with high academic performance, indicating again that some students are very aware of racism and continue to do well in school.

All of these studies point to the fact that race and social class background do not necessarily place students in an anti-school culture. It appears that some aspects of schooling make it difficult for certain students of color, such as schooling that is heavily based on European American norms and traditions and competitive systems of tracking. Both factors may push students toward greater involvement with peers as a way to avoid stress and find other ways to establish positive social identities. It is also important to note that some groups of students are able to combine strong academic performance with critical social identities and beliefs, so that peer cultures can be both supportive of social equality and of academic achievement. Many of these students were aided by the existence of school programs that supported minority achievement or school organizations based on political or cultural activities related to ethnicity.

Alternative Schools, School Practices, and Peer Groups

Given the importance of school practices and structures in helping students to bridge gaps between academic and social identities, a wide range of alternatives should be considered to help more students bridge these gaps. More cooperative learning situations and less focus on competition among peers would be fundamental changes to the ways many schools organize learning (American Association of University Women, 1995; Eder, Evans, & Parker, 1995; Oakes, 1985, 1994; Thorne, 1993). Cooperative learning promotes academic and social learning and friendships among students (Cohen, 1986). Participating in cooperative rather than competitive tasks makes individuals more likely to form friendships (Deutsch, 1968) and leads to a deeper level of interaction (Slavin, 1983). Cooperative learning has been shown to increase students' friendships with students from other racial groups compared to traditional learning formats (Devries, Edwards, & Slavin, 1978; Slavin & Hansell, 1983). However, in groups, high-status students tend to interact more than low-status students and research findings suggest that peer interaction leads to increased learning (Cohen, 1984). Consequently, the achievement gap may widen if cooperative groupwork is used in a classroom without adherence to the principles of cooperative learning (Cohen, Lotan, Scarloss, & Arellano, 1999).

These principles include positive interdependence, promotive interaction, individual accountability, social skills, and group processing. For cooperative learning to be effective, the teacher must properly prepare the task, the groups, and the students. Because of inequalities in power and status among students, teachers should set up heterogenous groups (e.g., by ability level, race, class, and gender). Teachers must set up cooperative tasks for which students are each assigned a role and must ensure that all group members do their part of the work (i.e., positive interdependence) and encourage each other (i.e., promotive interaction). Teachers must instruct students on interpersonal and small-group skills and emphasize these skills throughout the cooperative tasks. Finally, students must be taught to reflect on the cooperative process (i.e., group processing). Cooperative learning is not achieved merely by placing students in groups and expecting them to work together.

Research shows that institutional arrangements and schooling practices can alter the focus on competition or cooperation among peers in schools, with heterogeneous school groupings often facilitating interaction among peers, particularly across racial groups. Damico and Sparks (1986) compared two middle schools, one in which students were stratified by grade and ability level and one in which the students were randomly assigned to learning teams that were diverse in terms of grade, ability, race, and gender. In the latter school, classroom instruction consisted of a combination of multitask, individual, and cooperative learning as compared to the use of a recitation format in the more traditional school. Whites in the traditionally structured school interacted less with blacks than they did in the school with mixed teams. In the mixed-team school, whites talked to blacks as much as they talked to other whites and had more cross-racial friendships.

In a study of a Mexican middle school, Levinson (1998) found fewer social divisions in peer groups than are typically found in schools in the

United States. Students in this school were assigned to *grupos escolar*, small groups of 36 to 45 students that were designed to be heterogeneous by academic ability, social class, ethnicity, and gender. The students stayed with these groups for 3 years for most of their classes as well as for both academic and extracurricular activities. In addition, the teachers continually spoke of the need to help other students academically and socially and in other ways emphasized the importance of group solidarity. While a few friendships formed around social class and ethnic backgrounds, most of the lasting friendships were formed in these small groups and transcended boundaries of social class and ethnicity. Levinson found that the culture of solidarity in the school created equality in the peer groups. However, Levinson also found that students who did not agree with the group (and the group norms of cooperation and equality) were stigmatized—for example, if a student did not share his or her homework with others, he or she may be subject to social control and stigmatized in the group. Still, there was an amazing amount of solidarity and a similar identification with the school among the students within a *grupo escolar* compared to that among students at most schools in the United States. This seems to be encouraged by the heterogeneous groupings and focus on solidarity in the school.

Having and creating personal relationships—rather than distant, bureaucratized, and depersonalized authoritarian relationships—with adults and mentors in schools also leads to a more positive pro-school identity (Davidson, 1996; Loutzenheiser, 2002). Having school meetings promotes students' identification with the school and feelings of being heard (Eder et al., 1995; Proweller, 1998). Peer tutoring is another practice that facilitates positive peer relations and student involvement in the school and classroom (Boocock, 1978; Epstein, 1983; Kinney, Christensen, Casillas, & Christensen, 1997). Classroom projects by groups of students bring peers together, particularly when students are involved in major decisions regarding the project and when it is based on their experiences and ideas (Kinney et al., 1997). Alternative school structures such as various forms of detracking also influence the ease with which peer groups facilitate students' academic identities. Mehan and colleagues (1994) describe the strategies of Latino and African American youth in AVID, a program aimed at untracking low-achieving, minority students with high test scores, which began in the San Diego City schools and extended to 148 other schools in California. Many Latino and African American students in AVID became academically successful without losing or compromising their ethnic identity by adopting a strategy of "accommodating without assimilating." Many AVID students created academically oriented peer groups and developed strategies to manage or balance dual identities, particularly those related to academics and neighborhood/

community. Students formed new friendships through AVID that supported their attempts to accommodate without assimilation. Collaboration was used as an instructional strategy during the special elective class for AVID students to encourage them to work together and help each other. These students developed a critical consciousness about both the structures producing inequality and discrimination in society and the power of their own agency. AVID increased rates of college enrollment among low-income students and those from ethnic groups underrepresented in college. The structure that AVID provided previously low-achieving students permitted them to achieve positive social as well as academic outcomes and facilitated the formation of academically oriented peer groups and friendships (Mehan et al., 1994).

Some schools have developed other programs that empower minority students to maintain their racial/ethnic identity while learning skills that will help them in their quest for upward mobility. For example, the Movimiento Estudiantil Chicano de Aztlan (MEChA), the Chicano student movement organization program, teaches upwardly mobile students the skills and cultural resources they need to attend college while also upholding these students' Mexican heritage (Bettie, 2003). The Spanish Club in another school served a similar purpose by providing students an opportunity to focus on Spanish language and Mexican culture. They were able to build an academic identity that they viewed as compatible with their ethnic selves (Valenzuela, 1999). Finally, an innovative program at a Canadian school brings together 10–15 students and a teacher to discuss social issues and personal interests and concerns for social studies credit. As members of Positive Peer Culture, students are asked to respect cultural diversity and to challenge racism and sexism. This program supports positive racial identities while also empowering students to see school achievement as possible and positive (Yon, 2000).

In addition to altering school practices and creating new programs, schools can cultivate positive and inclusive peer structures through transforming the structure, mission, and identity of entire schools. Schools with specific missions and clear school identities, such as magnet schools, may help students form strong social ties and better academic outcomes. Gamoran (1996) found that social relationships were stronger in magnet schools than in comprehensive public schools, Catholic schools, and secular private schools. Furthermore, he attributed the higher academic outcomes of students in magnet schools to strong social relationships. More research is needed to determine how the type of instructional approach (e.g., the Montessori method or open classrooms) and subject (e.g., performing arts or science and mathematics) matter for students' friendships and identities.

Some alternative schools, designed to foster a reconnection to school, emphasize the school's—and particularly the teachers'—flexibility and caring for students' academic and nonacademic concerns (Loutzenheiser, 2002). In the school studied, students' peers and teachers were accepting of differences between students. For example, a Native American student, Guinevere, performed a traditional dance for students at the school and felt "different—but in a positive sense" (Loutzenheiser, 2002, p. 457). Special events at school and class projects create a school and peer environment that affirms students' racial/ethnic identities (Kinney et al., 1997; Loutzenheiser, 2002). In a study of an alternative school for adolescents who had been expelled or suspended or who dropped out of school, students felt connected to this alternative school and attributed their feelings partly to the teachers' caring and respect toward students (Kinney et al., 1997). Certain practices used in alternative schools, such as high levels of student participation in classrooms, also may be effective in more traditional school structures.

Alternative school programs and practices such as these can provide an environment in which students as well as adults can initiate a pro-academic peer culture. Yon (2000) found that some of the students who attend the Canadian high school with programs supporting positive peer cultures and racial identities formed their own informal group called the African Queens based on their association in a dance performance for African History Month. Their goal, similar to that of the Positive Peer Culture program, was to raise awareness and provide mutual support related to issues of race and gender. Through lunchtime meetings, they helped each other with schoolwork, which led to an improvement in their academic performance.

Other students have also taken an active role in facilitating this bridging of worlds. For example, Marbella Sanchez purposefully selected friends who supported both the academic and ethnic aspects of her identity (Davidson, 1996). She is an interesting case study because she merges a positive orientation to Mexico with a belief in working hard to do well in school and with a resistance to the school's pressure to assimilate ethnically—for example, she and her friends spoke only Spanish at school on Tuesdays and Thursdays. Marbella spoke often of the importance of schooling to "become someone" and this high regard is shared by her peer group—they have parties every 6 weeks, in accordance with school grading quarters, and only those peers with all A's and B's are allowed to attend. Although Marbella successfully fought her placement in basic mathematics, she often felt powerless to challenge the school's tracking by linguistic ability, which placed her in courses with low expectations (Davidson, 1996).

In yet another study, it is clear that a desire to create greater acceptance of difference brings some students together in what Hemmings (2000) has referred to as a "post-oppositional" subculture. The racially mixed peer group that she studied also included students who were gay, who were academically oriented, and who were single parents. Many had previously had difficulty with school and had been drawn to anti-school values, which were prevalent in this racially diverse working-class school. The leader of this group served as a "cultural therapist," helping her friends accept their unique identities and promoting respect for differences in general. When the black students in this group were labeled by others for "acting white," they responded by advocating the value of interaction across differences. Taken together, these studies show that student leaders as well as adult leaders can take the initiative in creating conditions that facilitate the formation of pro-academic peer cultures.

FRIENDS, PEERS, AND COLLEGE LIFE

The potential for conflict between academic and social concerns does not disappear with the transition from secondary school to college. The college environment, particularly dormitory life, differs from that in earlier levels of schooling. College students spend an increased amount of time with peers, as most traditional college students live with peers rather than with family. These changes in context influence peer relations, friendships, and the balance between academic and social identities. One of the potentially conflicting "multiple worlds" of younger adolescents, that of family life, seems to recede into the background in college, leaving academic life and individual social life to compete for older adolescents' time and identity.

In his ethnography of college life, Moffatt (1989) asserts that the college experience is as much about "social learning" as academic growth. Moffatt describes how students choose courses, their hierarchy of majors, and their academic practices. His observations and interviews suggest that friends help with academic matters—they may discuss poems written for class, form a study group, or advise friends on which classes to take and avoid. Moffatt states that anti-intellectual identities do exist among Rutgers students, but that most students have a "higher life of the mind in college." At the same time, he describes academics as important, but not central, to college life for most students. Several exceptionally academically oriented students adjust to the college environment by forming peer groups of similarly oriented students who they met through their participation in the honors program.

At earlier levels of education, peer relations are shaped by the existence of school subcultures and countercultures that are oppositional to school achievement (Kipnis, 2001; Willis, 1981; Yu, 1996). In her historical examination of undergraduate cultures, Horowitz (1987) identifies a trend toward increased blending of student subcultures. She identifies three "ideal types" of college students—college men and women, outsiders, and rebels—which have different relationships to the academic and social aspects of college. College men and women are invested in the social and are largely opposed to academic and professorial culture, whereas the outsiders, also referred to as "grinds," are invested in the academic and are outside the social culture of college. Many undergraduates are mixtures of these groups rather than pure ideal types. Still, Horowitz's typology, like that of others (e.g., Astin, 1993; Clark & Trow, 1966; Kuh, Hu, & Vesper, 2000), points to potential connections between peer relations and academics in undergraduates' lives.

Ethnographic research of men's collegiate basketball suggests that student-athletes are socialized to the norms regarding appropriate academic effort and involvement within and by the peer group (Adler & Adler, 1991). Furthermore, cliques on the basketball team are differentially invested in the social, athletic, and academic aspects of college life. Some peer groups are more invested in the social role (such as the "bad niggas"), some are more into the academic role (such as the squares—"L-7s"), while still others are more committed to the athletic role (such as the "candy-asses") (Adler & Adler, 1991).

Some research findings on student clubs and organizations illustrate how they shape the role of friends and peers in students' college experiences. McCannon and Bennett (1996) identified meeting peers with similar interests as among the top reasons for college students joining a student club or organization related to their major. In his research on African American students' participation in African American student organizations at a predominantly white university, Guiffrida (2003) found that most students value their participation in these organizations because they feel "comfortable" interacting with black peers in a predominantly black environment. Handler (1995) describes how joining a sorority structures women's relationships with other women, both within and outside of their sorority, and with men. The division between the academic and social aspects of college life appears strong in many student groups and organizations such as sororities. Indeed, academics are rarely mentioned in research on sorority and fraternity life. One of the few references discusses the value of academics versus social life in sorority life through contrasting the celebrations for milestones in romantic relationships—candlelight ceremonies when a sister is lavaliered as well as when she is given a fraternity pin, a promise ring, and an engagement ring—to the award for the sister with the highest grade point average—a bag of potato chips (Berkowitz & Padavic, 1999).

Although more women than men currently attend postsecondary education, gender norms emerge in college life as a factor influencing some young women's academic identities. As previously mentioned, research on younger working-class girls' peer groups suggests that these girls perform an exaggerated femininity and embrace romance while attempting to escape academics. Among older adolescents, this focus on romance rather than academics seems to be no longer linked to class background. Research on the peer cultures of some college women show that they may develop a "culture of romance" (Holland & Eisenhart, 1990) or a "culture of motherhood" (Stone & McKee, 2000), both of which are, at least somewhat, oppositional to school achievement.

In their study of undergraduate women at two southern universities, one predominantly black and one predominantly white, Holland and Eisenhart (1990) found that young women did not value academics; peers did not care whether women had serious career plans or excelled in classes. Holland and Eisenhart compare the women in their study to Horowitz's (1987) college men and women who value romantic relationships and identify more with peer culture than academics. About half of the young women in their study were majoring in mathematics- and science-related fields and all were high achievers in high school and were committed to pursuing a career in the future. In college these young women turned their interests and identity from schoolwork to romance.

Nearly all of the women in this study ended up with marginalized career and academic identities, and those who expressed resistance did so privately rather than publicly (Holland & Eisenhart, 1990). Women helped one another fare as well as possible on the "sexual auction block," but rarely formed deep bonds with other women and rarely discussed academic matters with friends. Peer culture at the predominantly black university viewed self-reliance and economic independence as essential and saw men both as potential economic providers and a financial drain, but those at the predominantly white university did not plan for economic independence and expected a husband who would be the primary breadwinner. Regardless of this difference, however, most ended up with fewer credentials and training, lower academic and career achievement, and less identification with their career than they expected.

Research at other universities shows a somewhat different, but not necessarily brighter, picture for undergraduate women. Based on research at a university in the Northwest United States, Stone and McKee (2000) argue that undergraduate women position themselves differently for careers, marriage, and parenthood than do undergraduate men. Women and men both discussed their immediate future as career oriented, but women's discussions of future motherhood implied that motherhood is incompatible with a career. They found that the "culture of motherhood" drew women away from career aspirations, although not necessarily from immediate academic achievement.

A recent study of Duke University undergraduates found peer culture characterized by superficial and unsupportive relationships for many students and revolving around heterosociability. Many young women struggle to conform to both strict norms of femininity and high standards of academic achievement (Roth, 2003). These two intense pressures characterize the everyday lives of many young women at Duke. Young women described the expectation that one be "smart, accomplished, fit, beautiful and popular, and that all this would happen without visible effort," what one sophomore termed, "effortless perfection" (Roth, 2003, p. 12). Young men also noted pressure regarding clothing and body ideals, but felt fewer consequences than did women when they violated these norms.

In most of these studies, peer cultures shape academic and social life and friendship is separated from academic life. If friends are discussed in relation to academics, they are often seen as a distraction or a dereliction of student duties. In contrast, Martinez Aleman (1997) argues for the intellectual and academic value of female friends for college women. She argues that such relationships are "risk-free testing sites" where students try out ideas with their female friends in a safe environment rather than in the classroom, which she argues is a "chilly climate" for women (see Hall, 1982). More recent research at the postsecondary level has noted complexities in the "chilly climate" for women—variations by subject or discipline, teaching style, teacher's gender, and/or the gender ratio of students in the class (e.g., Canada & Pringle, 1995; Constantinople, Cornelius, & Gray, 1988; Crawford & MacLeod, 1990).

Female friendships support students' ideas and function as sources of information, advice, and diverse perspectives because they have fewer obstacles to self-expression and learning than do classroom settings (Martinez Aleman, 1997). However, the primary purpose of female friendships differs for white students and students of color; women of color sought out these relationships to develop positive racial/ethnic identities as well as to give and receive academic encouragement and support, whereas white women sought out these relationships as a respite from academic pressures (Martinez Aleman, 2000). With their female friends, white women practice ideas they may later express in class discussions, papers, or projects. Female friendships for women of color are sites for discussions of racism and ethnocentricity in the classroom and for the production of a positive racial/ethnic identity. The small enrollment of women of color at this predominantly white liberal arts college, however, limits the friendship choices for women of color. Research with female African

American community college students shows that these women valued relationships that supported their academic performance and generally ignored unsupportive friends (Shaw & Coleman, 2000). In contrast to other research with traditional students at 4-year colleges and universities, these students discarded friendships they perceived to get in the way of educational success and sought new friendships with students with similar educational experiences and goals. This illustrates how institutional structure and practice influences college students' experiences of their friendships, specifically the role of friendships in academic life, and does so differently according to a student's race, gender, and the context of the college or university.

SCHOOL PRACTICES THAT INCREASE THE GAP BETWEEN FRIENDS AND ACADEMICS

The research examined so far offers us further insight into which school practices currently push students toward their peer culture and away from academic goals. In the area of extracurricular activities, we have shown that most extracurricular involvements in high school are compatible with academic goals. One possible exception would be those that involve intense competition in nonacademic areas such as varsity sports. At this point in time, the academic achievement of male students is somewhat more likely to be hurt by participation in highly competitive sports than females', although this could change as women's sports become increasingly competitive. In schools where this is the case, sports can distract from academics by causing students to be too tired or too nervous to concentrate, or by taking too much time away from academic work.

Intense competition in academic areas can also increase the gap between friends and academics. We were surprised to see that this can be a problem even in academically oriented schools where the top track is often seen as the "smart" one, leading students who fail to make it into the top track to identify themselves as "dummies." For some of them, it was easier to turn to their friends as a top priority and seek "coolness" instead of "smartness." When schools create environments in which only a few can get self-esteem through school success, more students will turn to peers for their source of self-esteem.

We also identified other problems with the practice of curriculum tracking. In both academically oriented high schools and regular schools, minority students were found to opt out of the highest track in order to keep from being socially isolated. Tracking creates additional divisions among students, making it difficult for many minority students to maintain both racial and academic identities. Low tracks often provide a context for a school counterculture where students see schools as reproducing race and class differences rather than providing meaningful educational experiences. These countercultures help students to develop alternative sources of self-esteem, but take them further away from academic goals.

Yet another problematic school practice is the focus on European American tradition, especially in schools with students from other traditions (such as Asian American or African American). When schools emphasize European American history, norms, and values, some non-white students experience so much stress from the cultural gap that they turn to their peers to restore a sense of security and belonging. For other students, it is difficult to do well academically when the focus is primarily on individualism rather than on cooperation or solidarity—values of their family and peers. Finally, this focus on the mainstream norms and values can further strengthen school countercultures as students see schooling as irrelevant to their cultural identity and background.

SCHOOL PRACTICES THAT SUPPORT THE RELATIONSHIP BETWEEN FRIENDS AND ACADEMICS

There are implications from our review of current research for increasing and strengthening practices that support the link between peers and academics. First, offering a wide variety of extracurricular activities, as occurs in most high schools today, increases the number of multiple and fragmented subcultures. As Kipnis (2001) notes, this breaks down the dichotomous peer cultures of pro- versus anti-school or social versus academic of Coleman's era. We see the growing number of academic clubs as being especially important for providing a social niche for "brains" who now coexist as one subculture among many.

Although high schools have increasingly diverse subcultures, many middle schools continue to have dichotomous subcultures, limiting students' options for positive social identities as well as positive academic identities (Brown et al., 1995; Eder et al., 1995). This is in part due to the limited number of extracurricular activities in most middle schools. While high school students are often allowed to form their own after-school clubs and organizations, this is seldom the case at the middle-school level where athletics, cheerleading, and sometimes music activities are all that are available. A more diverse range of extracurricular programs in middle school—either teacher or student organized—would help increase the range of subcultures and provide more support for academic identities.

We also found that specific clubs at the high school level were important for fostering a sense of ethnic identity and culture. In some cases, Spanish Clubs served this purpose while in other cases it was served by clubs that sponsored school-wide activities such as a Dance Club performing for African History Month. More clubs and organizations of this type are needed in high schools with students of color to reduce the gap that often exists between their ethnic and school identities. Because little evidence for such clubs at the middle school level exists, this would also be a valuable place to introduce such clubs and school-wide cultural events.

Our review also has important implications for academic practices at the secondary level of schooling. Some studies of middle schools found that heterogenous grouping served to break down racial and social class barriers. This practice is stronger if it is also part of a homeroom concept with an overall emphasis on group solidarity or if it is combined with cooperative learning of any type. We have less evidence of its success at the high school level, but it seems to be an appropriate practice for academically oriented high schools where there is less variance in ability. It could then reduce the social isolation so often felt by nonwhite students, who currently may reduce their academic goals by avoiding the top track.

In schools that do have curriculum tracking, greater use of cooperative learning within classrooms could strengthen the link between peers and academics. Any time students have structured opportunities to learn with peers, schools are reinforcing the importance and acceptability of the relationship between friends and academics. It is a further advantage for students who perform better in small-group environments, either because it fits their cultural values or because it is more supportive of their learning styles. Students for whom English is a second language also benefit from such groups when some of the peer instruction occurs in their native language (Goldstein, 2003). In such cases, peer culture can serve as a form of cultural capital to students who lack other forms of cultural resources.

Academic support groups are needed at all levels of curriculum tracking. Programs such as AVID have been found to be particularly important for minority students in higher tracks where the support group helps to create a new peer culture that supports academic achievement (Mehan et al., 1994). However, students at all levels of tracking might benefit from the existence of such peer support and peer mentoring programs.

Schools can also enhance the link between friends and academics through various alternative social practices. Programs like the Positive Peer Culture support groups address issues of racism, sexism, and other peer concerns, providing a model for ways in which peers can support racial, gender, and other social identities within the school environment. Student activist groups can also strengthen ethnic identities and create socially critical awareness. Chicano student organizations were key in allowing some students to perform well academically while keeping a strong ethnic profile in the school. Finally, programs that have been found to be successful in alternative schools, such as student participation in decision making, can be transferred to mainstream schools in ways that also further the relationship between peers and schooling.

At the college level, students could benefit from similar practices and programs. More peer-based learning in college classrooms could prove beneficial for both students of color and women, who often look to their peers for support and intellectual growth. At the same time, a wide range of clubs and organizations that support students' racial, gender, and academic identities are all important for keeping the link between academics and friendship strong.

IMPLICATIONS FOR FUTURE RESEARCH

Most of the research currently done in this area has been at the high school level. Here we have seen the importance of school and peer context on the link between friends and academics. It is likely that these contexts are also extremely important at the middle school level, yet little research has explored learning under different social and cultural middle school environments. Also, except for the studies of heterogeneous learning, we have little research on the way in which cooperative or peer-based learning might strengthen this link. Finally, more research on the social side of middle schools is needed, including a look at the impact of offering a wider range of extracurricular activities on students' academic and social identities.

At the high school level, we have considerable understandings of the importance of different social contexts on learning. However, even here more research is needed examining the impact of peer-based learning within different school practices (tracking as well as heterogeneous grouping). Also, more research on the impact of ethnic clubs, ethnic organizations, and school-wide ethnic events on students at all levels of ability is needed. By expanding the research on alternative schools, we can continue to discover new practices that might also benefit students in more mainstream schools. Finally, by studying students' own practices of initiating alternative peer cultures such as those identified by Davidson (1996) and Hemmings (2000), we can see that adolescents as well as adults are capable of creating new practices that enhance the link between peers and academics. These peer strategies might prove valuable for identifying more structural practices that adults could then introduce into other schools.

College-based research on this important link is also needed. As more students attend college from diverse backgrounds and as the number of women on campuses continues to increase, we need to examine the practices that currently limit the development of strong academic identities as well as those that enhance it. This will include studies of classroom practices as well as the study of a wide variety of social contexts. It is important to know which clubs and organizations currently provide support for either racial, gender, or academic identities and in what campus environments more support is needed. Also, as friendships become more complex at the college level, including cross-class, cross-race, and cross-gender friendships, it will be important to see how these friendships support or detract from academic roles and identities.

In summary, we have seen that there is no single answer to whether friends support or detract from adolescents' academic experiences. Instead, a variety of factors contribute to this relationship including the background of students as well as school structures and practices. Given that school programs and practices can help many students bridge gaps between their academic and social identities, it is critical that we continue to work toward implementing new programs and alternative practices in more schools.

ACKNOWLEDGMENT

We wish to thank Sandi Kawecka Nenga, Jenny Stuber, and Tim Urdan for their helpful suggestions on an earlier draft of this chapter.

REFERENCES

Adler, P. A., & Adler, P. (1991). *Backboards and blackboards: College athletes and role engulfment.* New York: Columbia University Press.

Akom, A. A. (2003). Reexamining resistance as oppositional behavior: The Nation of Islam and the creation of a black achievement ideology. *Sociology of Education, 76,* 305–325.

American Association of University Women. (1999). *Growing smart: What's working for girls in school.* Washington, DC: American Association of University Women Educational Foundation.

Amit-Talai, V. (1995). The waltz of sociability: Intimacy, dislocation and friendship in a Quebec high school. In V. Amit-Talai & H. Wulff (Eds.), *Youth cultures: A cross-cultural perspective* (pp. 144–165). New York: Routledge.

Astin, A. W. (1993). An empirical typology of college students. *Journal of College Student Development, 34,* 36–46.

Berkowitz, A., & Padavic, I. (1999). Getting a man or getting ahead: A comparison of white and black sororities. *Journal of Contemporary Ethnography, 27,* 530–557.

Bettie, J. (2003). *Women without class: Girls, race, and identity*. Berkeley: University of California Press.

Boocock, S. S. (1978). The social organization of the classroom. *Annual Review of Sociology, 4*, 1–28.

Brantlinger, E. A. (1993). *The politics of social class in secondary school: Views of affluent and impoverished youth*. New York: Teachers College Columbia University.

Broh, B. A. (2002). Linking extracurricular programming to academic achievement: Who benefits and why? *Sociology of Education, 75*, 287–305.

Brown, B., Morey, M., & Kinney, D. (1995). Casting adolescent crowds in a relational perspective: Caricature, channel, and context. In R. Mentemayor, G. Adams, & T. Gullotta (Eds.), *Personal relationships during adolescence* (pp. 123-167). London: Sage.

Canada, K., & Pringle, R. (1995). The role of gender in college classroom interactions: A social context approach. *Sociology of Education, 68*, 161–186.

Christian-Smith, L. K. (1990). *Becoming a woman through romance*. New York: Routledge.

Clark, B. R., & Trow, M. (1966). The organizational context. In T. M. Newcomb & E. K. Wilson (Eds.), *College peer groups: Problems and prospects for research*. Chicago: Aldine.

Cohen, E. G. (1984). Talking and working together: Status, interaction and learning. In P. Peterson, L. C. Wilkinson, & M. Hallinan (Eds.), *The social context of instruction: Group organization and group processes*. New York: Academic Press.

Cohen, E. G. (1986). *Designing groupwork: Strategies for the heterogeneous classroom*. New York: Teachers College Press.

Cohen, E. G., Lotan, R. A., Scarloss, B. A., & Arellano, A. R. (1999). Complex instruction: Equity in cooperative learning classrooms. *Theory into Practice, 38*(2), 80–85.

Coleman, J. (1961). *The adolescent society: The social life of the teenager and its impact on education*. New York: Free Press.

Constantinople, A., Cornelius, R., & Gray, J. (1988). The chilly climate: Fact or artifact? *Journal of Higher Education, 59*, 527–559.

Cousins, L. (1999). "Playing between classes": America's troubles with class, race and gender in a Black high school and community. *Anthropology & Education Quarterly, 30*, 294–316.

Crawford, M., & MacLeod, M. (1990). Gender in the college classroom: An assessment of the "chilly climate" for women. *Sex Roles, 23*, 101–122.

Crosnoe, R. (2002). High school curriculum track and adolescent association with delinquent friends. *Journal of Adolescent Research, 17*(2), 143–167.

Cusick, P. A. (1973). *Inside high school: The student's world*. New York: Holt, Rinehart & Winston.

Dagaz, M. (2004, April). *Gender and class effects of high school extracurricular participation on academic achievement*. Paper presented at the annual meeting of the North Central Sociological Association, Cleveland, OH.

Damico, S. B., & Sparks, C. (1986). Cross-group contact opportunities: Impact on interpersonal relationships in desegregated middle schools. *Sociology of Education, 59*, 113–123.

Davidson, A. L. (1996). *Making and molding identity in schools: Student narratives on race, gender, and academic achievement*. New York: State University of New York Press.

Deutsch, M. (1968). The effects of cooperation and competition upon group process. In D. Cartwright & A. Zander (Eds.), *Group dynamics* (pp. 461-482). New York: Harper & Row.

Devries, D. L., Edwards, K. J., & Slavin, R. E. (1978). Biracial learning teams and race relations in the classroom: Four field experiments on teams-games-tournament. *Journal of Educational Psychology, 70*, 356–362.

Eccles, J., & Barber, B. (1999). Student council, volunteering, basketball, or marching band: What kind of extracurricular involvement matters? *Journal of Adolescent Research, 14*, 10–43.

Eckert, P. (1989). *Jocks and burnouts: Social categories and identity in the high school*. New York: Teachers College.

Eder, D., Evans, C. C., & Parker, S. (1995). *School talk: Gender and adolescent culture*. New Brunswick, NJ: Rutgers University Press.

Eitle, T. M., & Eitle, D. J. (2002). Race, cultural capital, and the educational effects of participation in sports. *Sociology of Education, 75*, 123–146.

Epstein, J. L. (1983). Selection of friends in differently organized schools and classrooms. In J. L. Epstein & N. Karweit (Eds.), *Friends in school: Patterns of selection and influence in secondary schools* (pp. 73–90). New York: Academic Press.

Fine, G. A. (2001). *Gifted tongues: High school debate and adolescent culture*. Princeton, NJ: Princeton University Press.

Fordham, S. (1996). *Blacked out: Dilemmas of race, identity, and success at Capital High*. Chicago: University of Chicago Press.

Gamoran, A. (1992). The variable effects of high school tracking. *American Sociological Review, 57*, 812–828.

Gamoran, A. (1996, October). Do magnet schools boost achievement? *Educational Leadership*, 42–46.

Gamoran, A., & Mare, R. D. (1989). Secondary school tracking and educational inequality: Compensation, reinforcement or neutrality? *American Journal of Sociology, 94*, 1146–1183.

Gilbert, P., & Taylor, S. (1991). *Fashioning the feminine: Girls, popular culture, and schooling*. London: Routledge.

Goffman, E. (1963). *Stigma: Notes on the management of spoiled identity*. Upper Saddle River, NJ: Prentice Hall.

Goldstein, T. (2003). Contemporary bilingual life at a Canadian high school: Choices, risks, tensions, and dilemmas. *Sociology of Education, 76*, 247–264.

Gotto, S. (1997). Nerds, normal people, and homeboys: Accommodation and resistance among Chinese American students. *Anthropology and Education Quarterly, 28*, 70–84.

Guiffrida, D. A. (2003). African American student organizations as agents of social integration. *Journal of College Student Development, 44*(3), 304–319.

Hall, R. M. (1982). The classroom climate: A chilly one for women? *Project on the status of education for women*. Washington, DC: Association of American Colleges.

Hallinan, M. T., & Williams, R. A. (1989). Interracial friendship choices in secondary schools. *American Sociological Review, 54*, 67–78.

Handler, L. (1995). In the fraternal sisterhood: Sororities as gender strategy. *Gender and Society, 9*, 236–255.

Hanson, S., & Kraus, R. (1998). Women, sport, and science: Do female athletes have an advantage? *Sociology of Education, 71*, 93–110.

Hanson, S., & Kraus, R. (1999). Women in male domains: Sport and science. *Sociology of Sport Journal, 16*(2), 92–110.

Hargreaves, D. H. (1967). *Social relations in a secondary school*. London: Routledge & Kegan Paul.

Hauser, R. M., Sewell, W. H., & Alwin, D. F. (1976). High school effects on achievement. In W. H. Sewell, R. M. Hauser, & D. L. Featherman (Eds.), *Schooling and achievement in American society* (pp. 309–342). New York: Academic Press.

Hemmings, A. (1998). The self-transformation of African American achievers. *Youth and Society, 29*, 330–368.

Hemmings, A. (2000). Lona's links: Postoppositional identity work of urban youths. *Anthropology and Education Quarterly, 31*, 152–172.

Holland, D. C., & Eisenhart, M. A. (1990). *Educated in romance: Women, achievement, and college culture*. Chicago: University of Chicago Press.

Horowitz, H. L. (1987). *Campus life: Undergraduate cultures from the end of the eighteenth century to the present*. New York: Knopf.

Horvat, E. M., & Lewis, K. S. (2003). Reassessing the "burden of acting white": The importance of peer groups in managing academic success. *Sociology of Education, 76*, 265–280.

Kandel, D. B., & Lesser, G. S. (1972). *Youth in two worlds*. San Francisco: Jossey-Bass.

Karweit, N. (1983). Extracurricular activities and friendship selection. In J. L. Epstein & N. Karweit (Eds.), *Friends in school: Patterns of selection and influence in secondary schools* (pp. 131–140). New York: Academic Press.

Karweit, N., & Hansell, S. (1983). School organization and friendship selection. In J. L. Epstein & N. Karweit (Eds.), *Friends in school: Patterns of selection and influence in secondary schools* (pp. 29–38). New York: Academic Press.

Kinney, D. A., Christensen, J. K., Casillas, J. C., & Christensen, K. A. (1997, January). *The making of an academic epiphany: Delineating teenagers' transformations at a successful alternative high school*. Paper presented at the annual meeting of the American Sociological Association, Toronto.

Kipnis, A. (2001). Articulating school countercultures. *Anthropology and Education Quarterly, 32*, 472–492.

Kuh, G. D., Hu, S., & Vesper, N. (2000). 'They shall be known by what they do': An activities-based typology of college students. *Journal of College Student Development, 41*(2), 228–244.

Lamborn, S., Brown, B. B., Mounts, N., & Steinberg, L. (1992). Putting school in perspective: The influence of family, peers, extracurricular participation, and part-time work on academic achievement. In F. Newmann (Ed.), *Student engagement and achievement in secondary schools* (pp. 153–181). New York: Teachers College Press.

Larkin, R. W. (1979). *Suburban youth in cultural crisis*. New York: Oxford University Press.

Lee, S. (1996). *Unraveling the model minority stereotype*. New York: Teachers College Press.

Levinson, B. (1998). Student culture and the contradictions of equality at a Mexican secondary school. *Anthropology and Education Quarterly, 29*, 267–296.

Loutzenheiser, L. W. (2002). Being seen and heard: Listening to young women in alternative schools. *Anthropology and Education Quarterly, 33*, 441-464.

MacLeod, J. (1987). *Ain't no making it: Leveled aspirations in a low-income neighborhood*. Boulder, CO: Westview Press.

Martinez Aleman, A. M. (1997). Understanding and investigating female friendship's educative value. *Journal of Higher Education, 68*, 119–159.

Martinez Aleman, A. M. (2000). Race talks: Undergraduate women of color and female friendships. *Review of Higher Education, 23*(2), 133–152.

McCannon, M., & Bennett, P. (1996). Choosing to participate or not: A study of college students' involvement in student organizations. *College Student Journal, 30*, 312–315.

McRobbie, A. (1978). Working-class girls and the culture of femininity. In Women's Studies Group (Ed.), *Women take issue* (pp. 96–108). London: Hutchinson.

Mehan, H., Hubbard, L., & Villanueva, I. (1994). Forming academic identities: Accommodation without assimilation among involuntary minorities. *Anthropology and Education Quarterly, 25*, 91–117.

Moffatt, M. (1989). *Coming of age in New Jersey: College and American culture*. New Brunswick, NJ: Rutgers University Press.

Oakes, J. (1985). *Keeping track: How schools structure inequality*. New Haven, CT: Yale University Press.

Phelan, P., & Davidson, A. L. (Eds.). (1993). *Renegotiating cultural diversity in American schools*. New York: Teachers College Press.

Phelan, P., Davidson, A. L., & Cao, H. T. (1998). *Adolescents' worlds: Negotiating family, peers, and school*. New York: Teachers College Press.

Proweller, A. (1998). *Constructing female identities: Meaning making in an upper-middle class youth culture*. Albany: State University of New York Press.

Quiroz, P. A., Flores-Gonzalez, N., & Frank, K. A. (1996). Carving a niche in the high school social structure: Formal and informal constraints on participation in the extra curriculum. *Research in Sociology of Education and Socialization, 11*, 93–120.

Roth, S. (2003). *Report of the Steering Committee for the Women's Initiative at Duke University*. Retrieved from http://www.duke.edu/womens_initiative/report_report.htm

Shaw, K. M., & Coleman, A. B. (2000). Humble on Sundays: Family, friends, and faculty in the upward mobility experiences of African American females. *Anthropology and Education Quarterly, 31*, 449–470.

Slavin, R. (1983). *Cooperative learning*. New York: Longmann.

Slavin, R., & Hansell, S. (1983). Cooperative learning and intergroup relations: Contact theory in the classroom. In J. L. Epstein & N. Karweit (Eds.), *Friends in school: Patterns of selection and influence in secondary schools* (pp. 93-114). New York: Academic Press.

Stone, L., & McKee, N. P. (2000). Gendered futures: Student visions of career and family on a college campus. *Anthropology and Education Quarterly, 31,* 67–89.

Stryker, S. (1980). *Symbolic interactionism: A social structural version.* Menlo Park, CA: Benjamin/Cummings.

Thorne, B. (1993). *Gender play: Girls and boys in school.* New Brunswick, NJ: Rutgers University Press.

Valenzuela, A. (1999). *Subtractive schooling: U.S.-Mexican youth and the politics of caring.* Albany: State University of New York Press.

Willis, P. E. (1981). *Learning to labor: How working class kids get working class jobs.* New York: Columbia University Press.

Yon, D. (2000). *Elusive culture: Schooling, race, and identity in global times.* Albany: State University of New York Press.

CHAPTER 10

THE "IDENTITY–EDUCATION" LINK

Six Themes in an Educational Setting that Influence Adolescent Identity Development and Well-Being

Gerald R. Adams and Susan Palijan

It would be difficult in our current society to discuss the nature of adolescent identity formation without references to the social contexts in which identity emerges. Culture, family, school, work, church, and community are the contexts that are identified as the major institutions of socialization for identity development. Individuals interested in the history of change in institutional ideologies and the evolution of identity should read *Identity: Cultural Change and the Struggle for Self* (Baumeister, 1986). For some time, psychologists have recognized the influence of education on identity (Douvan & Adelson, 1966; Erikson, 1968; Kroger, 2000). Indeed, one's identity may not only be influenced by educational experiences, but also shape the very experience one receives in the formation of identity (Adams & Fitch, 1983). However, the nature of the identity–education link has seldom been discussed using published evidence on this

Educating Adolescents: Challenges and Strategies, 237–253
Copyright © 2004 by Information Age Publishing
All rights of reproduction in any form reserved.

possible connection. What evidence do we have to link identity and education?

In examining the relationship between identity development and education, a number of theoretical perspectives and empirical investigations can be found. Indeed, education has been found to be an integral part of the identity process for adolescents of varying ages and regardless of gender (Kalakoski & Nurmi, 1998). There are many factors to consider in the identity development of adolescents, and while family and school are key socialization units to examine, the cultural context within these units must also be acknowledged. The interplay of family, education, and culture has been studied in identity research (e.g., Mhloyi, 1998; Spencer, 1999), and it is clear that for culturally diverse adolescents, the impact of their ethnicity (and ethnic identity) is an important issue. A supportive family system is needed for a student's healthy identity development during adolescence within a school environment (Deslandes, Potvin, & Leclerc, 2000; Giddan, 1987), and having supportive academic departments has also been shown to be effective in the developmental process (Adams, Ryan, & Keating, 2000). Within a school environment, extracurricular activities play an important role in the development of an identity, and both community services and religious activities are forms of social involvement that adolescents often become involved in. These activities serve as a means of exploring personal values, beliefs, and goals, all of which comprise an ego identity, and as a way of discovering the meaning of ethnicity, as shown in ethnic identity.

Altogether, one's identity is a central aspect of adolescence that is developed within an educational setting, and while there is no particular structure to these findings, six general themes from our examination of published research have emerged, which are reviewed in this chapter. The themes are that of ego identity, ethnic identity, community service, extracurricular or leisure activities, religion, and school or academic climate. A commentary follows this review and some possible future directions for this research area are discussed.

EGO IDENTITY

Berzonsky and Adams (1999) have reviewed much of the evidence on the usefulness of what is known as the identity status paradigm. This review covered literature over 35 years of the paradigm used in empirical research. A comparison was made between a perspective of viewing identity from operationalizations using the dimension of *exploration* and *commitment* (Marcia, Waterman, Matteson, Archer, & Orlofsky, 1993) and a more constructionist identity *decision-making* perspective (Berzonsky,

1989). This analytic review supports the concept of four identity states or statuses: *diffusion* (no exploration, no commitment), *foreclosure* (no exploration, commitment), *moratorium* (exploration, no commitment), and *identity achieved* (exploration and commitment). Berzonsky and Adams's (1999) review also indicates that there are theoretically appropriate individual differences between the identity statuses. Furthermore, when comparisons are made between the identity status dimensions of exploration and commitment with another system of inquiry formulated by Berzonsky (1989), using an identity decision-making perspective and a measure of exploration and commitment, it appears that the four general types of identity states are confirmed. Berzonsky (1988) refers to these as identity achievement/*informational* style, moratorium/informational style, foreclosure/*normative* styles, and a diffusion/identity *avoidance* style.

Ego identity represents the goals, beliefs, and values of an individual. Survey and interview techniques have been used in empirical studies on ego identity formation. In a study by Archer (1989), gender differences in various aspects of identity formation were studied for students from Grades 6, 8, 10, and 12 using the Ego Identity Interview. When the ego identity statuses in the domains of vocational choice, religious beliefs, political ideology, and sex-role orientation were examined, males were more likely to be foreclosed than were females. Overall, however, there were few significant gender differences found on the variables of process, domain, and timing of identity formation. This suggests that ego identity formation is a similar process for males and females, although some argue that identity formation is more of an individuation process for men and a relational process for women. In a recent study, Lewis (2003) examined the differences in ego identity statuses of college students in relation to their age, ethnicity, and gender. The Revised Version of the Extended Objective Measure of Ego Identity Status (Bennion & Adams, 1986) was used, in which both ideological and interpersonal aspects of ego identity were measured. Although gender differences were not found for overall ego identity scores, men had higher levels of identity diffusion and foreclosure in the interpersonal dimension than did women. However, women were more likely to have higher levels of identity achievement than were men at most ages between 18 and 41. In terms of age and ethnicity, younger individuals and Asian students tended to have high identity foreclosure and diffusion scores. In non-Western cultures such as Asia, collectivism is often valued over the individualism that is typically representative of Western cultures in which achievement is measured by individual success. In collectivist cultures, there is a general belief that success is based on togetherness and helping one another. Undoubtedly, for Asian adolescents living in a Western culture, the value differences likely lead to states of confusion (high diffusion scores) or else there is an adherence to the family values being taught to them, and there is resistance to explore any other options (high foreclosure scores). Thus, it is critical to examine an individual's age, gender, and ethnicity, as all of these factors could affect ego identity status development, which in turn can affect experiences in family and school environments.

In a longitudinal study, Adams and colleagues (2000) examined the influence of family and university environments on college students' identity formation and ego strength. There were only a few developmental changes noted over a period of 2 years among the first- and second-year students on various family and school variables. A student's ego strength, however, was predicted by democratic family life and supportive academic environments, thus emphasizing the importance of support systems within and outside the school environment. By having a safe environment at home and at school, adolescents feel comfortable to more fully explore their identity options. Otherwise, they may feel pressured to adhere to certain values by the school or from their parents, especially in the case of adolescents from immigrant families.

In considering immigrant young adults, identity development becomes more complex. Arredondo (1984) found that both ego and identity development scores increased over a period of 5 years for a group of adolescents averaging 16 years of age and from 13 different ethnic backgrounds. According to Arredondo, typical immigrant young adults will develop a more integrated sense of self over time as well as maintain a strong bond with their family and ethnic culture, while also blending into the mainstream culture. Although this appears to be the typical developmental process, there are also many ethnic backgrounds to consider, all of which have varying cultural beliefs and practices. It is difficult to generalize findings across ethnic groups; however, it is encouraging to know that over a period of 5 years, young immigrant youth are able to form more integrated selves. Thus, it is important to consider the impact of family and schools, as both are critical to the development of ego identity for both immigrant and nonimmigrant adolescents.

University education is becoming the new standard of education for today's youth. With increasing technological advances and a constantly changing job market, many adolescents are pursuing higher education. The transition to university is an important factor in the identity formation process. Berzonksy and Kuk (2000) measured first-year university students' ego identity statuses, identity processing styles, and student developmental tasks to determine if these factors affected their transition to university. It was found that those with high achievement and moratorium scores were more prepared for the university context and needed less support from others. Thus, it appears that adolescents who have explored various aspects of their identity and have supportive families are more likely to be successful in an academic environment. We return to issues of education in a later section on academic climate.

In addition to considering ego identity and the family system, we have already shown that ethnicity is another dimension of identity that needs to be addressed. Next, we examine ethnic identity more closely.

ETHNIC IDENTITY

Ethnic identity represents the meaning of ethnicity in one's life and is an important facet of the identity formation of all adolescents, regardless of their ethnic background. When Phinney (1989) tested stages of ethnic identity development on a group of 10th graders, only minority adolescents could be accurately placed into one of the three ethnic identity stages. Half of the adolescents assessed were identified in the diffusion/foreclosure stage, while the other half was classified into either moratorium or ethnic identity achievement. In addition, those who had the highest scores on ego identity and psychological adjustment had achieved an ethnic identity. Thus, adolescents who explore and commit to the meaning of ethnicity in their lives will be more likely to have also formed an ego identity and are generally more adjusted than those who do not. Both an ego and ethnic identity can be seen as dimensions of one's identity and are important predictors of health and well-being. In terms of predicting college adjustment, gender differences have been found among Asian, Asian Indian, black, Hispanic, and white participants (Klasner & Pistole, 2003); thus, one's ethnic background and gender should also be considered. In a study of school success in college, Barajes and Pierce (2003) found that whereas young Latina women identified more with their ethnic culture and followed their values, young Latino men tended to have a less positive ethnic identity and defined their success according to values of the mainstream culture. As with any ethnocultural group, there are certain gender stereotypes and expectations that adolescents are expected to meet. As a result of an increasingly global culture, more countries are beginning to adhere to Western values. Consequently, males may be persuaded by mainstream culture, wheras females may continue to adhere to traditional values found within their cultural group. Thus, it is important to consider one's ethnic identity when measuring school-related variables.

Ethnic identity is an important aspect of an individual's personality and individual adjustment (Laursen & Williams, 2002). Numerous researchers have reported that among minority youth, ethnic identity is associated with improvement of self-esteem, academic achievement, and psychosocial adjustment. By belonging to a particular ethnic group, minority youth often feel more secure and better about themselves and their academic successes. The achievement of a positive ethnic identity has important implications for an individual's overall psychological adjustment (Phinney, Lochner, & Murphy, 1990). Furthermore, ethnic identity is a significant factor in minority students' adjustment to college. In a study by Saylor and Aries (1999), the strength of ethnic identity was measured among first-year minority students at the beginning, middle, and end of their college year using ethnic identity and adjustment measures. Results indicated that the strength of ethnic identity could be predicted by participation in cultural events (e.g., high school involvement). After a year, it was noted that an individual's involvement with on-campus cultural organizations and ethnic friends became more important than did family involvement. In addition, ethnic identity increased significantly over a period of a year, and joining various ethnic organizations did not have any negative effects on overall adjustment or involvement on the larger campus. Thus, an active involvement in ethnicity-based organizations allowed minority students to further explore the meaning of ethnicity in their lives by supporting the exploration of their identity.

Ethnic identity is a critical aspect of one's identity and should be incorporated into school programs. After examining various ethnic factors on students' social and academic competence, Sheets (1999) recommended that ethnic identity development should be incorporated into programs and that multiculturalism should be promoted in schools. After completing a classroom program to promote the development of ethnic identity, a group of at-risk ninth graders from various ethnic backgrounds showed higher levels of academic and social competence. Through an active discussion of issues of racism, prejudice, and discrimination, students in high schools can challenge their own beliefs and explore the meanings of ethnicity in their own lives. It is invaluable to learn more about other ethnic groups within a classroom setting. Issues of racism, prejudice, and discrimination are bound to arise within multiple settings throughout adulthood, including the workplace, community, and everyday life. Allowing adolescents to explore their ethnic backgrounds and learn more about those of others will not only allow their identities to develop but will teach them important lessons about respect and understanding. In addition to ego identity and ethnic identity, there is increasing attention being given to community service and its role in identity formation and school success.

COMMUNITY SERVICE

The formation of a civic identity is a fundamental aspect of community service. Numerous researchers have examined the importance of youth activism and community involvement in the identity development and well-being of adolescents. Youniss and Yates (1999) argued that morality is a component of one's identity that can be fostered through participation in the community, leading to the development of a moral-civic identity. The integration of this kind of service into a school curriculum will not only foster this identity development but will promote future adult moral-civic activism. The formation of a civic identity is an international phenomenon, and all over the world youth are becoming more active in both community service and political activism (Yates & Youniss, 1999). According to Youniss, McLellan, Su, and Yates (1999), the role of community service in identity development could potentially fall into three types of orientations. Normative orientations represent conventional political involvement such as voting; unconventional orientations deal with acts such as boycotting; and deviant orientations are represented by such things as marijuana use. It was found that varying increments of community service were most predictive of these different orientations. Furthermore, certain background characteristics are more predictive of community service than are others. For example, being female, attending Catholic school, having high socioeconomic status, and coming from an intact family predict service involvement. Also, an involvement in both extracurricular activities and some form of part-time work is associated with higher levels of community service. If adolescents are willing to take the time to join after-school activities or to commit to a job, it is likely that they will also use their time to join community organizations and become more involved.

Political involvement is an important part of community involvement and of overall identity, especially since an adherence to certain values, goals, and beliefs about political issues is an element of ego identity. Yates and Youniss (1998) argued that identity development and political commitment are interrelated processes that occur in adolescence. A case study of black urban adolescents who participated in a service learning program revealed that the development of social responsibility and an understanding of pertinent societal issues, along with participation in community service, led to increased political commitment. In a society that is becoming increasingly global, adolescents must consider many complex issues to develop their own political viewpoints and subsequent identities (see Adams, 1985). Increasing technological advancements and pertinent world issues have sparked numerous issues that demand a response from every individual. The formation of political viewpoints is an important part of one's identity because certain political issues may oppose one's values, goals, or beliefs. This is evidenced by recent government challenges in France to remove all apparel identifying one as being Islamic to either discourage overidentification with a religious identity or to encourage the identification as a French citizen over that of being a Muslim.

Various theories have been proposed regarding youth involvement in community service. Youniss and Yates (1997) have found that this form of involvement promotes both a personal and collective identity. By becoming actively involved in social causes, today's generation of youth is being socially responsible and caring for the well-being of society in general. The mandatory requirement of community service in schools is recommended because it has been shown to stimulate the formation of agency and responsibility. Although many youth become involved in community service, certain peer groups volunteer more than do others. In a recent study, Youniss, McLellan, and Mazer (2001) analyzed two suburban Catholic high schools and identified five crowd types and their commitments to voluntary services. The crowd types were labeled as School, Disengaged, All-Around, Fun, and Average. School crowd members were the most likely to volunteer for social service activities and join school clubs, and they had high scores on future service and political intentions. Adolescence is a time of exploration and, undoubtedly, students may feel that they belong to more than one crowd type at different points in their school life. It seems plausible that those in the School crowd would be more likely to volunteer their time, as their sense of responsibility is presumably greater than those in the Fun crowd. Thus, while involvement is beneficial, certain groups of students will likely become more active in their school or community than will others.

The promotion of these kinds of activities in a school environment can help to foster the identity development of students and to encourage them to believe that they can indeed make a difference in society. By believing that they can actively participate in solving social problems, adolescents are also developing their own identities (Youniss & Yates, 1997). Implementing community service in school programs is laudable. Although it is not mandatory in all schools, it is a valuable investment for students, as it allows them to become more socially aware of their surroundings and to explore their own identities. Participation in community service also allows adolescents to become more active citizens. In addition to community service, extracurricular activities are also critical aspects of a young person's identity development.

EXTRACURRICULAR/LEISURE ACTIVITIES

Extracurricular activities are essential to a school environment. Eccles and Barber (1999) examined the potential risks and benefits of the five types of activities for students over a period of 14 years. These activities were prosocial (church and volunteer activities), team sports, school involvement, performing arts, and academic clubs. Although prosocial activities and participation in team sports were related to more positive educational trajectories, high rates of drinking alcohol were more problematic for those involved in sports. Peer associations and activity-based identity formation could help explain these group differences. Peers influence the types of activities that students choose to join, and often there are stigmas attached to certain activities. When considering the various crowd types discussed earlier, it is likely that only those from the School crowd will join the academic clubs or volunteer their time in prosocial activities. There are numerous factors to consider in understanding the differences between engagement in extracurricular activities and an individual's sense of who he or she is to become.

Identity formation is a process that could be applied to the understanding of the effects of these kinds of activities because of the multiple roles that students acquire in school. Using a social psychological approach to identity formation, Wiggan (2002) explained that, depending on students' evaluations of themselves, they may or may not strive to succeed in school. Students who do not believe that school success is possible will likely alienate themselves from this setting and identify with those who can make them feel better about themselves. A balance of extracurricular activities and academics will allow students to form healthy self-concepts, and it is important that teachers and parents provide positive social support systems. In turn, students who feel as if they cannot achieve success in school may change their negative self-evaluations into more positive self-images and become more involved in school either through academic or extracurricular activities. The importance of healthy support systems cannot be overemphasized, and, in a school setting, teachers are often viewed as parents, friends, or mentors. A healthy family and school environment are essential in adolescent identity development and school involvement. By encouraging adolescents to have both academic and extracurricular activities as options, students are allowed the flexibility to feel good about their successes.

Interestingly, there are some dramatic differences between ethnic groups in terms of involvement in extracurricular activities. Davalos, Chavez, and Guardiola (1999) investigated the relationship between school retention rates and a variety of variables, including extracurricular activity, for Mexican American and white non-Hispanic students in Grades 7 through 12. Students who reported participating in an extracurricular activity were more likely to remain in school than were those who did not. Mexican American students who reported high ethnic identity levels were more likely to stay in school and to have more positive perceptions of school than were students with lower ethnic identity levels. Students who identify with their ethnic group and participate in extracurricular activities seem to stay in school longer and enjoy it more than those who do not. By joining these kinds of activities, Mexican American students are able to meet students with varying cultural backgrounds, which may lead to more exploration of their own ethnicity. On forming an ethnic identity, they will feel better about themselves and, consequently, their perceptions about school will improve.

Both in high school and college, leisure plays an important role in healthy development. According to Bloland (1987), leisure enhances student development and enhances creativity, self-expression, and character growth. Its benefits also include happiness and physical health. Leisure activities are integral aspects of the campus environment and provide good opportunities for planned interventions. Identity formation processes are also key features of leisure activities. Shaw, Kleiber, and Caldwell (1995) examined the relationship between identity development and participation in leisure activities for a group of 10th graders. Leisure activities and obligatory activities were assessed, and it was found that girls spent more time than did boys in obligatory activities, wheras boys were more likely to spend their time in paid work activities. In terms of identity development, sports and physical activities were associated only for girls, whereas social activities did not relate to identity variables for either gender.

RELIGION

Religion plays a significant role in many students' lives. Religious identity development can be composed of various factors, including church attendance, involvement in church activities, self-reported religiosity (or spirituality), and religious identity (King, Elder, & Whitbeck, 1997). King and colleagues (1997) attempted to identify developmental expressions of religion in the lives of Grade 7–10 students from two-parent, white, rural families in the United States. Adolescents who grew up on a farm expressed stronger commitments to religious values than did adolescents who did not. In addition, parent–child relationships and social identities were important influences on adherence to these values. Family relationships are central to the identity formation process, especially in the development of a religious identity, because religion may or may not have an important place in the family, which can lead to the questioning of religious issues.

The development of a religious identity during adolescence can be linked to ego identity formation. Hunsberger, Pratt, and Pancer (2001) examined the association between ego identity statuses and religious doubt for a group of senior high school and university students. The researchers reported that identity achievement scores were associated both with belief-confirming consultation and with belief-threatening consultation for religious doubts. However, more diffused individuals seemed to experience greater religious doubts, be religiously uncommitted, disagree with religious teachings, and avoid both belief-confirming and belief-threatening consultation. In terms of personal adjustment, identity-achieved individuals were healthier. It is possible that an exploration of and commitment to religious values and beliefs can be beneficial to adolescents' identity and well-being.

In an examination of religious beliefs of students from a private college, McAdams, Booth, and Selvik (1981) found that both ego stage and social motivation were critical factors. When college students who identified that religion was an important part of their lives described personal religious identity crises, interesting differences were found. Students who scored at higher levels of ego development were more likely to report identity crises that involved a lot of questioning of fundamental religious beliefs, compared to students at lower stages. In terms of motivation, religious experiences were described differently for students who were high in intimacy and power motivation.

The exploration of religious beliefs and values is not always possible. Simel (1996) investigated the impact of the prevalent Christian religion on the identity formation of Jewish and Islamic students in Bavaria, Germany. Although the Bavarian public education system promotes a civil Christian religion and provisions are made in schools for these kinds of religious classes, non-Christians are not encouraged to explore their religions, which is expected to be done by either family members or non-school institutions. Animosity may result in such school systems as non-Christians are seemingly forced to assimilate into a Bavarian Christian culture and avoid further exploration of their own religion.

Perhaps a religious education should be presented in a way that allows for students to examine various aspects of religion. McEniry (1982) suggested that both humanistic psychology and values clarification can be used to aid adolescent religious education. One way to go about this is to apply general religious principles to specific life situations by a decision-making process. By balancing religious theory with life experiences, adolescents are able to test and clarify their religious values and to develop a more permanent religious identity. The exploration of one's religion may be an important step in identity development.

SCHOOL AND ACADEMIC CLIMATE

In a recent examination placing identity formation into social contexts, Kroger (2000) reviewed several investigations of identity formation in educational contexts. This review includes an examination of teacher–student interactions, structural features of school, and educational curricula. Raphael, Feinberg, and Bachor (1987) investigated student teachers' perceptions and personal reactions to students with various identity states. These novice teachers most preferred adolescents who were in moratorium and least preferred those who were identity diffused. One can surmise that these perceptions might also influence the quality and nature of the educational experience that diffused versus moratorium students receive. Our own informal observations suggest that diffused students receive less attention, are disciplined more often, receive lower grades, and are more likely to be criticized in and out of the classroom. Of course, an empirical investigation is needed to confirm these observations.

Taylor, Gilligan, and Sullivan (1995) hypothesize that women's identity development requires educational environments that are supportive of building relationships. In a set of studies, these investigators found that the typical school structure is associated with female students feeling alienated and female teachers who report similar states of mind. Kroger (2000) summarizes these studies as follows:

> The desire of girls and women teachers for an experience of connection was generally strong, but the administrative school structure and overextended workloads mitigated against the establishment of meaningful interpersonal relationships. The transition to high school for many girls often brought experiences of disconnection and loss through inattention from teachers. Environments that provide opportunities for a strong sense of interpersonal connection are central to facilitating identity development for women, argues Gilligan and her colleagues. (p. 81)

Kroger further reported that comparisons between private and state-supported schools reveal that private school female students were more foreclosed and public school female students were more diffused or in a state of moratorium (see Roker & Banks, 1993). It is possible that public schools provide a wider or broader lens on life and may encourage more identity exploration. Much is yet to be known about the influence of school structure, student–teacher interactions, and interpersonal relationships on the identity formation of young women and young men.

Dryer (1994) advanced several ideas about the nature of educational environments and school curricula as regards the facilitation of identity formation. The general theme of his writing is that all curricula should stimulate exploration and commitment, through student exploration, responsible choice, and self-determination. In particular, this could be enhanced by role-playing and by greater interaction between generations of past students, community workers, and family members. A few small experimental studies have attempted to create conditions of exploration and encourage commitments as a way of promoting growth in identity formation. Findings from these studies suggest that educators may be able to create identity-enhancing conditions; however, findings also suggest that creating change may be difficult, with only modest change for considerable effort (Markstrom-Adams, Ascione, Braegger, & Adams, 1993).

In our own research on academic climates in university settings (e.g., Adams & Fitch, 1983), we have found that certain academic programs attract students with specific identity statuses. For example, programs that focus on rigor and intellectual ability attract students who are high in identity formation before even coming to university. Likewise, programs that promote intellectual and social awareness also promote higher levels of identity formation over the course of a university experience. We have also found that higher levels of identity achievement are associated with more complex thinking processes.

CONCLUSIONS

Evidence suggests that there is an identity–education link. Identity formation is a transformative process during the high school and college years. Our review of some recent literature indicates that involvement in school, community, family, and religion can be instrumental in facilitating identity formation. Regardless of an individual's ethnic background, both ego and ethnic identity are integral aspects of an adolescent's identity. Higher levels of ego identity and ethnic identity are associated with a number of positive indicators of well-being and adjustment. However, one's age, ethnicity, and gender also should be considered. As diversity in our society increases, the incorporation of multiculturalism into school programs is a necessary tool to allow students to explore all aspects of their identity and to understand other ethnic groups.

The identity formation process is also demonstrated by an individual's involvement in the community, in school, and in religious institutions. We found that community and political involvement are interrelated with identity development and that youth activism teaches individuals to explore these aspects of their identity. In terms of school involvement, the balance of both extracurricular and academic activities is important in the formation of a healthy identity, and students should be encouraged to participate in both in- and after-school programs and clubs. It may be that spirituality is another aspect of identity that may warrant greater attention, given the contention of some researchers that individuals who explore their religious beliefs are more likely to have higher levels of ego identity and well-being.

In our current society, a university education is becoming the new standard of education, which means that students will be staying in school for longer periods of time. A school's academic climate is a crucial component of identity development, and it has been shown to be related to ego identity. Different school systems and programs help to form the identity statuses of students, which may hinder the exploration of identity in students who are not favored by teachers. Curricula should encourage identity exploration and the commitment processes of identity, especially for women who can benefit greatly from a positive and encouraging educational environment. Teachers should be more aware of their students' identity statuses and should use a variety of identity-related activities in class.

Although culture, family, school, work, church, and community are often the contexts that are seen as the major institutions of socialization for identity development, the link between identity and education remains unclear. The family and school environment appear to be at the center of many of the issues involved in an individual's identity. Positive family and school environments not only facilitate identity formation but also promote health and well-being. It is clearly a complex process, and a person-in-context perspective is most likely to help integrate findings across evidence such as that reported in this chapter.

REFERENCES

Adams, G. R. (1985). Identity and political socialization. In A.S. Waterman (Ed.), *Identity in adolescence: Processes and contents* (pp. 61–77). San Francisco: Jossey-Bass.

Adams, G. R., & Fitch, S. (1983). Psychological environments of university departments: Effects on college students' identity status and ego stage development. *Journal of Personality and Social Psychology, 44,* 1266–1275.

Adams, G. R., Ryan, B. A., & Keating, L. (2000). Family relationships, academic environments and psychosocial development during the university experience: A longitudinal investigation. *Journal of Adolescent Research, 15,* 99–122.

Archer, S. L. (1989). Gender differences in identity development: Issues of process, domain, and timing. *Journal of Adolescence, 12,* 117–138.

Arredondo, P. M. (1984). Identity themes for immigrant young adults. *Adolescence, 19,* 997–993.

Barajas, H. L., & Pierce, J. L. (2001). The significance of race and gender in school success among Latinas and Latinos in college. *Gender and Society, 15,* 859–878.

Baumeister, R. (1986) *Identity: Cultural change and the struggle for self.* New York: Oxford University Press.

Bennion, L. D., & Adams, G. R. (1986). A revision of the extended version of the objective measure of ego identity status: An identity instrument for use with late adolescents. *Journal of Adolescent Research, 1*, 183–198.

Berzonsky, M. D. (1988). *The structure of identity.* Paper presented at the second biennial meeting of the Society for Research on Adolescence, Alexandria, VA.

Berzonsky, M. D. (1989). Identity style: Conceptualization and measurement. *Journal of Adolescent Research, 4*, 268–282.

Berzonsky, M. D., & Adams, G. R. (1999). Commentary: Reevaluating the identity status paradigm: Still useful after 35 years. *Developmental Review, 19*, 557–590.

Berzonsky, M. D., & Kuk, L. S. (2000). Identity status, identity processing style, and the transition to university. *Journal of Adolescent Research, 15*, 81–98.

Bloland, P. A. (1987). Leisure as a campus resource for fostering student development. *Journal of Counseling and Development, 65*, 291–294.

Davalos, D. B., Chavez, E. L., & Guardiola, R. J. (1999). The effects of extracurricular activity, ethnic identification, and perception of school on student dropout rates. *Hispanic Journal of Behavioral Sciences, 21*, 61–77.

Deslandes, R., Potvin, P., & Leclerc, D. (2000). Links between adolescent autonomy, parental involvement, and school success. *Canadian Journal of Behavioural Science, 32*, 208–217.

Douvan, E., & Adelson, J. (1966). *The adolescent experience.* New York: Wiley.

Dryer, P. H. (1994). Designing curricular identity interventions for secondary schools. In S. L. Archer (Ed.), *Interventions for adolescent identity development* (pp 121–140). Thousand Oaks, CA: Sage.

Eccles, J. S., & Barber, B. L. (1999). Student council, volunteering, basketball, or marching band: What kind of extracurricular involvement matters? *Journal of Adolescent Research, 14*, 10–43.

Erikson, E. H. (1968). *Identity: youth and crisis.* New York: Norton.

Giddan, N. S. (1987). Coping and identity development in college students. *Journal of College Student Psychotherapy, 2*, 33–58.

Hunsberger, B., Pratt, M., & Pancer, M. (2001). Adolescent identity formation: Religious exploration and commitment. *Identity, 1*, 365–386.

Kalakoski, V., & Nurmi, J-E. (1998). Identity and educational transitions: Age differences in adolescent exploration and commitment related to education, occupation, and family. *Journal of Research on Adolescence, 8*, 29–47.

King, V., Elder, G. H. Jr., & Whitbeck, L. B. (1997). Religious involvement among rural youth: An ecological and life-course perspective. *Journal of Research on Adolescence 7*, 431–456.

Klasner, L., & Pistole, M. C. (2003). College adjustment in a multiethnic sample: Attachment, separation-individuation, and ethnic identity. *Journal of College Student Development, 44*, 92–109.

Kroger, J. (2000). *Identity development: Adolescence through adulthood.* Thousand Oaks, CA: Sage.

Laursen, B., & Williams, V. (2002). The role of ethnic identity in personality development. In L. Pulkkinen & A. Caspi (Eds.), *Paths to successful development: Personality in the life course* (pp. 203–226). New York: Cambridge University Press.

Lewis, H. L. (2003). Difference in ego identity among college students across age, ethnicity, and gender. *Identity, 3*, 159–189.

Marcia, J. E., Waterman, A. S., Matteson, D. R., Archer, S. L., & Orlofsky, J. (Eds.). (1993). *Ego identity: A handbook for psychosocial research*. New York: Springer-Verlag.

Markstrom-Adams, C., Ascione, F. R., Braegger, D., & Adams, G. R. (1993). Promotion of ego-identity development: Can short-term intervention facilitate growth? *Journal of Adolescence, 16*, 217–224.

McAdams, D. P., Booth, L., & Selvik, R. (1981). Religious identity among students at a private college: Social motives, ego stage, and development. *Merrill-Palmer Quarterly, 27*, 219–239.

McEniry, R. (1982). Values clarification: An aid to adolescent religious education. *Counseling and Values, 27*, 40–51.

Mhloyi, M. M. (1998). Identity formation: Problems and prospects, the case of Zimbabwe. *Journal of Comparative Family Studies, 29*, 243–254.

Phinney, J. S. (1989). Stages of ethnic identity development in minority group adolescents. *Journal of Early Adolescence, 9*, 34–49.

Phinney, J. S., Lochner, B. T., & Murphy, R. (1990). Ethnic identity development and psychological adjustment in adolescence. In A. R. Stiffman & L. E. Davis (Eds.), *Ethnic issues in adolescent mental health* (pp. 53–72). Thousand Oaks, CA: Sage.

Raphael, D., Feinberg, R., & Bachor, D. (1987). Student teachers' perceptions of the identity formation process. *Journal of Youth and Adolescence, 16*, 331–344.

Roker, B., & Banks, M. H. (1993). Adolescent identity and school type. *British Journal of Psychology, 84*, 297–300.

Saylor, E. S., & Aries, E. (1999). Ethnic identity and change in social context. *Journal of Social Psychology, 139*, 549–566.

Shaw, S. M., Kleiber, D. A., & Caldwell, L. L. (1995). Leisure and identity formation in male and female adolescents: A preliminary examination. *Journal of Leisure Research, 27*, 245–263.

Sheets, R. H. (1999). Racial and ethnic identity in school practices: Aspects of human development. In R. H. Sheets & E. R. Hollins (Eds.), *Relating competence in an urban classroom to ethnic identity development* (pp. 157–178). Mahwah, NJ: Erlbaum.

Simel, D. L. (1996). Exclusionary Christian civil religion for Jewish and Islamic students in Bavarian schools. *Comparative Education Review, 40*, 28–46.

Spencer, M. B. (1999). Social and cultural influences on school adjustment: The application of an identity-focused cultural ecological perspective. *Educational Psychologist, 34*, 43–57.

Taylor, J. M., Gilligan, C., & Sullivan, A. M. (1995). *Between voice and silence: Women, girls, race and relationships*. Cambridge, MA: Harvard University Press.

Wiggan, G. (2002). *Student achievement: The social psychology of identity formation and multiple roles and role salience*. Atlanta, GA: Southern Sociological Society.

Yates, M., & Youniss, J. (1998). Community service and political identity development in adolescence. *Journal of Social Issues. Special Issue: Political development: Youth growing up in a global community, 54*, 495–512.

Yates, M., & Youniss, J. (Eds.). (1999). *Roots of civic identity: International perspectives on community service and activism in youth*. New York: Cambridge University Press.

Youniss, J., & Yates, M. (1997). *Community service and social responsibility in youth.* Chicago: University of Chicago Press.

Youniss, J., & Yates, M. (1999). Youth service and moral-civic identity: A case for everyday morality. *Educational Psychology Review. Special Issue: Moral Development in Adolescents and Adults, 11,* 361–376.

Youniss, J., McLellan, J. A., & Mazer, B. (2001). Voluntary service, peer group orientation, and civic engagement. *Journal of Adolescent Research, 16,* 456–468.

Youniss, J., McLellan, J. A., Su, Y., & Yates, M. (1999). The role of community service in identity development: Normative, unconventional, and deviant orientations. *Journal of Adolescent Research, 14,* 248–261.

CHAPTER 11

RELIGION AND THE EDUCATIONAL EXPERIENCES OF ADOLESCENTS

Geoffrey L. Ream and Ritch C. Savin-Williams

Whether young Americans do or do not participate in religion, religious and educational contexts overlap in their lives, and it is important to understand the place and nature of this overlap and its effects. For this review, religion is understood to be a multidimensional and multicontextual process, encompassing both spirituality, which is an individual-level search for the sacred and meaningful, and participation in religious organizations. Religious organizations, in turn, are defined as organizations that seek to provide individuals with human capital (a set of beliefs, values, practices, etc.) that compensates in part for aspects of life beyond human agency and understanding (e.g., death, evil) under supernatural assumptions (Stark & Bainbridge, 1985, 1987).

This chapter considers the influences of religious involvement and spiritual commitment on adolescent behavior and health, topics central to the research interests of scholars (Weaver et al., 2000). The focus shifts to more complex concerns of how religion influences adolescents' social world, including the school environment. Next, we survey the psychological processes underlying adolescent belief system development, including

Educating Adolescents: Challenges and Strategies, 255–286

religious socialization, normative development of spiritual commitment, and the processes by which young people become attracted to cults and the occult. Finally, we discuss the impact of religion within contexts broader than schools, including special issues related to race and ethnicity, religious organizations as youth-serving institutions, constructive cooperation between faith-based and secular youth work, and political conflict between religious organizations and schools. The main theme throughout is respect for young people's individual religious choices and agency, within appropriate boundaries that adults help them maintain.

PREVALENCE AND BENEFITS OF YOUTH RELIGIOUSNESS

Prevalence

Gallup poll data have tracked the proportion of American teenagers who attend religious services regularly as hovering just under half, and this has remained steady since 1977 (Gallup & Lindsay, 1999; Lyons, 2003). Young women are somewhat more faithful in attendance than young men (46% vs. 40%) (Lyons, 2003). With regard to denominational affiliation, 52% of American youth (and 51% of American adults) are Protestant, 26% (24%) Catholic, 2% (2%) are Jewish, 3% (2%) are Mormon, 8% (9%) are some other denomination, and 9% (9%) are unaffiliated with religion (Gallup Brain, 2003; Gallup & Lindsay, 1999). When asked to compare themselves to their parents, 65% of youth are "very" or "somewhat" confident that they will be more religious than their parents. In most respects, teens' rates of agreement with certain religious opinions are not meaningfully different from those of adults. Nearly all (95%) teens believe in God or a universal spirit and 86% believe that Jesus Christ is God or the Son of God, but only 67% believe in life after death and 52% have confidence in organized religion. Fewer give religion a central role in their lives: 42% pray alone frequently and 39% consider their own religious beliefs to be very important (Gallup & Lindsay, 1999).

Influences on Behavior

Classical sociological theory (Durkheim, 1915; Weber, 1922) conceptualizes religion as a creator and enforcer of behavioral norms. Religion functions well in these capacities. Personal religiousness as well as religious participation have inverse relationships with several behaviors conceptualized as problematic among adolescents, including drug use

(Benda & Corwyn, 2000; Benson, 1992; Brownfield & Sorenson, 1991), alcohol use (Ellison, Boardman, Williams, & Jackson, 2001; Mason & Windle, 2002), premarital sex (Beck, Cole, & Hammond, 1991; Donahue, 1995), and more serious forms of delinquency, including carrying a weapon, violence, and selling drugs (Benda, 2002).

Several caveats need to be made. Some argue that religion functions *only* as a creator and enforcer of norms, a social force through which society works to formalize rules necessary for people to live in community, and that personal spirituality or religious commitment has no independent relationship with outcomes over and above structural aspects of religion. This hypothesis emerges from psychoanalytic (Freud, 1927) and sociological secularization (Berger, 1967) understandings of religion, but empirical evidence has conclusively debunked it. Recent studies consistently demonstrate positive effects of personal spiritual commitment and religious involvement over and above structural (i.e., factors that are environmental/contextual rather than personal, such as family religiousness, peer influence, social support) aspects of religion (Benda, 1995; Benda & Corwyn, 2000; Donahue, 1995). The effect of personal religiousness is dependent on context. National findings support the "Hellfire effect," that a higher ambient level of religiousness in the neighborhood and community leads to a stronger influence of religion on behavior (Stark, 1996).

Religion's positive effects on prosocial behavior have also received significant research attention (Donahue, 1995; Forliti & Benson, 1986), particularly with regard to volunteerism and community service (Youniss, McLellan, & Yates, 1999). Attending Catholic school is also positively associated with volunteerism (Youniss, McLellan, Su, & Yates, 1999). Findings based on the Monitoring the Future study indicate that youth who are most involved in church are, according to their typology, *school-oriented youth*, who are strongly invested in school-based activities but not as strongly in fun activities with peers, and *all-around youth*, who are strongly invested in both school-based activities and fun activities. These same two categories of youth are also, of the five types, the most strongly invested in political activity, both conventional (e.g., voting) and unconventional (e.g., picketing, boycotting). The relatively high religiousness of all-around youth forestalls an argument that the correlation between religiousness and prosocial behavior is because religious youth are simply dull and compliant to the wishes of adults. Rather, they are "vibrant" and genuinely invested in their communities (Youniss et al., 1999).

Influences on Mental and Physical Health

Additionally, religion is positively associated with physical and mental health. A review of research not specific to adolescents indicates that religion is related to lower mortality and morbidity, both by facilitating psychological coping skills and by inhibiting self-destructive behaviors (such as alcohol abuse and smoking) that would otherwise be related to chronic illness (Koenig, McCullough, & Larson, 2001). Among religious individuals, greater use of positive religious coping (e.g., invoking a partnership with God, reappraising the situation as part of God's "perfect plan") mechanisms, which church-based social support encourages (Krause, Ellison, Shaw, Marcum, & Boardman, 2001), is associated with greater well-being. In contrast, negative religious coping behaviors (e.g., confusion and anger toward God, attributing the situation to God's punishment) have been identified as problematic for health (Krause, Ingersoll Dayton, Ellison, & Wulff, 1999; Pargament, Smith, Koenig, & Perez, 1998; Pargament, Tarakeshwar, Ellison, & Wulff, 2001). When studies distinguish between structural and personal aspects of religiousness, a difference emerges that is parallel to that found in problem behaviors. In a study of coping effectiveness of adults, although religious involvement and its associated social support and integration had a positive influence on psychological and physical health, personal religiousness and spirituality exerted a positive influence over and above structural aspects (Mattlin, Wethington, & Kessler, 1990).

Although most of these health-related findings have been extended to adolescents (Donahue, 1995), research in this area is not as well developed as the literature related to religion and problem behaviors during adolescence. For example, in a sample of rural high school students from low-income families, religious involvement was correlated with higher levels of "ego strengths," including hope, will, fidelity, love, and care (Markstrom, 1999).

RELIGION, YOUTH, AND SOCIETY

Religious Organizations' Commitment to Youth

Aside from the health impact of religious participation, the place of young people within religious organizations is important for understanding religion as a context of youth development. All major religious organizations include school-age youth, although a young person's place within that organization is understandably different from that of an adult. In a section of the recent *Handbook of Applied Developmental Science* devoted to faith perspectives, Catholic (Dowling & Dowling, 2002), Protestant (Roehlkepartain, 2002), Jewish (Friedland & Berkson, 2002), and Muslim (Hadi & Al-Fayez, 2002) voices all articulated their faiths' commitments to taking an active role in the positive development of children and adolescents. Beginning a family also figures prominently in adults' reasons for "returning to the fold" (Sherkat, 1991), because of the support that religious organizations provide to young families and because many parents believe that it is important for their children to learn religious beliefs and values.

It can be further argued that religious organizations are not entirely altruistic in reserving a place of honor for children and adolescents at their tables. The best predictor of adolescent religiousness is a secure attachment to religious parents who intentionally socialize religious habits in their children (Granqvist, 1998; Kirkpatrick & Shaver, 1990); the best predictor of young adult/college-age religiousness is intentional retention of religious social capital (Hoge, Johnson, & Luidens, 1993). The energy of youth is, in turn, the lifeblood of religious organizations, as it is of any social institution (Erikson, 1968). Thus, inasmuch as many involved young people seek to retain the religious human capital they acquired from the religious organization during childhood and adolescence, the religious organizations seek to retain the young people. Religious organizations interested in maintaining a ministry to youth intentionally adapt to be relevant to them and to include them at all levels appropriate to their interests and abilities (Ream & Witt, 2003). To do otherwise would be to deprive themselves of a vital source of energy and growth. For example, a publication of the Episcopal Society for Ministry in Higher Education (ESMHE) solidly blames that denomination's clergy shortage on neglecting ministry to college-age youth (Brewster, 1999).

Youths' Commitment to Religious Organizations

Contexts of religious and spiritual development in adolescence can either be specifically youth-oriented or involve people of all ages. Rituals such as Confirmation and Bar or Bat Mitzvah provide a context within which a young person can make a meaningful contribution to the intergenerational religious community. In the case of Bar Mitzvah, one such contribution is the *haftorah* reading, which affirms the family's religious identity and provides a means of continued connection among extended family members (Davis, 1989). Adolescents thus demonstrate a return on the investment the family has made in them since childhood. However, in a recent study of college students, although most participants had undergone such a rite-of-passage ritual, only a third indicated that it was meaningful to their spiritual development. Those who did claimed that it was a voluntary commitment for them and represented a real change in their status with respect to their religious communities (Ream & Witt, 2003).

Thus, in discerning the character of young people's religious participation, it is as important to understand *why* they attend religious services as it is to know that they are attending services. Obligatory, adult-oriented religious participation is unlikely to contribute meaningfully to a young person's spiritual development. It may even be counterproductive if it produces either immediate resentment and rebellion or religious identity foreclosure to be revisited in young adulthood, a life stage with fewer age-specific ministries targeted at it and, consequently, fewer spiritual growth and development resources available.

By contrast, 85% of participants in the above-mentioned study who had experienced a youth-oriented context of spiritual development, such as a church youth group or a youth trip to Israel, counted the experience as having been meaningful for their spiritual development (Ream & Witt, 2003). The other 15% had either wanted to find their own paths spiritually or had been turned off by youth cliques. It would be safe to conclude that voluntary religious involvement is beneficial to youth, but in order for this to occur, a religious organization has to first be available, then be ideologically in line with what the young person wants to believe or already believes, and be able to provide a place where the young person "fits in." An objective statement that religious involvement would be beneficial for young people who are not already involved in religion cannot be empirically supported because there will (hopefully) never be experimental evidence from a study in which adolescents are randomly assigned to religious treatment and nonreligious control groups.

Organized Religion as a Youth-Serving Institution

"Youth development," a perspective to which many youth-serving institutions adhere, conceptualizes religious involvement as a developmental asset (Benson, 1997). Youth development in general represents a departure from the usual focus of research on specific problem behaviors of adolescents, including drug use and teen pregnancy, and instead focuses on what is going *right* in the lives of adolescents—social support, appropriate boundaries, structured use of time, educational commitment, positive values, social competence, and so forth (Benson, 1997; Benson & Saito, 2000). Higher levels of developmental assets are consistently negatively correlated with problem behaviors in youth (Benson, 1997). Youth development theorists suggest that, similar to the known multiplicative detrimental effects of multiple risk factors (Sameroff, Seifer, Baldwin, & Baldwin, 1993), developmental assets accumulate to create resilient youth (Benson & Saito, 2000). Drawing upon findings regarding coping and prosocial behavior, it is clear that not only religious involvement but also an internalized spiritual commitment act as developmental assets, particularly by giving youth a sense of connection with things greater than themselves (Garbarino, 1999).

Search Institute, a national youth development organization, recently commissioned a study on the role of religious organizations in reaching high-risk youth (Trulear, 2000). Search Institute is particularly interested in working with religious congregations in inner cities because, after the exodus of community resources from the inner cities in America's post-industrial economy, religious congregations are sometimes the only organizations left to do the job (Benson, 1997). The first field report of this study (Trulear, 2000) and a later update (Branch, 2002) addressed the question of what religious organizations have to contribute to youth development that secular organizations do not. They recruited congregations that were engaged in sustained and organized service to youth and aided them in developing programs for high-risk youth in partnership with the justice system.

According to initial observations, these congregations experienced an intrinsic, faith-based "calling" to serve. Their faith-based approach was inclusive, welcoming everyone and providing a variety of services, which many of their workers perceived to be the historic role of congregations. The desire to serve anyone who presented a need, however, clashed with Search Institute's narrow focus on high-risk youth (Trulear, 2000). In the implementation of the study, this was a major problem for some of the participating congregations, along with the difficulty of the project's leadership in convincing congregations of the need to work with high-risk youth and maintaining a constructive relationship with a juvenile justice system which, in some cases, had its own ideas on how to best use the program (Branch, 2002).

The congregations' youth development efforts were personality driven, that is, not based on a defined mandate or set of rules, but on the visionary leadership of a pastor or other leader. One of these set an example, which some parishioners followed, of residing in the inner city along with youth in order to be more accessible to them. Although personality-driven interventions would seem to run afoul of the youth work field's penchant for tailored, research-based programs such as DARE and Communities that Care, it has several benefits. Many congregations find themselves beset by a "tyranny of need" and must accept that they cannot do everything for everyone. Visionary leaders help focus the congregation's efforts on specific goals and principles, encouraging and implementing changes that would otherwise take months of evaluation work. Furthermore, youth and youth workers alike report that the content of programs matters less than the relationships that youth establish with caring adults. These leaders provide role models for both youth and workers (Trulear, 2000).

There are predictable wrinkles in bringing faith-based organizations into partnership with secular organizations. In an investigation of faith-based initiatives (Chaves, 1999), the highest rate of public funding use was among African American congregations, and this was only 40%. Smaller congregations were, on average, less likely to use public money. Faith-based organizations were aware of the strings that may be attached to government grants. Other churches, more steeped in doctrines of being "in this world but not of it," cited theological reasons, such as the impossibility of funding "Moses's movement with Pharaoh's money" (Trulear, 2000). Although Search Institute found religious organizations surprisingly open to evaluation, viewing it as good stewardship, many congregations did not have the human resources necessary to do the grant writing and evaluation work that would be required to access public money. Small faith-based initiatives also tended to slip below the radar of philanthropic organizations. Secular foundations expressed various degrees of concern that their money would be used to fund proselytizing work, but the congregations in Search Institute's study made it clear that proselytizing was not their mission and benefactors of faith-based institutions recognized that the spiritual center of these organizations was beneficial to youth (Trulear, 2000).

Religious organizations, therefore, have much to offer youth that is unique (Kress & Elias, 2000), including a connection with spirituality, meaning, things greater than the self (Garbarino, 1999; Hall, 1904), social support, behavioral regulation (Bjarnason, 1998), and opportunities for positive relationships with caring adults (Trulear, 2000). To adults who work with youth, religion offers a strong "calling" to that type of ministry (Trulear, 2000), above and beyond the evolving and sometimes unclear ideologies of the youth development movement (Pittman, Irby, & Ferber, 2000). To organizations that wish to augment existing youth development efforts, religious congregations represent a "socializing system" (Benson & Saito, 2000) that, although multifaceted and intricate, is more accessible to evaluation efforts and easier to engage than entire communities.

Religion and Schools

Young people's spirituality and religious participation exist in the ecological context of the interaction between religious organizations and other spheres of their lives, particularly educational institutions. As long as students and/or their parents are religious, pure separation of church and state remains an American impossibility. Religious adults in communities vote, run for school boards and other public offices, lobby school boards and state and local legislatures, and are otherwise politically active. Evangelical Christianity in particular has a specific religious mandate to be involved in helping create social change (Noll, 1994), a considerable force given that, in a Gallup poll given February 17-19, 2003 (Gallup Brain, 2003), 41% of Americans responded "yes" to the question "Would you describe yourself as 'born-again' or evangelical?"

A caveat: Other research with a national sample (Kosmin & Lachman, 1993) found that, when asked for a single free response to the question of "What religion are you?" only .25% of Americans replied either "Born Again" or "Evangelical" rather than the name of a denomination. The obvious problem with this is that there is no Evangelical *denomination*, but there are individuals and congregations that are part of the Evangelical *movement,* many of which are part of other mainstream denominations, such as the Evangelical Lutheran Church of America, the Evangelical Presbyterian Church, and so on. Thus, Gallup's methodology reflects reality more clearly because it captures individuals' identification with a movement as well as a denomination.

Schools and school boards are often the target of religious organizations' efforts at social change (Diamond, 1998). Main issues include advocacy for student-led prayer in schools (Focus on the Family, 2003c), recasting evolution as a scientific theory and not fact, teaching creationism (Focus on the Family, 2003a), and preventing the dissemination of any information about homosexuality that is affirming or scientifically neutral (Focus on the Family, 2003b). Supporters of "abstinence-only" education, operating under the banner of the "parents' rights" movement that conservative religious organizations heavily support, pressure schools to restrict and control sexuality education, disregarding evidence that abstinence-only education has only occasionally been found effective at changing sexuality attitudes (Carter Jessop, Franklin, Heath, Jimenez Irizarry, & Peace, 2000; Roosa & Christopher, 1990; Sather & Zinn, 2002) and is very rarely found effective at decreasing behavior that place youth at risk for pregnancy or STDs (Aten, Siegel, Enaharo, & Auinger, 2002; Starkman & Rajani, 2002). In these respects, it does not compare favorably at all with comprehensive sexuality education (Haignere, Gold, & McDanel, 1999). Ethical and legal implications of schools' responses to this pressure are discussed later.

FAITH AND BELIEF SYSTEM DEVELOPMENT

Religious Socialization and the Learning of Beliefs

Concern with how adults can best facilitate the religious development of adolescents is arguably the first significant question asked in the field of research on adolescence. G. Stanley Hall, founder of the American Psychological Association, articulated a perspective on religious development that remains relevant to this day. According to Hall (1904), a didactic and authoritarian religious training process was unhelpful and counterproductive. Rather, parents and other invested adults were to facilitate a process of "conversion" in adolescents, broadly defined to include the adolescent's cognitive, social, and identity development as occurring alongside spiritual development. Actualization of youth, in Hall's view, was the all-encompassing goal, with doctrinal instruction only a part of that goal.

Empirical evidence has since confirmed and elaborated Hall's perspectives. Most adolescents follow the religious footsteps of their parents. Parents who wish to raise religious youth not only transmit religious values but also nurture and support their children's spiritual development (Bjarnason, 1998). Parental encouragement of the young person's own religious habits in adolescence is centrally important to this process (Erickson, 1992). Concerns that adolescent religious adherence may be derailed by doubt related to intellectual development or simple peer pressure are unfounded—parental religious socialization is the most important factor in creating a religious young person (Ozorak, 1989). Peer religious support is, however, helpful to adolescents in their spiritual development (King, Furrow, & Roth, 2002).

Effective religious socialization also nurtures and supports a young person's intellectual development with respect to religion. Contrary to uninformed stereotypes of religious people as unthinking or needing a "crutch" to get through life, empirical evidence has failed to support notions that religious people think less critically about religious matters or are less intelligent in general. A study of Catholic and conservative Protestant parents reported that, although they valued obedience of their children more than parents not involved with religion, they valued intellectual autonomy no less (Ellison & Sherkat, 1993). Other research reports sex differences in the relationship between religious and intellectual development. Having similar fundamentalist values to parents is helpful for the educational achievement of young men, but parental religious fundamentalism predicts lower achievement in higher education among young women if they do not share their parents' values (Sherkat & Darnell, 1999). The significance of this is that the religious socialization process has the power to oppress adherents and limit their options when the appropriate values are made part of a religious belief system; this issue is treated in greater detail below.

Several studies compare the relative influence of parents, religious organization, and peers. One compared samples of English 11- and 16-year-olds cross-sectionally and found parental church attendance significantly predictive of 11-year-olds' positive attitude toward prayer, but that parental religious socialization only influenced 16-year-olds' positive attitudes toward prayer indirectly through encouraging, or having encouraged in the past, the young person's religious attendance and prayer (Francis & Brown, 1991). Another study found a reciprocal relationship between parent socialization and youth religiousness: Young people influence their parents, in many cases, as much as parents influence them (Sherkat, 1991). A study of Jewish youth and families noted that the values of family cohesion and warmth that are so strong in Judaism influenced the family system as a whole to both function better as a family and nurture youths' religious development (Gamoran, 1992).

Collectively, these studies serve to describe possible best practices for religious organizations. These include investing in the family as a whole and the individuals therein, providing parents with support and resources in the religious socialization process, emulating the warm and nurturing family style that helps facilitate that process, and providing a place where young people are valued and included. Religiousness later in the life course, from a rational choice perspective, is largely a matter of holding onto religious human capital that had been invested in a young person during childhood and early adolescence (Sherkat & Wilson, 1995). Another process concerns acquiring human capital that a person wants but has not had for perhaps several years. Why a person would want this human capital is best explained by means of a psychological attachment model.

Attachment Theory of Belief System Development

Conceptualizing religion as an attachment process has brought clarity to the study of multiple paths of belief system development (Kirkpatrick, 1992, 1994, 1995). Attachment theory (Ainsworth, Blehar, Waters, & Wall, 1978; Bowlby, 1969) posits that individuals have various "attachment styles" based on their experience with their primary attachment figure in infancy, usually the mother, that are refined by later experiences with romantic partners (Hazan & Shaver, 1987). Attachment styles are classified as:

- *Secure* (roughly 60% of Americans): An individual expects a significant other to be appropriately responsive to his or her needs, trusts that this person will be there when needed, and is sad to see that person go but is not overly afraid of separation.
- *Ambivalent* (roughly 25% of Americans): An individual expects a significant other to read signals poorly and be responsive to his or her needs, but inappropriately so, and thus he or she clings to a partner anxiously, angry with any separation.

- *Avoidant* (roughly 10% of Americans): An individual expects a significant other to be unresponsive to his or her needs, and so is unwilling to let a person get too close and experiences strong separation anxiety while being afraid to display it overtly (Hazan & Shaver, 1987).

Psychologically, attachment to God, religion, and spirituality can *correspond* to a person's attachment to parents, or can *compensate* for what was never present in that relationship (Granqvist, 1998). A study comparing individuals' religious experiences based on attachment style revealed that securely attached respondents had higher religious commitment and more positive images of God than individuals in either insecure category (Kirkpatrick & Shaver, 1992). Avoidant participants were more likely to both describe themselves as agnostics (Kirkpatrick & Shaver, 1992) and to have had a sudden conversion experience (Kirkpatrick & Shaver, 1990). Also, if parents were relatively nonreligious, avoidantly attached individuals were more likely than individuals in other attachment categories with relatively nonreligious parents to become religious (Kirkpatrick & Shaver, 1990). Ambivalently attached individuals were more likely than others to have had a glossolalia (i.e., "speaking in tongues") experience.

Among college students, positive images of self and others (characteristic of secure attachment) were related cross-sectionally to positive images of God and religion, but negative images of self plus positive images of others (characteristic of insecure attachment) were related longitudinally to becoming more religious (Kirkpatrick, 1998). Object relations maturity (an operationalization of one's ability to relate in positive ways to others) was also correlated with spiritual maturity (Hall, Brokaw, Edwards, & Pike, 1998). In terms of the actual support function of a relationship with God, an important sex difference was discovered: controlling for available social support, a relationship with God was associated with decreased loneliness in young women, but was either unrelated or associated with increased loneliness among young men (Kirkpatrick, Shillito, & Kellas, 1999). Another study found, similarly, that religion was more useful as an emotional coping resource to young women than to young men (Feldman, Fisher, Ransom, & Dimiceli, 1995). These studies underscore the importance of considering sex differences in evaluating adolescents' use of religious coping.

Conversion and Apostasy Paths of Belief System Development

Conversion (becoming more religious or changing from an unsatisfactory to a more intensive and satisfactory pattern of religious involvement) and apostasy (discontinuing religious involvement completely or to a nominal level) are artifacts of a religious marketplace that encourages individual choice (Stark & Bainbridge, 1985, 1987). According to early theories (Lofland & Stark, 1965), in order for conversion to take place, a person must follow a series of steps or stages, each successively more predictive of joining a new religious group and each transitioned by successively fewer people. Potential converts must (in this order):

1. Experience enduring, acutely felt tensions,

2. within a religious problem-solving perspective,

3. which lead that person to self-identify as a religious seeker, then

4. encounter a new religious group at a turning point in life,

5. wherein that person forms an affective bond with other members of the group,

6. loses attachments to people outside that group, and

7. is exposed to intensive interaction with other group members.

Later empirical research tested this and similar models of conversion. Findings with a sample of Dutch adolescents (Kox, Meeus, & 't Hart, 1991) indicated that the Lofland and Stark (1965) model presents a set of circumstances that independently predicted adolescent conversion and thus described the life situations of many converts. However, it did not work as a stage model. A study of a 1970s-era American Jesus movement (Richardson, Stewart, & Simmonds, 1978) similarly found that lists of stages to conversion only work as lists of circumstances that make conversion more likely. Although most individuals' paths of belief system change shared many of the above features, not every path included all of the above experiences, nor did it always occur in the same order (e.g., an individual may experience positive interaction with new friends at a religious group and *then* begin to see the group as a significant context of life change).

DeHaan and Schulenberg (1997) found that converts in their sample of college undergraduates generally had undergone a period of religious searching or questioning. Furthermore, contrary to conventional wisdom of religious youth as conformist (discussed in Youniss et al., 1999), a low level of religious searching predicted low levels of religious commitment (DeHaan & Schulenberg, 1997). Youth are likely to join religious organizations if those organizations supply them with both something they believe is missing in their lives and satisfying relationships.

The noncorrelation among Lofland and Stark's (1965) conditions of conversion (Kox et al., 1991; Richardson et al., 1978) can be interpreted in two ways. One is that converts cannot be fairly characterized as pathologically lost and vulnerable individuals desperately seeking to fill a void in their lives. The other explanation is that the findings are at least partially a product of the time period in which the data were collected. Adolescents (as in Kox et al., 1991) in general are stuck with the "storm and stress" view of themselves that society imposes upon them (see Erikson, 1968, Preface, for a specific discussion of the "identity crisis" as possibly being an artificial social construction), and youth who lived in the 1960s and 1970s (as in Richardson et al., 1978) had lived through a time of rapid social change. Perhaps personal searching and family strain were prevalent in the lives of converts who participated in Lofland and Stark's research, but not to any greater extent than in the rest of the population.

Another pattern of conversion was found in a sample of rural farm youth (King, Elder, & Whitbeck, 1997). Increases in religiousness among young participants in the Iowa Youth and Families project tended to coincide with increases in religiousness in the youths' families. It is important to note here that the most prevalent forms of conversion, as described above, have little to do with family strain or doomsday cults, but rather with normative growth and change of individual belief systems and organizational attachments in the context of supportive interpersonal relationships. Allegiance to, and criticism of, social institutions and their ideology, religious or otherwise, are part of normative identity development (Erikson, 1968).

The Iowa rural youth study (King et al., 1997) also tracked a significant number of apostates. Apostate youth tend to identify less strongly with their parents than converted youth or continuously religious youth. Other apostasy research has found that parental factors such as perception of parent hypocrisy, difficult relationship with parents, and parental divorce contributed to alienation from religion in church-related youth. This does not explain nearly as much variance in the likelihood of apostasy, however, as perception of pastoral insincerity and lack of a positive relationship with a nonparent adult religious role model such as a youth pastor (Dudley & Laurent, 1988). A review of Hunsberger's research on Amazing Apostates revealed a similar finding: apostasy in church-related youth is generally the product of major disillusionment with religion (Dudley, 1999). Earlier theories that apostasy is the result of secularization that should naturally come with increasing education and life experience are not borne out by empirical research (Greeley, 1978).

CONTEXTUAL CONCERNS

African American Youth

Research on African American youth indicates that church involvement, particularly self-motivated church involvement, acts as a buffer against "subjective stigmatization," or internalized racism (Brega & Coleman, 1999). Although the authors found lower levels of subjective stigmatization in youth strongly committed to the church, they did not test for an interaction between the strength of those socialization messages and self-motivated church involvement. Because this study found differential levels of subjective stigmatization based on type of racial socialization, the African American church as a source of positive ethnic-minority identity is a prime target for future research. For example, Markstrom (1999) found different patterns of the effect of religiousness on ego strengths for African American and white youth. Although the influence of religiousness on ego strengths was more pronounced for white youth, religiousness uniquely affected positive ethnic-minority identification in African American youth.

Latino/a Youth

In immigrant groups, a second-generation rebellion has often been observed as the grandchildren of original immigrants seek to break loose of the ethnic community and become fully modern Americans (Hernandez & Dudley, 1990). In a sample of Latino/a Seventh-day Adventist adolescents, disaffiliation of youth from a "religio-ethnic community" of immigrants caused collateral damage to their religiousness. Family affluence and assimilation with American culture predicted lower religious commitment, lower religious saliency, and lower devotional behavior (Hernandez & Dudley, 1990).

Inner-City Youth

The potential of religious organizations to help revitalize inner-city areas has received redoubled attention within the community development literature (Johnson, Larson, Li, & Jang, 2000; Ramsay, 1998). Lower income, ethnicity (Hernandez & Dudley, 1990), and inner-city residence (Ramsay, 1998) contribute to a different role for religion in the lives of youth and different expressions of that religion. In general, factors that predict a lower stake in conformity with the rest of society also predict preferences for sects (i.e., new and innovative offshoots of churches) over churches (i.e., older and more established religious organizations) (Bader & Demaris, 1996).

Jewish Youth

Gamoran (1990) examined how Jewish youth adapt to the heavily Christian "civil religion" that has become an inescapable part of American schools. "One Nation under God" sounds inclusive enough on the surface, but when a Christmas tree is installed in the school library, Jewish youth have little trouble figuring out which God the nation is under. Jewish youth have the option to either mask their Jewish identity and assimilate, or assert their Jewish identity and be marginalized. Gamoran noted, however, how this civil religion (which includes holidays that are not explicitly religious) can work both ways; although celebrating Christmas in schools can marginalize Jewish youth, celebrating Martin Luther King Day can help include African American youth (Gamoran, 1990).

Conservative and Liberal

Public opinion data showed significant dips in confidence in organized religion and in religious participation during the televangelist scandals of 1987–1988 for both youth and adults. However, the same analyses run with fundamentalist beliefs and size of the electronic church audience as dependent variables showed no effect. The life-course event of the televangelist scandals had differential effects for liberals and conservatives (Smith, 1992). A possibly related finding is the differential effects of socialization for liberal/mainline Protestants and conservative/evangelical Protestants. Based on effect sizes, the evangelical groups were roughly twice as successful at socializing youth with an enduring religious commitment than mainline groups (Nelsen, 1981). Conservatives who were taught to hold to the faith no matter what, similarly to the adherents to fundamentalist beliefs mentioned above, were more resilient to both internal doubts and outside factors that caused them to question their faith.

SPECIAL ISSUES

Cults and the Occult

In evaluating youth involvement in cults and the occult, a proper perspective is important, particularly in defining terms. Social theory of religion defines a cult as any new religious movement, or NRM (Sherkat, 2001a, 2001b). In order to qualify for the label "dangerous cult," a group would have to use deceptive recruitment practices, be secretive about its practices, employ overt mind-control techniques, and threaten proselytes with harm should they leave. In contrast, Evangelical Christian sources (Gomes, 1995) hold that a cult is any group whose beliefs run counter to central doctrines of Christianity. From the perspective of the Evangelical countercult movement (details: http://www.religioustolerance.org/ccm. htm), groups such as Heaven's Gate (39 members of which attempted to reach a higher plane of existence via suicide in 1997) fall into the same category as groups that require a high investment from their members but that are not known to coerce retention or use mind control, including the Church of Latter-Day Saints (Mormons), the Jehovah's Witnesses, and the International Church of Christ. Educators and youth workers who find parents afraid of cult threats to youth may have to consider carefully the definition of "cult" that is being employed. In the middle of a social panic about cults and the harm they can do to youth, it is easy to overlook groups that are a real threat and instead be drawn into interdenominational politics.

A recently published warning to parents and practitioners about "cults" (Hunter, 1998) suggested reasons for joining "cults" that, according to conversion research, are reasons for joining any religious organization. Hunter made no distinction between conversion to churches, to sects, or to NRMs. His suggestion that youth-serving organizations attempt to serve youth in ways that forestall "cult" involvement is well grounded, but it must also be noted that youth-serving religious organizations may be best suited to the task of providing youth services and supports that serve as a viable and attractive alternative. This is not only because, as noted earlier, potential converts often are predisposed to seek solutions to problems from within a religious problem-solving perspective (Lofland & Stark, 1965). Religious organizations make unique contributions to youths' health and development (Ream & Witt, 2003) and often serve as part of a supportive network that includes both religious organizations and secular youth development organizations (Baker, 2002). Finally, in impoverished areas in which deviant or militant religious involvement may appear to be a particularly attractive option, religious organizations are often the only organizations capable of delivering services (Trulear, 2000).

Streib (1999) used narrative analysis of qualitative interview data to develop a typology of motivations and life themes associated with German youths' involvement in fundamentalism and the occult. Fundamentalists were either governed by the tradition in which they grew up, had grown up in another tradition and converted to a fundamentalist tradition, or were "accumulative heretics" who made a tour of several different religious traditions. Common life themes were childhood trauma or a long-felt need for love and acceptance. Motivations for being religious were not significantly different from those of nonfundamentalist youth (Streib, 1999). With regard to youth involved in the occult, Streib found several youth who only wanted to experiment. Seriously involved youth were engaged because they wanted relief and transformation, but as they used magical thinking to engage significant life themes, they also became more anxious because, unlike religious practices, occult rituals involve appeasement of and defense against powers greater than the self rather than a positive relationship with such powers. Streib related the story of a young woman whose involvement with the occult only made her more scared of her demons, but who found relief through exorcism in a strict Catholic church.

Generalizability of Findings

In discussing findings on the social psychology of religion, one critical question is, "Which religion?" Scholars who are uninitiated to the subject may be unwilling to believe that it is possible to operationalize religion in a manner that can be useful to research, and the field still suffers from this ideological prejudice (Donelson, 1999; Gorsuch, 1988). Scholars within the field, however, have given more attention to measurement and methodology than virtually any other issue. Intrinsic religion (Allport & Ross, 1967; Gorsuch & Venable, 1983) is a widely used measure of the degree to which a person participates in religion because of an internally motivated commitment and relies on his or her faith in everyday life. The intrinsic religion measure has been validated across cultures (Gorsuch, Mylvaganam, Gorsuch, & Johnson, 1997), although the concept has been criticized for artificially conflating too many dimensions of religious involvement (Kirkpatrick & Hood, 1990). In a multireligious sample, Protestants scored higher on intrinsic religion than Catholics or Jews, but the scale still reliably measured religious belief and commitment within Catholic and Jewish populations (Ream, 2001a). Other research found strong links between religious commitment and attachment processes (Kirkpatrick, 1992; Kirkpatrick & Shaver, 1992), indicating that certain psychological dimensions of religion are endemic to the human organism and not fundamentally different from one culture to the next.

Thus, although many studies quantify commitment and participation level and generalize across denominational lines, these are not regarded as problematically ignoring contextual factors, but rather as a valid generalization that can be confidently made based on extant work and theory. However, religion is simultaneously viewed as a source of human capital (Iannaccone, 1990; Stark & Bainbridge, 1985, 1987, 1996), that is, a learned set of values, beliefs, and behaviors that people acquire intentionally and that parents and other concerned adults confer upon children in order to provide them with resources for living. In contrast to attachment and motivational theories that regard universal aspects of religion, human capital perspectives inform observations that religions, responding to environmental influences, differ greatly in their social, cultural, and institutional features. Religious institutions may serve themselves by including, along with the package of religious belief and commitment, other religious social capital aimed more at perpetuating the institution than providing individuals with needed psychological resources, particularly to adolescents. Thus, the social psychological findings presented below about the connection between religion and certain attitudes must always include the caveat that the connection can never be said to be direct and that religion as a psychological process connects to social and political attitudes through a socialization process that is unique to specific institutions, however strong the hegemonic control of those institutions over society may be (Ream, 2001b, 2002).

Prejudice and School Shootings

Connections between certain dimensions of personal religiousness and prejudice toward religious outgroups (Jackson & Hunsberger, 1999), racial minorities, and sexual minorities (Laythe, Finkel, & Kirkpatrick, 2001) have been found among college-age youth. The classic and often-replicated finding holds that racial prejudice is more often part of an extrinsic and externally motivated religious belief system that uses religion as a means to an end (as well as its correlates, such as fundamentalism and right-wing authoritarianism), and that intrinsic and internally motivated religious beliefs are negatively correlated with racial prejudice (Allport & Ross, 1967; Kirkpatrick, 1993; McFarland, 1989). Prejudice against sexual minorities, however, has been observed to be tightly bonded with intrinsically religious belief systems, including those of college-age youth (Fulton, Gorsuch, & Maynard, 1999; Herek, 1987; Ream, 2002).

The latter is of particular importance to educators, given the known role that sexual prejudice plays in incidents of school bullying and victimization (Robinson, 2001). According to a *Washington Blade* (a widely circulated gay community newspaper based in Washington, D.C.) news report published after the Columbine shootings (Chibbaro, 1999), gay and lesbian students in Littleton and the greater Denver area were worried about a backlash against them due to homophobia. They knew that Eric Harris and Dylan Klebold had been called "gay" and thought that the shooting would be perceived as gay students lashing out against harassment received at school (see also Wilkinson, 1999). They believed they would face a strong and potentially violent reaction, which would not discriminate between youth such as Harris and Klebold who had only been labeled gay (although all available indications of the shooters' sexual orientation indicated that they were heterosexual) and those who actually were sexual minorities. Students interviewed for the article understood, as researchers are only recently coming to understand, they would be victimized based on *perceived*—not necessarily actual—sexual orientation, that this victimization would be far more severe than victimization based on other factors (Hershberger & D'Augelli, 1995), and that they would be in significant personal and emotional danger (Hershberger, Pilkington, & D'Augelli, 1997; Savin-Williams & Ream, 2003). According to the *Washington Blade* article,

> with this as a backdrop, many of the Gay teens who attended the Rainbow Alley meeting in Denver on the night of April 21 appeared to be bearing the weight of the world on their shoulders, said Mike Smith, executive director of the Colorado Gay, Lesbian, and Bisexual Community Services Center.
> "You could see it in their eyes," Smith said. "It was a real gut-level human emotion of being in fear for being different. A lot of them said they were afraid to go back to school the next day." (Chibbaro, 1999, pp. 1, 17)

The article reviews three other school shooting incidents (perpetrators included Michael Carneal in Paducha, Kentucky; Matthew Santoni in Northhampton, Massachusetts; Barry Loukaitis in Moses Lake, Washington) in which the perpetrator was reacting against having been a victim of antigay slurs. Additionally, a news report from the *San Diego Union-Tribune* (Green & Lieberman, 2001), kept on file at the Gay, Lesbian, and Straight Educators' Network (http://www.glsen.org/templates/news/record.html?section=12&record=608), indicates that Charles Andrew Williams, the school shooter in Santana, California, had also been the target of antigay epithets.

Religious Antigay Activism

Although the harm that sexual prejudice causes to sexual-minority youth is a matter of public record (Herr, 1997; Ryan & Futterman, 1997; Savin-Williams, 1996; Savin-Williams & Diamond, 1999), the evidence gleaned from several school shooting incidents reveals that sexual prejudice causes harm to high school–age youth even if neither the perpetrator nor the victim is a member of a sexual minority. Several antibullying programs developed in response to this evidence, however, were opposed by religious conservative organizations because the programs mentioned antigay prejudice as an inappropriate motive for victimizing students (Tomsho, 2002). These efforts proceeded along the same lines as the Christian Right's advocacy for abstinence-only education in place of comprehensive sex education: the proliferation of an ideology at the expense of the immediate goal of keeping youth safe.

Conservative activism of the type with which schools need to be most concerned is grassroots and local in its focus, but involves resources sent from and individuals trained by national organizations such as Focus on the Family or the Christian Coalition, or state organizations such as the Michigan Family Association (Diamond, 1998). Favorite tactics of these activists include overstating the strength of their case and understating the scope of their organizations. In support of their consistent position that homosexuality is a choice of adults and is harmful to youth, they cite antiquated psychoanalytic theory, raw prevalence data from the Centers for Disease Control, heavily biased and poorly conducted "research" by conservative think tanks such as the Family Research Institute, and the writings of their own opinion leaders such as James Dobson (Dobson, 2001; Herek, 1998; Herman, 1997). The activists themselves may not even understand that they have been misinformed, and are unlikely to want to believe that such a trusted authority as James Dobson would misinform them (Diamond, 1998). Rather, they are convinced that they are benefiting sexual minorities by encouraging them to acknowledge that they are unhappy with their existence (which is often made unhappy, ironically, by the efforts of conservative activists) and to embrace the possibility of change. When opposed, conservative activists cast themselves in the victim's role, claiming that their first amendment rights have been violated and that, despite the hegemonic power of their movement, they are a minority group being persecuted for their views (Herman, 1997; Stein, 2001).

It has been argued that, as a result of this ecological pressure, sexual-minority youth often find their failure preordained by their educational environment (Herr, 1997). However, recent research indicates that most youth with same-sex attractions are resilient to these environmental stressors, picking through the minefield laid for them and emerging with surprisingly few casualties. Large and diverse samples of sexual-minority youth reveal elevated rates of reported suicide attempts and other symptoms of marginalization and victimization, such as depression and low self-esteem (Savin-Williams & Ream, 2003), but not the astronomical suicide attempt rates reported in research based on clinical or support group samples (Savin-Williams, 1994, 2001).

Schools' Response to Religion-Based Sexual Prejudice

Educators' duty to counteract the sexual prejudice found in schools, in spite of the sometimes overt efforts by Christian conservative organizations to stop any antivictimization effort that makes an explicit mention of sexual orientation as a motivation for bullying (Tomsho, 2002), is further underscored by recent cases in which schools were successfully sued for failing to protect students against victimization. Jamie Nabozny (Buckel, 2000; Callahan, 2000; Taylor, 2003) won $900,000 from the Ashland County School District in Wisconsin in a high-profile ruling by the 7th U.S. Court of Appeals. Thomas McLaughlin's (Lewin, 2003; "National briefing," 2003) parents, with the help of the American Civil Liberties Union, forced the Pulaski County Special School District in Arkansas to settle out of court for $25,000 and clear Thomas's record of disciplinary actions that the school had taken against him in response to his disclosure of his sexual orientation. Religion figured prominently in the latter case. In Thomas McLaughlin's words, "Later, the science teacher wrote me a four-page handwritten letter about the Bible's teachings on homosexuality, telling me I would be condemned to hell. I threw it out." The parents also alleged that "a different assistant principal called Thomas to his office this year and made him read aloud a Bible passage condemning homosexuality" (Lewin, 2003, p. 10).

Although the link between religiousness and sexual prejudice has been established in the research literature, it must be noted that prejudice is not a necessary component of religion (Ream, 2002). Constructing religious messages to include sexual prejudice is a deliberate and intentional process of religious leaders (Diamond, 1998), but individuals often take the difficult path of constructing their beliefs differently (Fulton et al., 1999). Arguably, religious sexual-minority youth have the hardest time of this, because they are the targets of the prejudice that they are trying to extricate from belief systems that they want to trust and obey. However, some intrinsically religious sexual-minority youth are at an advantage, because, however marginalized they are within a religious organization, they can draw upon the resources of their faith to help them face homophobia (Ream, 2003). Schools may best serve this population of youth by first making sure that schools are safe and gay-positive places, then, rather than assuming that all sexual-minority youth are high risk, by attending to those who are having trouble with the same concern that any other at-risk youth would receive.

CONCLUSIONS

Voluntary religious involvement is generally a positive influence on young people's lives. Personal spiritual commitment, as well as religious involvement, are beneficial. The only caveat is that adolescents follow various developmental paths with respect to their religious development, and what is beneficial to one may not be helpful for another. Young women and ethnic minorities for whom religion is an important aspect of culture tend to receive more benefits resulting from religious involvement than do white, male youth, as if an increased role of religion in resiliency processes compensates for the status of membership in a nondominant group. For sexual minorities, however, religion has as much potential to be harmful as it does to be helpful. Religion is part of a whole-family and whole-community process, and its role in a young person's life depends on context.

Religious organizations make valuable partners to community organizations that serve youth. Far from fitting the stereotype of being only interested in proselytizing, religious organizations involved in youth work demonstrate a commitment to youth and to youth development ideology. They vary in the degree to which they are interested in using Charitable Choice and other sources of public funding. Religious organizations provide psychological and spiritual resources, such as a facilitated connection with a sentient entity greater than the self, that are beyond the scope of what secular organizations can offer. This has proven to be particularly important in the case of at-risk and high-risk youth, who often have a compromised sense of basic faith and trust, which religious attachments can help restore (Garbarino, 1999).

Regarding the interaction of religious and educational spheres in young people's lives, it is important to assume a youth development approach, placing the concerns of young people first and allowing them to take the lead in articulating their needs. The intersection of politics and religion is a fact of life for educators and skillful management is necessary to ensure parents are on board and youths' boundaries are respected. Although satanic cults, evolution, the homosexual lifestyle, and separation of church and state are of great concern to some parents and sectarian political action groups, moral panics over these issues have caused far more harm than the issues themselves ever could, and parents and community members must be encouraged to see past these illusory threats to their children and engage their youths' educational process in a more adaptive manner. Allowing schools to become a battleground for adults' political concerns is never appropriate, but neither is installing a sign that reads "religion-free school zone." Within secular educational contexts, adolescents learn how to define themselves as religious (or nonreligious) people in a religiously diverse world. Young people themselves are educators' best source for information on how to best facilitate that process and make sure that everyone is comfortable being who they are.

REFERENCES

Ainsworth, M. D. S., Blehar, M. C., Waters, E., & Wall, S. (1978). *Patterns of attachment*. Hillsdale, NJ: Erlbaum.

Allport, G. W., & Ross, J. M. (1967). Personal religious orientation and prejudice. *Journal of Personality and Social Psychology, 5*(4), 432–443.

Aten, M. J., Siegel, D. M., Enaharo, M., & Auinger, P. (2002). Keeping middle school students abstinent: Outcomes of a primary prevention intervention. *Journal of Adolescent Health, 31*(1), 70–78.

Bader, C., & Demaris, A. (1996). A test of the Stark-Bainbridge theory of affiliation with sects and cults. *Journal for the Scientific Study of Religion, 35*(3), 285–303.

Baker, J. M. (2002). *How homophobia hurts children: Nurturing diversity at home, at school, and in the community*: New York: Haworth Press.

Beck, S. H., Cole, B. S., & Hammond, J. A. (1991). Religious heritage and premarital sex: Evidence from a national sample of young adults. *Journal for the Scientific Study of Religion, 30*(2), 173–180.

Benda, B. B. (1995). The effect of religion on adolescent delinquency revisited. *Journal of Research in Crime and Delinquency, 32*(4), 446–466.

Benda, B. B. (2002). Religion and violent offenders in boot camp: A structural equation model. *Journal of Research in Crime and Delinquency, 39*(1), 91–121.

Benda, B. B., & Corwyn, R. F. (2000). A theoretical model of religiosity and drug use with reciprocal relationships: A test using structural equation modeling. *Journal of Social Service Research, 26*(4), 43–67.

Benson, P. L. (1992). Religion and substance use. In J. F. Schumaker (Ed.), *Religion and mental health* (pp. 211–220). New York: Oxford University Press.

Benson, P. L. (1997). *All kids are our kids: What communities must do to raise caring and responsible children and adolescents*. San Francisco: Jossey-Bass.

Benson, P. L., & Saito, R. N. (2000). The scientific foundations of youth development. In *Youth development: Issues, challenges and directions* (pp. 125–148). Philadelphia: Public/Private Ventures.

Berger, P. L. (1967). *The sacred canopy: Elements of a sociological theory of religion*. Garden City, NY: Doubleday.

Bjarnason, T. (1998). Parents, religion, and perceived social coherence: A Durkheimian framework of adolescent anomie. *Journal for the Scientific Study of Religion, 37*(4), 742–754.

Bowlby, J. (1969). *Attachment and loss: Vol. 1. Attachment*. New York: Basic Books.

Branch, A. Y. (2002). *Faith and action: Implementation of the national faith-based initiative for high-risk youth*. Retrieved January 11, 2003, from http://www.ppv.org

Brega, A. G., & Coleman, L. M. (1999). Effects of religiosity and racial socialization on subjective stigmatization in African American adolescents. *Journal of Adolescence, 22*, 223–242.

Brewster, G. (1999). *Ministry on the frontier: The contribution of Episcopal campus ministry to the present and future church*. Champaign, IL: Episcopal Society for Ministry in Higher Education.

Brownfield, D., & Sorenson, A. M. (1991). Religion and drug use among adolescents: A social support conceptualization and interpretation. *Deviant Behavior, 12*(3), 259–276.

Buckel, D. S. (2000). Legal perspective on ensuring a safe and nondiscriminatory school environment for gay, bisexual, and transgendered students. *Education and Urban Society, 32*(3), 390–398.

Callahan, C. (2000). Schools that have not protected and worked with gay and lesbian students have been sanctioned by the courts. *Education, 121*(2), 313–326.

Carter Jessop, L., Franklin, L. N., Heath, J. W., Jr., Jimenez Irizarry, G., & Peace, M. D. (2000). Abstinence education for urban youth. *Journal of Community Health: The Publication for Health Promotion and Disease Prevention, 25*(4), 293–304.

Chaves, M. (1999). Religious congregations and welfare reform: Who will take advantage of "Charitable Choice?" *American Sociological Review, 64*(6), 836–846.

Chibbaro, L. (1999, May 7). Young gays traumatized by shooting. *Washington Blade*, pp. 1, 17.

Davis, J. (1989). Mazel Tov: The Bar Mitzvah as a multigenerational ritual of change and continuity. In E. Imber-Black, R. Whiting, & J. Roberts (Eds.), *Rituals in families and family therapy* (pp. 177–208). New York: Norton.

DeHaan, L. G., & Schulenberg, J. (1997). The covariation of religion and politics during the transition to young adulthood: Challenging global identity assumptions. *Journal of Adolescence, 20*(5), 537–552.

Diamond, S. (1998). *Not by politics alone: The enduring influence of the Christian Right.* New York: Guilford Press.

Dobson, J. C. (2001). *Bringing up boys.* Wheaton, IL: Tyndale House.

Donahue, M. J. (1995). Religion and the well-being of adolescents. *Journal of Social Issues, 51*(2), 145–160.

Donelson, E. (1999). Psychology of religion and adolescents in the United States: Past to present. *Journal of Adolescence, 22*, 187–204.

Dowling, E. M., & Dowling, R. J. (2002). Youth development through youth ministry: A renewed emphasis of the Catholic Church. In R. M. Lerner, F. Jacobs, & D. Wertleib (Eds.), *Handbook of applied developmental science: Promoting positive child, adolescent, and family development through research, policies, and programs* (Vol. 3, pp. 475–494). Thousand Oaks, CA: Sage.

Dudley, R. L. (1999). Youth religious commitment over time: A longitudinal study of retention. *Review of Religious Research, 41*(1), 110–121.

Dudley, R. L., & Laurent, C. R. (1988). Alienation from religion in church-related adolescents. *Sociological Analysis, 49*(4), 408–420.

Durkheim, E. (1915). *The elementary forms of the religious life* (J. W. Swain, Trans.). London: Allen & Unwin.

Ellison, C. G., Boardman, J. D., Williams, D. R., & Jackson, J. S. (2001). Religious involvement, stress, and mental health: Findings from the 1995 Detroit Area Study. *Social Forces, 80*(1), 215–249.

Ellison, C. G., & Sherkat, D. E. (1993). Obedience and autonomy: Religion and parental values reconsidered. *Journal for the Scientific Study of Religion, 32*(4), 313–329.

Erickson, J. A. (1992). Adolescent religious development and commitment: A structural equation model of the role of family, peer group, and educational influences. *Journal for the Scientific Study of Religion, 31*(2), 131–152.

Erikson, E. H. (1968). *Identity, youth, and crisis.* New York: Norton.

Feldman, S. S., Fisher, L., Ransom, D. C., & Dimiceli, S. (1995). Is "what is good for the goose good for the gander?" Sex differences in relations between adolescent coping and adult adaptation. *Journal of Research on Adolescence, 5*(3), 333–359.

Focus on the Family. (2003a). *Creation/evolution debate.* Retrieved April 16, 2003, from http://www.family.org/cforum/topics/a0018793.cfm

Focus on the Family. (2003b). *Homosexuality in schools.* Retrieved April 16, 2003, from http://www.family.org/cforum/topics/a0018824.cfm

Focus on the Family. (2003c). *Religious expression in the classroom.* Retrieved April 16, 2003, from http://www.family.org/cforum/topics/a0018794.cfm

Forliti, J. E., & Benson, P. L. (1986). Young adolescents: A national study. *Religious Education, 81*(2), 199–224.

Francis, L. J., & Brown, L. B. (1991). The influence of home, church, and school on prayer among sixteen-year-old adolescents in England. *Review of Religious Research, 33*(2), 112–122.

Freud, S. (1927). *The future of an illusion* (J. Strachey, Trans.). Garden City, NY: Anchor Books.

Friedland, S. J., & Berkson, W. (2002). Jewish youth and family development programs. In R. M. Lerner, F. Jacobs, & D. Wertleib (Eds.), *Handbook of applied developmental science: Promoting positive child, adolescent, and family development through research, policies, and programs* (Vol. 3, pp. 495–514). Thousand Oaks, CA: Sage.

Fulton, A. S., Gorsuch, R. L., & Maynard, E. A. (1999). Religious orientation, anti-homosexual sentiment, and fundamentalism among Christians. *Journal for the Scientific Study of Religion, 38*(1), 14–35.

Gallup Brain. (2003). *Poll topics & trends: Religion.* Retrieved April 16, 2003, from http://www.gallup.com/poll/topics/religion.asp

Gallup, G. J., & Lindsay, D. M. (1999). *Surveying the religious landscape: Trends in U.S. beliefs.* Harrisburg, PA: Morehouse.

Gamoran, A. (1990). Civil religion in American schools. *Sociological Analysis, 51*(3), 235–256.

Gamoran, A. (1992). Religious participation and family values among American Jewish youth. *Contemporary Jewry*(13), 44–59.

Garbarino, J. (1999). *Lost boys: Why our sons turn violent and how we can save them.* New York: Free Press.

Gomes, A. W. (1995). *Unmasking the cults.* Grand Rapids, MI: Zondervan.

Gorsuch, R. L. (1988). Psychology of religion. *Annual Review of Psychology, 39*, 201–221.

Gorsuch, R. L., Mylvaganam, G., Gorsuch, K., & Johnson, R. (1997). Perceived religious motivation. *International Journal for the Psychology of Religion, 7*(4), 253–261.

Gorsuch, R. L., & Venable, G. D. (1983). Development of an "Age Universal" I-E scale. *Journal for the Scientific Study of Religion, 22*(2), 181–187.

Granqvist, P. (1998). Religiousness and perceived childhood attachment: On the question of compensation or correspondence. *Journal for the Scientific Study of Religion, 37*(2), 350–367.

Greeley, A. M. (1978). Religious musical chairs. *Society, 15*(4), 53–59.

Green, K., & Lieberman, B. (2001, March 10). Bullying, ridicule of Williams were routine, friends say. *San Diego Union-Tribune,* p. A1.

Hadi, F., & Al-Fayez, G. (2002). Islamic Arabic youth and youth development: An example from Kuwait. In R. M. Lerner, F. Jacobs, & D. Wertleib (Eds.), *Handbook of applied developmental science: Promoting positive child, adolescent, and family development through research, policies, and programs* (Vol. 3, pp. 455–473). Thousand Oaks, CA: Sage.

Haignere, C. S., Gold, R., & McDanel, H. J. (1999). Adolescent abstinence and condom use: Are we sure we are really teaching what is safe? *Health Education and Behavior, 26*(1), 43–54.

Hall, G. S. (1904). *Adolescence, its psychology, and its relations to physiology, anthropology, sociology, sex, crime, religion, and education.* (Vol. 2). New York: Appleton.

Hall, T. W., Brokaw, B. F., Edwards, K. J., & Pike, P. L. (1998). An empirical exploration of psychoanalysis and religion: Spiritual maturity and object relations development. *Journal for the Scientific Study of Religion, 37*(2), 303–313.

Hazan, C., & Shaver, P. (1987). Romantic love conceptualized as an attachment process. *Journal of Personality and Social Psychology, 52*(3), 511–524.

Herek, G. M. (1987). Religious orientation and prejudice: A comparison of racial and sexual attitudes. *Personality and Social Psychology Bulletin, 13*(1), 34–44.

Herek, G. M. (1998). Bad science in the service of stigma: A critique of the Cameron group's survey studies. In G. M. Herek (Ed.), *Stigma and sexual orientation: Understanding prejudice against lesbians, gay men, and bisexuals* (pp. 223–255). Thousand Oaks, CA: Sage.

Herman, D. (1997). *The antigay agenda.* Chicago: University of Chicago Press.

Hernandez, E. I., & Dudley, R. L. (1990). Persistence of religion through primary group ties among Hispanic Seventh-day Adventist young people. *Review of Religious Research, 32*(2), 157–172.

Herr, K. (1997). Learning lessons from school: Homophobia, heterosexism, and the construction of failure. In M. B. Harris (Ed.), *School experiences of gay and lesbian youth* (pp. 51–64). New York: Harrington Park Press.

Hershberger, S. L., & D'Augelli, A. R. (1995). The impact of victimization on the mental health and suicidality of lesbian, gay, and bisexual youths. *Developmental Psychology, 31*(1), 65–74.

Hershberger, S. L., Pilkington, N. W., & D'Augelli, A. R. (1997). Predictors of suicide attempts among gay, lesbian, and bisexual youth. *Journal of Adolescent Research, 12*(4), 477–497.

Hoge, D. R., Johnson, B., & Luidens, D. A. (1993). Determinants of church involvement of young adults who grew up in Presbyterian churches. *Journal for the Scientific Study of Religion, 32*(3), 242–255.

Hunter, E. (1998). Adolescent attraction to cults. *Adolescence, 33*(131), 709–714.

Iannaccone, L. R. (1990). Religious practice: A human capital approach. *Journal for the Scientific Study of Religion, 29*(3), 297–314.

Jackson, L. M., & Hunsberger, B. (1999). An intergroup perspective on religion and prejudice. *Journal for the Scientific Study of Religion, 38*(4), 509–523.

Johnson, B. R., Larson, D. B., Li, S. D., & Jang, S. J. (2000). Escaping from the crime of inner cities: Church attendance and religious salience among disadvantaged youth. *Justice Quarterly, 17*(2), 377–391.

King, P. E., Furrow, J. L., & Roth, N. (2002). The influence of families and peers on adolescent religiousness. *Journal of Psychology and Christianity, 21*(2), 109–120.

King, V., Elder, G. H. J., & Whitbeck, L. B. (1997). Religious involvement among rural youth: An ecological and life-course perspective. *Journal of Research on Adolescence, 7*(4), 431–456.

Kirkpatrick, L. A. (1992). An attachment-theory approach to the psychology of religion. *International Journal for the Psychology of Religion, 2*(1), 3–28.

Kirkpatrick, L. A. (1993). Fundamentalism, Christian orthodoxy, and intrinsic religious orientation as predictors of discriminatory attitudes. *Journal for the Scientific Study of Religion, 32*(3), 256–268.

Kirkpatrick, L. A. (1994). The role of attachment in religious belief and behavior. In K. Bartholomew & D. Perlman (Eds.), *Advances in personal relationships: Attachment processes in adulthood* (Vol. 5, pp. 239–265), Jessica Kingsley.

Kirkpatrick, L. A. (1995). Attachment theory and religious experience. In R. W. Hood (Ed.), *Handbook of religious experience* (pp. 446–475), Birmingham, AL: Religious Education Press.

Kirkpatrick, L. A. (1998). God as a substitute attachment figure: A longitudinal study of adult attachment style and religious change in college students. *Personality and Social Psychology Bulletin, 24*(9), 961–973.

Kirkpatrick, L. A., & Hood, R. W. (1990). Intrinsic-extrinsic religious orientation: The boon or bane of contemporary psychology of religion? *Journal for the Scientific Study of Religion, 29*(4), 442–462.

Kirkpatrick, L. A., & Shaver, P. R. (1990). Attachment theory and religion: Childhood attachments, religious beliefs, and conversion. *Journal for the Scientific Study of Religion, 29*(3), 315–334.

Kirkpatrick, L. A., & Shaver, P. R. (1992). An attachment-theoretical approach to romantic love and religious belief. *Personality and Social Psychology Bulletin, 18*(3), 266–275.

Kirkpatrick, L. A., Shillito, D. J., & Kellas, S. L. (1999). Loneliness, social support, and perceived relationships with God. *Journal of Social and Personal Relationships, 16*(4), 513–522.

Koenig, H. G., McCullough, M. E., & Larson, D. B. (2001). *Handbook of religion and health*. Oxford: Oxford University Press.

Kosmin, B. A., & Lachman, S. (1993). *One nation under God: Religion in contemporary American society*. New York: Harmony Books.

Kox, W., Meeus, W., & 't Hart, H. (1991). Religious conversion of adolescents: Testing the Lofland and Stark model of religious conversion. *Sociological Analysis, 52*(3), 227–240.

Krause, N., Ellison, C. G., Shaw, B. A., Marcum, J. P., & Boardman, J. D. (2001). Church-based social support and religious coping. *Journal for the Scientific Study of Religion, 40*(4), 637–656.

Krause, N., Ingersoll Dayton, B., Ellison, C. G., & Wulff, K. M. (1999). Aging, religious doubt, and psychological well-being. *Gerontologist, 39*(5), 525–533.

Kress, J. S., & Elias, M. J. (2000). Infusing community psychology and religion: Themes from an action-research project in Jewish identity development. *Journal of Community Psychology, 28*(2), 187–198.

Laythe, B., Finkel, D., & Kirkpatrick, L. A. (2001). Predicting prejudice from religious fundamentalism and right-wing authoritarianism: A multiple-regression approach. *Journal for the Scientific Study of Religion, 40*(1), 1–10.

Lewin, T. (2003, March 25). Arkansas school is accused of harassing a gay student. *New York Times*, p. A10.

Lofland, J., & Stark, R. (1965). Becoming a world saver: A theory of conversion to a deviant perspective. *American Sociological Review, 30*, 862–875.

Lyons, L. (2003). *Open the doors and see all the—teenagers?* Retrieved June 17, 2003, from http://www.gallup.com/poll/tb/religvalue/20030617.asp

Markstrom, C. A. (1999). Religious involvement and adolescent psychosocial development. *Journal of Adolescence, 22*(2), 205–221.

Mason, W. A., & Windle, M. (2002). A longitudinal study of the effects of religiosity on adolescent alcohol use and alcohol-related problems. *Journal of Adolescent Research, 17*(4), 346–363.

Mattlin, J. A., Wethington, E., & Kessler, R. C. (1990). Situational determinants of coping and coping effectiveness. *Journal of Health and Social Behavior, 31*, 103–122.

McFarland, S. (1989). Religious orientations and the targets of discrimination. *Journal for the Scientific Study of Religion, 28*(3), 324–336.

National briefing South: Arkansas: Gay student settles suit. (2003, July 18). *New York Times*, p. A15.

Nelsen, H. M. (1981). Religious conformity in an age of disbelief: Contextual effects of time, denomination, and family processes upon church decline and apostasy. *American Sociological Review, 46*(5), 632–640.

Noll, M. A. (1994). *The scandal of the Evangelical mind*. Grand Rapids, MI: Eerdmans.

Ozorak, E. W. (1989). Social and cognitive influences on the development of religious beliefs and commitment in adolescence. *Journal for the Scientific Study of Religion, 28*(4), 448–463.

Pargament, K. I., Smith, B. W., Koenig, H. G., & Perez, L. (1998). Patterns of positive and negative religious coping with major life stressors. *Journal for the Scientific Study of Religion, 37*(4), 710–724.

Pargament, K. I., Tarakeshwar, N., Ellison, C. G., & Wulff, K. M. (2001). Religious coping among the religious: The relationships between religious coping and well-being in a national sample of Presbyterian clergy, elders, and members. *Journal for the Scientific Study of Religion, 40*(3), 497–513.

Pittman, K., Irby, M., & Ferber, T. (2000). Unfinished business: Further reflections on a decade of promoting youth development. In *Youth development: Issues, challenges, directions* (pp. 17–64). Philadelphia: Public-Private Ventures.

Ramsay, M. (1998). Redeeming the city: Exploring the relationship between church and metropolis. *Urban Affairs Review, 33*(5), 595–626.

Ream, G. L. (2001a). *The development of intrinsic religious commitment and religious participation in young adulthood, and the religious development of gay, lesbian, and bisexual adolescents.* Unpublished master's thesis, Cornell University.

Ream, G. L. (2001b, August). *Intrinsic religion and internalized homophobia in sexual-minority youth.* Paper presented at the annual meeting of the American Psychological Association, San Francisco.

Ream, G. L. (2002, August). *Factors related to the development of religion-based homophobia.* Paper presented at the annual meeting of the American Psychological Association, Chicago.

Ream, G. L. (2003, August). *Religion as resiliency: Sex, sexual orientation and race differences.* Paper presented at the annual meeting of the American Psychological Association, Toronto.

Ream, G. L., & Witt, P. A. (2003). Organizations serving all ages. In S. F. Hamilton & M. A. Hamilton (Eds.), *Handbook of youth development* (pp. 49–74). Thousand Oaks, CA: Sage.

Richardson, J. T., Stewart, M. W., & Simmonds, R. B. (1978). Conversion to fundamentalism. *Society, 15*(4), 46–52.

Robinson, B. A. (2001). *Why did the Columbine shooting happen in Littleton, CO?* Retrieved July 15, 2003, from http://www.religioustolerance.org/sch_vio1.htm

Roehlkepartain, E. C. (2002). Building strengths, deepening faith: Understanding and enhancing youth development in Protestant congregations. In R. M. Lerner, F. Jacobs, & D. Wertleib (Eds.), *Handbook of applied developmental science: Promoting positive child, adolescent, and family development through research, policies, and programs* (Vol. 3, pp. 515–534). Thousand Oaks, CA: Sage.

Roosa, M. W., & Christopher, F. S. (1990). Evaluation of an abstinence-only adolescent pregnancy prevention program: A replication. *Family Relations: Journal of Applied Family and Child Studies, 39*(4), 363–367.

Ryan, C., & Futterman, D. (1997). *Lesbian and gay youth: Care and counseling.* Philadelphia: Hanley & Belfus.

Sameroff, A. J., Seifer, R., Baldwin, A., & Baldwin, C. (1993). Stability of intelligence from preschool to adolescence: The influence of social and family risk factors. *Child Development, 64,* 80–97.

Sather, L., & Zinn, K. (2002). Effects of abstinence-only education on adolescent attitudes and values concerning premarital sexual intercourse. *Family and Community Health, 25*(2), 1–15.

Savin-Williams, R. C. (1994). Verbal and physical abuse as stressors in the lives of lesbian, gay male, and bisexual youths: Associations with school problems, running away, substance abuse, prostitution, and suicide. *Journal of Consulting and Clinical Psychology, 62*(2), 261–269.

Savin-Williams, R. C. (1996). Ethnic- and sexual-minority youth. In R. C. Savin-Williams & K. M. Cohen (Eds.), *The lives of lesbians, gays, and bisexuals: Children to adults* (pp. 152–165). Orlando, FL: Harcourt Brace.

Savin-Williams, R. C. (2001). Suicide attempts among sexual-minority youths: Population and measurement issues. *Journal of Consulting and Clinical Psychology, 69*(6), 983–991.

Savin-Williams, R. C., & Diamond, L. M. (1999). Sexual orientation. In W. K. Silverman & T. H. Ollendick (Eds.), *Developmental issues in the clinical treatment of children* (pp. 241–258). Boston: Allyn & Bacon.

Savin-Williams, R. C., & Ream, G. L. (2003). Suicide attempts among sexual-minority male youth. *Journal of Clinical Child and Adolescent Psychology, 32*(4), 509–522.

Sherkat, D. E. (1991). *Religious socialization and the family: An examination of religious influence in the family over the life course.* Unpublished doctoral dissertation, Duke University.

Sherkat, D. E. (2001a). Investigating the sect-church-sect cycle: Cohort-specific attendance differences across African American denominations. *Journal for the Scientific Study of Religion, 40*(2), 221–233.

Sherkat, D. E. (2001b). Tracking the restructuring of American religion: Religious affiliation and patterns of religious mobility, 1973–1998. *Social Forces, 79*(4), 1459–1493.

Sherkat, D. E., & Darnell, A. (1999). The effect of parents' fundamentalism in children's educational attainment: Examining differences by gender and children's fundamentalism. *Journal for the Scientific Study of Religion, 38*(1), 23–35. Retrieved from http://www blackwellpublishers co uk/asp/journal asp?ref=0021-8294

Sherkat, D. E., & Wilson, J. (1995). Preferences, constraints, and choices in religious markets: An examination of religious switching and apostasy. *Social Forces, 73*(3), 993–1026.

Smith, T. W. (1992). Religious beliefs and behaviors and the televangelist scandals of 1987–1988. *Public Opinion Quarterly, 56*(3), 360–380.

Stark, R. (1996). Religion as context: Hellfire and delinquency one more time. *Sociology of Religion, 57*(2), 163–173.

Stark, R., & Bainbridge, W. S. (1985). *The future of religion.* Berkeley: University of California Press.

Stark, R., & Bainbridge, W. S. (1987). *A theory of religion.* New York: Peter Lang.

Stark, R., & Bainbridge, W. S. (1996). *Religion, deviance, and social control.* New York: Routledge.

Starkman, N., & Rajani, N. (2002). The case for comprehensive sex education. *AIDS Patient Care and STD's, 16*(7), 313–318.

Stein, A. (2001). *The stranger next door : the story of a small community's battle over sex, faith, and civil rights.* Boston: Beacon Press.

Streib, H. (1999). Off-road religion? A narrative approach to fundamentalist and occult orientations of adolescents. *Journal of Adolescence, 22*, 255–267.

Taylor, K. R. (2003, January). All for one? *Principal Leadership, 3*, 65–68.

Tomsho, R. (2002, February 20). Schools' efforts to protect gays face opposition. *Wall Street Journal*, p. B1.

Trulear, H. D. (2000). *Faith-based initiatives and high-risk youth: First report to the field.* Philadelphia: Public-Private Ventures.

Weaver, A. J., Samford, J. A., Morgan, V. J., Lichton, A. I., Larson, D. B., & Garbarino, J. (2000). Research on religious variables in five major adolescent research journals: 1992 to 1996. *Journal of Nervous and Mental Disease, 188*(1), 36–44.

Weber, M. (1922). *The sociology of religion* (E. Fischoff, Trans.). Boston: Beacon Press.

Wilkinson, P. (1999, June 10). Humiliation and revenge: The story of Reb and VodDkA. *Rolling Stone,* 49–54, 140–141.

Youniss, J., McLellan, J. A., Su, Y., & Yates, M. (1999). The role of community service in identity development: Normative, unconventional, and deviant orientations. *Journal of Adolescent Research, 14*(2), 248–261.

Youniss, J., McLellan, J. A., & Yates, M. (1999). Religion, community service, and identity in American youth. *Journal of Adolescence, 22*(2), 243–253.

INDEX

Printed in the United States
28482LVS00002B/4-6

9 781593 111540